The aesthetic exception

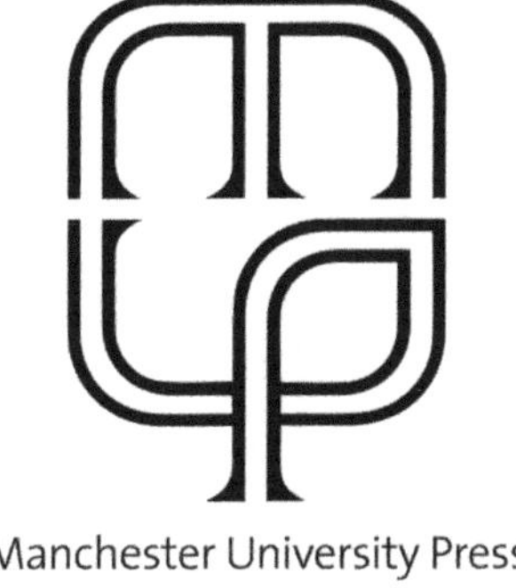

Manchester University Press

The aesthetic exception

Essays on art, theatre, and politics

Tony Fisher

MANCHESTER UNIVERSITY PRESS

Published by Manchester University Press
Oxford Road, Manchester M13 9PL
www.manchesteruniversitypress.co.uk

British Library Cataloguing-in-Publication Data
A catalogue record for this book is available from the British Library

ISBN 978 1 5261 7016 3 hardback
ISBN 978 1 5261 9115 1 paperback

First published 2023
Paperback published 2025

EU authorised representative for GPSR:
Easy Access System Europe – Mustamäe tee 50,
10621 Tallinn, Estonia
gpsr.requests@easproject.com

Typeset by Newgen Publishing UK

For Amanda, Beatrice, and Tilly

Contents

List of illustrations

Acknowledgements

The essays that comprise this book derive from over a decade of work, in which many friends, colleagues, and sometimes complete strangers played a significant role in shaping the thinking that led to them. To acknowledge the influence of interlocutors is to recognise a fundamental truth, of course – that no work arrives fully formed but is always bound by a debt owed to the knowledge, wisdom, and insight of others. To begin with the foremost of these 'debts', I would like to first acknowledge Janelle Reinelt, without whom this book would not have been written. It was only until (fairly) recently that our paths crossed – a fact that both of us found strange, given our mutual interests and political affinities. When they did, however, it sparked for me the kind of productive discussion that bears, as it were, the ripest fruit of disagreement, grown in the fertile soil of engagement with the opposing viewpoint. There is barely a word written in this book that was not prompted by that encounter. The second debt is to my close collaborator and Central colleague, Tom Six, who accompanied me along the haphazard path that led to the writing of this book, meticulously reading and responding to each draft I produced, providing invaluable criticism and, above all else, the kind of solidarity without which such an endeavour would simply not be possible. Eric Fromm once observed: 'Human solidarity is the necessary condition for the unfolding of any one individual' – something similar might be said of the unfolding task of writing.

To think the conjuncture, as this book seeks to do, is essentially a collective task. Those who also engage in this work, and who have generously contributed their own expertise, experience, time, patience, and discernment in helping my own efforts, include colleagues in India: Komita Dhanda, Bishnupriya Dutt, and Aparna Mahiyaria. I am extremely grateful to all three; each read drafts of the chapter on the Indian street theatre, suggesting key readings, correcting my blunders on Indian politics and history, and introducing me to a world of exemplary scholarship of which I have so far only been able to scratch the surface.

The chapter on the aesthetic exception benefitted from being read by friends – Louise Owen, whose feedback was as shrewd as her criticisms were perceptive, and Kélina Gotman, whose support and insights, as always, I greatly value. Joe Kelleher offered astute advice on an early plan for the book that enabled me to take up the slack and tighten its focus. Shanna Leigh Ketchum-Heap of Birds helped with the introduction. Conversations with Janelle, and Bishnupriya, and with Silvija Jestrovic, Liz Tomlin, Elaine Aston, Trish Read, Chantal Mouffe, and Nick Ridout, during our time together in Venice at the conference 'Cultures of the Left in the Age of Right-wing Populism', all helped shape the chapter on the communicative turn in art. This text was subsequently published in Spanish thanks to Wenceslao Garcia Puchades, as 'Arte Político después del Giro Comunicativo' in *Escritura e Imagen* 16, 2020: 285–305. The version printed here is a substantial reworking of that essay.

I thank Peter Boenisch for putting me in touch with the Schaubühne; and Chris Balme for our many conversations on German theatre, and much else besides! I am also profoundly appreciative of the support I've received from Maria Delgado, who has proven a steadfast and brilliant mentor to me over the past seven years. Indeed, it was on a trip to Manchester with Maria, which concluded in a meeting with Matthew Frost of Manchester University Press, that I was first able to pitch the nascent idea of the book to him. I am grateful to Matthew for his enthusiasm for the project both then, which kick-started everything, and now, as it finally reaches its conclusion. Thanks are also due to Radka Kunderova for the opportunity she gave me to present some of the research on the theatre of the conjuncture to her conference 'Redefining Theatre: Theatre and Society in Transition' at the Freie University in Berlin in 2021. My gratitude goes also to Nadine Deller and Natasha Bonnelame for putting up with my occasional forays into the topic of this book as I was researching it during our many conversations over the past few years; and to Barry Campbell for his help in constructing the book's index. I am also appreciative of the support I received from the Research Office at Royal Central School of Speech and Drama, when completing the book.

Finally, the labour of researching and writing this book was only made possible because of the unfaltering encouragement and support of my partner and compadre, Amanda Stuart Fisher, who held the world together for me, even in those darkest moments when everything seemed to totter on the brink of the abyss. Some debts cannot be repaid…

Introduction: The horizon of the aesthetic

Apropos this book

The question of the relation between art and politics may seem an inauspicious place to begin a book. 'Can art be political?' has become the most exasperating of questions. Its tiresomeness can be measured by the sheer volume of discourse it has generated over the decades. This is not to say these debates are without value or interest, but only that in circulating the same arguments and objections no-one can feign surprise if the same predictable results are obtained. Such threadbare outcomes would seem to confirm the indefatigability of the law of diminishing returns, and little else. All the same, if the circumstances behind the writing of a book are relevant to its meaning, informing the choice of its material and the disposition of its argument – in short, its positioning and its motivation – they may have some bearing on how that question should be understood here. Writing in 2022, in the midst of a deep political winter has meant that the question, to my mind at least, attains a degree of urgency that not only transforms it but for that very reason compels us to return to it once more in the hope of discovering new answers. Far from being otiose, it is precisely this question that must be posed for the simple reason that art itself cannot avoid it. That winter has been long and hard and, for far too many, particularly bitter. With mounting challenges on all fronts – not least escalating inequality due to climate breakdown, compounded by the devastating effects of a worldwide pandemic, and the deepening entrenchment of the 'neoliberal' hegemon (or rather its transformation through a naked power grab since 2011 into a global oligarchy[1]) – it is unlikely to abate any time soon. As humanity's collective horizon grows ever darker, any glimpse of future progressive possibility seems to be obscured by the ideological barriers erected by contemporary reality in relation to which, to coin a phrase, there appears to be 'no alternative' (or so goes the lie we are endlessly sold). But if this leads to the affirmation that pessimism is the only reasonable attitude that the intellect can strike today, then it is art that promises to promote a different outlook in which optimism of the spirit refuses to be subdued or dampened. From art, and particularly when it comes to the topic of this book, political art, more should be expected than mere consolation, or accounts of the present that underwrite despair. Equally, more can be demanded of it than measly promissory notes for some future but obscurely framed happiness. And this is precisely what this book expects and demands: that art offers both a means of understanding and confronting the present predicament and may even indicate directions of travel out of it. Let me state the central proposition of this book as unequivocally as is possible, then, for the avoidance of all doubt: '*political* art is political *art* "period"'. Of course, the question this raises should already be forming on the reader's lips: what is the meaning of this tautology?

To address this further question will require working through the tangled jumble of concepts that comprise the book's lexicology. It is a book that speaks of limits, borders, the crossing of thresholds, and the projection of horizons; of movements, transgressions, and traversals; and also, of terms cast on less metaphorical terrain: of aesthetic (and, yes, art's political) effects, and relatedly of autonomy and heteronomy in art practices. But it also deploys ideas drawn from elsewhere, from political philosophy and cultural theory. It speaks of conjunctures, mediations, of organicity and tendencies, and of the overdetermined structuration of the social formation within which art necessarily yet contingently appears. Above all, it is a book that treats the relation of art and politics not as an indeterminate but as a determinate relation, where, simply put, political context determines art's political possibilities. Determination cannot be thought univocally, however. It is not a one-way street (politics is not the master of art). Were that the case, then art would be propaganda pure and simple. The determining relation is instead thought as operating in both directions simultaneously, but above all as a relation that is highly conditional and that is forged whenever and wherever art becomes an articulatory practice. What I mean by this I shall come to shortly, but essentially it indicates an aesthetic operation that produces a specific political effect: radical art determines (in that it comprehends) the 'determinations' of the social structure. In one way or another, radical art exposes society's mediating forms in critical ways such that it permits a possible rearticulation of the subject of politics.

In this sense (and precisely because 'determining the determinations' is how art assumes a political character) it makes little sense to speak of a 'politics of the aesthetic' in general. The aesthetic (or aesthetic regime as Jacques Rancière has described it[2]) has no intrinsic political meaning beyond the possibility for art's political articulation, whether through practices or criticism (even if it might be said to contain that possibility as a potential *for* an egalitarian politics). Nicolas Bourriaud is right to indicate that it is not the aesthetic per se but art that 'exposes the world's non-definitive character',[3] even if (*pace* Bourriaud) I think it does more than merely 'affirm' the '*transitory* and *circumstantial* nature of the institutions that structure social life [and] the rules governing individual and collective behaviour'. If art intervenes in those institutions and behaviours, it does so by rearticulating them. It is owing to the determinate nature of articulatory practice that only specific aesthetic acts embodied in particular artworks relating to existing political reality will be considered in what follows. That limitation is not to be confused with the dogmatic claim that art is political only when it is responding to given political 'facts'. But it is a limitation that I argue is entirely consistent with the book's aim, insofar as it seeks to show how art as a material practice may claim a political existence, even if that existence is an inherently ambiguous one, since art also seeks (and as a precondition of its existence as art) to evade the laws of political gravity. That art and politics are yoked together in the form of a relationship that neither particularly wanted or desired, and which each side has, at times, had reason to resent, only highlights the problematic nature of the question that comprises the book's starting point. But it also reveals one end of the slender thread that runs through the essays that follow, and which I invite the reader to use as a guide. If this image suggests something labyrinthine, it is only because once the proper terms of the problem are known, it becomes apparent that what they imply indicates an irresolvable paradox, and not least because the phenomenon they describe is essentially a 'relation' that can equally be expressed as the disavowal of any relation whatsoever.

This phenomenon is named in the first essay of this book (from which it derives its title) as the paradox of the aesthetic exception. And while other concerns may dominate the ensuing essays, it is nevertheless this paradox that provides the book with its own horizon of thought, against which those concerns become thinkable. What the aesthetic exception describes is the language game that produces the critical space of distinction within which art practices appear as both separate from other social practices but also as being related to them through the construction of a frontier that is essentially contingent. The aesthetic exception is itself the result of an articulatory practice in which the discourse and institutions of art are formed: it shows that art's fabled autonomy rests on the provisional nature of this discourse and that it is constantly open to infiltration by so-called heteronomous influences (or 'determinations'). Art practices do not lose their distinguished status simply for being related to wider social praxes. Even so, to the extent that the aesthetic exception comprises what Rancière terms the 'dispositif' of art – the regime for its identification[4] – that exceptional status imposes discursive limits that can only be partially breached. This leads to two (im) possibilities: either art is a contingent practice that can never quite attain the full autonomy demanded of it by the logic of the aesthetic exception, or else it is an autonomous practice that seeks to redeem itself in the heteronomous world from which it is necessarily separated *by* the aesthetic exception. The latter is best illustrated by the transgression (of the aesthetic exception) by the historical avant-garde (examined in detail in the first essay). These, of course, are transgressions the aesthetic exception invites; what they demonstrate in practice, however, is that radical art is indeed able to rearticulate the space of art in relation to the space of the social – although not to the extent that it may disregard the threat posed by the eradication of the differential through which the radical work of art is constituted *as* a work of art. Were the aesthetic exception to disappear, so too would the frontier that distinguishes art as 'art'; but more to the point, what would also disappear with it is art's power as an articulatory practice, which this book asserts is the very basis of its political possibility. Understanding that political possibility, and its limits, is then the central task of the book. Its fundamental contention is that however much radical art may shed the requirement of aesthetic autonomy, it must nonetheless do so by navigating the exception and its discursive frontier; the very attempt places it within the space of a paradox. To extend the seafaring metaphor a little further: what the book examines are practices whose radicalism compels art to circumnavigate its space of exception – either it must attempt to cross that space or render it volatile by locating and occupying the extreme perimeter of that peculiar zone in which art's status of exception is established and maintained. The book takes this approach not to dismiss the familiar problem of aesthetic autonomy, but to resituate it as a problem of articulation thereby establishing a different starting point, hopefully unencumbered by earlier conceptual impasses.

Those impasses, of course, are not to be lightly dismissed. They appear within the book in the form of three discrete problematics. The first is the problem of the aesthetic – not the 'politics of the aesthetic' exactly, so much as the political limits and possibilities available to art afforded by the revolt it stages against the sequestrating logic of the aesthetic; the second is the familiar problem of art's social and political efficacy – and the question of whether art is able to directly intervene in a political situation while maintaining what Peter Osborne terms its 'art-character';[5] and the third is the problem of how art is able to articulate itself on the terrain of political struggle – that is, of art's relation to the field of actual political practices. These problems comprise the core thematic areas of the book, against which its sections can be mapped: The first essay ('The Aesthetic Exception') is a philosophical exploration of the problems raised by art's exceptional status, focusing particularly, as just indicated, on the example of the historical avant-garde. The second essay ('Political Art after the Communicative Turn') shifts to the cognate problem of how it is possible for art to communicate political effects given art's status of exception (through which it is apparently separated from the social world). Here I draw on the developments of the communicative turn to offer an alternative to the dichotomies of what I have previously called the 'efficacy debate', where art is claimed either to produce effects unproblematically, or else is seen to be so problematic as to induce a political coma (with the denial of any such capacity at all). The final essay of the book ('Taxonomy of the Political Theatre') comprises its longest section and examines the problem of how art articulates itself on the actual terrain of political practices. I take theatre to offer an exemplary site for such an articulation, not least because of the manifold ways in which questions of representation as well as the relation of art to the 'social' are condensed within its spaces of exception. Ostensibly, the essay apprehends, through several chapters, the problem of the political theatre, understood in the genitive sense, i.e., as the problem that emerges with and belongs to the very designation '*of* the political theatre'. The *problem* of the political theatre is a problem of its peculiar genealogy. In other words, it does not present the reader with a history of the political theatre but rather with the history of the problem that was both announced by and incarnated in the theatre as part of its conditions of emergence as a political idiom (conditions coinciding with the theatre of the Russian Revolution of 1917). In examining this genealogy, however, I also ask what I take to be the more fundamental question: what makes the political theatre 'political'? In answering this question, I develop two claims. The first is that no art is political that does not engage with the historical conjuncture of which it is a situated part; the second is that the politics of political theatre can only be analysed in the terms of its specific rearticulation of conjunctural elements that comprises its mode of intervention, and the extent and degree of its penetration, within a given social formation (I draw on examples including the political activism of the Indian street theatre, and in particular, Jana Natya Manch or 'Janam' – Peoples Theatre Front – as well as examine the 'closure' of the theatre of representation with the arrival of postdramatic theatre). I conclude that this articulatory practice is itself only fully realised through the projection of a political horizon, grasped as that which political theatre anticipates in the simulated form of the new or what I term a 'futurity-to-come'. Grasping the future-to-come is not simply a matter of inflating utopian fantasies, but, I argue, a practice of simulation performed within and critically directed at the present. The example I use, and where the book concludes, is drawn from the theatre of Milo Rau. His is a theatre that articulates the problematic of a futurity-to-come, constituted against the horizon of our own conjunctural moment under conditions of globalisation: what it projects is the counter-horizon of an alternative planetary future.

The promise of the aesthetic

But first: what exactly is the field of problematisation that is announced by the politics of the aesthetic? This formulation, as has already been noted, has become indissociably linked to the thought of Jacques Rancière. Rancière argues that aesthetics names an event that sees the collapse of the early modern regime of the arts (based on 'mimesis') while at the same time inaugurating a radically new epoch, describing it as a 'new and paradoxical regime for identifying what is recognisable as art ... [the] aesthetic regime of the arts'.[6] But where exactly is the radicality of art to be found insofar as it is appropriated under the regimen of the aesthetic? And in what sense should it be viewed as paradoxical? It is with the arrival of modernity, with which the aesthetic regime is essentially coterminous, that a fundamental displacement of the value regime that had governed art for the previous age occurred. What the aesthetic regime announced was a paradigm shift in which truth could no longer be ascribed to art on representationalist grounds, but rather on the grounds of aesthetic validity (the question posed is not whether the artwork is truthful, but whether it is tasteful, beautiful, sublime). The reason for this is to be found in the central problem of the newly emergent discourse of aesthetics which articulated a need to establish sensibility rather than representation as the basis of aesthetic experience. The consequence: art became entirely autonomous with respect to a concept of truth founded on *ratio* or representational correspondence. The issue is already present in one of the founding statements of aesthetic thought, Baumgarten's *Aesthetics*, published in 1750, where a clear distinction is made between aesthetic and logical truths – a distinction that is incorporated as the basic presupposition of aesthetic discourse thereafter. The end of the aesthetic, for Baumgarten, is the perfection of sensibility, whose object is the beautiful. Aesthetics is defined by him as the 'science of sensual cognition',[7] and, as such, describes a 'third concern' (*tertia cura*) of truth: 'truth ... as it is known to the sensory'.[8]

The distinction of the aesthetic achieves its most celebrated philosophical expression in Kant's *Critique of Judgement* with his dictum that the beautiful is formally purposeful, yet autonomous with respect to any positive (cognitive) or practical (moral) end: 'Beauty is the form of *finality* in an object, so far as perceived in it *apart from the representation of an end*'.[9] I judge a flower such as a tulip[10] beautiful not because my estimation of it attributes any end or purpose to it (the flower is not beautiful because I understand it to be the reproductive organ of the plant) but on the autonomous basis that I find the internal organisation of its elements delightful or pleasing. An aesthetic judgement is not a theoretical cognition. It is not concerned with concepts; it does not identify the particular as subsumed under general laws, as found in the natural sciences. Nor is it concerned with the nature of right action, with the 'science of ethics'. The discrimination of the aesthetic as a distinct sphere of judgement set apart from cognitive and moral acts not only constitutes aesthetic discourse as the foundation for the regime that identifies that which is specific to art, however; at the same time, it ensures the complete alienation of art from truth. Aesthetic validity provides art with its internal logic and the regime for identifying art with a means to preserve art's separation from the world of non-art. Aesthetic separation is most explicitly formulated by Kant with the claim that the aesthetic faculty of 'discriminating and estimating ... contributes nothing to knowledge'.[11] The consequences of this are far reaching, as the philosopher Jay Bernstein has observed: what Kant institutes is a fateful discordance between art and truth. Bernstein argues (as does Habermas in fact[12]) that this is not an accidental consequence of Kantian thought, but is fundamental to his theory of modernity: 'the Kantian categorial differentiation between truth, moral worth and aesthetic reflection [provides the] guiding thread [of modernity]'.[13] It describes a process of the 'separation of spheres, the becoming autonomous of truth, beauty and goodness from one another'.[14] To the extent that modernity is structured around divisions that leave aesthetics bereft of truth, the 'experience of art as *aesthetical* is the experience of art as having lost or been deprived of its power to speak the truth'.[15] Modernity becomes the 'site of beauty bereaved – bereaved of truth' while being simultaneously deformed by its reduction of truth to 'truth-only cognition'.[16]

This results, according to Bernstein, in the emergence of a paradox, however – one that will inform the 'fate' of art over the centuries that follow. No sooner is art ejected from the sphere of truth by aesthetic discourse than the autonomy to which it is consigned is reconstituted as a new and distinct scene of truth quite dissimilar from those governing the sciences and morality. From this point on, art constitutes itself as a third scene of truth, although one that stands in an equivocal and, crucially, critical relation to the way social objectivity is constructed under conditions of modernity. Relegated to the merely aesthetic, art nonetheless 'comes to speak about the fate of truth and art in modernity'.[17] And it is in relation to this idea that I think one can begin to understand the radical implications of the aesthetic as a distinct regime, as well as those contradictions that it embodies, summarised so memorably by Adorno in his striking aphorism: 'Art is the ever broken promise of happiness.'[18]

To discern the proper parameters of that promise, I would like to attend more closely to Rancière, as there can be no discussion of art and its relation to politics today without contending with the challenges set by Rancièrean aesthetics. Now essential to Rancière's conception of the aesthetic regime is that it stands in a homologous relation to politics understood as 'dissensus'. Both politics and aesthetics are modes of dissensus insofar as a dissensus, in each respective case, describes an activity in which the rules and norms governing unreflected experience are suspended, and in which the ordinary conditions of experience, or what we might call the 'common "distributions" of sense', are disrupted. Art (under the aesthetic regime) and politics (grasped as dissensus) both redistribute bodies beyond their given place; each dislocates the pre-arranged positions of bodies and subjects within the fixed space of community, where everyone is assigned a role, or a specific part to play; each thus dismantles hierarchical modes of organisation and presentation. To the extent that dissensus opposes itself to hierarchy in principle, it possesses an egalitarian logic – one whose levelling effects are capable of fundamentally dissolving the terms of the social order and throwing open the sensory world to reconfigurations of the visible, the sayable and the doable. In prioritising the logic of dissensus, Rancière highlights the non-reducible character of the aesthetic and its politics, but also that of politics itself. Dissensus, although found in determinate social, political, and artistic situations, is not exhausted by the actual circumstances of dissent. It is why Rancière insists that politics is not about the struggle for 'interests' or for 'power'. Lenin's question 'Who whom?', or in Raymond Geuss's less contracted form, 'who <does> what to whom for whose benefit', no longer suffices as a definition of politics.[19] (I think it does, but more on this later.) One reason Rancière holds this view is that wherever dissensus appears, it does so as a logic that supersedes any situation to which it can be applied: i.e., the logic of radical equality. This can be understood in the following way: radical equality is unlikely to ever be found in contexts of social struggle (hence the need for the struggle in the first place), and yet there can be no possibility for any political struggle that does not begin from the presupposition of equality. Equality is here understood as the *a priori* postulate of any dissensual activity whatsoever: its possibility must be assumed, even if in 'reality', no such equality exists. But it is also for this very reason that the assertion of an egalitarian logic enables both the suspension of what normally applies (an unequal distribution of the social) and the projection of an equal distribution where none can be found. Importantly, for Rancière, the very enactment of dissensus imposes an egalitarian logic on a situation where there is no equality. Dissensus becomes both an assertion of equality and a litigious demonstration of its absence.

But how then does this correspond to Rancière's view that the aesthetic comprises the immanent horizon for what is possible (and impossible) when it comes to political art, constituting for the latter, as it were, an insuperable difficulty owing to the problems that arise as a consequence of Rancière's association of aesthetics with dissensus? To fully understand this question,

I begin with a comparison of the aesthetic regime and the regime that preceded it – the representational or mimetic regime (Rancière also describes a third regime, the 'ethical regime of the image', but because this is less important to the argument, I will pass over it here). Where the representative regime of art is concerned with the ordering of bodies and subjects, assigned to their proper roles and functions, the aesthetic regime (because it is essentially dissensual) undoes all such hierarchical orderings – releasing art from the idea that there is a proper or 'true' subject of art. Rancière explains this in rather hyperbolic terms:

> With the triumph of the novel's page over the theatrical stage, the egalitarian intertwining of images and signs on pictorial and typographic surfaces, the elevation of artisan's art to the status of great art, and the new claim to bring art into the décor of each and every life, an entire well-ordered distribution of sensory experience was overturned.[20]

What each of these moments indicates and testifies to, for Rancière, is the 'equality of indifference' in which what is 'negated' is 'any relationship of necessity between a determined form and determined content'.[21] It is this 'equality of all subject matter' that fundamentally undermines, not representation per se, but the logic of representation insofar as it institutes the precession of privileged images and preferential themes (the decision over what is fit for representation and what is unfit), the subordination of artistic technique – its modes of making (*poiesis*) to representational meaning (*mimesis*), and of artistic affect (*aesthesis*) to a prescribed feeling and thus fixed point of reception (an assigned means by which art can be socially valued). What each of these features of the representative regime achieves is the subordination of art to a normative conception that regulates art, but which does not properly belong to it. This is why the aesthetic regime, insofar as it makes possible the autonomous space of art, must inevitably be seen to promote, through the new modes of art it enables, an experience of autonomy that does not belong to the world of necessity (a world governed by productive forces, or the instrumentalisation of knowledge, or the rule of economic rationality). Without requiring or possessing any explicit political content, art nonetheless comes to embody a metapolitics: 'The politics of art in the aesthetic regime of art, or rather its metapolitics, is determined by this founding paradox: in this regime, art is art insofar as it is also nonart, or is something other than art.'[22]

What does it mean to say that art is more than just art, is also 'nonart'? Under the aesthetic regime, art provides the possibility for an experience of autonomy and as such carries within it the 'promise of emancipation'[23] beyond the world of art. But it is also precisely with this promise that art discovers its political limit. The reason is simple: the fulfilment of that promise would lead, writes Rancière, to the 'elimination of art as a separate reality'.[24] What is meant by this, however, is somewhat ambiguous. There is nothing inherently paradoxical about art's desire to fulfil its promise of emancipation *unless* it is a self-negating promise. This can be understood in two ways. Either art eliminates freedom in the very attempt to transcend the autonomy it possesses, or it eliminates itself when an emancipated world is established. If art were indeed able to redeem that emancipatory promise, it would be because an emancipated form of life had been actualised. And reconciled life would have no further need for art as a separate sphere of activity. Autonomous art would simply disappear. This is to say, the promise of emancipation is a paradox for art under the aesthetic regime regardless of whether an emancipated world is possible. Viewed, however, from the perspective of the world in which the aesthetic regime maintains or preserves that emancipatory promise, then the paradox becomes somewhat sharper. What it says is that it is conceivable that a world free from necessity is possible by means of art (art just *is* that conception), but only insofar as art appears as the form by which the world for whom its promise appears to be empirically irredeemable is negated. Art is paradoxical because its metapolitics consigns it to the undecidable zone that opens between the formal possibility that the promise of emancipation it bears might be redeemable and the practical concession to the empirical world of the impossibility of being freed from the claims of necessity. To express this, as Adorno might have done, art promises to suspend the tyrannical hold of necessity over the world by introducing into it a moment of negative freedom. Art's promise is thus also its mode of conceding its bad faith.

To this can be added a final increment of ambiguity to Rancière's story, which indicates the deeper insufficiency of a politics founded on the aesthetic promise. There is a politics of art, but not a politics that can take place in or by means of art. It is why Rancière, as with Adorno before him, evinces a high degree of scepticism regarding art's supposed political effectiveness – something I will turn to shortly. Setting this issue aside, momentarily – are we not left nevertheless with a situation in which the politics of art can only be discerned from the vantage of the aesthetic – a perspective that is only available to the philosopher, who sets themselves up as the one able to fathom the secret meaning of art? There is no art *work* that makes a promise of emancipation – if it did, then it would immediately fall prey to the suspicion that it must be a *political* work of art, which Rancière rejects; and so, the promise of emancipation can only be conferred upon art from above. Art is the promise of emancipation that is denied any capacity to make such a promise. This ironic formula indicates that although Rancière denies art the power of interpreting the world, he does not deny the philosopher the power of interpreting the world through the appearance of art. In this sense, Rancière's aesthetic regime describes a regime of art criticism, rather than art practices. It is a hermeneutic regime designed to decide on the proper meaning of art's politics, while remaining wholly consistent with the earliest law of aesthetic discourse: the law that guards art against any infringement of its axiomatic separation from truth.

Not a cut but a threshold

This is not to deny the existence of the paradox that Rancière identifies with the development of the aesthetic regime. However, I would prefer to give an alternative account of that paradox as a means of indicating a different direction of travel for this book and its key concern with the political in art. What I term the aesthetic exception describes the instituting logics by which something called 'Art' emerges as an exceptional space within which works of art can appear. They appear as objects, statements, performances, images, texts, and compositions that are considered, in some sense, to be distinct from the world of non-art even if they share certain features in common – for instance, that they must possess a material substratum that partially locates them in a world of common things. The aesthetic exception is nonetheless a subtractive power: it acts to position artworks as if they were somehow beholden to an authority that is autonomous from everyday regulatory rules and the modes of legitimation governing quotidian life. This means, in whatever way that authority is constructed institutionally, it must be seen to embody the language game of the aesthetic exception. Only on this basis can it provide the means to decide where the boundary lies between art and non-art. The 'paradox of the aesthetic' emerges because in establishing itself as the 'validity regime' for deciding on what is or is not art, the aesthetic exception cannot but install the problem of autonomy in every work of art, however stealthily, as its very condition of existence. No work of art escapes the problem of autonomy because no work of art can evade the *dispositif* by which it is qualified as art. This does not mean that every work of art is an autonomous work, but rather that every work of art must, in one way or another, contend with the meaning of that autonomy. This problem finds its historical expression in the form of a fundamental contradiction that can be expressed thus: is the meaning of art's freedom decided by aesthetics (philosophy or art's critical discourse) – i.e., is it a regulated freedom? Or is it the absolute freedom of art to decide for itself how it should be defined, how it should be made, how it should be encountered, and how it should relate to the social world? I have noted that for Rancière, classification under the aesthetic regime takes priority over the world of practices. The aesthetic regime is limited by only one side of a double paradox: that art is art insofar as it is not art (which cannot be expressed through art without contradiction). However, the aesthetic exception is not primarily instituted because it consists in a paradoxical promise that artists may or may not be aware of; on the contrary, the paradox of the aesthetic is discovered at the very moment when artists sought to escape the aesthetic exception as a governing logic of art. The paradox lies here: that the aesthetic exception enables an art that claims complete autonomy from the validity regime that makes it possible. It is a paradox that is not imposed on art by a 'logic' that only philosophy can properly discern; it is a paradox that is discovered through artistic practices that rebel against it.

The paradox of the aesthetic exception is therefore entirely bound by this immanent historical contradiction. It flows through art's institutional and extra-institutional sites; and it inhabits art practices in their struggle to articulate themselves 'within' the world. For that reason, the aesthetic exception – graspable as the problematisation by art of the autonomy that constitutes it – is forever bound to an ambiguous exteriority in a relation that cannot be decided. Where art and the exception meet 'reality', it is always in the form of an indistinction in which the exceptional character of art becomes questionable. This means there are, in fact, two axes around which the paradox is expressed. The first becomes visible in relation to art's institutional meaning or rather 'framing conditions'; and the second concerns the visibility of art to the world that lies beyond it – both exteriorities have a significant bearing on how art can constitute itself in an articulatory relation to politics. In terms of the first aspect, plainly the question of art's institutional framing conditions cannot be divorced from the historical development of art under the aesthetic regime. The question I would like to pose here is whether or not it is true to say that art, or rather aesthetic experience – the experience of autonomy that the viewer has in the encounter with art – is necessarily dissensual; does it always 're-configure the fabric of sensory experience' in a way that can be defined as a '[meta]politics'?[25] The question can be addressed only through a transmutation of its terms. That the aesthetic was discovered in parallel with the emergence of bourgeois conditions of social reproduction is hardly an accident. To understand the emergence of the aesthetic is to understand it as a response to the conditions of existence of the bourgeois subject who emerged at the same time: a subject bound by the fundamental contradiction of possessing an ego that was split between freedom on the one hand and necessity on the other. Adorno and Horkheimer indicate the nature of that contradiction via Kant, for whom the subject is caught in the ambiguous relation of the 'transcendental to the empirical ego' – which they explain as follows:

> As the transcendental, supraindividual self, reason comprises the idea of a free, human social life in which men organize themselves as the universal subject and overcome the conflict between pure and empirical reason in the conscious solidarity of the whole. This represents the idea of true universality: utopia.

At the same time, however, reason constitutes the court of judgement of calculation, which adjusts the world for the ends of self-preservation and recognizes no function other than the preparation of the object from mere sensory material in order to make it the material of subjugation. The true nature of schematism, of the general and the particular, of concept and individual case reconciled from without, is ultimately revealed in contemporary science as the interest of industrial society. Being is apprehended under the aspect of manufacture and administration. Everything – even the human individual, not to speak of the animal – is converted into the repeatable, replaceable process, into a mere example for the conceptual models of the system.[26]

This originary scene of modern, instrumentalised (industrial) society, explored by Adorno and Horkheimer, shows that the question of freedom cannot be so easily divorced from 'interest'. In effect, the bourgeois subject insofar as they are constituted through the contradiction of an empirical ego (that is subjected to the world of material interests or 'necessity') can *also* be viewed as a transcendental ego, in which autonomy is discovered as an ideality. The question as to whether this should have a bearing on the politics of the aesthetic regime, in its earliest stages of formation, can be addressed as follows. For Kant, the aesthetic reveals the autonomy of the subject through the 'free play' of the categories of understanding insofar as they are liberated from necessity (they need not conform to the requirement of arriving at determining judgements bound by utility or usefulness, etc.); and they are thus freed up to enjoy the perceived object, not because it is useful, but as something possessing 'beauty'. In exercising aesthetic judgement, the subject discovers an autonomy that is entirely distinct from their involvement in the social world of production. However, as Kant is also at pains to point out, freedom in matters of taste is rationally constrained by the need to reach intersubjective agreement on the nature of the beautiful. An aesthetic judgement is not simply an expression of individual good taste; it is predicated on the alignment of all individual tastes and thus asserted *as if* all tastes *ought* to conform to that judgement. What aesthetic judgement seeks to confirm is the consensus that underpins the community of sense. The 'sensus communis' is produced as a community of critics: it is founded on a common taste and on a consensual disposition that each share, and which binds each to the other through the possession of 'good taste', deliberatively cultivated in the form of an aesthetic education. It is in art that bourgeois sensibility discovers what it also experiences in its encounter with nature: a means of partially reconciling the subject to the contradiction immanent to bourgeois society (a society that would otherwise be determined entirely by necessity – in Marx's terms, 'socially necessary labour time'). Art or rather aesthetic experience provides the subject with a taste for freedom, but – and here lies its essential ambiguity – not a preordained means for achieving full reconciliation (of its subjective and objective dimensions). Peter Bürger already pointed this out: the bourgeois self may appreciate art, but it remains an 'atrophied' self all the same.[27] Thus, within aesthetic experience, the social purpose of art under the aesthetic exception is discovered, whose aim is to adjust the subject to a form of necessity that only becomes bearable on condition that it does not wholly define them; thus, also, the tacit formula of recognition implied by art's validity regime: aesthetic recognition = social *consensus*. It becomes moot, therefore, whether the discovery of aesthetics implies a dissensual redistribution of the sensible or merely provides the means for adapting the subject to the demands of necessary production. The aesthetic exception bears within it two opposing but simultaneous possibilities, then: the first is the promise of reconciling the subject to necessity; the second is the promise of emancipating the subject from necessity. Dissensus is implied only in relation to the second possibility established by the aesthetic exception, but equally, according to the first, under the aesthetic exception, there is nothing inherently emancipatory about art. What makes it dissensual can only be determined by its relation to the institution of the exception and specifically by its rejection of the validity regime of art. And since this dissensual rejection of the aesthetic can only be enacted by means of art practices, then its proper locus is the institutional site in which it appears and which is seen to embody the authority of the aesthetic exception (such as the museum, the gallery, the theatre …). That these are contingent expressions of the aesthetic exception is quite irrelevant to those art practices discussed in this book that seek to disarticulate themselves from the material contexts of institutional practices and their discourses, in which they are captured.

But at this point a second and perhaps more fundamental issue raised by Rancière regarding the question of the relation of art to its exterior is encountered. It arises precisely because the aesthetic regime appears to inhibit the capacity of art to produce effects in 'reality' as found beyond its recondite institutional spaces. This matters because art's critical relation to the institution of the exception aims to break open art's enclosure within *its* institutions, to reach that which lies beyond art. The aesthetic regime prevents this from happening because it denies that there is an 'outside' to art – or at least one that can matter to it. Rancière writes: 'This politics of aesthetics … operates under the conditions prescribed by an original disjuncture. It produces effects, but it does so on the basis of an original effect that implies the suspension of any direct cause-effect relationship.'[28] What is the original effect of the aesthetic regime, for Rancière? It is the effect that he elsewhere describes as a consequence of the fundamental caesura produced by the aesthetic regime – an 'aesthetic cut that separates outcomes from intentions and precludes any direct path towards an "other side" of words and images'.[29] The image of a 'cut' is both pivotal and compelling. But it should also be noted that it rests on Rancière's decision to describe the aesthetic in terms of an image that appears to 'cut off' art from the social world. In imposing the image of the cut, Rancière imposes on art a fundamental injunction in relation to which all works that pretend to possess a 'direct' ability to influence the spectator 'politically' will need to be reprimanded (as demonstrated by his reading of Jenny Holzer). There are, however, a number of ambiguities in Rancière's formulation of the aesthetic cut. It seems that the door onto art's exterior is prised opened just a little when Rancière proclaims: 'all forms of art can rework the frame of our perceptions and the dynamism of our affects. As such, they can open up new passages towards forms of political subjectivation.'[30] However, before pushing too hard at that door, the following should be observed: art works are awarded the power to produce effects but at the same time, only those effects are allowed that are consistent with the logic of the aesthetic regime, with the logic of the cut – they are indirect effects. It is not just that the aesthetic regime breaks with the logic of mimesis, in other words; but rather, it breaks with the logic of mimesis precisely because it enacts an 'aesthetic break' in which there is no longer any possibility of a 'concordance between sense and sense',[31] i.e., the assumed link between *aisthesis* and *poiesis* under representation is severed. The consequence of the aesthetic cut is to separate art (understood as cause) from a determinate effect at the point of its reception. It is for this reason that there can be no legible way of attributing to art a politics beyond that of the politics of the aesthetic. The question arises, nonetheless: is the aesthetic cut the appropriate way to describe the situation of art under the aesthetic exception? I think there is one way to problematise this idea of the aesthetic cut, and it is by drawing a distinction between the two viewpoints made available by the levels of philosophy and practice. For the first, essentially the perspective of aesthetic discourse, the idea of an aesthetic cut is a valid outcome since it enshrines the primary axiom of that discourse. Aesthetics 'decides' the meaning of art by distinguishing art from all social praxis. When viewed from the perspective of art, understood as a social-human practice, however, the differential boundary between art and non-art is not experienced as a cut, but as a 'threshold' that can be traversed. This does not mean that all ambiguity disappears from art. It does mean, however, that art identifies in the peculiar ontology it possesses an epistemic privilege regarding the world of non-art and that in the space of the exception it is able to discover its critical and political voice.

The art 'interior' and its 'exterior'

The most tendentious aspect of debates concerning the question of art and politics can no longer be avoided: the problem of effect. As far as the polarities of the debate are concerned, its partisans can be distinguished according to the assumptions they hold regarding both the exterior of art and art's relation to that exteriority. Either the social meaning of art will be viewed as a matter of its 'enigmatic' interiority (encapsulated in Adorno's idea that 'art's social character is concealed and can only be grasped by its interpretation'[32]), or it is expressed through relational practices in which art openly converges on the scene of intersubjective communicative rationality as advocated by Habermas and his followers: art gives expression to a moment of pure sociality (exemplified in the artwork advocated by Nicolas Bourriaud). This problem has yielded a fair degree of controversy, across a number of debates, in recent years, motivated in large part by the publication of Rancière's essay, *The Emancipated Spectator* (2009). To give one example: in the field of theatre and performance scholarship, it has hardened around two irreconcilable positions. There are those, such as Alan Read, who insist on 'an incompatibility and a gap where there has been a presumption of comparability and relation'.[33] Read does not deny the possibility for a politics of performance; but he does argue, following Rancière, that there is no direct path available to theatre to a meaningful political consequence or result, at least of the kind imagined by the advocates of the political theatre: 'what does it mean to act politically?', Read ponders, once we 'surrender a latent and unfounded belief that *commitment* marks theatre's primary political will'.[34] Commitment in theatre is a redundant notion for Read, for the following reason: performance 'does not have to seek the political because it is already politics'.[35] This statement must be understood in relation to Rancière's notion of the aesthetic regime: it describes the dissensual or democratic redistribution of bodies, which works indirectly through the aesthetic field by opposing the order of the 'police'. In this way, Read counter-poses one understanding of politics against another that is to be excluded: 'The constitution of this scene of appearance is what performance does. It is this process of a continuous convening of litigious subjects, at odds with the effrontery of the political constitution of parties, that maintains the *efficacy* of politics.'[36] What Read disputes is the assumption that political art requires an explicit articulation of politics; he does not dispute the possibility of a political subjectivation by means of art. In this sense, his position aligns entirely with a Rancièrean 'politics of the aesthetic'. Less consistent, but no less interesting to observe, is the opposing position held by Liz Tomlin in her book *Political Dramaturgies and Theatre Spectatorship*, which articulates itself as a response to the 'sustained skepticism' she discerns regarding any 'ideological steer' in art (as found in Read).[37] Tomlin claims to challenge the 'prevailing narrative' that 'political dramaturgies holding ideological intention, or seeking political interpretations or effect beyond the theatre, are without significant currency'.[38] This scepticism, she argues, derives from the emphatic endorsement of autonomy in spectatorial practices whenever Rancière's aesthetic regime is embraced. She cites Rancière's claim that the 'very same thing that makes the aesthetic "political", stands in the way of all strategies for "politicizing art"', which she reads as a motive for 'discrediting' the idea that art possesses any 'ideological steer' capable of provoking a 'particular political response'.[39] She also argues – and I agree with her – for 'the importance of a material analysis of the context in which dissensus takes place'.[40] The problem arises when she attempts to align that dissensual context with her notion of the artist's ideological steer, since that notion bears certain commitments that would appear to impose the very order that dissensus disorders – the hierarchical relation of the one who possesses a degree of ideological mastery over the situation, and the one who must be thought to exist in a state of ignorance regarding its meaning. But even setting aside terminological considerations of this nature, it is hard to see how the idea of ideological steer offers anything other than a stipulation of the efficacy of authorial intent, with little else offered beyond the desire for it. Those who emphasise spectatorial autonomy, she writes, over the 'ideological intention of the artist … often fail to interrogate whether it is possible for the spectator to remain autonomous from the hegemonic narratives that construct the ideological norms and structures by which the spectator-subject lives'.[41] But by the same token, the reverse is surely also true: those who believe that ideological steer is sufficient, often fail to appreciate the difficulty of reaching those subjects who live within the folds of hegemonic narratives. This is compounded somewhat by the lack of specificity when it comes to Tomlin's understanding of what political effect is meant to look like. In a discussion of Kieran Hurley's celebrated one-man show *Head's Up* – first performed at the Edinburgh Fringe 2016 – political effect seems to be no more than an invitation for the audience to 'look beyond the utopian enclave of the theatre event' (after having encountered the 'searing critique of the neoliberal world inhabited by both performer and audience').[42] I do not doubt that the production intended this 'effect', but in what sense can one distinguish on this basis political effect from the interpretative act in which the spectator understands that the author intended the play to be read as possessing a political content (that it literally gives the spectator the 'heads up')? My point is not to deny that the audience *understood* the play's political intent, but to merely point to the weakness of what is actually involved in this 'understanding' in contrast to what is supposedly being defended.

In this sense, both Read and Tomlin may well land on contending positions, but they do so on the basis of the same understanding of effect, where the word 'effect' is meant to perform some kind of hydraulic function in which one 'will' does the heavy work of lifting another. Each articulates the political character of art thereby in relation either to art's exteriority, in which it asserts a cause-effect relation, or to its interiority, in which it claims that relation is definitively suspended. What each endorses is the presupposition behind Rancière's argument for the aesthetic cut that breaks any continuity between *aesthesis* and *poiesis*: that the possibility of 'political art' rests on a problematic conception in which art is connected to the external world via 'effect' and that effect must be modelled on a 'representative cause-effect schema'.[43] From this notion flow any number of heroes or villains, depending on your point of view: artistic intent, the message of the work, the codification of art and its decoding at the point of reception, ideological 'steer' .... The inadequacy of determining the political nature of art on the basis of such a conception becomes apparent when one interrogates the ambiguity of the term 'effect', which possesses a number of possible meanings in relation to art. The strongest meaning, and so the one that seems to loom largest, says there can be nothing adventitious in the cause-effect relation: the cause designates a power capable, not only of exercising a potent influence, but does so in a way that can be predicted (or at least strongly correlated). Here the meaning of the word effect is contained in the concept of causality. Effect must be directly determined by its cause, with the latter providing an explanatory ground for the former. This explanatory ground is grasped in terms of either the work's meaning ('content') or artistic 'intent', which initiates a causal sequence in which the artist is the possessor of a master code, or what Fredric Jameson called an 'allegorical key', which must also somehow be transmitted to the receiver, and which, by definition, must impose a hierarchy of knowing in the ordering of knowledge (meaning) and its transmission (reception).[44] For this conception, whoever knows the cause knows the meaning of the effect; but equally: the person who only knows the effect, knows nothing of the cause. As a consequence, the effect appears to them as blind fate. This is, of course, the paradigmatic basis for the possibility of critical realism in art. It is also where the conception of aesthetic efficacy blends seamlessly into that of social efficacy: the idea of political intent implies an art able to reveal 'the truth' of society; this, in turn, presupposes, within its hermeneutics, the structure of real causality in the production of ideological deception circulating within the social world. The claim, in other words, is that equipped with a knowledge of 'real' causes (in philosophy – *causa causans*), the subject is provided with the ability to alter their social fate – and this is the service provided by critical art.

Against this conception, Rancière holds that there is another kind of effect that is possible – an indirect effect, whose consequences cannot be discerned from the perspective of artistic intent, a work's meaning, its content, or its message. It is a conception that compels us to rethink 'the idea that there are apparatuses that automatically produce political effects'.[45] What this means is that the proper locus of the political for Rancière is something internal to art insofar as it is claimed by the aesthetic regime of the arts; on the other hand, should a work of art produce an actual political effect in the world beyond art, then this can only be understood in the weakest sense of effect – it is accidental: 'If [a work's] politics coincides with an act of constructing political dissensus, this is something that the art in question does not control.'[46] If artworks do not control these political effects, it is because that political meaning is 'in fact decided upon by a state of conflict that is exterior to them'.[47] Rancière gives the example of Victor Hugo's *Les Misérables* written in 1862. The novel, he claims, employs the 'formula' of a 'social narrative' but its political meaning depends 'on the times'. Hence, it has no fixed political meaning in any strictly intentional or 'internal' sense, but it is capable of taking any number of political meanings:

> [I]t has been seen as a catechism with socialist leanings, ignorant bourgeois sentimentalism over class struggle, or a first rate poem whose democratic meaning is not to be found in the din of revolutionary barricades but in the individual and quasi-subterranean obstinacy of [its hero] Jean Valjean.[48]

The point seems to be that there is no way to decide on the correct political interpretation of Hugo's novel, or any artwork for that matter, because the political meaning attributed to the text cannot be found within it: it can only be located in respect of circumstances that are external to it. Now, I entirely agree with Rancière, when he concludes: 'There is no criterion for establishing an appropriate correlation between the politics of aesthetics and the aesthetics of politics.'[49] One cannot identify it either with the concept of ideological steer or with any reductive conception of causality. But what Rancière inadvertently concedes is that there are indeed *other* tests that can be applied, and it is this concession that opens the way to a different account of art's relation to the political, even if the meaning of that relation is blithely passed over by Rancière, without further remark. It appears in the supposedly accidental relation of the work of art to a state of conflict that is 'exterior' to it. Evidently, Rancière does not deny that art *does* stand in such a relation although he thinks that relation as being unimportant to the question of art's politics. This book takes a different view on this crucial point. In fact, it really begins with the recognition that what is needed is an account of *how* those external or supposedly adventitious circumstances nonetheless confer upon art a determinate political character. This can be further understood in relation to an expression borrowed from the cultural theorist Stuart Hall (to which I will return in the third essay of the book): I agree with Rancière that there is no necessary relation between a work of art and its political effect; but to this I would add what he omits to say – namely, that there is no necessary 'non-correspondence' either. And it is because of this thought (that there is 'no necessary non-correspondence') that I would suggest a different way of conceiving art as relating to its exterior. If this does not provide a philosophical criterion for determining whether or not a work of art is political, it nonetheless provides a set of theoretical tests that can be applied. It is to those tests that I would like to turn in concluding the book's introduction, since – in essence – the elaboration of those tests, through their methodological application, is the primary concern of the essays that follow.

Four tests

Let me be clear: what is to be tested is not the degree of political effectivity of a work of art. Not only is the causal criterion unhelpful owing to the insufficiency of its concept (something I reconsider in the second essay), but it also obscures and (as seen in Rancière) even excludes other approaches. What interests me by contrast are precisely those conditions that appear external to the work of art but whose precise description enables its political character to be assayed. Still, am I not in danger of immediately running into an obstacle in speaking of the 'real' of politics and, in invoking exterior reality, setting my argument on a collision course with the heteronomous principle that is anathema to art? Am I not led then to either assume too much or make too little of the term politics, when it comes to political art, such that its meaning appears bewildering and confusing? How even should politics be grasped 'in its actuality'? In other words, before elaborating the four tests, a few clarifications are in order.

First, without further specification the word politics is beset by misconceptions precisely because it takes on any number of meanings, many of which, when applied to the domain of art, appear decidedly metaphorical; worse still, with this ambivalence comes the inevitable risk of conflating politics with opposing significations. Let me distinguish politics analytically then from two related but contrasting concepts: 'government' and 'state'. Bonnie Honig once pointed out that all political regimes (and many political theorists) tend to confuse 'politics with administration'. The reason why is not difficult to grasp: every insurgent force that manages to acquire power immediately sets about establishing a new status quo. In doing so, it seeks to 'close down the agon'.[50] It transforms itself, as if by dint of an inexorable process, into its opposite, into government. Government desires stability over instability; acquiescence over disobedience; the legitimacy that comes with holding the offices of state over popular politics and democratic disruption; the power of legislating over the act of rule breaking. Where politics is focused and organisational, government is dispersed and institutional. Insofar as the latter promotes 'Apollonian' calculation, painting itself in the grey of the legislature, it is implacably opposed to the 'Dionysian' fervour of the political. Once the State and its institutions are captured, political formations invariably subordinate political logics to the task of governing. Where political logics do persist, it tends to be in the effort of regimes to produce a new 'common sense' after their own image, by consolidating their hegemony over the entire social terrain. This means, by extension, the logic of government does not deprive a ruling regime of its political character. Governing merely confers upon a particular political project the appearance of universal legitimacy. The fact that every government is in the final analysis political indicates that its sovereignty is provisional and secular (not sempiternal and divine). One can see on this basis why government and politics are not just logically incompatible but opposed to one another in actual practice. Government 'displace[s] politics with bureaucratic administration, jurocratic rule, or communitarian consolidation, [and thus] tend[s] to remove politics from the reach of democratic contest'.[51] By contrast, politics proper paints itself in the primary colours of contest and struggle. It is produced from out of the agon which, in becoming a formative political force, exposes that which previously appeared settled and agreed to the 'supernumerary' demand of a subject born of disagreement and grievance.[52] Accordingly, the Schmittian distinction of 'friend and enemy' is entirely apposite in defining the political agon. (That said, Schmitt's definition only deduces the logic of the political as a formal, juristic abstraction. Politics also implies a 'real' terrain: a field of strategic possibility, a project around which it can assemble a coalition of different forces, and a set of determinable historical and social conditions that provide it with both an analysis and compelling demands rooted in material interests.)

In response to this it will be said: if this brief enumeration truly distinguishes the character of politics, then I have placed politics at a far remove indeed from the rarefied world of art practices and institutions. The reply to this depends entirely on how one conceives the terrain of political struggle. Should political struggle be restricted to a particular locus – party-based politics? What if on the contrary there is no one single terrain, but multiple terrains that incorporate *all* levels of a given social formation. To show this is indeed the case, briefly consider the old Marxian concept of mediation. Not only does mediation permit an understanding of how art can be articulated on the terrain of politics, it also shows that in spite of the language game of the aesthetic exception, art practices and institutions stand in a relation of what Stuart Hall termed 'mutual dependence' with other levels of the social formation.[53] The mutual dependence of art and its exterior can be elaborated further via Fredric Jameson's discussion, in *The Political Unconscious*, of Althusser's concept of structural overdetermination. Althusser argued that different levels of the social world possess a degree of semi-autonomy with respect to each other (rather than relations of strict dependency as found in orthodox Marxist accounts, particularly of the base-superstructure variety). Jameson follows Althusser but also asks what prevents these semi-autonomous levels (culture, law, politics, economics, etc.) from becoming *fully* autonomous, which would render the idea of a social totality incoherent.[54] The answer for Jameson is that there must be a form of structural interdependency between the different levels of the social – 'a mediation that passes through the structure, rather than a more immediate mediation in which one level folds into another directly'.[55] Thus, what Althusser refers to rather numinously as a 'final determining instance' is really the necessary 'interrelatedness of all elements in a social formation; only it relates them by way of their structural differences and distance from one another, rather than their ultimate identity'.[56] The autonomy of culture from economics, for example, or art from the sphere of law, rests on a differential logic and not an identarian logic in which each level of the social formation would merely appear as a chimera of a real essence or a reflection of a more fundamental level which it expresses (the 'economic' level). That said, in an overdetermined system, difference does not signify an absolute exteriority whose principles of divergence, separateness, or incommensurability would speak only of the indifference of levels to one another. It indicates a differential *relation*. That is to say, the identity of each level of the social world – including art – derives from its mediated relations, in which its difference with respect to all other levels is produced. Each is a distinct but interdependent part of a single ensemble. And if all levels belong together in the *same* social formation, bound by a common 'mode of production', then art can no longer be conceived as a free-floating sphere of autonomous activity. Rather, its autonomy can only be produced as a 'special instance' *within* an overdetermined structure. Art is not apart from but a part of the very structure from which it is 'excepted'.

It is on this basis that art's exteriority must be seen 'in the final instance', not as an absolute exteriority, but as a differential, mediating, and relational form, whose boundary is permeable; it is also on this basis that I propose four tests that enable an understanding of how art relates to its exterior in specifically political ways. Let me enumerate them briefly here. The first is the test of articulation: political art must be constituted as an *articulatory practice*.[57] Either it can articulate itself directly on the terrain of social struggle (as in activist art practices); or indirectly and critically by disarticulating those 'common sense' linkages through which social objectivity – or what Ernesto Laclau called the 'unity of common sense discourse' or 'doxa' – appears to people as natural as the air they breathe.[58] The concept of articulation refers to the very construction of the social formation. It describes the mechanism(s) by which different things are linked together to form a unified whole, however overdetermined or complexly structured it may be.[59] Thus, in saying that art practices can intervene in a political sense within this structure is to really say that they must be able to operate on what Hall terms 'the terrain of articulation'.[60] The aesthetic field is itself, of course, already an articulated level of the social formation: its autonomy is attenuated by the necessary but contingent mediations that connect it to other social levels, discourses, symbolic and semiotic systems, and communicative practices. Were it not so related, it could not constitute itself as an articulatory practice: art would possess an unconditional autonomy. It would then mean that no articulation was necessary; but it would also mean that art, as a closed system, and as a self-subsisting identity, could not comprehend the 'whole' from within (it could certainly not comprehend it 'politically'). Nor would art have any meaning within the social ensemble as such. The fact that art is immanent to the whole, and that it is essentially a mode of social semiosis, means that it is always already permeated by the world and its mediations. That the language game of the exception confers upon art an epistemic privilege that appears to distance it with respect to the social world, only means that it is not directly bound by its governing principles – its ideological values, economic priorities, and norms of conduct (at least not in the same way that other social practices are). As earlier noted, it is from the vantage point of the exception that radical art can 'determine the determinations', a phrase whose meaning can now be qualified: it intervenes in the sphere of such naturalised discourses as constitute the world of everyday opinion in which social determinations are articulated (as they so often are) in disingenuous ways. As an articulatory practice, art breaks into the system of articulations, in order to break open, disrupt, or reveal the tacit links by which common sense 'truths' appear in the form of a coherently distributed order governing the sensible world.

The second test shows that political art must be defined in the historically contingent terms of the conjuncture that organises the terrain of its intervention. *Political art is conjunctural*; just as the specific encounter with a work of art, insofar as it is experienced as political, will be entirely conditioned by the conjunctural circumstances of the encounter (indeed even the experience of so-called spectatorial autonomy is conditioned by the special character of the conjuncture of which it is also *an* experience). As such, political art must be able to give an account of its context as informed by its historical moment. The conjuncture is 'not just a date on the calendar', then.[61] It 'designates', write Hall et al., 'a specific moment in the life of a social formation … [and they add:] so long as a period is dominated by roughly the same struggles and contradictions and the same efforts to resolve them, it can be said to constitute the same conjuncture'.[62] Furthermore, insofar as it is an articulatory practice, political art will deepen our understanding of those determinations that comprise their conjunctural moment. A concise but pertinent example demonstrates the complexity of this conjunctural task: when the Southern Cheyenne artist Edgar Heap of Birds exhibited a monoprint in the aftermath of the killing of Osama Bin Laden in 2011 that stated: 'Indian Still Target Obama Bin Laden Geronimo',[63] he condensed in the most elliptical form that which the US 'war on terror' had fused together in the form of a historical synthesis, comprising a number of intersecting historical axes. What the poster exposed was a parapraxis or 'Freudian slip' that broke open the political unconscious by which the war on terror was constituted at the level of the political imaginary. It showed how that imaginary projected itself historically through the identification of Bin Laden with the Apache chief Geronimo, used as a code name for Bin Laden by the US Navy SEALs who carried out the operation. It is not just that two unrelated conflicts, over a century apart, were somehow accidentally conflated, however; but rather that in being articulated together, what the conflation inadvertently revealed was the 'obscene supplement' or the 'underside' (as Slavoj Žižek terms it) of America's sense of its own moral purpose.[64] The obscenity of the genocidal logics upon which America was historically founded are shown to *persist* – as disclosed by the use of the popular iconography of Geronimo, which once again imagined the Native American as the 'enemy' to be destroyed. The present conjuncture, however else it may be characterised, is founded on complex layers of history and ideology – and it is those concealed determinations that Heap of Birds articulated in his monoprint.

The third test identifies political art in relation to the dimension of the historical horizon (often referred to as art's 'utopian' or pre-figurative aspect), i.e., *political art is horizonal*. Test three, in other words, examines the extent to which a political work of art projects an alternative futural horizon, and/or disrupts the horizon of present expectations. What this somewhat complex formulation means can be clarified with reference to two concepts developed by the German historian Reinhart Koselleck in his discussion of the 'temporality of history': the 'horizon of expectation' and the 'space of experience'. Koselleck writes: 'concrete history was produced within the medium of particular experiences and particular expectations.'[65] Simply put, the horizon of expectation establishes the conditions of intelligibility for present political experience. In other words: that which is expected is essentially a futural projection that builds on that which has already been

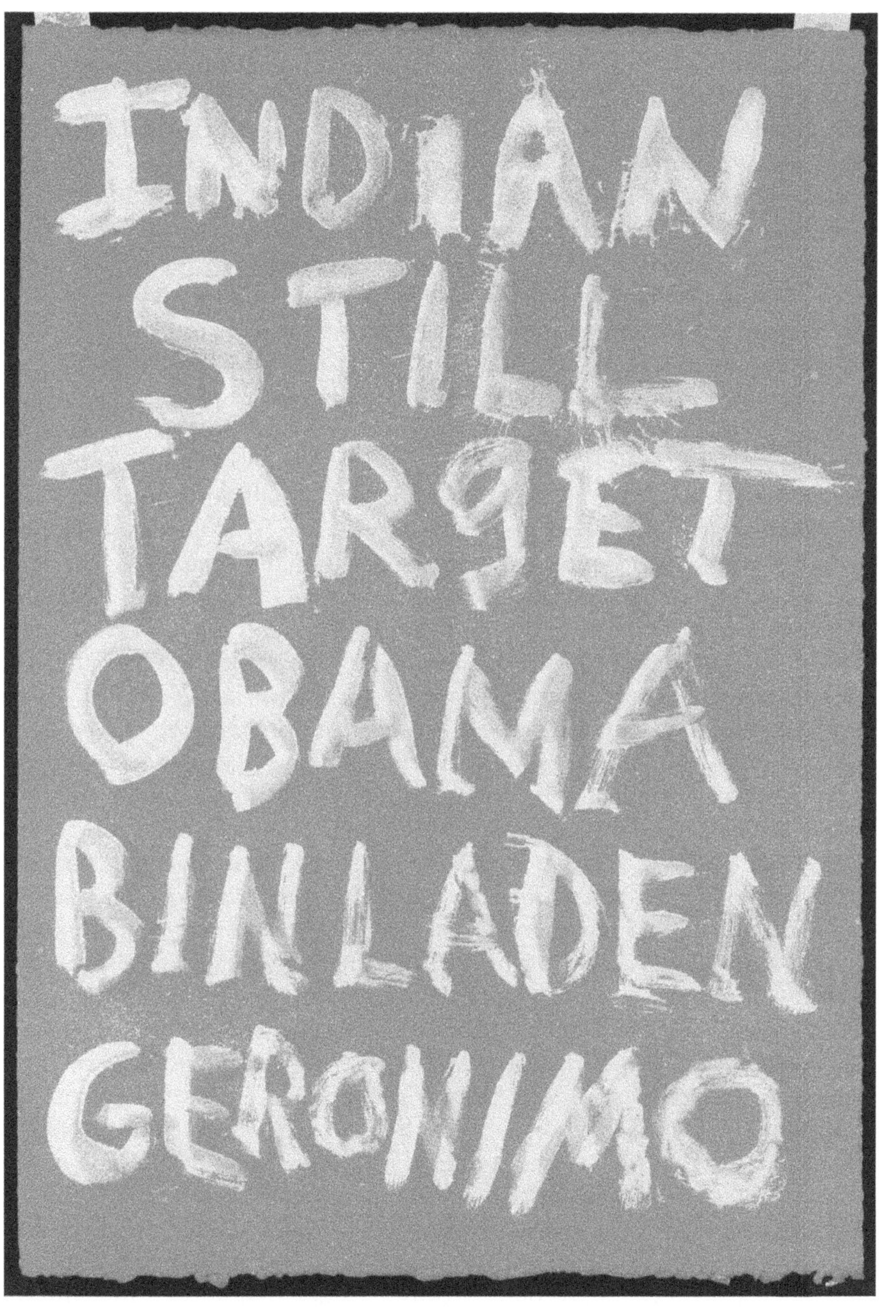

Figure 1 Edgar Heap of Birds, *Indian Still Target*, Mono print, ink on rag paper, 2016.

experienced. Future, present and past thereby converge in the 'horizon of expectation'. To understand the importance of this for a political project: the horizon of expectation signifies a delimitation of the range of possible (or permissible) experiences for a given age, in which past experience acts as a determining constraint on how the present is imagined, and a strategically projected future can be anticipated, and its effects predetermined. Every political project that becomes hegemonic attempts to constitute itself as the 'horizon of horizons', as it were, for its age. Where it succeeds, it presents itself as the horizon for any conceivable political alternative. In our own time, globalisation, with its logics of perpetual growth and capital accumulation, represents our contemporary 'horizon of horizons'. It is precisely that project of ceaseless growth that limits the space of possible political experience today. To the extent that different political formations project themselves upon it, whatever their political 'stripe', whether 'left' or 'right', 'republican' or 'democrat', etc., the global system of transnational capital appears as the horizon of all contemporary political horizons. Peter Osborne has objected, however, to this conception: what horizonal thought appears to foreclose, he argues, is the unexpected, which is essential to radical art practices. Moreover, he writes contra Koselleck: 'we will not reclaim a future qualitatively different from the present by reclaiming the idea of horizon, but rather by attempting to puncture it. In this respect, one can say in relation to art, at its best contemporary art models experimental practices of negation that puncture horizons of expectations.'[66] While I have a degree of sympathy for Osborne's argument, two things might nonetheless be observed. The first concerns Osborne's stipulation – essentially driven by his commitment to Adorno – that radical art should be restricted to the negating function of 'puncturing' the present horizon; the second concerns political practice, since it is difficult to make sense of the idea of 'reclaiming a qualitatively different future' *unless* one can project a qualitatively different politics – that is to say, a politics that can *displace* the present 'horizon of horizons' and *replace* it with another. The political task according to Koselleck is to sever the dominance of the horizon of expectation as it currently exists over the 'space of experience' such that '[h]istorical experience descending from the past could no longer be directly extended into the future'.[67] In relation to this, I propose that one way that radical art is able to model a qualitatively different politics – something that I explore in section three of this book – is to simulate a 'space of experience' that is 'no longer limited', as Koselleck says, 'by the [present] horizon of expectation'.[68] It is art's radical untimeliness that opens the way, in other words, for the possibility of imagining a *new* horizon of expectation. I argue that political art today is less concerned with simply 'negating' the existing horizon, and increasingly concerned with exploring that new space of experience that lies beyond the horizon line of globalisation: what it projects is the possibility of an alternative planetary future. 'Planet-thought', a term developed by Gayatri Spivak (and more recently by Achille Mbembe and others[69]), asks us to 'imagine ourselves as planetary subjects rather than global agents, planetary creatures rather than global entities'.[70] The planetary, I propose, names the horizon of horizons which displaces that of the horizon of globalisation.[71]

The fourth and final test comes down to the question of whether a work of art activates the 'bios politikos' – meaning: *political art activates the political life of the spectator*. The concept of the *bios politikos* (or 'vita activa'), deriving originally from the political thought of Aristotle, was taken up in a remarkable way by Hannah Arendt in *The Human Condition*, in relation to the dual problem of freedom and necessity. For Aristotle, it designated a 'life devoted to public-political matters'.[72] This entailed that every citizen of the *polis* must have a share in the *bios politikos*. It demanded the active participation of every citizen in public life: 'a citizen is one who shares in governing and being governed'[73] – and thus the activation of their own 'bios politikos'. Only by activating the *bios politikos* would the subject attain the kind of excellence that characterised what Aristotle referred to as the 'good life': 'a state exists for the sake of the good life, and not for the sake of life only.'[74]

What differentiates mere life from a good life? It is found in the difference between a life based on choice and a 'share in happiness' and a life that is based on necessity – the kind of reduced life that determines the basic condition of the enslaved, the worker, and – 'brute animals'.[75] It is in relation to this distinction that Arendt observes that the '*bios politikos* denoted explicitly only the realm of human affairs, stressing the action, *praxis*, needed to establish and sustain it. Neither labor nor work was considered to possess sufficient dignity to constitute a bios at all, an autonomous and authentically human way of life.'[76] The *bios politikos*, the genuinely political life, is genuinely human life. It expresses the fundamental freedom by which human existence is distinguished from mere animal existence. Only those considered free, however, possessed the *bios politikos* for Aristotle. It was not available to a life burdened by servitude or labour. Those who 'served and produced what was necessary and useful [to sustain life ...] could not be free, independent of human needs and wants'.[77] Today, of course, the situation of contemporary biopolitics, whose analysis was very much anticipated in Arendt's book, manifests the kind of society that condemns the vast majority to a life of mere labour – to the status of *animal laborens*, as Arendt described it – whose compensations are, at best, to be found in consumerism and in a limited amount of leisure time. Those compensations are granted on condition that participation in the *bios politikos* is – for the most part – abjured. It is only in reversing this general effect, and in reconnecting the subject to the *bios politikos*, that one can speak of political art – and at the same time understand that whenever art activates the *bios politikos* it does so on the grounds of a political articulation, in relation to a specific conjuncture, and against a particular horizon of expectation. The activation of the *bios politikos* of the spectator should not be confused with the problem of effect, as delineated earlier. There are innumerable ways in which art can induce within the spectator a sense of the political outside of issues of intent, explicitness of the message, and ideological direction. To explain what I mean, I would like to conclude with a final example, an excerpt from Peter Weiss's last great novel, *The Aesthetics of Resistance* (1975), which concerns a small group of German workers in the early years of the Nazi regime, who – despite being denied the rights of political organisation and assembly – nonetheless develop their political understanding through their encounter with great works of art, through an auto-didacticism in which the encounter with art precisely activates their *bios politikos*. I will cite the passage at length so as to permit it to bring to the fore the conjunctural 'effect' it evokes:

> The history of art likewise resembled a spiral in which we were always near the past and all components perpetually looked modulated and varied anew, and if any alteration was important for us it was because we had rediscovered the initial value of art, for as long as thinking had existed art had been everyone's property, interlaced with our impulses and reflexes. We refused to accept the notion of an exclusive art created for specifically educated people, nor, likewise, could we be satisfied that there had to be an artistic parlance customized for the working class, a language that had to be very intelligible, solid, and vigorous. For us, art could not be versatile and inventive enough. We agreed with many studying comrades that the paintings that were supposed to mislead us about antithesis had little in common with our goal, no matter how well defended they were. We wanted to find out for ourselves what spoke to us and what was worn out, what was in the services of the demagogues and what might help us in our efforts to track these things down. Painters, poets, philosophers reported on the crises and confrontations, the concretions and awakenings of their time. In the passages from one style to another, in a sudden liberation of movement, gesture, color, one might read social upheavals, yet in the multiplicity of mirrorings, of visual concentrations, one could always find a unity, everything nourished, questioned, answered everything else, and nothing was so remote as to be unfathomable.[78]

There is no way of predetermining the effect produced by art; just as there is no way of freighting the artwork with a meaning whose load it bears, as though it were a cargo shipped from one destination to another, solely in virtue of the political commitments or investments of its maker. Whether an artwork has a political meaning for its time, and whether that meaning then falls into abeyance once its time has passed – or whether, on the contrary, it acquires a political meaning (in a different time and place) whose denotation is something its maker could not have envisaged for it, indicates only the difficulty of attributing a proper locus to the politics of art. This does not mean art must be a total stranger to politics, nor is it to forbid artists any 'engagement' in political contexts.

It is rather to fundamentally recalibrate the meaning of that engagement, and in doing so, to uproot some of our deepest held convictions regarding the problem of the political in art. The essays in this book are the product – no doubt flawed – of my own attempt at digging over this familiar ground. What they offer, I hope, will at least suggest ways of opening the political character of art up to new understandings, able to better account for the dispersions of the artwork's 'political effect'. I do not hold that it is denigrative to assert that political effect cannot be found 'in' the work of art as such. The political meanings claimed on behalf of art cannot be made on the basis that it is conceived as the organising principle of all meaning – on the contrary, and as far as this book is concerned, political 'effect' is always an effect-in-dispersal. What this indicates is the contextual, relational, contingent, and aleatoric aspect of art's politics – in a word, its conjunctural character.

Part I

The aesthetic exception

I fully expect the argument that follows will seem anachronistic to some. It is this: that the work of art, under conditions of modernity, is constituted within a space of exception that brokers no relationality. The familiar sense in which the work of art is said to possess autonomy (is non-relational) is produced as a direct effect of the space of exception that constitutes its condition of visibility as art. I shall designate that space, the aesthetic exception; and in the extended essay that follows, I will develop a number of lines of enquiry that raise it to a level whereby its peculiar and paradoxical nature becomes visible, specifically in the way that its non-relational character is historically problematised in radical art practices.

That art should be articulated on the grounds of its exceptionality has long since fallen out of favour with both artist and critic. Whoever shares the objective of democratising art would happily confirm its redundancy. Whereas once Matthew Arnold could assert, as a radical proposition, 'culture lays on us the same obligation as religion', today, the fact that visiting a gallery is seen as almost liturgical, and the treatment of art as sacrosanct, has only confirmed culture has become part of the problem.[1] The sanctified space of art is at best empty of meaning; at worst, it belies the interests as well as the considerable symbolic capital invested in cultural institutions. Who today, excluding the conservative parvenu and the highbrow snob, would disagree with Pierre Bourdieu's acerbic assessment of the work of art's *status of exception*?[2] Those who proclaimed it, he observed, did so as a ruse for invalidating *a priori* any scientific or 'ordinary' understanding of art and its relation to society. The discourse of the exceptional work of art rests only on 'vapid reflections' about its ineffability and its 'inexpressible singularity'.[3] It also speaks to the self-aggrandisement on the part of those who claim to know art's true power – its ability to transform base matter into spiritual gold. To pronounce on the exceptional in art is to inevitably assert, usually by the one who is doing the asserting, the intellectual transcendence and superiority (at least in matters of taste) of the doyen, the expert, and the connoisseur. By implication at least they thereby mean to distinguish themselves from the boor, the philistine, the pleb – and from anyone else for that matter who fails to recognise, understand, or appreciate it.

In a statement by Alain Badiou, the idea of art's exceptionalism, however, appears to have been made permissible again. It is the purpose of art, he writes, to show exceptional things: 'Truth is exceptional and for art the exception is also the goal.' The trespassing of art onto the domain of truth – the domain of what is truly exceptional – is the reason, the philosopher alleges, for Plato's distrust of art.[4] Badiou's insight is more than useful in terms of what comes next, and I duly offer tribute to its importance here: 'the goal of artistic philosophy, or art in philosophy, is to create a new means to represent the possibility of the impossible, as a goal for new thinking.'[5] Nevertheless, what Badiou has in mind is quite distinct from the problem that I seek to identify in this essay. Badiou is not concerned with the exceptional status of the work of art, but with the representational means by which a new or exceptional thought is produced through art. The problem that interests me cannot be reduced to the question of either means or ends. It would be more accurate to call it a problematic of presupposition. It is the problematic, essentially, of art's condition of emergence; the condition of the very possibility for its appearance in the modern period, which it has still to surpass.[6] This does not mean that every work of art is exceptional, only that its visible difference from other objects is constituted by the space of an exception. It is this space that confers upon every artistic object or performance its sense of autonomy, which is to say, its meaning as art. The hypothesis I wish to examine in relation to this is that art – modern art specifically – rests on, or is bound, as if by an *ontological presupposition*, to inhabit the space of the 'aesthetic exception'.

1

The paradox of the aesthetic exception

The aesthetic exception is both paradigmatic and constitutive. As such, it describes the basic *dispositif* or 'apparatus' of art under conditions of modernity. Giorgio Agamben provides a succinct definition of the concept when he describes the *dispositif* of Christian *oeconomia*: '[it] articulates in God being and praxis.' In the broadest sense of the term, a *dispositif* determines both what something *is* and how it must be strategically administered or governed.[1] It is in virtue of the *dispositif* of the aesthetic exception that art's cultural and institutional location is produced; it is also in virtue of this *dispositif* that art is able to exist in the space of autonomy with respect to the norms that govern social practices. The aesthetic exception relieves art of its social responsibility. It is not that art is thereby made irresponsible; but rather that its foundations rest on something entirely distinct to the forms of regularity by which everyday life praxes are arranged and ordered. This is what classical aesthetics was struggling with when it formulated those foundations around the problem of aesthetic validity, which came to be seen as the proper means of evaluating artistic products. For this same reason, the condition of art must be defined, not simply in light of an 'autonomy' that it won by breaking free of its subservience to religious and sacral forms of aesthetic production, and which characterised the artistic activity of the premodern period – disintegrating finally during the period of the Baroque. It must be defined, rather, in relation to what the aesthetic exception institutes: a space of autonomy that constitutes the artwork's condition of appearance as art. There is no modern work of art that does not occupy the space of the aesthetic exception.

This does not mean that the aesthetic exception fixes art's meaning as though it were impervious to historical development. As modernity progresses, so also the demands placed on the space of aesthetic autonomy begin to intensify, producing an escalation of 'exceptional' effects, which articulate the struggle of art with its own condition, with its status of exception. From Romanticism to Dada, and beyond, its mode of appearance assumes a bewildering degree of variation. What gives tolerance to art's shifting ways of appearing – to the various Schools and movements, to the rhapsodic ruptures with tradition, to declared breaks with the past, and to the production of ceaseless new beginnings and false starts … – announces itself increasingly as the appearance of the exceptional form and as the demand for the new. The discovery of the precedent becomes the criterion for advanced and experimental art, while at the same time – as shall be seen – conceals a point of common derivation with its opposite, with conservative and conventional form. However, precisely because experimentation in art rests on an escalation of the exception, pressing at the limits of what it can tolerate and permit, it is inevitable that with every precedent – with every new discovery – there will be another subsequent discovery that eclipses it; and so, the innovative form that startles the world one day is rendered obsolete the next by a process oriented to the production of ever greater novelty.

To be sure, the story of the birth of experimental form in art is well-known and it is not my intention to retell it here. My task is limited to that of unearthing the space of exception that underpins it, and to do so, primarily, at the point when, through an escalation of its effects, it reveals itself as a crisis at the level of artistic institutions. For that reason, my analysis is focused on the development of avant-garde art in the twentieth century – a period spanning approximately seventy years, ending in the mid-1970s – where the space of the aesthetic exception is radicalised *within* artistic production in order to engineer a crisis for art and culture more generally.

It is in relation to this crisis that the avant-garde should be defined: the avant-gardist gesture is any artistic procedure, characteristically emerging in the first decades of the twentieth century, that reconfigures the space of the aesthetic exception in the form of a crisis of aesthetic validity – a crisis of the validity of art's autonomy from society. It advances as a mode of art that organises itself as a revolt against art. If it inaugurates something paradoxical thereby, something contradictory, and – as it transpires – something bound ultimately to 'fail', as so many have observed, it is because in order to resolve that crisis, art must attempt the impossible feat of surpassing its status of exception. This is the ambition of the avant-garde. That art rests on the presupposition of an exception, then, and that this leads art into a crisis, becomes unambiguously stated in the insurrection of the avant-garde against the aesthetic attitude of modernity. From Dada to the emergence of Fluxus and the conceptual art of the late 1960s, the crisis of aesthetic autonomy not only constituted a motive for anti-aesthetic radicalism, it reflected the truth content of the works produced. Art works came to embody the crisis of their own autonomous status. Its most extreme effect was to transform art into 'anti-art'. Indeed, the very name for this art, 'dada', encapsulated the exceptional status of art at the same time as it parodied it as nonsensical. An art form dedicated to the production of nonsense exists, by definition, beyond the expectations of ordinary communicative 'sense'; it constitutes an 'exception' to the means-ends logics that characterise common and everyday forms of intelligibility:

> Dada: the abolition of logic, the dance of the impotents of creation; Dada: abolition of all social hierarchies and equations set up by our valets to preserve values; Dada: every object, all objects, sentiments and observations, phantoms and the precise shock of parallel lines, are weapons in the fight; Dada: abolition of memory; Dada: abolition of archaeology; Dada: abolition of the prophets; Dada: abolition of the future; Dada: absolute and unquestionable faith in every god that is the product of spontaneity.[2]

Before long the new anti-art would be able to define itself according to the number of commitments it had accumulated, among which the following can be listed:

- To enact an emphatic search for the new, embracing experimentalism over continuity with existing tradition, Schools, and methods.
- To transgress the conventional disciplinary boundaries that demarcated the arts.
- To radicalise the exceptional position of art as a mode of critique vis-à-vis the social world against which it defined itself as antagonistic.
- To align art practices with political radicalism of one sort or another (Fascism in the case of Marinetti's Futurism; the social revolution in the case of Breton's Surrealism).
- To seek to blur, if not dissolve entirely, the frontier separating life and art.
- To reject the existing critical consensus over the meaning of art.
- To evolve a counter-discourse to that of the critic – exemplified by artists' manifestos and publications such as the Fluxus newspaper *Cvv TRE* in the 1960s or, earlier, Duchamp's periodical *The Blind Man*.

With respect, then, to the problem of the position of classical aesthetics, of how to establish art's autonomy from society, the avant-garde sought to 'open up' the very thing that its adversary, so-called academic art had 'closed': art as a social praxis.

However, with this radicalisation what comes into view is the paradox by which radical art will, increasingly, find itself circumscribed; a paradox that confines art to a space of exception from which it cannot break free no matter how hard it tries to do so. The reason why poses something of a conundrum. In common with every invocation of the exception, the aesthetic exception summons the very thing the word apparently excludes, such that one is invariably led to associate with the exception the internalisation of the rule within it. Art is both exceptional (its terms of social acceptance rest on the presupposition that it is to be excepted from the norm; simply put: it does not 'take' but 'breaks' rules) and, because of this paradox, not exceptional: the social conditions by which the novel form is produced already places it under what Bourdieu has called the 'rules of art', i.e., the radically new remains cognisable 'as' art; it belongs to an aesthetic *habitus* 'indissociable from the emergence of an autonomous artistic field capable of posing and imposing its own goals in the face of external demands'.[3]

Belonging to the rule and the radically new that breaks with the rule are, accordingly, the two contradictory terms inevitably at play in the paradox of the aesthetic exception.

On the exception and the rule

The following question arises therefore: How to understand the nature of this paradox in order to identify more precisely the peculiar dynamic at play in the problem of the aesthetic exception?

To answer this, allow me to indulge in a short but necessary digression from my topic. Consider the example of the exception in law, where a form of structural filiation with the aesthetic exception can be discerned. The dialectic of the exception and the rule, which derives from Roman law, scarcely needs repeating. The legal maxim 'Exceptio probat regulum in casibus non exceptis' – a phrase, common enough to be known by almost everyone, irrespective of whether or not they possess the slightest grasp of Latin, is, however, deceptive. The two popular forms it takes, 'For every rule there must be an exception' and 'the exception proves the rule', neglect to translate the second part of the phrase, which qualifies it with a caveat – *in casibus non exceptis* ('in cases not excepted'). In doing so they miss the full rationality of what resides in the intended meaning of the maxim. It is not that the rule points to the inevitability of the exception, as if there existed, outside of the law, a legitimate space of exception populated by a number of exemptions. On the contrary, in law, the exception points in one direction only: back to the rule – back to that which conforms to the norm and to that which it must be applied (i.e., the 'cases not excepted'). What does this say other than that the exception to the rule demonstrates the existence – the validity and authority – of the law, and the requirement of conforming to it?

The exception consequently possesses no power to invalidate the rule of law. In the very act of suspending its application, the exception confirms the rule. And the very thing that appears to be rescinded – the authority of the norm, the statute, the regulation – produces precisely the opposite effect. It inscribes the law within the exception at the exact moment it is declared.

For this reason, the exception is suffused by an ambiguity it cannot shed. This is not only due to the peculiar fact that the exception must be contained in law, but because the exception is established in an ambiguous relation to that which is beyond the law. The exception occupies the space that exists between *anomie* (lawlessness) and *nomos* (law). Or rather, it *institutes* what the Italian philosopher, Giorgio Agamben, has termed a 'zone of indistinction between outside and inside, exclusion and inclusion'.[4]

If the dialectic of the exception is meant to confer authority back on the law, it also opens the difficult question of how to account for that which is outside the law altogether: an outside and a zone of exclusion nevertheless constituted in law. The extreme example is that of the banishment or exclusion of the criminal from society. The criminal is not so defined because of their disregard for the law; they operate within the space of *anomie* as declared by law. Literally speaking, they are 'out' lawed; thus already 'banished'. Outlawing produces a parallel topological problem to that of the exception, since only the law can decree that which is 'extra legem positus' – that which is to be cast, placed, or positioned outside of the law. To be an outlaw is not only to be removed from the protection of the law, to forgo rights, property, and the privileges of suffrage: it is to be uncognisable within it. This is why legal protections are not contradicted by that which is outlawed, since illegality is determined in juridical and discursive terms as a space of non-being. Edward Coke would write that the felon is not only 'Extra legem positus', but thereby 'accounted in Law civiliter mortuus'[5] – they are dead as citizens: civilly dead, dead in the eyes of the law. A similar sense of banishment characterised the extra-legal status of monastic life. Because the monk had entirely retreated from secular existence, he was considered, like the sentenced convict, 'effectually dead in law'.[6] The ambiguity nonetheless remains apparent, constituting an ontological paradox, since the civilly dead, unlike the actually dead, possess a corporeal existence.

The ambiguity is homologous to that of the paradox of the exception and why it constituted a dilemma of law. It is because the rule and standard by which law demarcates itself stands in a necessary relation to a threshold of exception beyond which it can no longer apply, but whose existence is both denied and affirmed. The political legal order requires a constitutive outside, something excessive, something supplementary to it, in order to define itself as a relation to an exteriority. The exception demarcates the outer perimeter of law by establishing a zone of exclusion. In Agamben's terms, it seeks to include that which it excludes. The exception establishes a legal threshold of possible exemptions, on the one hand, but also – on the other – the space of non-being and *anomie*. It refers also therefore to that which is entirely beyond the pale and must be wholly removed from legal protection.

The exception indicates this twofold deviation from the norm: there is the atypical case that nonetheless is recuperable by law and then there is the irrecuperable case, which constitutes the peculiarity of a presence that cannot be counted as being, but which is nonetheless conjurable, 'there'. The figures of legal anomaly, of those who cannot be admitted into the space of legal protections, are prodigious. They include not only historically the criminal, the mad and the monstrous, but also, today, the *sans papier*, the migrant, the camp detainee – any number of wretched figures defined by law as external to its protections.

What can be generalised from the example of the legal exception?

I think it is precisely this constitutive paradox of the exception, which states that the rule is proven by means of that which cannot be counted under it; by the fact of a presence that threatens to negate it. The exception has the power to take on a disturbing existence insofar as it not only designates that which should not be, or that which cannot be permitted, but also indicates an intolerable form that nonetheless necessitates a degree of acknowledgement without which the dimension and domain of 'proper' being could not be established.

The uncognisable must therefore nonetheless be recognised.

It is why the problem of the exception in general always exhibits to a greater or lesser extent the peculiarity of this discursive composition – of including that which it excludes. In order for it to assert the law of its own being, and this certainly applies to the law of art under the aesthetic exception, the norm must posit the existence of an excluded alternative, whose secret power is that of the negation of the norm, a power capable of imperilling the entire dimension of what is accepted as legitimate being.

That the discursive complication, revealed by the paradox, is insuperable stems directly from what is implicated in the relation that is established between rule and the exception. It is that the identity of the excluded other cannot, in fact, be wholly other; it cannot in *fact* be radically external or entirely banished. If it was, not only could it have no relevance for the law, but it would also not be able to take the form of a relation, it could not constitute the excluded other as an identity that could be excluded, however abject, inferior, or subordinate. As such, the excepted 'other' would be equally incapable of serving its constitutive function of creating an 'outside' whereby an 'inside', a domain of inclusion, can be designated.

Exception and autonomy in art

What this establishes is that the paradox of the exception derives from the principle that every rule institutes a relation between that which is counted under it and that which must be excluded from it. It must be thought consequently as an 'irrelational' relation – an impossible relation between being and non-being, between reason and excess, between *nomos* and *anomie*.

Accordingly, it is in accounting for this paradoxical relation that the problem of art under the aesthetic exception is to be understood. A formulation, again borrowed from Agamben, will help elucidate its strategic effect. It is the aesthetic exception that can be said to define art's 'threshold and limit concept'.[7] As both threshold and limit, the aesthetic exception defines the dimension internal to art that inscribes into every work of art an 'originary indistinction' concerning its relation to the world beyond it: its meaning and purpose as art and its ways of appearing. It configures the relation between form and content and between the act of perceiving and the perception of an object, between art's modes of production, and its modes of reception.

This is not to claim that the work of art is without meaning or without content, only that under the aesthetic exception the work of art is always vulnerable to the imposition of a meaning and a content that would threaten its social reabsorption, its loss of autonomy, and its becoming inoperative as a work of art. This is also why the struggle that can be found within the historical development of the exception in modern art is very much the story of the struggle between heteronomous interpretations of art and the claim to the autonomous life of the artwork, which art is compelled endlessly to rediscover in order to proclaim its distinctness from quotidian reality. Even a heteronomous interpretation, however, cannot entirely collapse the space of the aesthetic exception or render it void. A purely economic evaluation of art – the most basic and reductive of heteronomous interpretations, in which the autonomy of art is almost entirely vanquished – is only possible on the basis that it presupposes the aesthetic exception.

The effect of heteronomous interpretation within cultural as opposed to economic spheres of circulation is also widespread and invariably pernicious in its effect. It immobilises the artwork – freezes it, while still preserving its exceptional status. The becoming historical of the contemporary work, its relocation into the fixed space of the art historical past, its entrance into museological space or into the archive – either as entombed emblem of art's glorious accomplishments or as object of curiosity within a wider depiction of the teleological development of art – appropriates the work to a meaning that is wholly objectified, while at the same time objectifying the exceptional status of the work of art in a mythic and entranced form. The fragile balance that establishes the artwork's 'living' relation to the social world, by contrast, also depends on this joint or hinge, this fulcrum established by the aesthetic exception, which places the work in a space of immense precarity – between the opening of meaning and its final closure. The work of art is established on the terrain of a ceaseless oscillation between legibility and illegibility, meaning and non-meaning, purpose and purposelessness, aesthetic 'sense' and historical 'reference', closure and openness. It is (in Stuart Hall's terms) a 'signifying practice' that, at the same time, refuses to be subsumed into the 'natural' order constituting the world of ordinary social significations.[8] In this way the artwork becomes the extreme embodiment of the aesthetic form of the exception.

It is also the infinite controvertability of aesthetic sense into meaning – conferring a conditional, situational and circumstantial character on modern art that permits its differentiation from the art of the premodern period, where the codifications bestowed by religious convention, its pedagogical systems inscribing their lessons onto art's visible surfaces in the form of symbols, parables and allegories, determined the intelligibility of the experience of art according to the prescribed signification imposed on every aesthetic object. This applied as much to the painted icon as it did to the passion play. Premodern art pointed to an exceptional realm, provided a window upon it, while remaining on the side of 'this' world: the exception was not art, but the suprasensible world it imagined; with modernity, the exception becomes wholly immanent to art, constituting its very being. With that immanence the aesthetic exception can be understood to have introduced a certain pathology into art: that of an imaginary without transcendence. It constantly threatens it with the catastrophe of a paradigmatic disordering of meaning that it bears within itself but from which it also draws its disruptive power. The theatre of Samuel Beckett and *Endgame* exemplifies this duality. 'I love order. It's my dream. A world where all would be silent and still and each thing in its last place, under the last dust.'[9] Yet Beckett's play could not be clearer: there can be no order that is not bound, at least as far as radical modernity is concerned, to the disordering of the dream of a perfected semiosis, in which the given world is always already blighted by the petrification of language. The world to which radical art addresses itself is as ruptured as the strange eventide environments inhabited by Beckett's clowns: they confront reality ('commonsense') but in its perpetual state of disintegration.

Another – earlier – example. In Mallarmé's free verse poem of 1897, *Un coup de dés jamais n'aborlira les hazard* ('A throw of the dice will never abolish chance') the disintegrative logic of the exception constitutes the very principle of its composition, such that it challenges the very principle *of* composition – of its formal rules of configuration and conformation. Mallarmé writes in his preface to the poem that his intention was not to 'transgress the measure, only disperse it'.[10] On the one hand, it is the goal of dispersal to suspend the apparatus of scansion, so that the hidden surface behind the organisation and production of poetic sense is revealed as an abstruse presence; it produces effects that never really coalesce in a locatable meaning. On the other hand, the order of meaning is not abandoned, so much as interrupted by gaps, apertures, holes, and cavities, which reveal the bare '*il y a*', so to speak, the bare 'there is ...' – and thus presentational being – of the page, albeit as an asignifying, uninterpretable, anonymous presence.

Already, with Mallarmé, two tendencies can be discerned that will thread their way through the historical development of avant-garde art under the influence of a radical orientation towards the exception – both are incorporated as responses to the problematic of presentation. One refers to the problem of presentational ground and can be called 'phenomenological', the other, that of the presentational act, and can be described as 'performative'.

(1) A new schematisation and spatialisation of the text occurs in Mallarmé: the assemblage of lines and of spacings that do not themselves 'signify' nonetheless reveal the ground that produces signification the moment the page, or to be more precise, 'blankness' itself, trespasses onto the terrain of a hitherto idealised space of poetry – i.e., space conceived as a plenitude of language and being. With this, art is released from a series of formal conventions designed to assert the privileging of meaning and the subsuming of form to the regularity of the established precept. It stages, instead, a play of formal contradictions between elements that can no longer be resolved by recourse to rules of composition that appear now as externally imposed and alien. The artwork is compelled to resolve the interplay of elements for itself, according to a logic that is entirely immanent to it.[11] This mobilisation of the tension that is discovered between the privileged space of meaning, and the impenetrable density of the material ground that, prior to modernism, is considered little more than mere scaffolding, will drive the development of formalism, for instance, abstraction in painting (exemplified in the paintings of Barnett Newman), to the point where the entire *dispositif* of art becomes questionable (as is found, for example, in the work of *Arte Povera* or in the architectural deconstructions of Gordon Matta-Clark).

(2) In dislocating the standard topographical distribution of lines governing the regularity of metre, the standard system of reading – the 'old' law of poetry that once determined the interplay of form and textual meaning also transforms the relation of poem to the reader and in doing so transforms the reader into a performer. Mallarmé confirms it, the poem becomes a performance score: 'this use of the bare thought with its retreats, prolongations, and flights, by means of its very design, for anyone wishing to read it aloud, results in a score.'[12] Kélina Gotman has consequently described Mallarmé's disruptive use of lexicological form as a 'choreotextual event', produced in the form of 'a tangible score whose mode of operation is to reach toward actualization'.[13] It undoes the configurations of poetry in order to reconfigure the poem as a work that 'stages *work* itself'[14] – a choreography of decompositional meanings that, as found half a century later, in the free notational musical compositions of John Cage, requires a performative activation on the part of the reader (or player) in order to complete it.

With the example of Mallarmé, the aesthetic exception is not so much revealed as the condition of the modern work of art – the forgetfulness of the 'law' of its being – but rather, it is 'radicalised' – recalled and awakened; it is mobilised to the task of unmaking the old rules of art. In rendering the distinction between presentational ground and presented object unstable, however, the radical exception reveals not just the exceptional status of art but also its *conditional status*. The de-limiting of form and signification, the essence of experimental art, thus announces, at the close of the nineteenth century, the vastly utopian project at the heart of the avant-garde, which amounts to nothing less than the great task of exorcising from the sphere of the production of art the hegemony of the rule *over* art.

As such, the aesthetic exception grants radical art the power to suspend the rule it institutes, not for the sake of greater aesthetic autonomisation – not to better realise the dream of art for art's sake (the *sine qua non* of aesthetic autonomy) – but on the contrary, for the sake of reconnecting art to the world.

The doctrine of exceptional production and the production of the exceptional subject

But it is for this very reason that radical art cannot but return to the problem of the aesthetic exception – and inevitably the questionability of its own exceptional status.

This means, the limit and threshold of the possibility of the work of art is discovered in the paradoxical movement that simultaneously makes and unmakes the 'law' of the aesthetic exception. So, what of this rule that must be suspended only to be rediscovered within the work of art, and discovered as its very being, and thus precisely in all works of art, even in those where one would least expect to find it?

To begin to answer this question, it is necessary to return to the problem of how the threshold and determinate limits of art are constructed at the commencement of the modern period.

Let us retread our steps for a moment. It has been said that in demarcating the boundary or frontier of art, the aesthetic exception establishes art within a threshold defined by a certain limit that withdraws it from social praxis and from the world. With this withdrawal, not only is art fundamentally displaced in terms of its prior social and religious function, but it is also removed to the novel space of the aesthetic exception. The consequence is that the work of art cannot be constituted as art without being so excepted. In being excepted, the world becomes inoperative for it. The aesthetic exception thereby provides the presupposition for the identification of art in the modern period as something that is apparently 'autonomous'. It constitutes the law of modern art insofar as it is characterised by the peculiarity of art's self-withdrawal from the social world. Associated with this withdrawal, with this displacement, with this well-known social alienation of art,[15] the name donated to modern art by philosophy, 'autonomy', signalled both the autonomy of the art object as well as the autonomous production of the artist. The point of recalling this association, however, is not in order to restage the problem of autonomy but to show the exception's inevitable hold over art; and that consequently if philosophy provided the withdrawal of art from the social world with a concept, it is because it saw the ground of the aesthetic as already distinct from that of social life.

Jean-Luc Nancy points to the pre-eminent role played in the development of modern understandings of aesthetics by Kantian thought. What is Kantianism, after all, if not a critical philosophy of limits and thresholds, of inclusions and exclusions – a philosophy that thinks the aesthetic exception even if it never explicitly names it? Thus, although the aesthetic exception cannot be said to be the sole invention of Kantian thought, it nonetheless receives its first theoretical codification there, and specifically through the development of what Nancy terms the 'Kantian schema'.

Nancy specifies its originality as follows: Kant's schema, he writes, 'forms a pure image *of* the image as a gathering together and unifying of the manifold: a pure image of how something *presents itself* in general'.[16] The aesthetic schema, introduced through the Kantian 'a priori', which already crafts a transcendental space of exception that is entirely consistent with the logic peculiar to the modern project, describes the pure formalism of the self-presenting presentation of any image whatsoever; it is the schema of a presentation in general that brings 'itself out of the confused and incessantly dissolved dispersion of the sensible givens in order to give itself to be seen. In order to make something be seen.'[17] In Kant, this presentational schema, or '*bild*', Nancy notes, 'gives us an understanding of the image that is completely different from the ordinary version of representation, figuration or fiction'[18] – that is to say, it is not the presentation of some particularity but rather of the image as such, grasped as the universal form of presentation, whose ground will be found in the transcendental subject.

It is in light of this that one encounters the consistency of Kantianism, and its congruence with the wider formation of aesthetic modernity; and that subsequently it can be said to adequately express the conditions under which art and aesthetic experience in general will inevitably develop towards greater autonomisation. Art will consequently no longer be bound to some determinate order of being (representation/mimesis, as elaborated in Rancière's representative regime); nor will it be beholden to a given or socially prescribed content. Instead, it will find meaning in form (presentation/*Darstellung*) and in the fact that it is form-giving (auto-*presentational*, i.e., performative: it produces itself from out of itself).

This is also why the term 'formal' aptly describes the space into which art during the modern period is increasingly withdrawn. The formal in art is coterminous – precisely so – with the idea of autonomy that emerges with the Kantian discovery of the subject, grasped as a constitutive or transcendental power, who gives form to the world and to its objects. If the aesthetic exception can thus be mapped against Kantian thought, it is because the latter had already begun to demarcate the boundary of aesthetic experience as founded on the power of the subject to subtract themselves from the mundane world of everyday involvements in order to discover an 'innate' power that is wholly formal and empty of determinate content. It is also this double power of subtraction-formation that enables the inscription of art (and the artist) into an economic logic of autonomous production, and it is this that accounts for art's necessary withdrawal from the heteronomous being of the social, rooted in human interests. It is also why, for Kant, art is irreducible to the productions of the social world – the world of customary work, of the squalidness of toiling labour, of the exertions of man the fabricator, and of the instrumental involvements that define what is commonplace. The artist and the artwork constitute exceptions precisely because they offer an image of production that is different in kind to the mode of production that will be envisaged by eighteenth-century political economists.

Given the Kantian emphasis on the auto-presenting subject, whose faculty of sensibility is emancipated by free play, it is entirely understandable why the first formulation of the aesthetic exception should coincide with Kant's doctrine of artistic genius. If fine art, according to Kant, is the 'art of genius', it is because it designates a mode of production that owes its existence to a sphere of influence that is unequivocally distinct to that of the world of mere social reproduction. It refers to a world of the imagination, unsullied by any association with human praxis, with work: '*Genius* is the innate mental aptitude (*ingenium*) through *which* nature gives the rule to art.'[19] Genius is to be thus distinguished from the ordinary cleverness associated with technical skill, with *technē*, with mere handicraft.[20] Where the latter is defined by the ability to learn according to the established rule, to become proficient in it, to be practised or accomplished even, as for instance is found in the technical arts or industry, the case of artistic genius is different. It cannot be understood on the basis of the rule of *technē*. Nor therefore can it be the product of technical training. That is why art stands in an ambiguous relation to the academic rules of art and why the products of art depend not on the artist's ability to master those rules but on their 'originality'. Only nature can bestow originality on the man of genius, and only originality can explain genius. It is this faculty of originality – or rather, it is the artist's exceptional ability to 'harmonise' their faculties according to the 'rule' set by nature – that makes their aesthetic products 'exemplary'.[21] Genius in art cannot be considered 'imitative' for the simple reason that genius cannot be taught. Equally, because it stands in 'complete opposition' to the 'spirit of imitation', where the mechanical arts are dependent 'upon industry and learning' – are 'simply comprehended and followed in obedience to [the] rule' – genius cannot be 'set down in a formula'.[22] It is impossible to conceive of any equivalence between a derivative technical know-how, no matter how well developed it may be in an individual, and artistic genius that produces itself from itself in the form of free play. Know-how rests on the capacity of the individual to follow a pre-established lead (the 'result of industry backed up by imitation'), and that is precisely why originality remains alien to it. With art, the ability to produce 'excellent' models, the exemplary and original form for others to follow, constitutes the sign of its essential difference.[23] For Kant, art is the product of *homo ludens* not *homo faber*.

The aesthetic exception is, therefore, at the outset, indistinguishable from both the idea of the exceptional individual and a mode of production that is distinct from all others. Its product, 'art', has no parallel in the human world; it is closer to the products of nature in that it appears, just as do ripples running across the surface of a body of water, 'with an absence of labored effect'.[24]

Nevertheless, every exception implies a rule, without which it cannot be comprehended. If genius designates the domain of the exception and is the means by which art appears as autonomous; *technē*, subordinated to the demands of the productive economy, constitutes the rule that governs the world of available things, subject to use. But in fact, in Kant the problem of the rule and the exception that applies to the production of art is – no less than any other form of exception – bound to a dialectic that exposes art to an inherent ambiguity. On the one hand, Kant asserts the priority of the rule of nature: 'a product can never be called art unless there is a preceding rule' and it is nature that provides that rule.[25] On the other hand, this rule that enables the genius to generate the products of art as original productions can only be viewed as a necessary but not as a sufficient condition. Taken in itself originality indicates a certain *anomie* that would destroy the possibility of art. Thus, what is excepted as the product of nature must be made to conform to the production of the very thing it seems to exclude, *technē*. Kant explains the problem as follows: 'Genius can do no more than furnish rich *material* for [the] products of fine art; its elaboration and its *form* require a talent academically trained.'[26] The originality of the genius, and the talent of the technician, are thus brought into alignment by means of the subordination of one to the other, of nature to the rules of art – and of the exception to the law of aesthetic validity. Art is a product of what Kant terms the 'originality of talent' – an amphibology.[27] The ambiguity is encapsulated in the analogy Kant draws between an 'ill-tempered' and a 'trained' horse. The equestrian image is mildly amusing but it also makes the forceful point: untamed genius must be brought under the law of the aesthetic exception if there is to be art. Hence the power of genius must be made to serve the rule, even as it departs from it. Only then can the force of genius's naked 'originality' produce both 'freedom from the constraint of rules' and the appearance of a 'new rule' that constitutes the exemplar for others to follow.[28]

Thus, the threshold established by the aesthetic exception, within which modern art is to be produced, and the limits that it institutes, in order to define art in its autonomy, are already fully operative in Kant's aesthetics, where art is constituted in its difference to the rule and as the exception that proves the rule. Its limits are demarcated by a distinctive mode of production, founded on 'play' not 'pay',[29] and by its separation from the world of routine utility and commonplace convenience (labour). As with nature, its products – aesthetic products – are of no concern to the world viewed from a utilitarian perspective. They are the beautiful and the sublime, which can only be encountered in an aesthetic attitude that suspends the relation to the norms that govern the economics of ordinary social praxis. Nevertheless, even here, too, the exception just as surely implies the rule. Art, Kant notes, is a mode of representation that is 'devoid of an end', but nonetheless, serves the 'interests of social communication'.[30] Although it must suspend the values of the social world, it does so without fundamentally challenging those values; nor does its autonomy permit it to do so, since it owes its existence to the 'rule of social communication' to which it is the exception.

It is important to touch on one final dimension of Kant's analysis, which concerns the possibility of *anomie* in art, even if it is only dealt with there as a kind of precautionary measure or perhaps as an attempted exorcism. It is found in the idea that something disturbing, unsettling, and even humiliating haunts art, against which it must be defended, insofar as it presses in at the outer perimeter or edges of the aesthetic exception. In Kant this disturbance makes its appearance in relation to two exclusions concerning objects of sensibility that are considered neither beautiful nor sublime and that open up the subject to an alterity for which it is not prepared, and that the 'man of taste' is bound to reject as abject. The first relates to the problem of ugliness, which Kant by no means excludes from art – quite the reverse. It is only art that is able to discover the beautiful in otherwise ugly things, such as war, violence, the furies, as can be found in tragic drama. These are objects that can be represented without threatening the pleasure or delight taken in them as representations.[31] The exception that cannot be considered a permissible exception, but rather comprises a type of ugliness that is to be excluded from the realm of aesthetic experience, is found in any object that provokes a sense of disgust in its beholder.[32] Disgust intrudes on the space of the aesthetic exception by means of representations of disgusting objects, which themselves must inspire the same feeling of disgust: 'the artificial representation of the object is no longer distinguishable from the nature of the object itself.'[33] The second exclusion is that of the 'monstrous', which relates to the cognition of the sublime. The sublime belongs to the aesthetic exception because it concerns the feeling of that which is immense yet untainted by any specifiable concept; strictly speaking, it is not an object but a feeling. Sublimity concerns the feeling that is generated in the subject by the presentation of that which is objectively immeasurable, infinite, unintuitable – the 'boundless' – invoking neither feelings of fear nor disgust but rather respect.[34] The monstrous, by contrast, deals with an intuitable object (it can be seen) that is nonetheless 'too great for our faculty of apprehension' – in other words, is presented within the field of visibility as an improbable object. Such improbable objects will be things to which a determinable concept such as 'animal' can nonetheless be attached, but whose size exceeds the capacity for presentation or comprehension at a human scale.[35] The colossus, for instance, or so Kant writes, verges on the monstrous.

2

Crossing the threshold

It should hardly be a surprise to discover that the language of disgust and monstrosity permeates the avant-garde, insofar as it offers art a means to escape the self-enclosure imposed by the aesthetic exception. It equips it with the means, and with a level discursive violence, capable of upending aesthetic modernity. From the expletive 'Merdre!' on Jarry's stage, to Tristan Tzara's proclamation: 'All pictorial or plastic work is useless: let it then be a monstrosity that frightens senile minds'; or, equally, his identification of the Dadaist work with those 'product[s] of disgust capable of becoming a negation of the family' – each statement places contradiction, contrariety, grotesquery, thus abjected and shunned things, at the service of art and, with this radical attitude, art at the service of 'LIFE'.[1]

This double movement, simultaneously propelling art towards life while rejecting the norms of the bourgeois aesthetic tradition and its validity regime, which compels art to surpass its own condition, to discover a sensorium unlike any other, has become the quintessential trope for the identification of the avant-gardist work of art. Agamben notes, for example, 'the work of art must be abolished in the name of something that, in art itself, goes beyond the work and demands to be realized not in a work but in life.'[2] But it is precisely this demand, to not simply reflect but to give shape to society, to transform the praxis of life itself, that ensures that the avant-gardist work of art runs into an insurmountable contradiction. Peter Bürger, in his seminal study on the avant-garde, summarised the issue as follows:

> When art and the praxis of life are one, when the praxis is aesthetic and art is practical, art's purpose can no longer be discovered, because the existence of two distinct spheres (art and the praxis of life) that is constitutive of the concept of purpose or intended use has come to an end.[3]

For Bürger, the unsurpassable horizon for art is that of its own institutionalisation, beyond which it would simply cease to be relevant because it would cease to be art. The achievement of the avant-garde lies, by contrast, not in the destruction of art as an institution – there it obviously failed – but in demonstrating the impossibility of 'positing aesthetic norms as valid ones'.[4] What is of interest in this claim is not simply that the avant-gardist art-work, seeking to surpass its condition as art, by deactivating what Agamben calls the 'work-artist-operation machine',[5] discovered that it nonetheless remained captive, if not exactly to the institution of art, then to its insti-tuting logic. Nor is it the observation that it consequently discovered that failure was the inevitable price to be paid for the boldness of its ambition, which is true of every vanguard movement. Rather, it is how, in attempting to cross the threshold of the aesthetic exception, the avant-garde nonethe-less created multiple breaches in the *dispositif* of the exception, whose pur-pose as art's validity regime is to ensure the legitimate autonomy of art by securing its separation from society. To reduce the avant-garde to failure, however heroic, is to misunderstand the significance of its transgressions; it is better understood in relation to the multiple infractions, incursions, and openings it made onto the world, which redefined the scope of the threshold of the aesthetic exception. It is to see how it revealed the nature of its own limits, without thereby entirely annulling the force of its presupposition – and the hold of the aesthetic exception over art.

Two issues arise: it is evident that art cannot merge with life unless the threshold of the aesthetic exception is crossed and that its limits are, at least partially, breached; it is also evident that the aesthetic exception, for the very reason that it institutes art's difference from life, places art in a relation to that which it apparently excludes. Only on this basis does an opening onto life become conceivable. This is why avant-gardism is not a style of art but the practice of crossing the paradoxical space of the exception that constitutes art. As crossing, it is always made – or attempted – in relation to art's excluded zones onto which the avant-gardist gesture trespasses in defiance of the norms of aesthetic validity that otherwise prohibit such a crossing. It should already be apparent that, in the very act of negating the aesthetic norm, the relation of art to that which it rejects or excludes as non-art is revealed and that it is revealed precisely as a relation of exception, i.e., that it includes what it excludes. Because the relation of art to non-art cannot be made visible without suspending the norm that maintains art in a space of legitimacy and non-art in a space of exclusion, where it can be pro-duced as pure exteriority, the very act of attempting to cross the threshold of the aesthetic exception necessarily renders its force inoperative – even if only for a fleeting moment, it implies a transposition of aesthetic experience from the interior of art to its exterior. That is why the crossing of the threshold produces an opening that possesses potentially radical and transfigurative possibilities for both art and for life. That which is interior becomes exteri-orised; that which is exterior, interiorised. What the avant-garde opens up, in other words, is the space of the aesthetic exception in terms that might be described – to employ a Foucauldian notion – as a 'field of problematisation', in which aesthetic objects, modes of aesthetic production and reception, norms and values of taste, the status of objects, things, bodies, and the very exceptionalism of art itself are able to be put to the test. I identify three such openings:

The first is onto the space of the everyday. It is exemplified above all by Duchamp's readymades, such as *Fountain* (1917) – Duchamp's notorious (and unsuccessful) attempt at presenting a common-or-garden urinal bearing the signature 'R. Mutt' at the exhibition of the Society of Independent Artists in New York. The readymade object comprises the exemplary avant-gardist gesture because it denies the claim that art possesses any exceptional value, or rather and more precisely stated, it denies that its value emanates from the work as the aura of autonomous artistic production. It opens art up to objects, products, and performances that belong to the mass economy of the living. Agamben notes that with *Fountain* 'in reality nothing ... comes to presence: not the work, because we are dealing with some industrial produced object of use, nor the artistic operation, because in no way is there a *poiesis* or production'.[6] What is the readymade if not the artistic procedure of deactivating the authority of poetic judgement over the work of art? During a symposium held at MOMA in 1961, Duchamp remarked, 'The choice of readymade is always based on visual indifference and, at the same time, a total absence of good or bad taste.'[7] But it is also, and this is Agamben's point, a deactivation of *poiesis* – since there is an absence of artistic production, there is no 'work' in the artwork.[8]

Except something is at work in the readymade – and it is the aesthetic exception. The appearance of the readymade necessarily remains within the nomenclature of gestures classifiable as art, even as it cancels its defining characteristic: the autonomy of artistic labour (first identified with genius). Although it enacts a suspension of the social destiny of the non-art object, conceived as the anonymous product of work, dislocating it from the domain of reification (from factory floor to shop floor) from which it originates, it fails to make questionable the idea that there can be no exceptional spaces in the administered world of industrial capitalism. Reified life remains more or less untouched by the readymade, for all its radicality. It might be said that the radical gesture of the readymade toward the everyday is a democratising gesture, but that it remains a *gesture*. The condition of excepting that which cannot be excepted is itself an exception that confirms the rule. That said, it is no less significant for having done so. Transformed by a radical gesture that brings an object of no significance into the space of the aesthetic exception, with the appearance of the readymade, that which constitutes art becomes exceptionally volatile; the norms of taste governing the work of art are shown to be only contingently related to the quality of the object and the mode of its production. Its radicality lies in the fact that it emancipates art from its role as a transmitter of norms and the obligation of art's conformity to the prescriptions of good taste. Duchamp, defending his work in *The Blind Man*, wrote: 'Whether Mr. Mutt with his own hands made the fountain or not has no importance. He CHOSE it. He took an ordinary article of life, placed it so that its useful significance disappeared under the new title and point of view – creating a new thought for that object.'[9] The paradox of the readymade, co-opted by Duchamp as irony, is however only possible because of the aesthetic exception. In problematising the aesthetic field, the readymade problematises itself. Thus, its rhetorical mode, which articulates the found object as art from the position of art's imagined self-dispossession, as the voluntary revocation of its exceptional status, nonetheless presupposes the very thing it seeks to erase: the exceptional status of the work of art. On the other hand, the discovery of the readymade provokes a significant transformation in the *dispositif* of art: whereas prior to the avant-garde, the work of art is determined according to its conformity with the rules of aesthetic judgement, with the avant-gardist gesture, the power of declaring the aesthetic exception is wrested from aesthetics by the artist who now 'chooses' what will henceforth constitute a work of art. The aesthetic exception remains in force; but it is now declared by the producers of art. The paradox of the readymade can be understood in light of this, accordingly: it confirms art's distinctiveness in the ironic form of the object it has appropriated and as something now insulated from the world of purposeful things; and at the same time, by successfully usurping the heteronomous object as art, it suspends the law of autonomous production from which art supposedly derives its meaning as a mode of 'work' whose unique privilege is to find its being solely in an activity that is meaningful in and for itself. It demonstrates art as simultaneously exceptional (in terms of its institutional location) and unexceptional (in terms of what can henceforth count as art). Thus, even the most banal object or image can become art.

The second opening the avant-garde makes is onto a space of racialised alterity. This is the space occupied by what Thomas McEvilley once termed the 'culturally Other'[10] (the appropriation of African masks, by Picasso, is just one instance); it is unlocked through radical art's embrace of 'primitivism'. As a designator, the term 'primitivism' remains highly problematic and profoundly ambiguous. Its ambiguity resides in the fact that it refers neither to a style of art (there is not one single primitivist style – there are many styles, from Fauvism to Cubism and beyond); nor does it denote the art of so-called 'primitive' cultures (from folk art to the art of the Easter Islands). Primitivism is closer to what Robert Goldwater once described as an 'artistic attitude'.[11] But this needs to be further qualified: it is a *radical* attitude forged by the avant-gardist attempt to contest the space of the aesthetic exception; to cancel it by crossing its threshold in order to collapse the differential that maintains art in relation to its zones of exclusion. Its problematic aspect therefore lies in how it discursively constructs those forms of art that must be simultaneously constituted as non-art – as existing in a space of exteriority, and at the same time, as somehow preserving the 'essence' of art that has been forfeited by the Western aesthetic tradition and which must be retrieved. Goldwater writes: 'Primitivism presupposes the primitive, and at the core of an artistic primitivism we may expect to find a nucleus of "primitive" works of art.'[12] The question, then, is how was that nucleus to be discursively constructed? Let us say, briefly, that primitivism is a discourse that *produces* the 'primitive' in the exact sense that Edward Said intended when he described orientalism as an 'invention' of the West.[13] This does not mean it is simply a fictionalisation; it is also a 'veridic discourse'.[14] It develops a systematic epistemology of Europe's others in the form of a mode of knowledge that enabled European culture to '[gain] in strength and identity by setting itself off against the Orient as a sort of surrogate and even underground self'.[15] Its initial colonial context, in the nineteenth century, coincided with an emergent ethnological interest founded on the encounter with 'other' cultures. Led by developments in the science of ethnology, primitivist discourse produced grotesque efforts such as Alfred Haddon's *Evolution of Art* (1895), predicated on the assumption of Western cultural exceptionalism, and which advanced a baseless Darwinian thesis that non-European art could be explained as a process of 'degeneration' of mimetic and naturalistic form, leading to an ever-increasing simplification of design and thus a cultural lapse or regression into mere ornamentation; but it also produced more respectful attempts such as Leo Frobenius's *Kulturgeschichte Afrikas* (1933), admired by both Léopold Senghor and Aimé Césaire, not least because Frobenius's anthropology restored to Africa the civilisation that European colonialism, with its depiction of Africa as a savage society, had denied to it.[16]

Inescapably, with the expansion of Western colonialism, the aesthetic exception, during the nineteenth century, is framed by ethnological assumptions that articulated European art in relation to the aesthetic achievements of those it plundered, as being wholly different in kind. That ethnographers relocated artworks taken from African and Oceanic cultures in the museums of the Western metropolis, presenting them as ethnological artefacts, merely confirmed that difference. By definition, it associated the primitive with other forms of heteronomous aesthetic production such as folk art and the archaeological remnants of prehistorical societies. The value of these objects was viewed therefore entirely in ethnographic, not aesthetic, terms. It is only with the development of the avant-garde attitude that those assumptions would be fundamentally challenged; with this, the primitive would begin to be inscribed into art in the form of a curatorial critique. Apollinaire, following a visit to the Trocadéro ethnographic museum in Paris, would complain that the masterpieces of African and Oceanic art exhibited there were 'arranged to appeal to ethnic curiosity, not to aesthetic sensibility' and that 'objects of a principally artistic nature should be separated from the ethnography [display] and placed in another museum'.[17] André Malraux's proposed 'museum without walls' went further: 'The multitude of works created in every civilization known to man doesn't "enrich" the Louvre; it calls the Louvre into question.'[18] Moreover, as early as 1919 African art began to be sold through the commercial galleries in Paris,[19] an unsurprising development given the growing interest among both artists and private collectors (Picasso himself had several African masks and fetishes in his atelier). The effect of these developments was twofold. On the one hand, by drawing the tribal artefact out of the objectified space of the ethnological museum and relocating it within the space of the art gallery, an avant-gardist curatorial gesture was able to significantly expand what could count as art. It did so in a way that inevitably destabilised the imagined supremacy of the European aesthetic tradition, exposing it to the cultural and historical contingencies at work in every aesthetic system. The exceptionalism of Western art, as constituted by the aesthetic exception, could no longer be taken as 'exceptional'. On the other hand, in drawing attention to its aesthetic qualities, the same gesture reobjectified tribal art by disregarding its lifeworld context and the forms of consciousness that produced it. Hal Foster observed that the process of the 'repositioning of the tribal object as art' led to its 'aestheticisation' – and that its 'commercialisation' was predicated on its 'decontextualisation'.[20] The aesthetic exception is thus reinstalled at the very moment it appears to have been suspended. As such, the division of art and life is itself reinstated.

It goes without saying that the avant-garde attitude of primitivism was by no means confined to curatorial interventions. Radical art deployed culturally determined and so-called 'primitivist' form as a means of emancipating itself from the staleness of a tradition whose closure it sought; in doing so, it evoked a radical discourse that aimed at rediscovering an authenticity perceived to have been lost to Western art. Malraux, in his writing on Picasso, captured the experience of the many artists at the time who, like Picasso, were 'dumbfounded by their discovery of an inexhaustible inventiveness [in African art] which they called the language of freedom'.[21] The 'plurality of African forms', he wrote, 'endowed that art with a virulent force'[22] against which all the familiar landmarks of Western art were shattered. Picasso, in particular, exemplified for Malraux the far-reaching nature of the encounter of European modernism with African and Oceanic art. Picasso's interest, he argued, was not simply formal – contrary to the suggestion of Goldwater, who claimed it was employed only for the sake of 'strengthening the plastic design'.[23] More than that, Picasso saw African art as endowed with 'supernatural' force and is even reported to have described masks and fetishes as 'weapons' capable of revealing the 'unknown'.[24]

It is precisely here, in the use of art as a weapon for revealing that which is unknown, that the aesthetic exception is inscribed by the avant-garde into the space of that which rational thought bars: the unconscious. Malraux's association of primitivism with the unconscious dimension of repressed and primitive impulses is hardly accidental. It understands aesthetic primitivism as providing the means by which art is able to cross the threshold that divides reason from unreason in order to reach that which Western culture exorcises from consciousness as irrational. The African mask, like Picasso's art,

> represent[s] what our unconscious might recognise, what the diver was able to bring up from the lowest depths. Painting was to bring up, from the depths of the unconscious, all that is so alien to man that he is unaware of it, but close enough to him so that he can recognise it.[25]

What is encountered and recognised in African art is therefore not simply an irrepressible will to art but the will to conjure a netherworld through art – a world of ancestors and spirits, and of unconscious and primal forces, that would otherwise remain unknown.[26] Primitivism constructs its encounter with African art by reconfiguring its animating principles: it incorporates them into an avant-gardism that pits itself against a European aesthetic episteme which, deriving from a Hellenic legacy, understands itself only as a will to represent.

Yet even here must one not enquire whether it is not, in fact, African art, used as a means of radicalising the aesthetic exception, that finds itself entirely dispossessed? It surrenders tribal art to aesthetic autonomy in the name of surpassing the autonomy of the work of art, and of reconnecting it to vital life-impulses. Its power derives from the fact that it can be appropriated to the aesthetic field while persisting in being 'immemorial' and therefore defined against the 'modern'. It remains 'outside' of art, which is to say that its value for the avant-garde lay primarily in the fact that as non-art it could not be fully assimilated. It is why Malraux sees virtue in the idea that 'African art has no history'.[27] And it is also why it is entirely legitimate to write, as Rasheed Araeen does, that

> It is not Picasso's interest in African art that should be objectionable, but his perception of Africa that reduces it perpetually to its past and prevents it from moving forward through its own consciousness of itself and the world around it.

> For Europe, Africa has always been, and still is, its Other, its suppressed
> unconscious, the land of savages and primitives frozen in a state of blissful
> ignorance.[28]

To deny African art a history is to deny that Africa has a place within the
contemporary world that constituted aesthetic modernity.[29] The bad faith
operative in the avant-garde is that it gives with one hand while taking
with the other. Nevertheless, something is given – or rather something gives
with the traversal of the aesthetic exception by the 'primitivist attitude'.
Souleymane Bachir Diagne draws out the paradox involved in primitivism in relation to Picasso who, he concedes, viewed African art as 'art in
its infancy';[30] Picasso thereby returned the African mask to the same discursive milieu of childishness and savageness that had been developed by
the ethnologists before him. But Diagne also suggests another, and rather
more intriguing way of reading Picasso, and that is as an enquirer who
sought answers to profound questions: how does one give 'form to the
spirits'?, how does one make the 'unconscious speak'?, how does one provoke, through art, 'strange emotions'?[31] Picasso understood that African
art was 'unable to be domesticated', as ethnographers had attempted in
reducing it to the level of mere curiosity. On the contrary, in the African
work of art, Picasso found 'the riddle of a way of seeing, thinking and feeling of which these objects are the writing'.[32] Picasso's art – perhaps more
than anyone else's – draws European modernity toward this other sensibility: towards a radically distinct way of thinking art, a different way of
experiencing reality, indeed, an alternative way of objectivating the world
through art. As for the aesthetic exception, then – the artefacts of tribal art
that Picasso exposed it to, revealed an aesthetic syntax and an artistic logic,
an entire vocabulary of art in fact, that had nothing to do with European
norms of perception or structures of feeling, and whose enigmatic power
was capable of bursting its assumptions and prejudices apart. Rather than a
reductive primitivist attitude, Diagne discovers, in Picasso, something more
radical: a becoming-African of modernist art,[33] and an attitude that disclosed the very thing European coloniality disavowed: an African way of
'being-in-the-world'.[34]

The third opening, made by the avant-garde, is onto the space of
'pathological' aesthetic production. It is expressed as an interest in what
Michel Thévoz describes as a 'kind of domestic, pathologised exoticism'[35]
identified with the 'naïve' art of the schizophrenic, the Sunday painter,
and an assortment of other gifted amateurs, in short, with art's 'outsiders'. It is also associated with the French artist, Jean Dubuffet, although
he was by no means the first to express an interest in the art of non-artists.
What he did was provide it with a name: 'Art Brut', or 'outsider art'. He
also attached to that name a radical thesis: it is a form of art that '[owes]

nothing (or as little as possible) to the imitation of art that one can see in museums, salons and galleries'. It is an art of 'spontaneous and personal invention', whose 'manner of expression' derives entirely from the artist's 'own impulses and humors, without regard for the rules, without regard for current convention'.[36] In expressing outright indifference to the rules and conventions of art, not only does it appear to reject socially acceptable estimations of art, but, along with it, the entire cultural and institutional milieu in which art is invested. It is why Dubuffet linked it to the all-out war he declared against 'asphyxiating culture': 'We can only rid ourselves of the Western bourgeois caste by unmasking and demystifying its phony culture.'[37] The avant-garde interest in outsider art develops as both an interest in the artistic efforts of those individuals who exist on the extreme margins of culture, as its excluded members; but it is also linked to an identification of 'genuine' art with a self-consciously asocial attitude by which the artist is necessarily opposed to society. The 'production of art', Dubuffet writes, 'is a strictly and strongly individual function, and consequently entirely antagonistic to any social function. It can only be an antisocial function, or at least an asocial one.'[38] To be outside art and to be outside of society are the two preconditions of being an outsider artist.

With Art Brut, it is not simply that the space of the aesthetic exception is crossed, however; better to say that it is entirely crossed out. The mechanism for accomplishing this – essentially a coup against art – is to declare that a form of art, which is excluded from being art, *is* 'art'. The objective was not simply to thereby expand the threshold of what could be accepted as a legitimate work of art. With Dubuffet, the gesture is rather more extreme: it aimed to collapse the aesthetic exception altogether into the space of *anomie*, where the existing laws, rules, and conventions of art are made senseless. What bourgeois culture proclaimed to be legitimate art was, in reality, for him, its 'falsified substitute'.[39] The subversive potential of Art Brut resides in the fact that the objects of outsider art maintained their 'outside' status. They are incorruptible since they cannot be assimilated to any aesthetic tradition or to any art historical School; but, also, it derives from this: that in being declared art they are nonetheless seen to express the truth of art, or at least the truth of art in its difference from art. The 'outside' is constituted as the real 'inside', because – in the face of illegitimate and inauthentic culture – only that which is outside is truly capable of expressing the interior character of art. It is able to do this for two reasons. First, because outsider art establishes a direct connection between art and life: even if the conditions of its production are typically institutional (the prison or the asylum) and its context thus circumscribed by therapeutic discourses – it remains the spontaneous product of life; second, because as the self-assertion of life, outsider art designated an art that belonged to the domain of a commonality that had all but been cast out from culture. Ordinary life, lacking expertise or even seriousness, does not consummate culture, still less does it produce it.[40] The audacity of Dubuffet's proposition is that it upends the aesthetic exception, decomposes it as a *dispositif* that preserves the insularity of art, segregating it from life, and elevating art above it. In its refusal to identify art with the products of permissible autonomy, the essence of art is located elsewhere. It emerges from the naïve productions of the lifeworld, from a heterological dispersion that bears no real affinity to the aesthetic morphologies of bourgeois culture; it appears in the form of an art that serves no function as art. For Dubuffet, its presence is a deliberate offence against institutional culture, a disturbance within the enunciative field of art. It would be truer to say that outsider art merely masquerades as art; in reality, it derives from something entirely heteronomous to it – from the pathological interests and desires of its makers, consequently from life itself.

Nevertheless, in order that outsider art can be made tangible, can serve the function it does, it also needed to be produced as an object.

That enunciative function was provided by the counter-aesthetic discourse of the avant-garde. Outsider art does not precede the appearance of the discourse that deciphers it. Rather than say that there existed a savage interior to art that merely awaited discovery, better to say this instead: that it was owing to an avant-garde counter-discourse that a dimension of objects that did not exist prior to its appearance was capable of becoming manifest within the field of art. This is not to say that works of art were not made by the mad, by the incarcerated, by the naïve producer, or any number of amateur artists. It is to say that they could not enter the field of artistic production as its outsiders until a discourse on outsider art had opened up the space according to which their presence there could be accounted for and understood – a space, in short, of legibility. Owing to this peculiarity, a counter-discourse must itself be constituted *as* discourse. Foucault's question: 'Who is speaking?' 'Who is qualified to speak?' cannot be eluded.[41] Whoever speaks authoritatively about art, exhibits a discerning intelligence, has an eye that, in touching art's tangible surfaces, perceives its inner qualities, decrypts its modes of expression, is able to articulate its intrinsic meaning. That is why the very act of making legible the outsider artist serves a discursive function: it is to incorporate them within the space of the aesthetic exception as the paradoxical presence of those who must be excluded from art. The discourse on outsider art is itself a manifestation of the aesthetic exception: its logics enable it to admit, into the field of legitimate art, objects that cannot otherwise appear there, giving form to that which is excepted. The very act of decentring the cultural norm serves also to recentre it as a poetics of the marginal and of the artwork that is non-art. The aesthetic exception proves itself to be the threshold that is at once crossed and conserved. Expressed in the language of Bourdieu, the exception reveals itself to be a 'game' in which one flouts the rules so as to more strongly affirm them. It can do so because the logic of an apparent exception derives directly from the fact that the artistic field has attained a 'high degree of autonomy and is inhabited by a tradition of permanent rupture with aesthetic tradition'.[42] This apparent oxymoron is resolvable once one understands the implicit conservatism that permeates the aesthetic exception and that permits the outlier only insofar as it confirms the authority of the regulatory field that constitutes it. With the avant-garde, that authority, as has already been said, passes into the hands of the artist, who is now granted the status of the expert – and thus the authority to declare what art *is*.[43] Consequently:

> [The] 'theoreticians' of outsider art can only constitute the artistic productions of children or of schizophrenics as an extreme form of art for art's sake, in a sort of absolute misinterpretation, because they overlook the fact that they cannot appear as such except to an eye produced as theirs is, by the artistic field which determines (or makes possible) the essentially contradictory approach, one necessarily doomed to failure, by which they aim to constitute the artist against the historical definition of the artist.[44]

Given that the theoretician does not speak as a 'private person' but as an authority, and with an eye possessing the power to 'except', it is evident that the radicality of Art Brut lies not in the work produced but rather resides in the gesture of declaring non-art to be art. Once again, the impossibility of the avant-garde is discovered in its most fundamental gesture: it seeks to surpass the condition of art by means of art. It is why the outsider artist can only ever be positioned as – to employ Bourdieu's colourful term – a 'creature-creator'.[45] The outsider artist possesses no authority with which to declare the aesthetic exception. They lack autonomy in the precise sense that they are denied the capacity to declare themselves 'artists'. Rather, the outsider artist must be produced as an artist by being inscribed within a 'space of artistic possibilities' that they neither command nor understand. Their function is to realise possibilities 'objectively' present within a field of aesthetic production about which they have little comprehension. In this sense, for the outsider, the opening of outsider art proves to be an illusion: in Bourdieu's terms, it reinforces, all the more firmly, the absolute closure of the artistic field. What retains its validity, however, is the aesthetic exception that once again is brought to visibility by the effect of its cancellation.

Art at the absolute limits: conceptual art and performance as Happening

From all that has been said above, it seems that the aesthetic exception, once radicalised by the attitude of the avant-garde, held art in the grip of a compulsion that relentlessly propelled it in the direction of non-art, according to the question it constantly posed: of whether or not art is capable of producing an art of the living. Every attempt to answer that question necessarily maintained art in an equivocal position. The avant-garde could no more resolve the question by surpassing its status of exception (in order to establish art as a redemptive social praxis) than it could redeem life by elevating it to the status of art. Each attempted crossing of the threshold confirmed the impasse of the avant-garde; just as every transformative vision it advanced foundered on the internal contradiction that it both aroused and yet left unresolved: art's incorporating of life (in an 'art of living') threatened the incorporation of art by life (art's absorption into the social world of everyday practices).

But it would be incorrect to conclude from this that the avant-garde experiment simply exhausted itself through repeated failure. It also led to a discovery that suggested a way out of the impasse of the exception, and a way for art to productively occupy the space of its own contradiction. Only by calling itself into question could the function of art be rediscovered; only at the very limit of its own impossibility, could art find itself again, in its political being, as essentially oriented by an instruction stemming from (and in recognition of) the immanent needs and demands located in the lifeworld. In the former case, art learned how to conceptualise itself as a discursive practice. It originates with the investigative developments of conceptual art as theorised by Joseph Kosuth and also Art & Language, but it also leads eventually to the realisation that the limit of art is by no means conceptual: it is found in the institutional site in which art is able to be socially reproduced. In the case of the latter, what was discovered was that for art to break with itself, so that practices may experiment with art as a form of life, art must *attenuate* itself to the point of dissolution, it must become wholly performance. The significant theorist here is Allan Kaprow, but equally important are the experimental writings and practices of the Fluxus movement that he helped establish. Between the mid-1950s and early 1970s, it is these two tendencies that come to embody a singular dynamic that pressed art to answer the question of its own 'limit' – no longer so as to breach it, or to overcome it, as with the earlier avant-garde, but rather to discover a way of constituting a practice of art that could subsist at the extreme limit of the aesthetic exception. For the first, art is discovered as a limiting-concept; for the second, art becomes a limit-experience.

What differentiates them is:

(1) To discover art in the form of a limiting-concept is to understand the precise specialism of the artist as being primarily a conceptual thinker concerned with the analytic conditions by which art is distinguishable as art. An artist is someone engaged in the attempt to question the meaning of art through an artistic process of permanent interrogation and enquiry into its concept. Dick Higgins provided a useful definition of such an artist-enquirer when he wrote: 'The artist is whoever researches aesthetic functions in practice.'[46] But what exactly is it to research the aesthetic *function* of art through the practice of making art? Kosuth's essay *Art after Philosophy* attempted to provide an answer to this question. It did so in two ways: first, negatively, by denying that the answer could be located in aesthetics ('there is no conceptual connection between art and aesthetics', i.e., art cannot be decided on the basis of an aesthetic judgement);[47] second, and in a more positive manner, by defining 'function' as art's 'reason-to-be'.[48] This minimal definition required amplification; it resolved the problem but only insofar as it appealed to a tautological concept in which art is reduced to an 'analytic proposition', as effectively summarised by Donald Judd's succinct aphorism: 'If someone calls it art, it's art.'[49] Kosuth's interpretation, nevertheless, adds an important qualification to the analytic definition of art: something is art 'by virtue of its presentation in terms of its art "idea" '.[50] Now, what is it to interrogate art on the basis of its idea, if not to attempt a pure distillation of the aesthetic exception, where the latter is understood as a limit-operator on what can count as art? Thus: to make art conceptually is effectively to reduce its reason for being to the task of answering the analytic question, 'what semantic conditions must be satisfied for something to be designated as art?' But it also opens up the way to a more critical question concerning the discursive conditions according to which the aesthetic exception is instituted. In doing the latter, the conceptual enquiry into art's reason-for-being reopens the ontological question central to the aesthetic exception regarding the nature of the ground of art: how is the 'mode of being' of art to be decided?

The radical implications of Kosuth's approach to conceptual art, although never expressly stated by Kosuth as such, can nonetheless be found in the later attempt to formulate an art practice that could also constitute a discursive critique of art: to interrogate the idea of art, not on the idealist grounds developed by Kosuth, but on the grounds of material and institutional analysis. Such a possibility is both implied and constrained by Kosuth's own analysis. In articulating the conceptual basis of art, one must begin, of necessity, he argues, with a critique of the traditional conception of art which is in reality a morphological interpretation of art. According to this interpretation, something is art if it *looks* like art. But Kosuth notes, similitude provides a weak ground for determining the 'nature or function'[51] of art. A morphological interpretation of art rests on the presupposition of established or conventional form and genre. It is why for all the apparent radicalism of formalist experimentation, it remained entirely bound to the limits of morphological interpretation, and so possessed an inherently conservative outlook. Since the formalist must presuppose what a given form *is*, it becomes 'impossible to question the nature of art'[52] on its basis – for the painter, art is painting. It is also why, for Kosuth, the history of the avant-garde reveals a tendency to conserve form rather than fundamentally question it. Cubism may say 'new things', but only from within the constraints established by the old language of painting.[53]

The exception is Duchamp, who understood that a critique of the *dispositif* of art necessitated a practice that could actively question the very conception of art; only Duchamp grasped that such a critique required a fundamental transformation at the level of the language of art and that consequently art must be compelled, as Kosuth puts it, to 'speak another language'[54] (a language that was adequate to the ideative problem of art, the language of its function). If Duchamp was the first to pose the question of art's function, it is because he was the first to break with the morphological interpretation of art, whereby the morphological identity of art is reproduced by means of its identification with a given or pre-existent form. To break with this conservative logic, art began to 'question the nature of art by presenting new propositions as to art's nature'.[55] Thus with conceptual art, the question of morphological identity is replaced by that of art's *logical* identity – in other words, with the question of the instituting language of art.

Understanding art conceptually, as the presentation of a radical proposition regarding art's 'nature', not only shattered the presumption that the nature of art can be located in reference to the conventional techniques employed in the identification of art – through a hermeneutic process of the continuous transmission of rules, genres, and aesthetic forms; it also demonstrated – and decisively so – that art could jettison almost every prior conception as to what constituted art while nonetheless remaining art. It is this discovery that gives conceptual art its peculiar Janus face, however. On the one hand, it becomes increasingly Calvinist in its adherence to the limiting-condition it discovers: the law of art that it inscribes within itself as its own reason-for-being and which defines the very interiority of the aesthetic exception as a space of exception becomes a kind of dogma or article of true faith; on the other hand, its increasing concern for the material aspects of language leads it toward a materialist critique of the institution of art itself. This tension, which resolves itself later through artists such as Hans Haacke, Jenny Holzer, and Andrea Fraser, is already palpable in Kosuth's essay.

In the first place, conceptual art is almost entirely defined by the logical reduction of the terms of the aesthetic exception: it produces an art that is fixated on advancing propositions regarding the nature of art, and as such cannot but limit itself to a solipsistic universe in which art is a commentary on art and its processes. Viewed from this perspective, it imposes on itself a definition of art that severely limits its ability to produce a critical discourse on art by means of art. Kosuth appears to confirm the problem when he writes: 'a work of art is a kind of *proposition* presented within the context of art as a comment on art.'[56] The question of what is constitutive for art, restricted to an examination of the semantic processes involved in producing it as 'language', necessarily also restricts it to a purely linguistic delimitation of art that refuses all 'matter of fact'.[57] Conceptual art becomes nothing less than a purified logic of art; it only *is* to the extent that it adheres absolutely to the idea of the limit-concept, which is to say, to an art whose role is simply to provide 'definitions of art'.[58] It is also why, in discovering art as limiting-concept, Kosuth affirms the law of the aesthetic exception in a way that denies art any social function: 'Art indeed exists for its own sake.'[59] To the extent that art is its own concept and thus autonomous with respect to the world, it cannot interpret the world without losing its claim to logical identity; at the same time, it cannot be interpreted by the world since only art can interpret art ('Art's only claim is for art. Art is the definition of art'[60]). Art verifies nothing that belongs to the domain of facts. Nor can it confirm lived experience by means of art's supposed 'expressive' capacity.

But it is precisely the quest for the analytic definition of art – for an art that has purified itself to the point of becoming a tautology – that also inevitably leads conceptual art into a confrontation with its own constitutive paradox: its logical autonomy must nonetheless be expressible as a facticity that is penetrated by non-logical elements. That the artwork has a presence in the world of things is not reducible to a mere accident of little or no import. Even the dematerialised work of art, which dispenses with the object altogether, cannot evade the aesthetic exception by which it is constituted as art. That it is fated to reproduce art's status of exception appears as the inviolable presupposition of every artwork, regardless of the question of form. Thus, while conceptual art correctly identified the question of the language of art as being bound to the problem of morphology – that is, to a language of conventions that bears the traces of stultifying and socially prescriptive norms such that even the most radical formal experiment unwittingly harbours within itself the secretions of the degraded sensorium of the world of late modernity – it nonetheless overlooked the constitutive role played by the logics of exclusion that relates art to all that is 'outside' of art and that belies the claim to any pure identity of art. The more art becomes distilled as a 'logic', the greater the amplification of the exception that is inscribed within the very structure of its being; correlatively – the more one is led to understand that art is indeed constituted by means of a social relation whose peculiarity is that it appears discursively by omission, in a negated form. It is true, the aesthetic exception can indeed be expressed in the form of a logical identity but only at the cost of concealing art's underpinning material relations, and it is this paradox that returns art to the constitutive question of its relation to the world: the aesthetic exception, grasped as the *dispositif* of art, determines art according to a logic of separation that is irreducible to form.

No doubt, the conceptual amplification of the language of art's logical autonomy served to reveal the *dispositif* of the aesthetic exception all the more acutely – indeed, to the point where it could no longer be evaded. At that point, art began to be made that thematised its own exceptional status critically; it did so by interrogating the structural and institutional forms of exclusion according to which it is circumscribed. In doing so, it reinterpreted the limit-condition of art, no longer in relation of a 'logic of identity', but in terms of a critique of the nexus of art institutions and material interests in which it found itself discursively, culturally, and economically articulated.[61]

(2) Where Kosuth conceived art in entirely analytic terms, for Kaprow, art 'happens' as an event of 'synthesis' in which art and non-art converge to produce the integral form of 'nonart art'[62] or 'performance'. Just as Kosuth sought to establish art at the logical limit of the aesthetic exception without seeking to eliminate it, so too, in Kaprow, the limit is also sought but not the abolition of art. However, Kaprow seeks that limit elsewhere and consequently confronts a wholly distinct problematic in relation to it: that of encountering the 'limit-experience' of art.

To understand what this entails, two initial observations:

First, it is clear that the Happening also breaks with the language of morphology – with identifiable genres, with the formal typologies of art, with all the old classifications – but it does so with an entirely different motive in mind to that of conceptual art. In pushing art to the limit, where it could no longer function according to the traditional mechanisms that serve the purpose of identifying the work of art, Kaprow located the Happening within the 'zone of indistinction' that defines the outer perimeter of the aesthetic exception; the Happening occurs at the point at which art is poised at the threshold of aesthetic *anomie* yet without entirely collapsing into senselessness and formlessness. Higgins defined the Happening as follows: '[it] developed as an intermedia, an uncharted land that lies between collage, music, and the theatre. It is not governed by rules; each work determines its own medium and form according to its needs.'[63] Kaprow himself would describe the Happening as a way 'to "do" [art] that was distinct from any known genre (or any combination of genres)'.[64]

A second, related observation, is this: to locate art at the very border of the aesthetic exception is not to seek to overcome art, but to discover a different way of living with art, one that seeks the closest possible proximity between art and life, while eschewing the utopianism of the early avant-garde that imagined their sublation in the form of a reconciled world, emancipated from both art and work. Kaprow notes: 'the models for these early Happenings were not the arts ... [but the] abundant alternatives [found] in everyday life routines: brushing your teeth, getting on a bus, washing dinner dishes ....'[65] The aim does not appear to assign art the task of redeeming life, so much as to make art out of its very material, out of its routines, its rituals, its unobserved performances. The Happening produces an intermedial conjunction of elements drawn from life and art; it evades art's confinement in form, but without forsaking its comprehensibility as art. Its interest lies in the development of an art of experience or rather an experiential art that is encompassed by and is capable of encompassing forms of life. But while it eludes the enclosure of traditional forms and innovates a practice that redefines what art can be, it is not interested in defining art as such. That is why it is better to say of the Happening that what it seeks is the limit-experience of art, not its limit-concept.

What does it mean to seek the limit-experience of art?

The concept of limit-experience, developed in the writings of Bataille – influencing both Michel Foucault and Maurice Blanchot – suggests an experience that transgresses the limits at which the subject experiences itself as the coherent centre of its own world; on the contrary, it is – Foucault notes – reached at the point where the subject 'leaves itself, at the limits of its own impossibility'.[66] Martin Jay offers a useful gloss on Foucault's explanation, which might just as well describe the experience of the Happening in Kaprow: '[it] is a curiously contradictory mixture of self-expansion and self-annihilation, immediate, proactive spontaneity and fictional retrospection, personal inwardness and communal interaction.'[67] Its applicability to Kaprow lies in the way the Happening situates art at the point of its own impossible possibility. To formulate art as Happening is to approach the very threshold of art's decomposition; not to cross it, but to occupy it. It is to establish an existence for art in the zone where a threatened indiscernibility from life pervades it. For the Happening to occur it must imagine that art and life might attain a degree of – if not perfect – congruence, that such an impossibility is nonetheless a possibility for it; but at the same time, it must recognise that the space it imagines for itself is unattainable and that it will remain on the side of art. Thus, in the Happening the limit-experience of art becomes operative, without which Kaprow's nonart art, could not be imagined: it is an art that is envisaged as the ideal that art and life form a composite whole. But because it remains an impossible possibility, it can never enter actual experience. Hence it is a limit-experience that must be invoked in order to make sense of the conflict that exists between the spheres of art and life that gives the Happening its reason-for-being. To express the same point otherwise, the limit-experience is the projection of a necessary fiction of the future anterior of art in which the moment when life and art are transformed into one another is represented as an ideality. Its impossible aspect lies in the aesthetic exception, proclaimed as starkly and bluntly as a Kantian 'fact of reason', in every work of art. Were it ever to be realised, art would be immediately released from the grip of the ontological differ-ence that separates it from life; but since that difference is constitutive of the aesthetic exception, it is also constitutive of art.

In an important essay written shortly after the death of Jackson Pollock, Kaprow speculated that a path, or a passage, and thus a return to the living world could be accomplished through the transformation of art into gesture and into performance.[68] In a remarkably prophetic passage, he imagines an art of the future in which all limits and bounds of genre and form will be transgressed – an art that makes use of:

> [the] specific substances of sight, sound, movement, people, odors, touch, objects of every sort and materials for the new art: paint, chairs, food, electric and neon lights, smoke, water, old socks, a dog, movies, a thousand other things that will be discovered by the present generation of artists ... they will disclose entirely unheard-of happenings and events, found in garbage cans, police files, hotel lobbies; seen as store windows and on the streets; and sensed in dreams and horrible accidents. An odor of crushed strawberries, a letter from a friend, or a billboard selling Drano ... all will become materials for this new concrete art.

> The young artist of today need no longer say, 'I am a painter' or 'a poet' or 'a dancer'. They are simply 'artists'. All of life will be open to them. They will discover out of the ordinary things, the meaning of ordinariness. They will not try to make them extraordinary. Only state their real meaning.[69]

It is almost as if Kaprow announces an entirely new axiom for art: that it must be non-exceptional. And yet two dilemmas arise as a consequence of this axiomatic transformation of art, which cannot but turn its emphatic embrace of the idea of art's immanence to life back upon itself – and back upon the problematic of art's status of exception.

In the first place, to do something, rather than to spectate something, is to experience something directly for oneself, without the medium of a rep-resenter. But a subtle contradiction can be discerned here. Life – by which is intended life as it is unselfconsciously lived or what the phenomenol-ogists once termed 'antepredicative' life – cannot also be a 'performance'. On the contrary, performance is not life as it is immediately lived; and the performance-Happening cannot be anything other than a staging of the everyday that fundamentally transforms its character. Kaprow writes of 'doing life, consciously'[70] – but he also means by this: doing life with the consciousness of being an artist – doing life 'artistically' – in the self-reflexive and estranging attitude that characterises the very act of making art: 'when you do life consciously ... life becomes pretty strange – paying attention changes the thing attended to – so the Happenings were not nearly as lifelike as I had supposed they might be.'[71] Moreover, the Happening established a new genre of art, whose function was barely distinguishable from ethnographic observation: '[it] disclosed the hidden performances, taken for granted, in the theatre of the everyday.'[72] What this confirms is that an art that adopts an 'ethnological attitude' cannot but be a means of appropriating life, rather than a means of establishing art on a continuum with the everyday. An attitude that 'exaggerates the normally unattended aspects of everyday life'[73] cannot be said to coexist in the same universe as the objects that interest it – the very act of incorporating the everyday destroys its ordinary character, and the distinction that separates aesthetic experience from reality is reimposed with the effect of rendering the everyday inoperative.

The second issue concerns the consequences of situating art at the limit-experience of art: the practice of making 'art, which isn't perceived as art, is not so much a contradiction as a paradox', Kaprow observes.[74] What this paradox suggests is something we have already encountered: that the power of art to confer upon nonart the 'status of art' necessarily bears the signature of the aesthetic exception. It is a power that is also at play in the Happening and can only be realised in recognition of the unsurpassable horizon of autonomy that modern art nonetheless dreams can be surpassed – what Kaprow termed 'this lifelike impulse [that] dominated the vanguard'.[75] It eventually produces the paradox of 'an artist ... who does and does not make art'.[76] The Happening thus represents something profoundly terminal for radical art: it is the moment in art when the aesthetic exception manifests the paradoxical essence of art in a form of art that refuses to abide by the knowledge contained in its own experience: that its ownmost possibility is also an impossibility – that nothing can be salvaged from the fact that precisely when it achieves its closest proximity to life, the difference that separates art from life – the exception – is experienced aesthetically as both chiasm and chasm.

Should the realisation of the inescapability of art's difference from life disturb or overwhelm us; does it present an insuperable obstacle on the path to the deliverance of life from that which remorselessly diminishes it? Must it lead to despair at radical art's repeated failures to irreversibly traverse, once and for all, the space of the aesthetic exception, thereby emancipating art from its own *dispositif*? Or, by contrast, might the vanity of the exercise, and the cost of its failure, serve to legitimate, at least after a certain fashion, a different attitude – one suffused with exorbitant irony, as is found in the new traditionalisms that emerged in the 1980s and 1990s – the 'return to painting' is the most obvious example that comes to mind – with all the complacency that that entailed; a return to forms of art that in proclaiming themselves 'post-avant-garde' presented themselves as being comfortable with their exceptional status?

Such questions, however, soon prove fatuous. It is inevitable that the problematic of the aesthetic exception continues to provoke different responses from art: its solutions are in turn both 'conservative' and 'radical'. Regarding the claims of radical art today – of an art that can be said to bear the traces, however faintly, of the avant-garde, the question of whether or not it is ever possible to realistically conceive of a society where art could renounce its status of exception continues to haunt it (as has been witnessed over the past two decades with the 'social turn' in art and the embrace of 'relational aesthetics'). Only insofar as it is haunted by life, however, is art provoked to ceaselessly return to examine its own limits, to explore its own radical impossibility.

After all, what does impossibility name if not art's dissatisfaction with reality? It compels it to return to the question of its own utopian horizon, where once again it imagines itself capable of reanimating the Schillerian dream of an 'art of living', in which art might be returned to life as a force capable of redeeming it. No doubt the history of avànt-garde art has revealed the severe limitations of the radical attitude that sought to overturn aesthetic modernity; but it is also plain that the question of art's exceptionalism unerringly returns to art in order to impose upon it the obligation to attempt further crossings of the threshold. That same history also shows that whenever life is absorbed into the space of the aesthetic exception, the paradox that structures it produces unpredictable consequences, that it is not without effect, and that it can transform both how the *dispositif* of art is instituted and how art itself conceives itself in practice. The paradox at the heart of the aesthetic exception holds open the possibility of an impossible (because *anomic*) relation that is nonetheless constitutive for it – the consequence is that radical art always bears within itself the sign of its own disappearance. By the same token, it is owing to this paradox that the aesthetic exception will always show that art and life are never wholly indifferent to one another.

Indeed, they are fated by modernity to perpetually meet at the point where each must either lose its identity and disappear, or else recoil from one another so as to re-establish their difference – with life sunk back into abjected reality, and art taking flight into its old recondite fantasies of an aesthetic autonomy that preserves it from the expropriations of the social-instrumental communicative system. If the paradox of the aesthetic exception reveals itself in the form of an irrelational relation, it is because under conditions of modernity, art is constituted in a differential play between two separable spheres – a separation that is and is not absolute. It is why, in this paradoxical play, which constitutes the ontological difference by which art is identified, in being divided from life, anomic pressures will always be present, as a persistent threat to the very possibility of art. To the extent that the aesthetic exception can never perfect itself (which in any case would see the discursive closure of art), what is held open is the promise of a possible emancipation through art, however limited; that the discursive limit set by art's *dispositif* cannot be exceeded, by no means prohibits art from testing those limits.

This is why modern art is essentially defined by its own problematisation: to problematise the aesthetic exception is fundamental to the possibility of a genuinely radical gesture in art, which is compelled to refuse its 'status of exception'; just as art's radical gestures provide the locus where the most extreme possibility contained in the *dispositif* of art is fully realised in the form of the paradox of an exception that both proves and exceeds the rule.

3

The institution of art: Critical and theoretical reflections

There are, no doubt, a number of objections that can be made to the thesis of the aesthetic exception, as I have elaborated it in this essay. A principal concern may well lie in the presumption that it discovers a 'dispositif' of art, as if there existed a law of being for art as such. It is as though in identifying that law one would be able to state unequivocally the governing principle for every form of art. Is there not, as a consequence, a tension in what I have described, between the social conditioning of art and its claim to an exceptional status, which my analysis side-steps, and where the aesthetic exception appears merely as a conceptual conceit, but not the product of the patient and somewhat laborious task of material analysis that is required if we are serious about understanding the 'contradictions of the avant-gardist undertaking'?[1] If there is a decisive question, and one that bears on art's social mediations, it is not how to understand the exceptional status of art, but how to identify art as the locus of social power, a concentration of symbolic capital – only in this way can one begin to understand how art is assigned to its social fate. To derive from the aesthetic exception a *dispositif* for any art whatsoever more than risks imposing a transcendental and idealistic construction on art – in doing so it overlooks the historical and material conditions of its existence. Bürger's point that it is the 'institution of art' that determines its 'framing conditions',[2] might appear apposite in this regard, since the institutionalisation of art he describes incorporates the historical processes by which art assumes its objective appearance in the world. Nevertheless, it is notable that Bürger writes specifically of framing *conditions*, suggesting that it is the institution of art (not art institutions) that determines what can count as art, and which 'frames' what is possible as art – a point I elaborate on below.

Another objection comes from contemporary art itself, where one need only attend to art practices themselves to understand the problem with the thesis of the aesthetic exception. It is only in respect of a historical and material process that one can begin to understand the nature of relational and institutional critiques that emerge within contemporary critical art practices, and that such art forms are already produced in the full knowledge that they are the bearers of social and communicative norms, which they are happy to adapt to their own ends and purposes. Arguably, the social norm becomes the material of the work – as is found in so-called 'relational' art, which is happy to call itself 'heteronomous'. For the new 'engaged' artist, the aim is to use art in order to release a social communicative power by means of artistic practices that would otherwise be suppressed by reified forms of life. Relational works that tap directly into the arteries and bloodstream of what Habermas once claimed to have identified as a 'network of a bodily and interactively shaped, historically situated reason',[3] cannot but view the thesis of art's exceptional status as otiose and as unwelcome as the belief that art is only capable of being itself when it is 'autonomous'.

To this last claim, I would point to Bürger's observation, which still retains its salience almost half a century after it was first written: 'An art no longer distinct from the praxis of life but wholly absorbed in it will lose the capacity to criticize it, along with its distance.'[4] It is undeniable that today it is the social relation that matters most to radical art practices. Alas, the risk that such practices run is that the social truth content they seek to make manifest or even liberate soon collapses back into social untruth ('relation-ality' elevates an idealised abstraction to the level of a social power, which is in reality nothing but a hyperbolic 'relation' not a real relation: 'the sphere of human relations as art-work venue'[5]). Where the sociality of art is viewed as an end in itself then the social truth of art cannot but be conflated with the relationality of its form of engagement, which in turn becomes its form. The 'truth' in art, for these practices, requires art to become a social communicative praxis; while social praxis, once it enters the space of the aesthetic exception, is deprived of its communicative and pragmatic content and autonomised as aesthetic form. The problems that arise with this contradiction are complex; but to simplify things one might borrow from Marcuse, for whom the principal dilemma was that in seeking to offer a 'counter image' to our present 'affirmative culture', what such practices risk is the 'transformation of the earth into a gigantic community centre'.[6] Marcuse would no doubt have added: what they fail to see is that at stake is not simply the transformation of culture, but its abolition. On this latter point, one must admit a degree of weary scepticism today. What can be said, however, is this: that the neo-avant-gardist undertaking, substituting the revolutionary fervour of their forebears for a tamer image of art as a kind of therapeutic panacea for various social ills, appears to neglect the lesson to be drawn from the crisis of aesthetic autonomy engendered by the avant-garde – that to forsake the institution of art is also to cede the grounds of autonomy upon which any artistic critique of the social senso-rium rests.

It is this latter point, this paradox of the avant-gardist gesture, that returns the focus of the argument to the difficult question of the relation between art's *dispositif* and art's institutional 'framing conditions'. The question here is how to understand the problematic of art as being bound both to a governing or conditioning principle in which art's exceptional status is declared and its modes of institutionalisation, by means of which (regardless of the material and determinate form it takes) art is granted its autonomy.

Now, to say – as I did at the outset – that the aesthetic exception is no more than the presupposition that governs the identification of art as a distinct and autonomous realm of objects, gestures, forms, or activities, is also to indicate toward the discursive formation within which 'statements of art' – i.e., any artwork – can be produced. The artwork is whatever can be articulated *as* art within a given aesthetic configuration; while, for its part, an aesthetic configuration is nothing other than the totality of artistic possibilities at play in a system of dispersed practices, where heterogeneous objects can coexist, no matter how contradictory they may appear when taken as an ensemble – hence what can count as art is indeed capacious and open. The question of the *institutionalisation* of those possibilities concerns, by contrast, their incorporation under specific validity conditions, which is in turn determinative of the range of positions made available by the aesthetic field at a given moment. Where the latter holds possibilities 'open', institutionalisation must be seen as relatively 'closed', according to its specific sites of reception (galleries, museums, theatres, and so on), modes of production, distribution and reception, access to subsidy, artistic networks, educational institutions, and their legitimating functions. It is for this reason that the aesthetic exception should not be conflated with the question of the institution of art. In itself it says nothing concrete about what the objects of art are, or which gestures and performances can be counted as art (and which discounted). Nor does it prescribe the proper form that art should take or stipulate the means for discerning acts of aesthetic impropriety or stylistic transgressions; or, alternatively, provide the critic with the measure of artistic success or failure. It says nothing about what art must look or be like, and it prohibits no activity from entering the expansive domain of art practices. More fundamental than this: to assert the aesthetic exception as a presupposition is not to discover an absolute point of origin or an unconditioned beginning; still less is it to discern the shadow of a metaphysics cast over art by aesthetic philosophy in order to mystify it.

In which case, what is it? And if it does none of these things, of what conceptual use is it?

In answer to this question, I would say, regarding the aesthetic exception, that it is no more nor less than a logic. To be precise, it is the logic by which a regime for the identification of art was able to be instituted under the new conditions that emerged with the development of bourgeois-capitalist society; a regime of art that first came to prominence around the time of the Enlightenment. Nevertheless, for such a regime to take hold, to acquire, as it would do, such comprehensive dominance over the production and reception of art, configuring art as an autonomous 'field', the aesthetic exception had to be necessitated by something. Consequently, it cannot be viewed merely as a fortuitous or accidental effect of Enlightenment thought, any more than it can be said to hover above art as an imperious principle of aesthetic judgement. On the contrary, to constitute itself as a *dispositif*, the aesthetic exception had to provide art with a function that made it indispensable to society. That function is succinctly described by Bürger as 'the neutralization of critique [and] of impulses to change society'.[7]

Thus, for aesthetic modernity, art served as a kind of release valve; it alleviated the alienating effects on the individual of a social existence that would otherwise be intolerably subordinated to the demands of bourgeois production and the maximisation profit;[8] it compensated for the depletion of the lifeworld under the ever-expanding reach of its instrumental and appropriative logics. It is not that the function of art provided the subject with a means of escape or the promise of an exodus, but it did provide 'an imagined satisfaction of individual needs that are repressed in daily praxis. Through the enjoyment of art, the atrophied bourgeois individual can experience the self as personality.'[9] To serve that function, art necessarily entered into a process of autonomisation in which the logics of the exception would be fully developed in the form of the autonomous work of art (just as, from the perspective of the bourgeois subject, particularly during the late eighteenth and early nineteenth centuries, to engage one's aesthetic faculties, to engage in a programme of self-cultivation or 'sentimental' education, was to discover, at least through the assertion of taste, one's own subjecthood as a realm of autonomous being). Autonomisation, however, required art's institutionalisation – the development of a 'social subsystem' whose functional mode constituted art in its '(relative) independence in the face of demands that it be socially useful'.[10] That is why, the suggestion that the aesthetic exception constitutes the *dispositif* of art by no means represents a refusal of the importance of the processes by which art is absorbed into its various institutional contexts. The emergence of a specific *dispositif* of art is, in this sense, inseparable from those institutional forms for which it provided the possibility of an axiological system that permitted judgements based on purely aesthetic considerations. Even if one cannot say that the *dispositif* of the aesthetic exception and the particular ways in which the institution of art appeared are identical, they are nonetheless entirely isomorphic in material terms.

Still, they are differentiated from each other as necessity is differentiated from contingency. Thus, while the aesthetic exception provides a necessary logic for the identification of art, the institutional 'framing conditions' that instantiates that logic in actual practice remain historically contingent and open to constant revision. The institution of art is the strategic amplification and unfolding of the aesthetic exception in situ, which is to say, it is configured in relation to wider mediations, corresponding to the social formation of which it is a part. As such, it contains the play of multiple and contingent elements that comprise the artwork, a genre, a field of production, a site of reception ... – art, with its assemblages and disassemblages, its universe of calculated risks and fortunate accidents, its inculcated techniques and disciplinary methods – imposed on practices in the hope of governing them – not to mention the experimental and intermedial forms that are invented to disrupt them – all of these language games and countless others belong to the coagulative processes that seek to amass symbolic power and cultural capital in an accumulative concentration called the 'institution of art', whose logic is that of the exception.

Given its undeniable structural domination of the aesthetic field, two critical responses to the problem of institutionality prove particularly instructive in the contemporary framing of art's status of exception. The first, which can be identified, most recently, with the philosopher, Alain Badiou, holds that art is only genuinely art when it is viewed in terms of an autonomy that is entirely immanent to it. The work of art is the 'subject' of the 'thinking of art as an immanent production of truths'; it is part of an infinite multiple that 'exposes its own organisation in and by the finite framing of its presentation'.[11] The question of its institutional context only becomes relevant to art insofar as its 'imperialism' must be defied – given that institutional logics tend primarily to be concerned, as I have said, with art's validity conditions, and thus are structured around an inherent conservatism, the institution of art could only represent for Badiou the corrupted scene in which the 'truth' that is immanent to art can no longer be encountered.[12] It becomes a moot question, as a consequence, where exactly the immanent truth of the art work is able to appear in and of itself. Badiou's solution, insofar as it can be discerned, is to advocate for a kind of militant autonomy, which defines the character of the genuine work of art, but only at the cost of sweeping aside all consideration of the 'de facto' institutional context that confers upon the work its salience as a work of art. In this sense, Badiou can be said to view art in terms that tend toward the absolutisation, or 'Platonisation', of the *dispositif* of the exception. Art's autonomy is taken as something 'de jure', albeit implicitly by Badiou (he would scarcely recognise the term) such that its coruscating 'truth', exploding as an immanent and singular event – a dazzling burst which illuminates, suddenly and without warning, the entire ideative constellation within which the work sits – has nothing to say about the social power that informs the development of art's institutionalisation.[13]

In complete contrast to Badiou, the sociology of Pierre Bourdieu, in all its sobriety and seriousness, submits art entirely to the social power that captures its institutions. Nor is there any discernible difference between the *dispositif* of art and its institutional form; the result is a conflation that leaves art wholly compromised. For Bourdieu, art is indeed subject to processes of autonomisation, but they are to be grasped entirely in terms of art's reduction to 'the autonomy of the field of cultural production',[14] with the consequence that art becomes only one 'relationship of distinction'[15] among many others (within the cultural sphere). Whatever autonomy art possesses it is grasped on entirely de facto terms; social distinction provides art's supposed exceptional status with its empirical meaning – and the work of art, whatever it may be, is nothing other than the cultural expression of those differentials that permeate the social sphere in the form of entrenched class positions: 'objectified cultural capital only exists and subsists in and through the struggles of which the fields of cultural production ... are the site'.[16] Since 'taste' expresses one's position in the 'whole habitus',[17] it also gives expression to one's complicity in its reproduction: taste becomes the means by which art assumes a socially regulative function. Taste – the subjective expression of enculturated dispositions – both locates the subject in the aesthetic field, according to his or her relative privilege, or degree of dispossession, and positions them, whether they are aware of it or not, as combatants in the underlying social war that is waged under the cover of culture. Thus: '[dispositions] are adjusted not only to a class condition presenting itself as a set of possibilities and impossibilities, but also to a relationally defined position, a rank in the class structure.'[18] On the one hand, the potential for social antagonism is permanently rehearsed in the cultural sphere; on the other hand, it is also permanently held in check or suppressed – by participation in the cultural sphere itself. There are several reasons for this.

First, it is a function of the aesthetic field, or 'institution of art', to insulate it from the very antagonisms – inequalities in the distribution of subjective competencies and aesthetic dispositions – to which its existence gives expression. The institution of art is, we have already said, coterminous with the process of art's autonomisation, and it is this that lifts the artwork above the fray of 'real' social conflict. The very schema of distinction through which culture is hierarchically divided – explicit in the differential positions that it founds between the popular arts and light entertainment and serious art – also conceals the symbolic struggle that is prosecuted by means of it. It accomplishes this precisely because it holds the monopoly on art's 'validity' conditions – or, in Bourdieu's terms, a monopoly on 'symbolic violence'.[19]

Hence, in asserting disinterestedness as its highest value, in judgements of taste, culture disguises the actual interests invested in it. Bourdieu's conclusion is bleak: 'The struggle ... produces effects which tend to disguise the very existence of the struggle.'[20] Relegating struggle to the level of the political unconscious is to deprive it precisely of a politics. Second, autonomisation, which declares art to be an exclusive sphere of human activity, with privileges that distinguish it from common life, must also be effectively policed. The means for doing so are embodied in a network of interlacing institutions – cultural, educational, and economic. It is this nexus of institutions that populates the field of culture with its experts, insiders, and professionals – with those who have accrued a degree of cultural capital, and whose qualifications represent their discursive authority .... They are those who uphold art's 'status of exception', and thereby maintain the social hierarchy, as the elite functionaries, lackeys, and civil servants of stratified culture. Included in this are both artists and audiences, whose productions and acts of consumption reproduce the *doxa* that produces them – each is stamped with the indelible mark of the position they hold within the 'field of classes and class fractions'.[21]

In this sense, Bourdieu speaks of the centrality of struggle and antagonism, but at the same time his sociology appears to reproduce it as an ossified form. It is frozen in the great edifices of power, and in the tundras and wastelands of inequality that seem to dissolve into the shade cast by the great meritocratic educational, cultural, and economic institutions. Needless to say, before this edifice, all claims to the de jure autonomy of the work of art must necessarily appear as a sham or fraud.

But it is precisely at this point that the aesthetic exception – and its central paradox – makes a surprising reappearance.

It is all the more surprising because it is produced from within the deepest recesses of de facto autonomy, which its own historical progress makes possible, as it accumulates ever greater symbolic and cultural capital within the institution of art. Bourdieu observes that as the aesthetic field develops or matures, so it becomes ever more 'autonomous', so that autonomy exerts ever greater influence over the practices immanent to it. Autonomy is not simply a matter of the institutional preservation of art against exogenous appropriative forces; it is also the claim that it constitutes a world beholden to laws that apply only to it. How do those laws become manifest to art on de facto grounds? The answer can only be because de facto processes of autonomisation already contain as a presupposition a de jure or 'formal' way of distinguishing art in its difference to non-art. Autonomisation is also a process by which art discovers that it occupies a space of exception. That presupposition is not an ideality but rather the formal realisation of the *dispositif* by which art is identifiable; that it presents art with an intolerable

prohibition – that it cannot cross the threshold of the aesthetic exception –
belongs entirely to the historical development of critical art practices.

Hence Bourdieu writes: 'The evolution of the field of cultural production
[leads] towards a greater *reflexivity*, which leads each of the "genres" to a
sort of critical turning in on itself, as its own principle, as its own premises.'[22]
Autonomisation – the material process of instituting art's exceptionalism
for the purpose of capturing cultural capital – inadvertently leads art to an
autonomous, i.e., 'reflexive' and 'critical', understanding of itself that must
be seen to be independent of that aim and even opposed to it. Art becomes
a '*vanitas*, which betrays itself as such', writes a sceptical Bourdieu.[23] But
in the betrayal of the 'as such' he cannot but identify the point at which art
discovers the nature of the ontological difference – the *dispositif* by which it
can be constituted as art – even as it is compelled to reject it. After all, that
'vanitas' finds its apotheosis for Bourdieu in the 'autoderision' of the avant-
garde, where the ontological difference is parodied in an effort to dismantle
the *dispositif* of art. The paradox of the avant-garde flows directly from this
fact. In 'breaking with tradition', the avant-garde necessitates a gesture of
autoderision that confirms the irreversibility of the historical development
of the field of cultural production. In rejecting the value of autonomy in art,
the avant-garde gives expression to it all the more firmly. The 'avant-garde
producers ... are controlled by the past when it comes to their intention to
surpass it, an intention itself linked to a state of the history of the field'.[24] It
is clear that here Bourdieu confirms the paradox of the aesthetic exception,
even as he seeks to limit art to a de facto autonomy – the avant-garde revolt
against autonomisation cannot but articulate itself as the exception that
confirms the rule: 'It is the very logic of the field which tends to select and
consecrate all legitimate ruptures with the history objectified in the structures of the field.'[25] The very logic of the field, however, can only legitimate
that which disrupts it because it is capable of appropriating radical art back
into the dominion of the aesthetic exception – as a logic it possesses 'legislative' or de jure powers of consecration.

Nevertheless, I would like to derive a different, less sceptical, conclusion to Bourdieu, at this point, by returning to Bürger's idea that the function of – as I have termed it – the *dispositif* of art, the aesthetic exception,
was to neutralise critique. If the historical process of autonomisation which
solidified or consolidated itself in the institution of art is understood to
be oriented by the social function of neutralising critique – of neutralising
social opposition to a world subordinated to capital, by offering the subject
respite from that world, in the illusions of an aesthetic sphere set apart from
it – then we must also understand that it led directly to a counter-movement
in which an entirely different function for art was discovered. What was
newly discovered aimed at nothing less than the comprehensive reversal of

art's original function. The term 'avant-garde' provides the name for the moment at which an historical threshold is reached, after which the process of autonomisation necessitated a reaction that pushed art toward a radicalisation of the aesthetic exception. Autonomy – the game of art's apparent independence from the social world – since it is bound up with the paradox of the aesthetic exception already contained within itself the principle of its reversal. Thus, in exposing the 'inside' of art to art's 'outside', radical art discovered – not that it possessed a political and social content – but rather the politics of its function vis-à-vis the social world as such: that all art is the embodiment of a social truth – that it has both 'form and content' *and* a 'social truth content'.

What effect does this insight have on the problem of art's institutionalisation? I think this remains the most fundamental question for art today. On the one hand, to say that art has a social truth content is to say that every work of art, one way or another, stands in a critical relation to the problem of objectivity – or, to put it otherwise, its very condition as art presents the work as a problematisation of the social construction of reality. Even the most conservative work of art testifies, by virtue of the aesthetic exception, to the irreconcilable nature of art in its 'irrelational relation' to the social world from which it stands apart. On the other hand, the inescapable lesson of the avant-garde is that art cannot escape its own 'dispositif', and thus institutionalisation is its 'de facto' condition. The attempt to believe it could escape that institution trapped the avant-garde in an ambiguity that proved insuperable. It made the redemption of the social world dependent on art, at the same time that it required the social world to bring about the end of the *dispositif* that perpetuated art as a deception. Badiou is right to say that the schema it developed, both romantic and pedagogical, condemned it to failure. Yet there is more to the avant-garde than failure 'on its own terms'. In discovering that the limiting effect of the institution of art, with its framing conditions, is unavoidable, art could nonetheless articulate itself as critique. That critique should not be limited to institutional critique alone, which would be to mistake the nature of the institution of art for art institutions. The institution of art describes the manifest ways in which the logic of the aesthetic exception is realised, which cannot simply be reduced to art's institutions per se. Rather, it testifies to art's problematic relation to the social world. Adorno writes: 'Art … is in no way simply equivalent with artworks, for artists are always also at work on art and not only on artworks.'[26] I think one finds, in this sentence, which on the surface seems to be so self-evident as to be hardly worth remarking on, nonetheless a profound insight into how we might consider the problem of the institution of art. The institution of art is not simply the function of ensuring art's autonomous status; it is also the guarantor that any individual work of art, regardless of genre, is indeed a 'work'. Hence it becomes the locus of de jure claims in which the work of art presents itself as a surface of inscription for wider critical discourses about the nature of art. But it also reveals something else about the character of the artwork: that every work of art reproduces the de facto conflict that exists between particularity and universality.

In fact, the fundamental 'function' of the *dispositif* of art is to appropriate the individual work of art under the universal category of 'art'. Yet, at the same time, the aesthetic exception cannot undo the fact of its radicalisation by the historical avant-garde, in which the paradox through which it is constituted, and which it embodies, is revealed to art in the form of a practice that discovers within itself the power to suspend the aesthetic norm. This means, first, that there can be no governing norm that applies to art, but merely contingent norms that vie with each other in the space of a universality without content. To the extent that it represents an empty universality, 'Art' names a problem that each individual work of art must contend with. Thus, second, every individual work of art must nonetheless discover or rather invent for itself the norm of art as a condition of its production. Every work becomes intrinsically problematic. For this reason, there can be no 'authentic' work of art, and eo ipso, no authentic response to art that is not already bound to the conflict immanent to art under the paradoxical condition of the aesthetic exception. That every work of art is at war with itself means that each constitutes the locus for an engagement in the war that is permanently underway within the broader community of sense.

Part II

Political art after the communicative turn

Writing in response to Sartre's essay on engaged literature, Adorno proclaimed: 'This is not the time for political works of art; rather politics has migrated into the autonomous work of art, and it has penetrated most deeply into works that present themselves as politically dead.'[1] For Adorno, committed and autonomous works captured two 'attitudes to objectivity' that were forever 'at war with one another' within the field of art.[2] In this essay, I would like to re-examine that war, since it is no doubt still being waged, even if the battlefield has subsequently changed beyond recognition, the combatants are quite different, and the strategic lines between the opposing sides have been redrawn in fundamental ways. The question of the political efficacy of art has been restated in forceful terms by Janelle Reinelt, in a rebuke – not just to me, but to Alan Read and Joe Kelleher. The 'tendency to minimize or denigrate the political impact of theatre' is identified by Reinelt with 'scepticism about their connection';[3] and she goes on to decry the way I advocate for a 'notional politicality for theatre and performance' but without the 'burden of having instrumental impact'.[4] To speak of the possibility of the political effectivity of art today, as many, such as Reinelt, are currently keen to do – and I sympathise with their frustrations – requires more than a dismissive response to those obituary writers who pronounce on the death of political art. While it may be tempting to answer Adorno's locution 'This is not the time ...' with an exasperated plea: 'if not now, then, when?' – things, alas, are seldom so easy than such academic handwringing tends to assume. If now *is* the time for political works of art, then it becomes ever more necessary to return to a number of questions one would have assumed have long since been answered, yet remain a source of confusion and controversy: What do we mean when we say a work of art can be political? What is a political effect? What is it exactly that makes a work of art political? Only in reopening these questions can the assumptions that inform much of the thinking about the nature of political works of art that has dominated aesthetic debates since Adorno be challenged. It is my hope that in doing so, we will find a way, if not exactly of bringing that war to an end, of nonetheless showing how irreconcilable positions might appear to be less irreconcilable than they at first seemed, and – if that is not possible – at the very least, of better understanding the underlying aims, motives, and philosophical commitments that each position requires us to adopt.

This essay is divided into three sections. The first addresses the controversy over the political efficacy of engaged art. I begin by loosely restating the basic terms of (what I have elsewhere described as) the 'efficacy debate', in its classical form, before moving on to examine its contemporary iteration.[5] What distinguishes classical and contemporary debates on political effect is the 'communicative turn' whose inflections have come to characterise many of the developments in contemporary art and performance practices over the past forty years or so. In the second chapter, I turn to offer a more precise articulation of how a political work of art is able indeed to produce political effects, on condition that those effects – insofar as they are *political* – must be construed as 'dissensual' effects. Here my principal interlocutor is not Rancière but Habermas. However, unlike Habermas, who reads the effects of communicative action in terms of its 'illocutionary' or socially binding 'force', I articulate the communicative effects of political art around a 'perlocutionary' or what might be termed an aleatory theory of political effect in the work of art. In the concluding section of the essay, I consider the analytical potential of such a perlocutionary theory in relation to a work by the African American artist, Dread Scott, *What Is the Proper Way to Display a US Flag?*[6]

1

The classical debate revisited: Sartre, Brecht, Adorno

The classical debate about the political efficacy of art revolved broadly around two mutually implicated yet opposing sets of claims. I will begin with the first, which is, stated simply enough, that the political work of art is political in virtue of its power to induce such desired or imagined political effects as its author intended it to have on its viewer. Although the way in which these effects are to be achieved vary considerably, depending on the position advanced, the general structure of the claim tends to revolve around two interlocking ideas. In the first instance, one must demystify reality in some way, in order to then make possible a Pauline-style conversion in the viewer or spectator. Art effectuates a political subjectification because it compels the viewer to confront a reality that has hoodwinked them in some way. Once that reality has been exposed, or so the claim goes, the subject would naturally align themselves politically with those who represent their true interests. As a consequence, the specific political power attributed to art also imbues it with a critical task: that of lifting the Veil of Maya. To the extent that it claims to know what reality is, political art is essentially 'realist' by nature; while, correlatively, it is realism that provides art with a critical arsenal, a set of aesthetic techniques and reasoned protocols, to combat the illusions and mystifications of bourgeois ideology. The classical expression of this position was first fully articulated by Lukács for whom the goal of politically aware art was to 'penetrate the laws governing objective reality and to uncover the deeper, hidden, mediated, not immediately perceptible network of relationships that go to make up society'.[1] Although Lukács and Brecht diverged considerably on what exactly a commitment to realism entailed – Brecht argued that Lukács had reduced realism to a set of merely formal literary criteria and sought to counter Lukács's inherent conservatism by greatly expanding on what could count as realism in art – they nonetheless agreed that political art was necessarily realistic in outlook: 'Realist means', wrote Brecht, 'discovering the causal complexes of society/ unmasking the prevailing view of things, as the view of those who are in power/ writing from the viewpoint of the class which offers the broadest solutions for the pressing difficulties in which human society is caught up/ emphasising the element of development/ making possible the concrete, and making possible abstraction from it.'[2]

Developing an existential variant of the debate in *What Is Literature?* Sartre would place essentially realist presuppositions at the heart of committed art by drawing an axiomatic distinction between poetry and prose forms, where only the latter is capable of intervening purposefully in the world. For Sartre, only an unembellished, descriptive language could express, with sufficient urgency, the pressing issues of the present age. 'I distrust the incommunicable,' he avowed, 'it is the source of all violence.'[3] Thus, while Sartre, unlike Brecht, did not see commitment in necessarily didactic terms, he nonetheless believed in art's potential as a direct, transformative force for change: 'To write for one's age is not to reflect it passively; it is to want to maintain it or change it, thus to go beyond it towards the future, and it is this effort to change it that places us most deeply within it.'[4] In fact, Sartre offers perhaps the most explicit articulation of how a work of art must function if it is to produce political change. In the first instance, it must operate on language, and in two senses: first it must be 'analytical', hence words must be cleansed of their 'adventitious' meanings, that is, of those aleatoric qualities of language that frustrate an intended meaning and that produce unforeseen, unplanned, and unpremeditated – or, in a word, unintentional effects (in speech act theory: effects that are termed 'perlocutions'). A political art must take measures to mitigate against the possibility of the corruption of meaning and its passage from author to reader. The second way it must work on language is, after having analytically cleansed it, to then 'synthetically enlarge it',[5] by which he meant the enlargement of the descriptive power of words to render them adequate to the 'historical situation' – the conjuncture – upon which they must work. This is why the artist must be assiduous in resisting the mystifications and opacities of language, which carries the unacknowledged beliefs, representations, values – in short, the existing *doxa* of the world within it. To demystify language is to dissolve the illusions of existing reality. Only in this way, Sartre insisted, is the political artist able to act upon the 'opinion of [his or her] fellow citizens'.[6] Moreover, the fundamental aim of the political artist is to create, through art, nothing less than a subject capable of acting in the world: 'to show the world is to disclose it in the perspectives of a possible change, then, in this age of fatalism, we must reveal to the reader his power, in each concrete case, of doing and undoing, in short, of acting.'[7]

It is in relation to Sartre's injunction 'to act', which expresses the goal of political art in the most unswerving and unambiguous of ways, that the second set of claims, implicated in the classical debate over the political efficacy of art, must be viewed as a startling inversion of the avowed goal of political art. Not only does it place a prohibition on the idea that aesthetic experience should result in an action on the part of the subject of that experience, it argues that far from persuading anyone, committed, realist, and political works of art merely 'preach to the already converted' – this was the accusation Adorno levelled at Brecht's theatre. For Adorno, the political character of the artwork must be located not at the level of its message, intention, or content, but elsewhere, at the level of its style and form. In refuting its core claims, Adorno not only offered an important critique of the underlying assumptions of politically committed art, but he also inspired a separate debate that even today continues to cast an immense shadow of doubt over the affirmative claims of the proponents of art's supposed political efficacy. This opposing and critical discourse can be called the 'autonomy debate'. According to Adorno, and those who later followed him, autonomy comprises an important feature in rearticulating the political nature not just of a work of art but of art as such. The autonomous work of art is political not because of any ideological directive its producer may have imbued it with, or any effect it may pretend to have, but because in its rejection of all instrumentalisation it opposes the encroachments of the administered world. The autonomy of art is established as a single source of illumination in a world otherwise darkened by the remorseless progress of that discursive power Adorno famously qualified in terms of the identitarian logic intrinsic to rationality itself. By holding fast to a promise of freedom in a world otherwise held captive by the total incorporation of the social by the productive, reifying, and subordinating logics of capital, art discovered its power of resistance. It did so not in the representational language of realism, but through a formal (autonomous) reconfiguration of its elements: 'Art is not a matter of pointing up alternatives but rather of resisting, solely through artistic form, the course of the world, which continues to hold a pistol to the heads of human beings.'[8] The (negative) utopian aspirations, invested by Adorno in art's autonomy, are succinctly summarised in his *Minima Moralia*, where he wrote:

> Total purposelessness gives the lie to the totality of purposefulness in the world of domination, and only by virtue of this negation, which consummates the established order by drawing the conclusion from its own principle of reason, has existing society up to now become aware of another that is possible.[9]

But the question I want to ask is why these two interlocking debates, the efficacy and the autonomy debates, necessarily lead to such irreconcilable differences. It is this question, posed in the acutest terms by Adorno, that addresses itself to the very foundations of what is meant whenever the term 'political art' is invoked. I would briefly like to consider some of the core criticisms levelled at committed art by Adorno. The first is that committed art contains a contradiction that cannot be resolved on the basis of its own realist assumptions. In seeking to reflect reality, committed art risks collapsing the difference between art and the real. No committed work can shed itself of the accompanying ambiguity created by its overt political intent, without the risk of 'reducing' itself to 'propaganda' and it is for this reason that, Adorno wryly observes how, in order to escape that risk, 'Sartrean goats' turn out to be, when all is said and done, inseparable from 'Valéryan sheep'.[10] Sartre's own novels err on the side of literature, not propaganda. A second criticism directly targets the idea that committed works, because they profess a virtuous relation to language, can induce what today might be called pragmatic communicational effects. What Sartre overlooks is the fact that once a communicative act enters the dimension of art, it loses its pragmatic link to an everyday speech situation, no matter how purified it may be of unwanted meanings. While the representation of pragmatic signifying practices retains a 'residue'[11] of the world beyond the committed work, at the same time they are transformed by the work's formal properties into something rather more ambiguous than the realist author would like to admit. To introduce pragmatic meaning into the exceptional space of art is to deprive it of any power to produce conventional effects. Without superimposing them, one might nevertheless see a helpful parallel here in J.L. Austin. According to Austin, a performative utterance, when spoken in the theatre by an actor, while intelligible, is also non-serious in the sense that, where in reality it would produce an effect on the world, the self-same utterance on stage is considered 'hollow and void'.[12] That said, if Austin thereby dismisses any further consideration of the issue, for Adorno, what is further revealed, is not simply an 'infelicity' of speech but something rather more substantive: that in the work of art, the signifying dimension of language is 'fused' with a-signifying and sensual elements. The very opacity of language shatters the conventional power of linguistic effect insofar as opacity/sensuality belongs to the formal configuration of art (rather than its alleged transparency that would allow a 'true' representation to penetrate the fog of ideological illusion).

But Adorno goes further: he alleges that those who argue in favour of the committed work end up the unwitting accomplices of the very forces they claim to oppose. This is not simply to claim that eventual co-option is the fate of the committed work – for example, in the way it might be said that Brecht has now become 'culinary' because he is taught in schools or is incorporated into the repertoire of the National Theatre, i.e., has become 'canonised'; it is to claim something far worse: that the antagonistic stance the committed work adopts toward the world was a chimera in the first place – its supposed radicalism is immediately dissipated by the stultification inherent in its conventionalism. One finds this conventionalism in both Sartre's praise of prose and the anti-intellectualism of Lukács, who denounced – just as fascists, Stalinists, and all cultural conservatives do – the decadence of so-called 'elitist' avant-garde art movements. The realist allies themselves, writes Adorno, with this 'antagonistic attitude toward everything strange or upsetting';[13] and it is why he later accuses committed works of tacit complicity in a mythology – essential bourgeois – that proclaims the subject's agency is enabled through art, simply in virtue of having correctly 'received' its meaning. The problem, to employ McLuhan's terminology, lies not with the message but with the medium:

> Hidden in the notion of a 'message', of art's manifesto, even if it is politically radical, is a moment of accommodation to the world; the gesture of addressing the listener contains a secret complicity with those being addressed, who can, however, be released from their illusions only if that complicity is rescinded.[14]

The accusation Adorno makes is that the claim of committed art to enact a political subjectification trades on a false prospectus. Instead of emancipating the subject, the work betrays them. For sure, the committed work enjoins the subject to act, to be free, to break with the deceptions that immobilise them, but only by sermonising them. Its implicit moralism restricts thought and its promise of truth degenerates into the rigidities of the existing system of representations, into ideology – into the existing medium or environment of complicity. This will be Adorno's criticism of Sartre. In claiming to effectuate change, Sartre merely reaffirms what already is, since the subject – imbued by the philosopher with the power of existential choice – soon learns of the hollowness of that choice once they attempt to exercise it. Thus, returned to the world, the subject discovers the extent to which the freedom to choose is contradicted and constrained by the brute facticity imposed by real world circumstances. Moreover, Adorno adds: the conservatism behind realism's 'unshakeable faith in meanings that are to be transferred from art to reality' is easily exposed as naïve once one considers that the culture industry finds such an idea perfectly acceptable.[15]

There is a final criticism that has a great deal of significance for how a political work of art might be conceived in its relation to the problem of representational truth. This becomes most explicitly evident in Adorno's critique of Brecht, where the 'process of aesthetic reduction' – Brecht's dramaturgical methodology – which he 'undertakes for the sake of political truth works against political truth'.[16] This failure springs directly from the didactic spirit at work in Brecht. To dispel the illusions propagated by bourgeois ideology, the aim of realism such as Brecht's is 'to capture the inherent nature of capitalism in an image'.[17] The same problem can be found in Chaplin. Adorno points as an example to the scene in *The Great Dictator* where a young Jewish girl retaliates against a group of

Nazi stormtroopers by hitting each of them on the head with a frying pan. Adorno writes: 'Political reality is sold short for the sake of political commitment';[18] the reality is she would have been torn apart by them. A more acerbic critique along these lines is made of Brecht's play *The Resistible Rise of Arturo Ui*, where Brecht's simplification of social reality constitutes a form of 'alienating infantilism'.[19] The more Brecht seeks to instruct his spectator, the more he is compelled to reduce reality to the level of a fairy tale and his parables miss the essence of the very thing they purport to lay bare. This was no more evident than in Brecht's misrepresentation of the true nature of fascism:

> In place of a conspiracy of the highly placed and powerful we have a silly gangster organisation, the cauliflower trust. The true horror of fascism is conjured away; fascism is no longer the product of the concentration of social power but rather an accident, like misfortunes and crimes.[20]

It is for the sake of the didactic lesson that the didactic theatre substitutes doctrine for truth. This is because the underlying imperative of the committed work is to demonstrate its commitment to whatever it deems politically correct; and it is why, at the same time, Adorno states that the 'very objectivity whose distillation the didactic play strives for is falsified'.[21] If political theatre makes for bad theatre and even worse politics, it is because in it 'aesthetic form' is defiled by 'political untruth'.[22] The real crisis that Adorno forced political art to confront was its impotence before its own professed aim. This is perhaps best summarised by inverting the eleventh of Marx's theses on Feuerbach: instead of changing the world, political art has merely interpreted it badly.

Adorno's essay on the problems of commitment in art sealed the fate of political effect for the classical debate. The question must be asked, nonetheless: does it still hold true today? Viewed half a century or so later, Adorno's essay appears to represent the apotheosis of autonomy in art. Consider the contemporary situation and one witnesses not only a reversal in fortunes in the dispute between autonomy and engagement in art, but that the very idea of aesthetic autonomy is almost entirely vanquished. One reason for this has to do with the sheer kinetic force of the present moment, with all its calamities and crises – from climate and economic breakdown, to reinvigorated social and protest movements, thence to the rise of the populist right. This not only appears to compel the 'return' of political art but brings with it the risk that for those who express any scepticism over its conditions of possibility the charge will be one of advocating quietism. Grant Kester had already predicted this as early as 1998: 'As we move toward a society in which the buffering institutions of the liberal state gradually disappear, artists will be confronted with the difficult choice between quietism and withdrawal or renewed engagement.'[23] The other reason, which expresses a wider set of contextual implications and motives, has to do with the communicative turn itself and what that turn enables, and it is this context that I would now like to consider.

Contemporary debates and the retrieval of 'effect'

I think it is true to say that contemporary debates exhibit a high degree of ambivalence when it comes to the question of art's political efficacy insofar as it relates to the problem of autonomy in art, and it is worth remarking some of the reasons for this before delving into the detail. First, and self-evidently, the nature of artistic practices has changed substantially since the period when Adorno was writing, with various advances he could barely have foreseen – from the development of conceptual art, the performance turn, the arrival of postdramatic theatre, and the emergence of socially engaged, relational ('new institutional'), and participatory art practices. With these have come subtler, tempered, and thus rather more nuanced understandings of what is implicated in art's social and political utility. Nothing could be further from Adorno's conception of autonomous art than the kinds of contemporary relational works, described by Nicolas Bourriaud, for example, that 'involve methods of social exchanges, interactivity with the viewer within the aesthetic experience being offered to him/her, and the various communication processes, in their tangible dimension as tools serving to link individuals and human groups together'.[24] Even those who retain the concept of autonomy do so on a fundamentally different conceptual basis to that of Adorno. Theorists such as Claire Bishop, who follows in Rancière's footsteps, argue that autonomy is not a quality that inheres in the work of art; it refers rather to the 'autonomy of our *experience* in relation to art'.[25] The shift from object to experiencer indicated here should not be confused with the space of individualistic (autonomous) absorption, once imagined by Michael Fried, as the antidote to what he viewed as minimalism's corrupting theatricality. On the contrary, it is an experience of autonomy that possesses the power to reshape the social space of art, however ambiguously, in which the participatory nature of that experience is more often than not foregrounded. The effect, as Rancière conceives it, is to create an aesthetic space of dissensus (the aesthetic redistributes bodies by configuring them outside of and even against the social norms to which they are usually made to conform). Shannon Jackson goes somewhat further: for her, the space of autonomy in art has been thoroughly contradicted by its appropriation by the art market. Consequently, the task today, she argues, is to understand the 'de-autonomising' tendency of contemporary art practices. For this reason, Jackson seeks a new critical language commensurate with the various ways 'forms of artistic works produce a consciousness of artistic heteronomy and social interdependence'.[26] And she writes:

> While the perpetual pursuit of autonomy continues to animate a theory of democracy as well as a critical concept of aesthetics, the bounded referents for autonomous personhood and autonomous art become less stable and more permeable in contemporary critical imagining.[27]

But it is not simply that art has increasingly tended toward the space of heteronomy (the so-called social turn in art) which is most important in this respect. What matters more, perhaps, are the social transformations that underpin the tendency towards socially oriented art practices. Particularly unforgiving to Adorno's conception of autonomy in art is the transformation of labour under Fordist conditions of production to those of post-Fordism.[28] According to Paulo Virno, for example, it is the very nature of the subject, whose labour has been transformed by the cognitive and 'virtuosic' character of post-Fordist modes of production, that collapses the distinction between *poiesis* and *praxis* upon which the thesis of the autonomous work of art rested, and which renders it invalid today:

> Virtuosity becomes labor for the masses with the onset of a culture industry. It is here that the virtuoso begins to punch a time card. Within the sphere of a culture industry … communicative activity … has itself as an end … But exactly for this reason, it is above all within the culture industry that the structure of wage labor has overlapped with political action.[29]

Artistic labour has become the model for today's cognitive labour. Of course, for some – insofar as contemporary labour practices are installed on the very ground of autonomous production that was once the sole preserve of art – this appears to realise the worst of all of Adorno's nightmares. There are others, however, such as Chantal Mouffe, who argue that what this transformation does, is create an opportunity for 'new forms of production [that allow] for new types of resistance'. Provided we jettison the 'analysis of Adorno and Horkheimer, based as it is on the fordist model',[30] these new conditions, she argues:

> [open] the way for novel forms of social relations in which art and work can exist in a new configuration. The objective of artistic practices should be to foster the development of those new social relations that are made possible by the transformation of the work process. Their main task is the production of new subjectivities and the elaboration of new worlds. What is needed in the current situation is a widening of the field of artistic intervention, with artists working in a multiplicity of social spaces outside traditional institutions in order to oppose the total social mobilization of capitalism.[31]

What is found in these kinds of theoretical developments are three ideas being advanced. First, the claim that radical artistic practices derive a power of resistance solely in virtue of their occupying the autonomous space of the aesthetic exception must be considered more or less redundant today. Mouffe, for instance, points to art's subsumption by 'biopolitical capitalism', making 'autonomous production' no longer feasible.[32] Even those who might be seen as the direct heirs of Adorno, such as Hans-Thies Lehmann, have declared the 'historical phase of the autonomy of "art"' all but dead: 'the notion of an autonomous art which emphasises the sphere of non-will, non-action cannot be the answer.'[33] The second claim, which follows as a corollary of the first, is that artistic practices need no longer worry about the problem of efficacy. On the contrary, such positions tend to assume effect as already built in. It is why, when Mouffe claims that 'artistic practices can play a decisive role' in transforming the prevailing 'common-sense' through 'counter-hegemonic interventions',[34] she does so without really explaining what potential limits should be placed on art's power to influence social and political practices. The question she leaves unanswered is: in what sense decisive? The third claim is this: that artworks can help effectuate social transformation in virtue of the fact that artistic practices having shed the requirement of being autonomous are able to embrace their role in challenging the reproduction of the social – not by negating it – but by directly exploiting the communicative dimension of art. This embrace of art as a communicative power can be found in Cuban artist, Tania Bruguera's concept of 'Arte Útil' (a term originating as early as 1934, with the eponymous manifesto of the architect Juan O'Gorman). For Bruguera, *arte útil* is not about the production of the objects of art, but about what can be implemented through an engaged arts practice: 'For me,' she writes, 'political art is creating a political situation, to put people into a political situation they have to deal with and solve.'[35] Bruguera's example epitomises the communicative turn in art: Following the reopening of diplomatic ties between the US and Cuba, under President Obama she installed a microphone in Habana's Revolution Square, inviting people to speak for one minute on what kind of future they wanted to see for the nation. When she was arrested (along with over eighty other participants), she used her interrogation to educate her interrogators on how to properly criticise art. And when she was released, she set up loudspeakers outside her home and broadcast herself reading Hannah Arendt's *The Origins of Totalitarianism* in a performance that lasted for a hundred hours – observing:

> As political artists, we have to learn the language of the politicians … For this project, I was proud that I could get the government to talk to me through a gesture. The resource I used for the piece was sound through loud speakers because sound can travel freely. The government's gesture was to put a group

of people with jack-hammers in front of the house so that no one could hear the reading. I was very proud to turn the government into a performance.[36]

The key point to observe at this juncture, however, is not the reassertion of a discourse which proclaims art to be a political power capable of generating consequences in the social world; it is rather the shift in aesthetic practices themselves, as announced by artists such as Bruguera, which has transformed the paradigmatic basis of the debate. Quite simply, over the past few years, the battlefield over the political efficacy of art has been transposed onto an entirely new terrain by art practices themselves. It has moved decisively away from the old hermeneutic paradigm of art where the classical debate was primarily concerned with the effects of art's representations on ideology, or was invested in the disruption of the ideological effects of representation as such (let us call this the semantic-interpretative paradigm of art), to what might be termed the communicative and performative paradigm, where relational art forms operate pragmatically and immediately on the terrain of social praxes. The assertion of the communicative dimension of art, particularly over the past thirty years or so, represents an essential shift in how artistic practices have been deployed within the social sphere and how they must be conceptualised, and it is unquestionably this tendency that opens up new ways of conceiving the nature of political commitment in the production of art (for example, around participatory forms of spectatorship).

The question, however, is whether the new practices have resolved the controversy over art's political efficacy, or merely recast old problems in a new light. If the terms of the debate, in other words, have been displaced, away from Lukács's old distinction between 'realism' and 'anti-realism', then the new fronts in the war over the problem posed by art's supposed social and political efficacy have merely opened up on the terrain of the communicative turn itself. Thus, at one end of the spectrum, we find positions such as those advocated by Rancière who '[dreams] of disrupting the relationship between the visible, the sayable, and the thinkable without having to use the terms of a message as a vehicle'.[37] Here the specifically political aspect of art is located in its disruptive power to enact a dissensus that far from being communicative seeks to disturb the existing logics of communication altogether – and its capacity to relay 'messages'; while what is foreclosed by Rancière's dissensual 'metapolitics' of art is the old 'cause-effect' relation through which the earlier hermeneutic paradigm assumed the possibility of an implicit communication between art and the world of non-art. Rancière thus asks us to rethink 'the idea that there are apparatuses that automatically produce political effects'.[38] By contrast, the other end of the spectrum is occupied by those who emphasise the potential of art to enhance social communication directly, prioritising its capacity to build a sense of 'social interdependence' both within its audiences and within the wider communities that it engages: positive effects are prioritised, in other words, over the negativity of 'critical' art practices that seek to frustrate or negate meaning.

For example, in a critical response to my own work, Reinelt has warned: 'in a discipline like ours, "dissensus" can be valorized as the only political goal available to performance while any positive politics with content or a program is diminished as over-reaching.'[39] Not only does this form of theory 'discourage sustained and engaged political artistry', it overlooks or dismisses out of hand, 'the dedicated political theatre of community, identity, and "applied" theatre'.[40] And she goes on to argue that 'consensus' and 'dissensus' should not be seen in such polarised terms – the conflicting and opposing ends on a spectrum of aesthetic practices – but are 'better employed to describe aspects of the social processes these artists engage with rather than seeing them as mutually exclusive options'.[41] I think this is undeniably true of many contemporary art practices. But still Reinelt's appeal to the terminology of a 'dedicated *political* theatre'[42] helps itself rather too hastily to the very thing that is in question – if it is not exactly question begging, it certainly invites the question of what specifically is meant by (the) 'political'. The argument is not simply about practice but also about the nature of theory and what it must presuppose. That said, there is one way of understanding the theoretical side of the argument whereby the disagreement between Reinelt's position and my own becomes so negligible that, in fact, I think it disappears altogether – for if what is meant is that a critical or dissensual art practice simply 'negates' or opposes for no other reason than for the sake of opposing – is an act of refusing meaning pure and simple – then not only would that be insufficient for the purposes of understanding the political possibilities of art, but it would indeed be an invitation to what I have elsewhere described as 'a noisy form of quietism'.[43] It would represent a position of aesthetic dissidence whose secret complicity with the orthodoxy it rejects resides in the fact that its dissidence is permitted precisely because there is an acceptance that it will have a negligible effect on the world.

One reason why such an extreme adherence to the spirit of Adorno's negative dialectics – if that is what it is – will not do is because the corollary of stating that political art is impossible today must be that it is impossible for the reason that the political subject is not possible. That impossibility is a luxury many believe we cannot afford to indulge. Those who do indulge it indeed come within a hair's breadth of advocating quietism. Hans-Thies Lehmann comes perilously close, for instance, when he defines contemporary tragedy as 'the inner breakdown of the subject as a political agent'.[44] This is also why politics for him only works 'modo obliquo' through theatre insofar as it can '[lay] bare ideological structures in our everyday way of seeing the world'.[45] A theatre that challenges the structures of 'perception', for Lehmann, necessarily works against that 'melodramatic consciousness' that Althusser once identified as the real target of Brecht's theatre, even if it does so now in a form that no longer correlates with Brecht's pedagogical vision of the stage. I understand why such a claim would be frustrating to anyone wanting to grapple with the political in the form of a realistic response to pressing issues when today doing politics clearly involves more than simply 'exposing' ideological structures. Mouffe has helpfully pointed to the conceptual limits of any critical art that adopts a purely negative approach to the world. For her, the word 'critical' must be retrieved from the 'essentialist' logics of ideology critique: 'Critical art practices', she writes, 'do not aspire to lift a supposedly false consciousness so as to reveal the "true reality".'[46] Rather, they intervene in the 'discourses and language games' in which specific political identities are inscribed. What this does is explode the old realist-anti-realist presuppositions of the past insofar as they still dictate, however distantly, the critical terms of the debate on art to the practices of the present. Why this is compelling is that it forces us to rethink the nature of the political subject and its performative modes of identification. It is around this question of performativity that the efficacy debate derives something of an advantage from the idea of the communicative turn, but it is also here that we need to tread most carefully. If Mouffe is correct, and I think she is, when she argues that it is 'not enough to simply foster a process of "de-identification"', since that 'negative moment' is insufficient in itself to 'bring about something positive' – i.e., a new form of political identity – then a 'second move is necessary',[47] one that 'rearticulates' the subject within a wider political (or counter-hegemonic) bloc. But given the strategic 'nature of hegemonic struggle and the complex process of the construction of identities',[48] it behoves us to question more thoroughly how art engages the subject in these political processes, and to do so in terms that are not simply stipulative or reductive or plain simplistic. If now really is the time for political art, then we really must ask: How does a political articulation of the subject occur through art?

For that reason, I would like to examine the problem of effect in relation to concepts that the communicative turn makes available to us. By communicative turn, I mean three interlocking sets of phenomena. First, the emergence of theories of signifying practices that emphasise, albeit in quite different ways, the communicative, pragmatic, performative, and discursive dimensions of language – found variously in late Wittgenstein's theory of language games, in speech act theory, in the discourse theory of Michel Foucault, and the cultural theory of Stuart Hall, etc.; second, the socio-political, economic, and cultural developments of post-Fordist modes of capitalism – where the social, affective, and linguistic capabilities of the worker are cultivated; and third the rise of aesthetic practices that embrace the new forms of sociality opened up within and by the communicative turn – in which the audience, as noted by Bojana Kunst, 'works with its social, cognitive and emotional skills, i.e., the skills central to contemporary forms of post-Fordist production'.[49] Now, if this can be summarised by saying that the 'communicative turn' appears on the terrain of post-Fordism, then it is evidently on this terrain that the debates over art's politics must be played out. Thus, it should be noted that for Kunst, post-Fordist conditions are pessimistically linked to what she terms the 'processes of the disappearance of sociality and political articulations of the public', which thereby 'places in question the emancipatory role played by art', locating her within the ranks of the new sceptics.[50] Others are more sanguine in this regard, with Jackson proclaiming that performance art 'activates and depends upon a relational system' – a 'contingency' that she celebrates as a 'prime venue for reflecting on the social and for exposing the dependencies of convivial and expressive spheres'.[51]

To sharpen the terms of the argument at this point: it is worth underscoring Jackson's influential term 'social works' here, which, she argues, 'gestures to the realm of the socio-political recalling the activist and community-building ethics of socially engaged performance research',[52] since it is precisely this so-called 'social' gesture that I think needs to be analytically suspended if we are to separate out, so as to understand more fully, the question of art's political effectivity. This is not to say that the two are not intimately related, and in practice often inseparable; but it is to point to an ideative complication that circulates within discussions of socially engaged performance whose meanings ought to be decomposed rather than conveniently elided – namely, that one cannot derive a concept of the political from the concept of the social. By this I mean related concepts such as sociality, intercommunicative agreement, consensus, cooperation, communality, and conviviality may well describe an attitude that underpins a 'politics', the political commitments and socially progressive aspirations of artists, and the forms of social expression that may be incorporated into an engaged artwork, but they do not describe the dimension of the political as such, nor its implications for art. Social practices in art are seldom defined from the political per se; and precisely for this reason the kinds of function that many commentators wish to attribute to political works lead them toward equivocating over the meaning of the word 'political'. When it is said that ameliorative or emancipatory social practices can be built on contemporary art's inherent relationality, for example, as a means of developing or strengthening community cohesion, and when we have this kind of social practice in mind when we speak of the political encounter in art, then we must ask whether the problematic of political art has been surreptitiously superseded and the problematic of the social substituted in its place. To conflate both is to run the risk of a sociological reduction of the political; while such a conflation at the level of practices – something Jen Harvie has critically examined in great detail in her book *Fair Play: Art, Performance and Neoliberalism* (2013)[53] – risks inadvertent collusion in the often-concealed political agendas of stakeholders and arts funders. I am not claiming that works that aim at developing forms of social cohesion (many forms of 'applied theatre' for example) cannot be motivated by explicitly political aims or are simply naïve (although it is worth bearing in mind James Thompson's scepticism regarding the actual 'social utility' of applied or social theatre, which he claims has 'reduced the scope of its politics');[54] what I would suggest is that to understand the political in art from the orientation such social practices set collapses it into a form of sociologism. What defines the tendency toward sociologism? To take Durkheim, who is the principal originator of the tendency, it is two things: first, it is the reduction of social antagonism to the 'pathologised' state of what he termed 'juridical and moral anomy';[55] and second, it is the search for a means of binding individuals together in a moral totality in order to assure 'social cohesion'.[56] Even if they share different motives, Bourriaud's notion of relational art as inventing 'new models of sociability' is entirely in keeping with a Durkheimian vision of art.[57] In this respect, it is interesting to note in Jackson's case that when she explicitly refers to the political, she does so not in relation to the idea of social interdependence but by reaching for a quite different concept – that of 'antagonism', which she finds in the work of Mouffe. It is a significant concession since it indicates that a social paradigm of the arts does not automatically entail that social works are political simply because they are pro-social. Her interesting idea of 'the infrastructural politics of performance',[58] by which she means the politics involved in negotiating aesthetic spaces for projects taking place in non-artistic contexts (anything from prisons to car parking lots), while it does serve to open up new discursive and praxical levels at which works can be seen to be politically activated, must, to fully develop the analysis, consequently refer us to what she terms 'infrastructural antagonism'.[59] And rightly so, since it is precisely in relation to the appearance of antagonism within the social that one encounters that which limits it, namely, the political.[60] It is this claim that allows for the specification of the political possibilities of art in relation to the question of its efficacy, under the conditions of the communicative turn, without simply snatching at the idea as though it were low-hanging fruit. It is only by descending into the undergrowth of the communicative turn, in other words – setting aside the goal of perfected sociality, or the dream of a *communitas* attained through art (that quiver in the eye of the social turn theorist!) – that we will be able draw out both the conceptual and practical limits of political effect in art, in response to contemporary critical discourse.

2

Art of the communicative turn: Habermas and the political

In order to analyse the possibilities opened up by the communicative turn, as well as identify a few of the difficulties with some of its more fundamental notions, I would like to consider one of its most influential proponents – Jürgen Habermas. The profound implications of the communicative turn are expressed in Habermas's critique of Adorno, when he writes: 'I want to maintain that the program of early critical theory foundered not on this or that contingent circumstance, but from the exhaustion of the paradigm of the philosophy of consciousness' – and he adds '[only] a change of paradigm to the theory of communicative action makes it possible to take up once again the since neglected task of a critical theory of society'.[1] In brief, where Adorno and Horkheimer remained trapped by the stultification inherent in the dialectic of the subject and object, leading them to view all rationality as intrinsically appropriative, coercive, and instrumental, Habermas, by switching paradigm, was able to identify a non-coercive dimension of reason that was overlooked by – indeed could not be seen from – the perspective of the *Dialectic of Enlightenment*, a form of reason based on intersubjective relations and whose aim is fundamentally bound by the task of fostering mutual understanding. 'Fundamental to the paradigm of mutual understanding', Habermas writes, 'is ... the performative attitude of participants in interaction, who coordinate their plans for action by coming to an understanding about something in the world.'[2] Communicative action, rather than being driven by teleological goals, aims at establishing agreement between social agents. In combatting the 'contingent interests' of private individuals, and in promoting 'the conditions of symmetry and of reciprocal dependencies of an intersubjectively constituted life-context',[3] what it founds is a community based on a rational *sensus communis*. Seen from the perspective of a theory of social action enabled through art, what the theory of communicative action makes space for is a positive determination of social effect without thereby reducing art to the claims of means-ends, purposive, or instrumentalised reason. In embracing the communicative dimension of art, aesthetic practices are reconfigured as a medium for the reconciliation of the social.

This is why Habermas is able to maintain that art provides a 'sanctuary [...
for] the satisfaction of those needs which become quasi illegal in the material process of bourgeois society', such as 'solidary living with others', and
the 'happiness of a communicative experience which is not subject to the
imperatives of means-ends rationality'.[4]

It is not difficult to understand contemporary art of the social turn in
these kinds of terms, where aesthetic practices offer a site for the social coordination of forms of action that require the cooperation of social agents; and
where participatory practices rehearse or even enact forms of social binding
among the participants. Hence the communicative paradigm of art, locating
its effects in the 'interpersonal relations'[5] established between participators,
provides the basis for a theory of art's social efficacy: where communication skills, linguistic competence, relational sociation, intersubjectivity, and
empathic identification constitute a medium for creating enhanced forms of
sociality through engagement in art practices. One informative consequence
of such a formal-pragmatic rethinking of the efficacy of art is how 'aesthetic experience', under the communicative turn, finds an identity with the
'speech situation'. This provides the basis for the paradigm shift indicated
earlier. Involved in uncovering the communicative dimension of art, there
is a subtle but significant displacement of meaning and effect: no longer
founded on the hermeneutic or interpretative paradigm, as it was even for
Adorno, meaning develops on the basis of a communicative theory that is
either derived from or resonant with speech act theory. It is on this basis
that a renewed claim for the social efficacy of art is enabled, which draws
a subtle but necessary general equivalence between aesthetic effect and the
formal pragmatics of the speech situation. This means, in speaking of the
communicative efficacy of art we have in mind either one of two possible
kinds of effect: art contributes either to the production of something akin to
an illocutionary effect, or it is conceived based on a perlocutionary outcome.
The difference between these two approaches will turn out to be fundamental to the question of what is meant by the political 'efficacy' of art. Let us
consider first the idea that the efficacy of art is equivalent to the effect produced by the illocutionary act.

For Habermas, the illocutionary act is identified with the consensual,
collaborative, and cooperative aspects of performance. It is through the
illocutionary act that a speaker's utterance is able to 'motivate a hearer
to accept the offer contained in his speech act and thereby to accede to
a rationally motivated binding (or bonding: *Bindung*) *force*'.[6] To say an
utterance has illocutionary force is to say it has made a claim on the space
of universality that transcends the contingency of 'worlds', and in so
doing, has placed a demand on the hearer that in accepting such a claim
they are necessarily bound by it: to recognise the legitimacy of the claim

contained in the utterance is to acquiesce to its illocutionary force. If the speech act has an 'illocutionary binding (or bonding) effect'[7] it is because intersubjective linguistic competencies are directed at, and accomplished through, the binding of individual speakers by their uncoerced agreement with, and acceptance of, illocutionary norms. Habermas is explicit on this point: speech acts are 'unambiguously regulated by accompanying institutions or norms of action'.[8] One potential problem with this claim, however, especially if the illocutionary act is to be used as a way of understanding art's political efficacy, is that it threatens to return us to the earlier problem of sociologism. In the first place, communicative action, in striving for consensus, is predicated on the idea that the social relation can be rendered transparent to all participants. What this does is overstate the effectivity of social relations insofar as communicative action leaves the question of effect 'underdetermined', relying instead on the metaphysical assumption that a rational foundation underpins illocutionary forces. Second, and relatedly, illocutionary acts are conceived on the basis of a form of direct reference where the motives and intentions of social agents are immediately apparent and in which the social structure loses its opacity – becoming fully transparent. Thirdly, the aim of communicative action – and its primary effect insofar as it achieves the condition of social transparency – is to dispel the antagonistic or anomic dimension of sociality. True, by stressing the illocutionary dimension of the speech situation, communicative action is able to highlight the power of intersubjective agreement to create forms of rational sociality. The downside is that the price to be paid for this accomplishment is that the illocutionary mechanism for accomplishing the task of bonding or binding, central to the discourse on social cohesion, overlooks the conformism inherent in conventional and habitual performatives. This is the true implication of sociologism: illocutionary forces indeed bind the social group into a coherent social totality but at the cost of omitting the political – that is to say, potentially antagonistic – character of the social relation and the differential construction of identity. In other words, what the 'social cohesion' or 'illocutionary' thesis conceals is the dimension of antagonism at play in the social construction and performance of political identities – the essential criticism of Habermas made by agonistic theorists such as Chantal Mouffe.[9] As a consequence, far from resolving the question of coercion, illocutionary acts – in aiming at the 'moral integration' of subjects – necessarily reproduce existing social relations, which they tacitly institutionalise: relations of subordination and discursive authorisation are implicit in the idea of speech conventions if one understands the illocutionary act, as Habermas does, in terms of the logic of social binding. Can one really distinguish the *symbolic violence of illocutionary forces* under *the given levels of productive forces in a society* from 'illocutionary acts' *conceived in a general idealised sense* without succumbing to the illusion that speech is essentially 'outside' of relations of power? If they cannot be so considered – and if, like Foucault, one insists that questions of truth and validity cannot be separated from questions of institutionalised power – then the illocutionary and consensualist paradigm must be fundamentally rethought if the political efficacy of art is to be grasped.

What, by contrast, of the perlocutionary act, whose effect is, according to Habermas, utterly different to that of the illocutionary binding of the social? Is it possible to visualise, without having recourse to sociological categories, the political efficacy of art in terms of a perlocutionary theory of political effect? The only way to address these questions is to challenge two of Habermas's basic assumptions: first, that 'Reaching an understanding is the inherent telos of human speech';[10] and, second, that the 'use of language with an orientation to reaching understanding is the *original mode* of language use'.[11] On this basis, for Habermas, any deviation from that telos is by definition a corruption of the communicative resources of language and a 'parasitic' or 'secondary' mode of use.[12] It is in this secondary and parasitic sense that the perlocutionary act is understood as derivative and not 'original'. Where an illocutionary act invokes intercommunicative assent – the consensus of the speakers – in the very act of performing a symbolic action through speech, the perlocutionary act is used in order to produce an 'effect', namely, to manipulate the addressee in some way; not to establish agreement, then, but to change the addressee's behaviour or beliefs about the world. For this reason, Habermas identifies perlocutions with 'contexts of strategic interaction', where speech acts are 'instrumentalised … for purposes that are only contingently related to the meaning of what is said'.[13] For this reason, also, the perlocutionary act is characterised by irrationality, and in two senses. First, as Austin had already emphasised in *How to Do Things with Words*, perlocutions are 'not conventional' and so their effects cannot be predicted – often those effects are 'unintentional';[14] second, the perlocution has no 'content', it must inhabit existing discourse but in such a way that it does not respect its normal functionality – it breaks with or challenges illocutionary norms, even as it inhabits them – hence their parasitic quality. But it is precisely because of this perlocutionary use of language – this use oriented by strategy – that one can begin to understand the political in the context of the communicative turn and thus the way in which art works can have political effects as distinct to social effects. To do so, however, it is necessary to retrieve the political, and specifically the dissensual or agonistic, dimension of social performance. The agonic dimension is not a deficient state of what, originally, must be presupposed as a noncoercive sociality based on a rational community of speakers. If the political is to be understood in agonistic terms, then speech or performance cannot be fundamentally defined by the efforts of consensual striving any more than sociality can be thought of as originally founded on what Kant termed a *Gemeinschaftlichen Sinnes* – the idea of 'communal sense'. Rather, social performance is just as likely to be motivated by strategic considerations that cannot be accounted for on a deliberative basis, but precisely because of disagreement over the very authority of illocutionary norms and the discourses they authorise. To be sure there are discursive contexts in which reaching mutual understanding between all participants in a communication is the goal, and that a space of contestation exists only to assist in the deliberative process – enabled by the construction of a space free from all interests other than those of verifying the supportability of a given deliberation (the ideal of science). However, a neutral space, free of interests and desires, hardly defines the reality of politics or what is at stake for political actors. Perhaps one must distinguish between communicative and political rationality, where political rationality is defined = strategic aim + tactics + coordination of interests. Political reason is not concerned with defending a criticisable assertion, but a *position* within a given terrain of struggle. In this sense, while political groups require coordinated action and cooperation among themselves, the aim of political speech or performance is by no means consensual; on the contrary, it essentially dissents from a given consensus.

I call this dissenting form of speech, 'dissensual speech'. Dissensual speech is any form of speech, symbolic act, or performance that seeks to break with the *sensus communis*, and which does so through a strategic and productive use of incivility. By this I mean, the dissensual act rejects the hegemony of norms instituted by whatever discursive structure it targets and that governs its particular conventional speech patterns. They do so not by vacating those structures – this is where Habermas is quite right to say they are parasitic – but by doing the opposite: by inhabiting them, by vampirising them. To say that political acts are 'strategic' is indeed to say that they aim at making an 'intervention in the world'[15] by challenging whatever counts as a norm of action for a given speech context. The norm gains its validity, after all, from commanding universal assent; so, where that assent can no longer be demonstrated, then the validity of the norm is placed in question: it is contested. However, precisely because dissensual speech acts are perlocutionary – precisely because they reject the authority of conventional speech situations – there is by definition no institutional, discursive or other power that can authorise dissensual speech; and that means that nothing can guarantee it will have, in Austin's terms, anything other than a perlocutionary effect. This is how the political efficacy of art, insofar as it constitutes an intervention in the symbolic sphere, must be considered by its very nature to be 'aleatoric' and unpredictable. Think of the tactical mobility of the activist interventions of the Yes Men, who disregard the norms governing illocutionary acts while at the same time occupying their discursive terrain – the legal nexus of corporate transnational capital and its symbolic modes of image-management promoted via public relations exercises; the Yes Men make use of its conventional illocutionary forms, not to reproduce them, but to subvert their discursive authority. They do so by 'cloning' that authority through a form of identity fraud or, as they put it, 'correction' – for example, by posturing as corporate spokesmen on news channels. What does the Yes Men's strategy of 'identity correction' aim to accomplish? This is a hard question to answer: it may seek to gain 'discursive "leverage"',[16] in Louise Owen's memorable phrase, over the corporate entity, by parodically disrupting its communicative strategies, in order to transform how the public perceives it; but the leveraging effect remains capricious, perlocutionary. Take the specific example of the Yes Men's intervention in Dow's involvement in the Bhopal scandal, the industrial disaster in which an estimated 8000 people are thought to have died following a gas leak from Union Carbide's pesticide plant: when the Yes Men's Jude Finisterra appeared on TV news channels, posing as a Dow exec, proclaiming: 'Today I am very happy to announce that for the first time Dow is accepting full responsibility for the Bhopal catastrophe ... we have resolved to liquidate Union Carbide, this nightmare for the world and this headache for Dow',[17] it resulted in $2bn being knocked off the share price of the company. The consequence of this is that an 'efficacy claim' can be legitimately ascribed to the intervention, but its political effect remains, regardless of the validity of that claim, limited to the nomenclature of the perlocutionary act. This is not to trivialise the political efficacy of art; on the contrary, it is to begin to understand what is involved in talk of a political intervention through art. I think it is to commit to the following claims:

- First, that political art cannot be adequately thought on the basis of a model of social engagement, that is, solely from the logics of social binding; on the contrary, it can only be sufficiently understood by returning to a conception of the political and its logics of dissent (or strategic incivility as I have described it above).
- Second, that the communicative turn provides a means for rethinking the idea of committed art – albeit not in the manner proposed by Habermas. It is possible, however, to follow Habermas's lead to the extent that he encourages us to view the communicative dimension of art as the locus of a potential effect: the difference is that, in keeping with the first claim, that effect is understood to be strategic or perlocutionary by design, not illocutionary.

- Third, that by understanding the communicative dimension of art as analogous to the speech act, we mean that a political work of art, inasmuch as it aims at producing political effects, operates on the basis of an equivalence with dissensual or what might otherwise be termed 'disruptive' speech.

There is, to be sure, a great deal of ambiguity in the word 'equivalence', which requires further analysis. In the first instance, it does not mean that a work of art must be literally taken as an 'act of speaking' (and it shouldn't be forgotten that Austin had already included nonverbal performances under 'illocutionary acts'). Its equivalence lies, as I noted above, in the element of a communicative *potentia* where the idea of effect is no longer thought in terms of hermeneutic meanings, or interpretative depth, but opened up to the wider performative context of the perlocution. Like the dissensual speech act, the political work operates by making public its gesture of dissent. Dissensual performance is always public, even if, in its strategic aspect, it appears as a public deception, as is clearly the case when it comes to the activities and impostures of the Yes Men. Nevertheless, it occurs in the public sphere, and it aims to reproduce that public sphere, not as a *sensus communis*, but as something in which 'meaning' is made volatile – it produces a *dissensus communis*. On this basis, the political work of art seeks to activate the public sphere in three ways that define it as dissensual speech: it will be 'agonistic', insofar as it stages a disagreement; it will be 'phatic', in that by breaking with an illocutionary consensus it seeks to rearticulate the subject as part of a wider counter-hegemonic identity or bloc; and it is 'parrhesiastic' – in the sense attributed to the term by Foucault – that is, it entails a risk to the speaker insofar as a dissensual act lays claim to a truth that directly and frontally challenges the discursive orthodoxy that underpins an accepted relation of power, its recognised processes of veridiction, and the order of knowledge it establishes.

3

What is the proper way to display a US flag? The work of 'dissensual speech' in art

In order to examine the idea of the equivalence of a political work of art with dissensual speech, and its particular (and peculiar) form of discursive leverage (understood as a perlocutionary 'effect' of the work, insofar as it operates as a disruptive element in the context of the monopolistic production of communicable meaning in capitalist societies), I would like to consider, in the final section, a work by the African American artist, Dread Scott. The work, entitled *American Newspeak... Please Feel Free*, was exhibited in February 1989 as part of a student show at the Chicago Institute of Art. Comprising a series of twelve installations, each consisted of an image (typically a photomontage print), a small shelf (that protruded from the wall beneath the image, which contained a notebook and pen) and a 'political' provocation – in the form of propositions such as: 'War is Peace', 'Freedom is Slavery', and 'Don't Suspect a Friend Report Him'. The work encouraged audience participation by inviting viewers to take copies of the prints, provided they recorded their reasons for doing so in the ledgers Scott had made available to gallery visitors. It was the twelfth work in the series, however, that would provoke a controversy that would reach to the very highest levels of government, invoking a Senate ban, an admonishment from the president, and finally an action in the US Supreme Court resulting in a change in the law. What is of specific note is the discrepant relation between the actual political effect that resulted from the work and the work itself, from which no specific intention to elicit a ban, provoke a president, or change the law can be derived. Indeed, Scott could hardly have foreseen where his provocation would lead. Nor therefore can it be said that those effects were due to anything immanent to the work as such: the work did not 'cause' in any predictive sense an intended 'effect'. To the extent that it produced political effects, those effects were perlocutionary and by no means assured by the fact the work had a specifiable political content. They arose out of the conjunctural nexus of mutable, contingent, aleatory, and conditional relations any work has to its wider world. In one sense, this simply affirms a trivial truth: that even where works contain an explicitly political intent – and not even the most ardent adherent of the efficacy debate would claim otherwise – those effects ('intentions') cannot be guaranteed as if by virtue of some iron-clad law of the work. But that is to invite the non-trivial question: then what does guarantee them? And if they cannot be guaranteed, then in what sense can it be said that a work is politically effective? It is this question that a perlocutionary theory of political effect in art must answer. It does not deny that works can be motivated by the explicit political intentions of its producer, contain 'messages' and 'meanings' for its audience, or offer critical interpretations of 'reality'. What it denies is that any of these propositions provide an explanation for the political efficacy of art. Nor, conversely, does it claim that political effects are merely contingent, accidental, the result of caprice or chance. What it argues is that the work contains a content that is 'virtually' oriented by its 'perlocutionary potential' – its potential to produce an effect – and that, correlatively, effects stemming from the work at best only partially realise the potential of the work to make its content real. The partial realisation of the effect testifies to the peculiarity of the perlocutionary nature of the work: firstly, that its potential to produce effects is always activated by circumstances that far exceed the original frame of the work – it is 'conjunctural'; but that, secondly, those effects cannot be said to have exhausted the work. The latter point is crucial here: after all, if the meaning or intent were indeed able to be fully realised, then the work would have been exhausted; but since the effects of the work are perlocutionary, no strict correlation between content and effect can be established – the work, in other words, retains a degree of autonomy. In the event that the work fails to produce an effect, then one should say that its perlocutionary potential is unrealised, and the work's social content remains 'unarticulated' or 'sealed'.

Let us return to the twelfth element in Scott's installation series, since what can be discerned through this piece is how the work constitutes itself performatively as a kind of discursive surface upon which a plurality of subject positions can be inscribed and an agonistic politics staged.

The title of the twelfth part of Scott's installation took the form of an open question: *What Is the Proper Way to Display a US Flag?* Like its eleven preceding parts, the twelfth work presented a photomontage to the viewer, comprising images taken during the Korean peninsula war, with photos of Korean students burning American flags while holding up signs stating, 'Yankee go home, son of a bitch', juxtaposed with images of the coffins of US troops killed in action, draped in the US flag, being loaded onto a troop transportation plane for repatriation and burial. The title of the piece is printed across the montage; this is affixed to the gallery wall. Beneath it, once again, a small shelf with a book and pen can be found – but what differentiates this piece from the eleven that preceded it is that underneath the

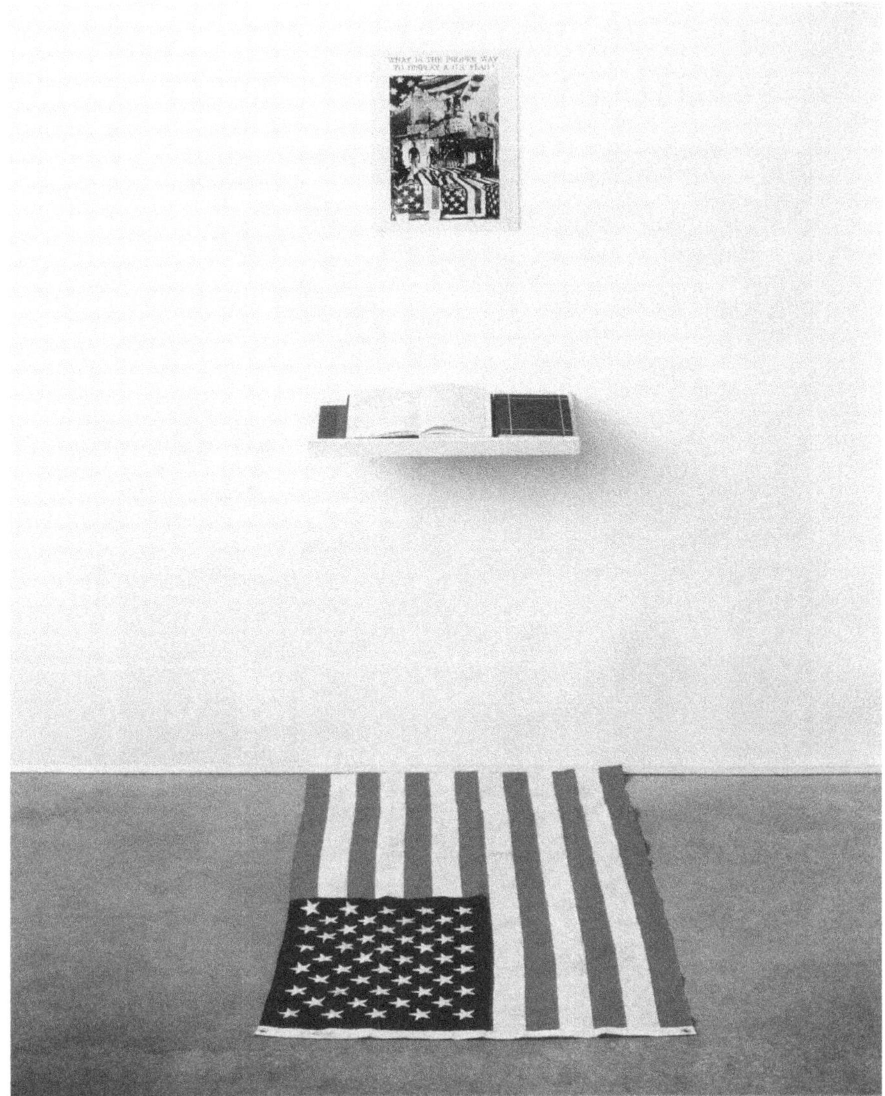

Figure 2 Dread Scott, *What is the proper way to display a US flag?*, exhibited as part of the installation *American Newspeak… Please Feel Free*, Chicago, 1989.

shelf, spread out across the gallery floor, is a large US flag. This compels the audience, who constitute the final element of the work, to walk across the flag in order to view the image and record their response in the ledger. Needless to say, those responses revealed a wide range of ways individuals

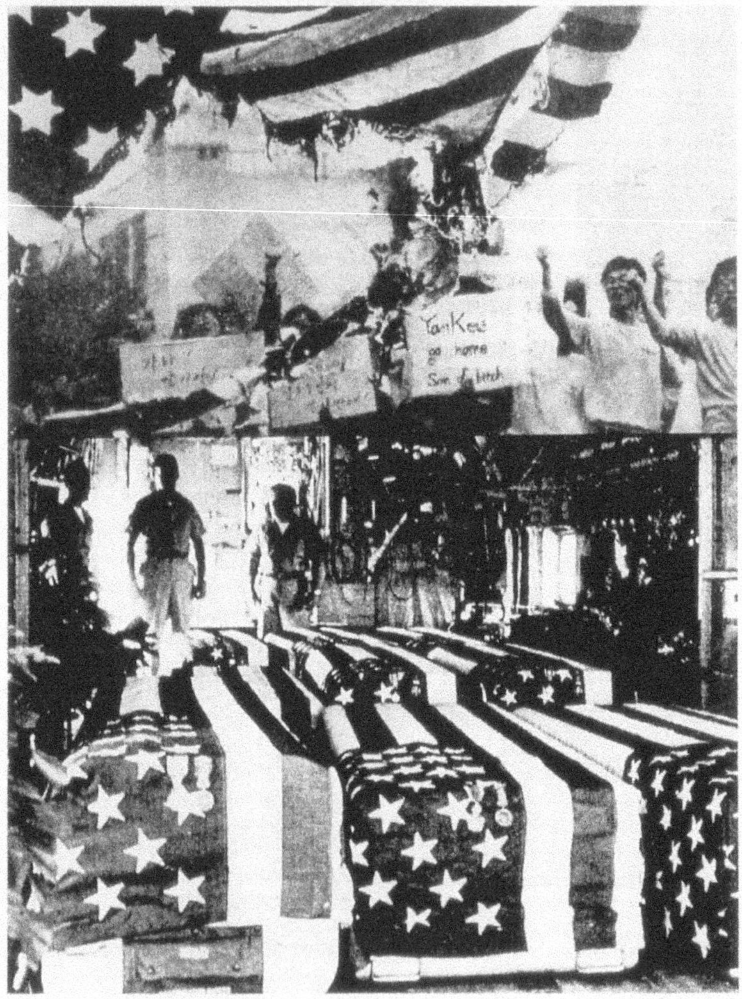

Figure 3 Dread Scott, *What is the proper way to display a US flag?*, detail.

oriented themselves to the work – which included: 'phatic' statements from a number of viewers, i.e., statements that indicated the assent, agreement, alignment of the viewer with Scott – articulating a bond of sociality and equality, as for instance when a Vietnam veteran wrote: 'Let it burn, Let it burn, let the Fucker Burn, Burn, Burn. The first time I had to confront the flag was in Vietnam – Black GIs in my unit refused to stand & salute it! After much debate & anguish I did the same ....' The phatic allocution constitutes an important moment in dissensual speech, incorporating expressions of solidarity into a political discourse – what Bronisław Malinowski once referred to as the moment of 'communal bonding' established by the phatic act.[1] They also included, however, antagonistic statements – many overtly racist: 'Dread, go back to the foreign country where you belong'; or openly hostile: 'As a veteran defending the flag I personally would never defend your stupid ass! You should be shot.'[2]

It is not only of interest that the work elicited these responses but that in doing so it constituted itself as an agonistic surface upon which a range of differential subject positions were able to be articulated. The open frame of the work, taking the form of a question posed to the viewer, did not tell the viewer *what* to think – it provoked them to *say* what they thought – establishing a dialogic and at times adversarial relation to both Scott and to the other participants in the work. Moreover, in using the symbol of the US flag, the symbolic embodiment of American patriotism – Scott allowed for multiple forms of identification and, crucially, disidentification ('This flag I'm standing on stands for everything oppressive in this system', as one viewer wrote) to striate the space of the work. It is not so much that the work disrupted an existing consensus on patriotism, in other words, but that it revealed (insofar as it configured itself *as*) American patriotism's disrupted surface – the work became striated by agonistic effects and was shaped – perhaps disfigured – by the forms of identification that entered the inherently contested space of the political. What it produced, in short, was a 'dissensus communis'. In disturbing the smooth surface constituting the symbol of national unity, one begins to understand how the work operated as a kind of dissensual speech act: the profound disagreements it provoked, inciting both affective and cognitive responses from viewers, arose from what I earlier termed a tactical use of incivility. Rather than confirm a civil convention – there are indeed accepted and conventional ways to display the US flag – the work defied convention; but it did so, not for the sake of defiance or incivility per se, but for the sake of realising a political, i.e., strategic goal. What was that goal? Ostensibly, it was to oblige the viewer to question for themselves the fundamental basis of an established convention, and – in confirming or rejecting it – to express their political identities; but beyond this ostensible goal, a further perlocutionary dynamic was set in play in the work, since to ask the question of what constitutes 'proper use' when displaying a national symbol, is to also bring into question the forms of consent, the norms, and the discourses of truth upon which the underlying convention is founded (to determine its determinations) and thus it is to put its legitimacy to the test. What this brings to mind is the hegemonic strategy advocated by Laclau and Mouffe, which seeks to build a counter-hegemony, bringing about 'new modes of identification'[3] – to break with the norm in order to coalesce opinion around a different norm, a different way of acting and being in the world.

It is this more profound challenge to the status quo, enclosed in the work, that provoked a series of responses that extended its effects; what it unleashed was a series of unpredictable consequences that both exceeded the work while further realising its perlocutionary potential through what might be termed *ancillary* effects. First, the display provoked protests outside the gallery from veterans, and a number of personal threats made against Scott, but as a consequence of the publicity it attracted it soon got the attention of Chicago city councillors who responded to the work with a proposed ordinance that would make it illegal to 'place the US flag on the floor or ground', thus outlawing the exhibit. The artist, they complained, had invited the act of 'trampling on the flag'. The controversy would gain the attention of the President, with G.H.W. Bush decrying the work as 'disgraceful' – and proclaiming 'I don't approve of it at all'. Eventually, it would lead to the 101st Congress passing a law – the 'Flag Protection Act of 1989' – amending a statute passed in 1968 at the height of anti-Vietnam war protests, to render the work illegal. The statute of 1968, *An Act to Prohibit Desecration of the Flag, and for Other Purposes*, stated: 'Whoever knowingly casts contempt upon any flag of the United States by publicly mutilating, defacing, defiling, burning, or trampling upon it, shall be fined not more than $1000 or imprisoned for not more than one year, or both.'[4]

In response to the ruling, Scott, accompanied by two friends, staged a protest on the steps of the US Capitol, publicly burning the flag – a performative act of civil disobedience that exposed Scott to risk of arrest and prosecution, and which, I think, makes the parrhesiastic nature of the act of dissensual speech plainly visible. As I noted earlier, the parrhesiastic mode of enunciation belongs to dissensual speech, and thus as a mode of 'truth-telling', it must also characterise the performativity of the political work of art. It can be defined in the first instance by its difference from modes of authorised or legitimated speech that rest on illocutionary or conventional discursive norms. The question for authorised speech – to paraphrase Michel Foucault – is: who, out of the totality comprising the community of speakers, is accorded the right to speak? Who is qualified to speak in virtue of their knowledge, their competence, their institutional position; who is sanctioned by law, by tradition, or by the force of convention to speak?[5] The parrhesiast, by contrast, occupies a position that is diametrically opposed to the authorised speaker, and for whom the very act of speaking incurs immense personal risk. In fact, the parrhesiast is the one who, to pursue Foucault's analysis of ancient practices of 'truth-telling', by definition, speaks from an unauthorised position and whose speech, from a legal, juridical, or merely conventional point of view, is regarded – if not always as necessarily proscribed – even so, as illegitimate. Nevertheless, it is the parrhesiast who 'stands up, speaks, tells the truth to a tyrant, and risks his life'.[6] This is why the act of dissensual speech requires courage to the extent that it involves defying, confronting, or subverting established forms of authority, customary relations of power, and systems of authorisation. *Parrhēsia*, Foucault writes, is exercised as a 'dangerous practice with ambiguous effects'[7] and the reason for this comes down to one simple fact: that the sole condition of parrhesiastic speech is that the parrhesiast must necessarily risk conflicting with the power they contest, and in so doing challenge that power through the assertion of a truth that confounds the existing system of veridiction upon which its authority is established.

For this reason, and to the extent that dissensual speech operates on the terrain of truth, it can be seen as an intervention in what counts as 'true' for a given discourse and its conventional matrix of speech. In this sense, like the perlocutionary act, it occupies the terrain of the illocutionary convention to achieve some form of 'discursive leverage' over it. When, in 1990, Scott's case was heard at the Supreme Court,[8] which led to the overturning of the statute of the previous year, the perlocutionary effect that flowed from the work reached its conclusion. The Supreme Court judgement ruled in favour of Scott: 'prosecution for burning a flag in violation of the Act is inconsistent with the First Amendment.' Flag burning, the Court went on to argue, 'constituted expressive conduct' and for that reason enjoys the 'First Amendment's full protection'.[9] If it is a 'mode of expressive conduct', i.e., if it is art – if it is excepted – it is guaranteed under the right to freedom of speech. It is at this point – of let's call it maximum discursive leverage – that the 'content' of the work was realised in the most precise sense through the poignancy of the question that it essentially posed to the Supreme Court: can one mandate patriotism?

Nevertheless, and this is the point on which I would like to conclude, the Supreme Court's answer did not provide the work with a meaning, a point of discursive closure, in which its intention was fully realised in the juridical act that overturned a bad law. Quite the opposite, irrespective of the decision of the court, the work retains its power to disturb what is concealed within the murky sediments that lie beneath the public *doxa* and, in this sense, it remains what it always was: a locus for a wider nexus of effects, a distributor and amplifier of perlocutions.

Part III

Taxonomy of the political theatre

Imagine the taxonomic table of the political theatre. Composed of complex codifications and intricate mappings, the table systematically crystallises the proxemics of form and function. It charts various theatrical methods in relation to political practices. It observes the variables of style and expression; but also takes into account the arts of rhetoric and persuasion. Through a chronology comprising ancestry, lineage, and succession, it patiently adumbrates the inner workings that traverse the political theatre's entire genealogy. Imagine for a moment this table and what it represents – a final envoi of the political theatre? Or a demonstration of a form that produces endless differences within itself, illustrating that the political theatre unfolds rather like a controlled experiment, combining elements of chance and design, twisting and turning as if in syncopation with the very rhythm of historical events? Imagine this table as if it could lay bare, in a *coup d'œil*, none other than the entire anatomy of the political theatre. Needless to say, no such thing exists; needless to say, that no practice could ever be fixed in the tendentious space of a taxonomy without being deformed beyond recognition.

Even so, I would like to explore the idea that such a taxonomy is possible if only as a thought experiment. To begin with, how would one go about constructing such a table? It would require the painstaking work of collating, sifting, and cataloguing the range of theatre practices that claimed to be political. The first priority for the taxonomist would be that of deciding the basic taxon. What is the appropriate means for identifying an individual instance classifiable as a type under the general rubric of 'the political theatre'? What would the criteria be for selecting and distinguishing between different types and for configuring further subtypes? And just as one methodological problem paves the way for another, a code determining nomenclature would also need to be agreed. Its purpose would be to govern the assignment of a typology (what determines the 'political' character of the political theatre?) and to attribute valid designators to it ('agit-prop' as opposed to 'epic theatre' … etc.) while authorising the invalidation of others (satire would be omitted, for instance, for being too protean a genre). Assuming there is a domain of political theatre that can be properly distinguished from that other domain (the realm of non-political theatre) then the problem of phylogenetically relating types of theatre together into a variety of groupings would still present considerable difficulties. One would need to be attentive to category errors, to problems of morphology and derivations of form. One would soon be bogged down in the snags and snares of phenetic analysis and the headache of collocating examples while mapping multiple variations across them to produce proximities (between similar types) and distances (between dissimilar ones), which would considerably exacerbate the problem of ordination (whose literal meaning is to 'put in order').

No doubt the attempt would be condemned as fatuous by some, while others would denounce it as misguided. How could one think of imposing a method of analysis on the theatre that was designed for the evolutionary sciences? The risk would be one of fixing the mobile specificities of the form in crude and reductive ways. Nevertheless, as a thought experiment, imagine that such a systematic analysis was indeed viable, and that a near comprehensive descent of the political theatre could be produced, with its branches and subdivisions, according to its various categories, specifications, and differentiations; its stratagems, forms, and structures; its underlying aims and its motivating forces. The results would surely be open to question – the limitations of taxonomy are well known (the choice between an 'evolutionary' model or a 'dialectical' pattern in constructing the political theatre's genealogy, or something else entirely different, would hardly be innocent). But setting aside practical drawbacks and procedural reservations, would there not also be some value in conducting the exercise? One could plausibly speculate on what discoveries it might lead to, and on the questions it would compel; and that, regardless of the improbability of its guiding purpose, it would have salience for anyone who had an interest in the political possibilities of the theatre. From the attempt at a taxonomic analysis, the following might be deduced: the underpinning principles of any-political-theatre-whatsoever; the discovery of those family resemblances that explain the contiguities between a range of broadly similar things; the ruptures in practices (themselves founded on deeper epistemic breaks) in which the phantom conjured by 'the political theatre' is seen only to arrogate dissimilar things mistakenly gathered under the force of a common name. The exercise would show that between Piscator and the postdramatic theatre there is a yawning chasm, but that at the same time one can barely slip a piece of paper between them.

To play such a taxonomic game, the political theatre would need to be classified as per its own self-ascriptions, and according to what it professed itself to be, all the while considering the key criticisms levelled against it and its (all too familiar) presumptions. Such an approach would require an assiduous neutrality on the part of the taxonomist of the political theatre. They would refrain from piously adjudicating between this or that form or experiment; they would eschew the temptation to arbitrate between the various positions that accrue, like so many debtors and creditors, to the question of what technique or method produced better or worse results or led to a greater or lesser effect. The essential task, as per the rules of the game of taxonomic analysis, would be at once simple (the production of value free division, categorisation, and classification) and immensely complex (every categorical term would prove treacherous and mutable – how does one distinguish between different understandings of propaganda in theatre? to take one example). There would still be the 'bad' traditional theatre of Lehmann, and the theatre – not of the good old days, but the bad new ones of Brecht. But the judgements 'good' and 'bad' would lose their meaning for the analyst. Taxonomic methodology would prohibit them from making such judgements, just as it would compel them to defer indefinitely the answer to the question of which was the 'real' political theatre, and which the imposter, the fake, the producer of mere chicanery.

If there is a persuasive reason to play this taxonomic game, I think it is this: to imagine the taxonomy of the political theatre is to imagine that the political theatre exists (or once existed). It is implied whenever critical discourse differentiates, as it does today, between 'making theatre in a political way' and making 'political theatre'.[1] Even for the most sceptical commentator on the problem of political theatre, such a taxonomy must already have been secretly imagined; but, above all, to problematise the political theatre requires the construction of a taxonomy, if only that it may then be decomposed and the proper name 'political theatre' dethroned – a taxonomic exercise then, but one that works against its own inherent tendency to capture, in any definitive sense, its object. Getting to grips with this problematic taxonomy would be cardinal for anyone who wished to develop a critical awareness of the problem of the political theatre.

There is perhaps one more reason for playing this game: if those who assert the possibility of the political theatre and those who deny its possibility share a tacit knowledge of its taxonomy, however ill-formed and misbegotten it may be, they also thereby claim to know what the political theatre is and what it isn't. Folded into the question regarding the taxonomy of the political theatre there lies the prospect of unfolding an entire ontology of the theatre.

1

Foundational problems and problems of foundation

Taxonomy, which addresses itself to foundational problems of origination, descent, ancestry, and succession, presents an obvious difficulty when applied to the political theatre. It would take no more than a cursory survey of theatre's history to show that political theatre was always already 'there' from the outset, as if it took root in the very essence of the thing. Yet from this supposition little else can be deduced. No tradition of political theatre can be discovered by returning to the theatre of antiquity; no clear line of ancestral descent established, and no foundation discovered – only an order of succession whose datability appears arbitrary and whose modes of appearance haphazard and infrequent.[1] How is it possible to speak of a line of descent if, lacking an origin, political theatre could only be traced to the contingency of events? And if there is no line of descent then to what aspects of theatre's long history should the analysis restrict itself?

On the one hand, it is evident that the political problem of the theatre is as old as the theatre itself and that the shadow cast by the State and by government falls across the stage wherever it has appeared. This does not represent an open horizon of historical possibility for the political theatre, however; it only indicates the lamentable fact of the matter – the relative scarcity of its appearance and the reason for it. It is precisely because the idea of political theatre was considered a problem by the State that its appearance, with a few notable exceptions, which were swiftly suppressed, was by and large permanently inhibited by legislators. One possible response would be to follow Alain Badiou and claim that theatre, precisely because it is so problematic, has an intrinsic connection to the political sphere, regardless of whether or not it expressly deals with the theme of politics: 'What does the theatre talk about if not the state of the State, the state of society, the state of the revolution, the state of consciousness relative to the State, to society, to revolution, to politics?'[2] While Badiou's question may open up theatre to the wider philosophical problem of the State, it does little to further the present enquiry into the taxonomy of the political theatre, or explain what distinguishes the political theatre from other forms of theatre. 'The theatre text *is* a text exposed to politics, by necessity,' he writes, '[because] it always subordinates its incompletion to the open gap of *conflict*.'[3] The quantifier 'always' suggests that there is no theatre that is not political, by simple virtue of its inherent conflictuality, and no theatre that is without a relation to the State, since theatre according to this definition is founded on two axioms of political life that applies equally to the State and to the theatre. Each deals with states of affairs; and each deals with conflicts arising within those states. The political theatre is everywhere (where there is theatre) but it is also consequently nowhere in particular – its meaning stretched to the point that it breaks with any determinable referent.

On the other hand, it is also clear that at a certain point in its history something called the political theatre did come into being – and it did so concretely, incisively, and above all else self-consciously. When it eventually appeared, it produced two significant effects. First, it made itself felt at the level of dramaturgical practices, where new and experimental forms proliferated at an astonishing rate. But it also did so in a more discrete manner, in the form of the problematic it introduced. It is this problem that has proven difficult if not impossible to resolve, such that even today it remains a source of controversy: namely, that of the ultimate meaning, purpose, and destiny of the political theatre. Considered thus, an 'origin' for the political theatre can be identified on a historical basis without recourse to the abstractions of Badiou's theoreticism. I am, of course, referring to the theatre that was produced under revolutionary conditions, in that smelting furnace of ideas, passions, and aesthetic experiments which erupted with the revolution in Russia in October 1917. Of course, it is undeniable that political theatres preceded the theatre of the Russian Revolution; but none condensed within themselves the problem of the political theatre in the way the Russian theatre did. There are innumerable reasons for this that I can merely touch on here – these are to do with the specific conjunctural conditions of the period: a dysfunctional state, with an underdeveloped bourgeois class, diminished by the residual strength of the *Ancien Régime* concentrated in centres of aristocratic power; a well-armed proletarian class, radicalised by the immediate experience of war; and the needs of a small group of intellectuals seeking to forge a broad and somewhat improbable coalition of classes. During the period leading up to the October Revolution, not only were the structural contradictions of everyday life palpable for all to see, but they also lent the idea of a political theatre a sudden clarity of purpose that it had at best only previously grasped in the form of an inchoate sentiment: that theatre should be 'for the people'.

To avoid any misunderstanding on this point: one publication in particular demonstrates that the political theatre did not emerge entirely without precedent – Romain Rolland's polemic, *Théâtre du Peuple*, translated for publication in Russia in 1908, and in English, as 'The People's Theatre', in 1918, served as an important touchstone that galvanised critical thought. Principally, it served to demarcate the terrain upon which the political theatre would necessarily emerge – the terrain of futurity and of the theatre-to-come:

> among those who claim to represent the aims of the people's theatre there are two diametrically opposed ideals: the adherents of the first seek to give the people the theatre as it now exists, any theatre so long as it is theatre; those of the second attempt to extract from this new force, the people, an entirely new theatre. The first believe in the theatre, the others in the People. The two have nothing in common: one is the champion of the past, the other of the future.[4]

With Rolland, the quest for the new theatre demanded the production of a fundamental break: first, between the theatre of the people and that of the 'State', which he writes '[by] its very definition … belongs to the past'.[5] The second aspect of this break concerned the relation of the new theatre to the canon (which could no longer be relied upon since it does not belong to the people) and the repertoire of the middle-class theatre that had emerged in the previous century ('what do the people care about bourgeois problems, limited as they are to the Bourgeoisie?'[6]); only a theatre that shares their 'struggles, their worries, their hopes, and their battles' will truly constitute itself as the people's theatre.[7] In order to establish the people's theatre, historical necessity dictated a complete and irreversible rupture with 'all the dramatic impedimenta of the past'.[8] A twofold requisite makes 'rupture' a constitutive element of the conditions of existence for the political theatre: it must be differentiated from the old high-minded theatre of the State – that old theatre of address favoured by governments as exemplary sites of moral exhortation with their laborious hortatory and declamatory style; and it must rid itself of the vices of the theatrical past, more or less in its entirety, to rid itself of the elite interests invested in it. The break must be radical since the people's theatre cannot simply be a rival and still less poor cousin to the existing theatre; its novelty lies in the fact that it usurps the very name of the theatre. It is precisely for this reason that the people's theatre is the precursor for the political theatre that developed in the wake of the Russian Revolution, even if Rolland's theatre of the future, could only grasp that future in incipient form.[9]

It is with the theatre inaugurated by the October Revolution, the political theatre in its 'classical' period (the 'classical political theatre'), that Rolland's theatre of the future enters theatre practice as a problem for the theatre of the present. Not only did the Russian Revolution impel the theatre to seize the idea of a people's theatre and propel it into actuality, but it also set the political theatre on a genealogical trajectory that makes visible the foundational problematic internal to it. On the one hand, the political theatre's conditions of emergence are rooted entirely in the revolutionary conditions that compelled it into being. On the other, it commences with the recognition of the epochal struggle being played out between two antagonistic historical forces, in relation to which it discovered a new designation for itself – one that transformed the people's theatre into the vanguard theatre of the proletariat. As Meyerhold would write in 1920, when the revolution was still in its infancy:

> The most up-to-date new spectator (I mean the proletariat), the most capable in my opinion of freeing itself from the hypnosis of illusionism, and specifically under those conditions that it must (and I am sure will) know that what it's watching is acting, will approach that acting consciously, for through acting it wants to express itself as coactive and *creating a new essence*, since for a living being (as for a new human being reborn in communism), every kind of theatrical essence is only an occasional pretext to proclaim in the spotlight's excitement the *joy of a new everyday life*.[10]

Only in professing the cause of establishing a 'new everyday life' and the creation of a 'new essence' as its own, in other words – only then – could the political theatre, after centuries of aborted attempts and false starts, be born. Nevertheless, what do we know of this birth, when all is said and done, other than that it occurred within the nexus of chaotic events, precipitated by ongoing crisis? That the political theatre was emboldened by events to give expression to the energy of its historical moment by no means guaranteed its inner coherence – particularly since the revolution, far from being a rational outcome of the historical process, in fact 'fused' a number of contradictions which it exposed but did not necessarily resolve.[11] In this perspective, the political theatre came into being in the lacunary space that opened between the disorders of a fevered present and a new order that was as unfathomable to it as a dream. Edward Braun, writing on the theatre of Meyerhold, suitably observed, 'Soviet theatre … is rightly considered a *locus classicus* in the history of the political theatre.'[12] It could hardly be otherwise insofar as the mytheme from which the revolution drew sustenance, formulated it as an 'epistemological break' that disrupted the very order of history itself: thus does it epitomise the founding event of the twentieth century. Theatre could scarcely remain unchanged when all around it nothing in the world appeared the same. Either theatre became political, and lent its power to the indignant, or it became irrelevant. But here we confront the essential dilemma of 'foundation', inscribed at the heart of the revolutionary theatre of Russia: how exactly should the theatre *demonstrate* its relevance to the new society? And in what way is the new able to be produced through the old – and by means of what fundamental dislocation? It is true to say that the facts on the ground to an extent pre-empted how that question would be answered in practical terms. As early as October 1917, the Bolsheviks began to take control of Petrograd's state theatres, immediately recognising their usefulness for broadcasting the propaganda that would win over an at times recalcitrant public. Already one understands from this that the classical political theatre, indebted to political forces to which it was subordinate, was required to fulfil a set of limited but determinate functions – the classical political theatre is by necessity and by definition a theatre of propaganda. All the same, this only provides a limited account of its function; it by no means answers the question of what the epistemological rupture of revolution meant for the theatre as an aesthetic practice. It was Meyerhold who sought to address this question in respect of its most radical implications. More than anyone, it was Meyerhold who grasped that revolution entailed an hour of reckoning for the old theatre, hostile – as it could only be – to the new society. The revolution, for him, turned superseded culture into little more than compost. At best it provided the fertiliser that fed the growth of a new culture and art. Within a few months of the upheaval, he established the arrival of the political theatre in its most radical aspect through the wholesale appropriation (and violation) of the old apparatus of the bourgeois stage. He used the flies to lower political slogans, and the walls of the auditorium to display the political poetry of his fellow futurist, and collaborator, Mayakovsky, to advance through theatrical means the idea that the revolution announced an absolute break with the culture of the past. In an essay written in 1918, 'The Proletarian and Art', Mayakovsky would emphatically proclaim that the idea of the new demanded the evisceration of all that had gone before:

> The new has to be discovered with new words. We need a new form of art .... On the left are we, who portray the new; on the right are those who regard art as a means of all kinds of acquisition .... There is no classless art. Only the proletariat will create the new, and only we, the futurists, are traveling the same road as the proletariat.[13]

That the avant-gardism of Meyerhold and Mayakovsky would put both on a direct collision course with the Soviet state is well known. Even if it was not immediately apparent to either of them in the first years of the revolution, the structural contradiction that would lead each to personal calamity was present from the outset. It can be discerned in the way the theatre was compelled to adapt itself to the altered political circumstances of the day, which installed within it a twofold tendency that pulled it in two different directions at once: into increasing conformity with the new orthodoxy that it was compelled to uphold, and to become a spontaneous demonstration of the political emancipation of the worker through their direct democratic participation.

For example, almost immediately, the revolutionary theatre was made to coalesce around new organisational forms and structures which orchestrated the opening up of the cultural front on an immense scale. This occurred under the leadership of Anatoly Lunacharsky – a close collaborator of Lenin's – with his newly formed Commissariat of Enlightenment. Lunacharsky's approach, however, was quite at odds with the avant-gardist insistence on experimental radicalism. It sought, instead, to address, not the individual needs of the artist, but the collective needs of the proletariat. In his address to the actors and technicians of the State Theatre in Petrograd, in December 1917, Lunacharsky would make the following exhortation: that while the new Soviet government did not demand conformity to a 'definite political credo', all the same, the theatres must recognise 'a new master in this land – the common working man'.[14] How – Lunacharsky's speech demanded to know – can the theatre best serve this new master? One way in which that question was answered was through an organisation, already initiated by the political economist Aleksandr Aleksandrovich Bogdanov, called 'Proletkult' ('proletarian culture') – a cultural and educational organisation formed a year prior to the revolution to educate the working classes. Proletkult had three immediate goals: first, to educate the masses in past cultural forms; second, to create a proletarian art strong enough to eventually supplant the existing bourgeois cultural formation that persisted; and third, to instil in the working classes, by means of a cultural education, a proletarian consciousness – in short, to enculturate the worker, the peasant, and the intellectual into the ideals and principles of the revolution. In fact, with the rapid success of the revolution, Lunacharsky soon grasped the need to transform and extend the cultural front into a wide-ranging educational programme designed to promote 'proletarian enlightenment'.[15] The very idea of proletarian enlightenment, however, carried a number of implicit meanings that belied its paternalistic impulse. The first of these is underscored by an obvious implication that is intrinsic to the very articulation of Lunacharsky's programme – that the worker required educating and so was seen to be in need of cultural enlightenment, without which they remained a mere 'barbarian'.[16] Second, it meant the production and dissemination of 'pure proletarian ideas' – not least because the prole existed in a state of ignorance concerning the proper meaning of the revolution and what it required of them. The objective, according to Lunacharsky, was – concisely put – the promotion of 'our political propaganda ... conducted through all government agencies'.[17] In the cultural arena this meant resisting the 'few radical [but deluded] voices' of the Futurists who proclaimed the irrelevance of the achievements of the past. Instead, the 'proletariat', he argued, 'must be *armed with the entirety of human education*'.[18] This leads to a further and final implication that inhered in the question Lunacharsky posed: it is not a matter of whether culture provides a means for transmitting the tastes and dispositions of the working class, since it was already obvious to him that the worker's taste and dispositions were themselves corrupted – were an expression of the vicious and degraded state to which the worker had been reduced. What is called for instead should therefore in no way be confused with a romantic validation of popular culture. Because taste was lacking in the worker, it had to be inculcated in them. The ambiguity that arises with this derives straightforwardly from the fact that proletarian culture does not exist. On the contrary, it needed to be produced. Consequently, this question of how to constitute a genuinely proletarian art and culture permeates artistic debates within the first decade of the revolution – just as much as the question of how much of the past is to be carried over into the present and in what form. To give a brief example, in 'The Proletarian Actor', Valentin Tikhonovich reflecting on the criticism that much of the new theatre was amateurish, conceded the 'proletarian class has not yet recognised its path of proletarian art'.[19] The contradiction is manifest in the distinction he draws between the substandard nature of much worker's and peasant's theatre, and the training that provides the professional actor with all the requisite skills of art. The problem remains, however: for the proletariat, professional training leads to the 'separation from one's own class, and the *declassification of the* proletariat'.[20] It is 'associated', he added, 'with an art that is saturated with the *old* ideology and clothed in the *old* form'.[21]

But on the other hand, it is precisely due to the emergence of the 'amateur' theatre in revolutionary Russia that a theatre of the proletariat can be said to have developed at all. Only through the participation of the workers and the peasantry did the classical political theatre come close to cultivating that new democratic habit of mind that testified to their political emancipation. In practice, it led to the discovery of further theatrical innovations that would prove to be just as influential as the avant-gardism of Meyerhold. In particular, the period of the civil war (1919–1921) saw the development of experimental forms of theatre that combined a democratic outlook with propagandistic purpose – the 'Agitki' or agit-theatre. These highly satirical forms of popular propaganda were closely attuned to the class disposition of the audience. Often employing short-form performances, which could be inserted into everyday life contexts without disrupting them, they mocked well-established political targets and so were deliberately crafted to elicit from the audience the most vigorous expression of contempt for the opponents of the revolution. One eyewitness to a street performance described the following: 'The erstwhile enemy is constantly ridiculed and combated in symbolic form on the open street, with the masses encouraged to join in.'[22] Troupes such as *Teresvat* ('Theatre of Revolutionary Satire'), formed in Vitebsk in 1919, would inspire countless imitators, producing a wider Teresvat movement – mainly comprising amateur or semi-professional theatre troupes – appearing throughout the country. The 'Blue Blouse' movement, perhaps the most celebrated of all the agit-theatre groups, and named after the apparel worn by workers, was formed through the Moscow Institute for Journalism in 1923 to create the 'Living Newspaper'. It began to seek out audiences at their places of work, in working men's clubs, on farms, and even on street corners, with the explicit aim of bringing to a largely illiterate population both news and information that would otherwise be inaccessible to them. Its performances included declamatory speeches that quoted Lenin and Trotsky; it deployed banners, posters, and political slogans; it incorporated choral singing; and with its display of crude effigies, reminded the audience of its class enemies: the priest, the bourgeois, the banker .... One popular way in which the audience was encouraged to become engaged in political debate was through a decidedly agonistic form of performance that made use of theatricalised 'agit-trials'. These theatre trials combined all the core features of an actual prosecution: 'indictment, the debates from both sides, the questioning of the witnesses, the performance of their roles with make-up on ...'[23] – often with audiences motivated to make impromptu interventions with improvised speeches. Hence, with the agit-trial, the audience went from 'being spectators to active participants'.[24] The agit-theatre, at least before its novelty eventually wore off, became immensely popular; it was without doubt genuinely democratic, while also promoting the 'political and social education of the masses'.[25] It is why the first decade of the revolution coincided with an extraordinary explosion of theatrical activity and invention, producing a theatre of 'agitation' and 'propaganda' that swept across Russia – what Lars Kleberg has elegantly described as a 'new type of ambulatory "street theatre"'.[26] And yet even as the revolution transformed the destiny of the stage, propelling it toward new forms that it could scarcely have imagined before, points of diffraction began to bifurcate the field of experimental practices that the new political theatre had made possible, which only helped to make questionable how exactly political theatre was to be defined, where it might appear and in what form, and what political purposes, ends, or interests it should serve.

To understand this, it is necessary to return to the intractable and insistent problem of the new: of establishing a new art, of cultivating a new social disposition in the people, of forming a new state, and of creating a new world. This problem underpins the tension that is always implicit in the encounter between the classical political theatre and actual power – with the forceful assertion of government power, concerned with the pressing exigencies of the immediate political context. The dilemma is not simply exterior to the classical political theatre, however – something imposed upon it by circumstance. It is more fundamental than that: it defines the basic ambiguity of the classical political theatre insofar as it is bound to the irreconcilable contradiction which itself constituted a key cornerstone of the revolution. What, after all, is at stake in the demand that the masses should be awakened to their condition, and specifically the demand that the theatre contribute to the awakening of a consciousness that otherwise remained either dormant or in a state of incompletion? What does this 'awakening' entail, in other words? It is firstly and above all this: that only through the production of class consciousness is an understanding of those existing conditions able to be generated and widely broadcast (conditions that only the social revolution could transform). Secondly, and somewhat more problematically: that this understanding required an awakening of the consciousness of the worker as a self-conscious proletarian – as the one whose essential being is determined by work and thus by the social ontology of material reproduction as embodied through their labour. For the worker, labour = being. This is what theatrical propaganda must establish for the workers' state: a *proletarian* consciousness – and it is therefore unsurprising that it pervades much governmental discourse on the function of the stage in early Soviet Russia. This is nowhere more in evidence than in the vexed debates over how to form a repertoire appropriate to the character and purpose of the new theatre. V.V. Ignatov, the secretary of the Petrograd Proletkult, and member of the presidium of the Central Committee of the All-Russia Soviet of the Proletkult, could not have put the point more plainly:

> the repertoire of proletarian theatres must be made up of play, which awakens in the masses creative energy, a joyous acceptance of life, audacity, a thirst for tireless struggle for a socialist future .... A proletarian theatre must carol constructive labor of the creative human being as one of his wondrous capabilities and thereby evoke, arouse, modulate in the masses a stalwart, unyielding, and joyous will to labor.[27]

Even Meyerhold, despite his iconoclasm, would connect the enjoyment of theatre, and recreation more generally, to the primacy of work:

> Now, where the whole infrastructure of Russian life is being reconstructed, every citizen in the land must know that for the building of a new, socialist government, we need to have a new resource of strength. Everyone will become a worker, in whatever trade he works – in the trade of intellectual labor or manual labor.[28]

It is clear from this why recreation is to be maximised. It is not so that the workers are to work less, but that they may find within themselves, and specifically through the engagement with art, 'ever newer and newer resources of strength' – to evolve a will to (labour) power.[29] The emancipation of the worker is not to be misunderstood as freedom from necessity then. This is because emancipation from necessity in no way constitutes the central promise of the revolution. Rather, emancipation comes from participating in the social reproduction of society, albeit recast on the basis of a corporate and socially totalising connection that ties the proletarian, the peasant, and the intellectual together through the common denominator of human labour. It is with grim irony that a revolution which exalted the figure of the emancipated proletarian should condemn its actual workers to a life of drudgery and toil in the service of the new Soviet state.

But there is a final point to be made here, which returns us to the tendency that leads the classical political theatre towards its eventual absorption by government; a tendency that increasingly subordinated the early radicalism and vanguardism of the political theatre to statist propaganda, at the expense of democratic agitation. In fact, arguably, it is the agitational element that proves ultimately to be the most problematic aspect of the political theatre for the new state, if what is meant by agitation is the attempt to provoke free and independent thought in an audience – to activate the *bios politikos* of the spectator, as it were. It belongs to the very nature of government to banish from the polity that which appears troublesome and subversive; and so, it is no surprise that under Stalin, the Soviets eventually did what all governments do when confronted with an art form whose interventions produce social meanings inconvenient to them: they suppressed the political theatre entirely. What this reveals, is a critical distinction that must be made between the political theatre, on the one hand, and a governmental theatre, on the other, in which the political logic of revolution is evermore constrained by the conservative forces that would prefer an art whose ultimate purpose is the stultification of critical thought – and in a word, the suppression of the new. To be sure, the tendency is one of gradual absorption, rather than a sudden manifestation of state censorship. It thus moves through uncertain and barely perceptible phases, where the early aesthetics of revolutionary rupture is supplanted by the project of the proletarianisation of culture, before finally being eradicated altogether, with the conventions imposed by Soviet realism. It can no more be associated with a coarsening of style, a sudden loss of ambition, a faintness of heart, a desire to re-establish control over art and culture, than it can be attributed to this or that government edict. The internal nature of this tendency, in other words, inhabits the classical political theatre as a contradictory logic in which emancipation becomes its opposite.

One final and notable example will demonstrate this tendency: when theatre director Nikolai Evreinov staged a mass participatory spectacle in 1920, by inviting citizen-performers to reenact *The Storming of the Winter Palace*, the political theatre had already acquired a meaning quite at odds with Meyerhold's utopian vision of a theatrical art that could conjure, in outline at least, the future society from the resources of aesthetic experiment; it was also quite separate from the agitational theatre that harnessed the militant sense of democracy in the early twenties. In fact, other prerogatives prevailed: rather than taking theatre to the people, Evreinov's theatre took a decisive step toward political pageantry, and towards the State. It presented itself as the scene in which an event of foundation was not simply celebrated but effectively reverse engineered through a performative abridgement of reality, producing what amounted to the curated distillation of the cultural memory of the events of 1917. What resulted was an unprecedented theatrical event, a 'celebratory mass spectacle … heralding the proletariat's final victory' and 'performed by a mass of eight thousand strong … the first theatrical army of the world'.[30] Commencing with immense fanfare, and with the explosive staging of the collapse of Kerenski's Provisional Government amid the blistering noise of artillery and gun fire, along with the closing celebratory torchlight parade, those who beheld *The Storming* were left awestruck (it is estimated that between 60,000–150,000 spectators attended the event).[31] Its purpose, according to one contemporary observer, was not so much to win over the people to the cause as reveal 'the natural essence of the mass as such'.[32] It was as though the actual events that had taken place three years earlier in Petrograd were a mere dress rehearsal for the theatrical performance-to-come; as if only through the simulacral power of performance was the reality of the revolution able to be consummated as historical image, as myth. That Evreinov's spectacular production paid little regard to historical accuracy is entirely beside the point. In it, history is made to serve the political theatre, not the other way around. Nor was Evreinov's theatre concerned merely with transfiguring the violence of revolution into popular entertainment, although it concluded with an exorbitant firework display. It provided a theatrical frame for the conjuring of a collective body – a demonstration that the new Soviet state and the people coincided in that homogenous identity designated by the abstract noun: the 'masses'. The total State required a total theatre for which it acted as both accomplice and stenographer. Theatre thus wrote the people's history in the shorthand of statist propaganda.

Consequently, there is an original splitting within the classical political theatre, yielding two discrete branches that divide the taxonomic table of the political theatre as if genetically from the outset. In one column, there is the revolutionary theatre – a fecund theatre of ideas, full of the *élan vital*

of a new beginning, vanguardist in outlook and democratic in tempera-
ment, which combined circus and satire, and dreamt of an audience that
would proclaim: 'This is our theatre!'[33] In the other, the political theatre is
grasped as the ideological and cultural expression of the political state: a
shrewd puppet-master, a cunning theatre for the masses, but essentially anti-
democratic by disposition. Where one had the aim of overturning the status
quo, the other wished only to establish the State anew – to give birth to a
new establishment. The tension between them directly results from their different political functions and from their contending aims, which ultimately
could not be reconciled (the fate of the avant-garde under Stalin is well
known). For the classical political theatre, what characterises its innermost
tendency, is also what leads it to an inexorable reversal: problems of foundation transmute into foundational problems, which the political theatre
thereafter never ceases to grapple with, in one way or another.

What is meant by this can be expressed in the form of a preliminary
conclusion. Firstly, although I have said that the theatre of the Russian
Revolution establishes the classical political theatre, it by no means can be
said to have established a 'foundation' for the political theatre as such. It
cannot be found either in the rupture of revolution or in any given aesthetic
form or experiment that emerged in its wake. All that is established is the
peculiarity of an origin that produces an endless dispersal of forms, which
never quite consolidate at the level of practice. This is not to say that the
classical political theatre thereby represents only a form of revolutionary
phantasmagoria. What is at stake, rather, is the taxonomic identification
of the classical political theatre understood as the inaugural name for a
problem which that theatre could neither resolve nor fully understand or
articulate. This problem, all the same, constitutes the basis for a genealogy –
at least of sorts – and it does so to the extent that the problem of foundation
(the problem of establishing the 'new') is present in every appearance of
the political theatre insofar as it testifies to the irreconcilable meaning of its
name: if the political theatre designates a problem it is because it contains
an affirmation in which the promise of political transformation is somehow
realised in or enabled through the theatre; at the same time, this promise can
only be enunciated at the very point that the political theatre renounces its
own realisation.

The political theatre is epic theatre

'All theatre is political!' – this epigrammatic statement remains a mere plati-
tude without the added caveat: 'but not all theatre is political in the same
way.' What this indicates is a wholly original problem that in truth only

becomes legible with the emergence of the political theatre. By articulating itself as a reckoning with theatre's past, as the agent of radical discontinuity, and as possessed by the exuberance and creativity that accompanies every new beginning, the founding theatre of the future – the theatre of a new political dawn – of necessity becomes a locus for the surfacing not just of a new concept of theatre but of new theatre concepts. But evidently the new can only manifest itself in contradistinction to the old. It is not a simple negation, but requires a critical and diagnostic operation, yielding a fundamental recalibration of the theatre. Nowhere is this better understood than in Germany in its adoption of the spirit of radical innovation that animated the revolutionary theatre in Russia, particularly in the pyretic atmosphere that characterised the politics of the Weimar Republic in the immediate aftermath of the First World War.[34] What the strained cultural moment in interwar Germany demanded was an analysis of the theatre situation in light of the political situation. It was dictated not just by immediate practical exigencies but also the need to establish the new practices on a rigorous theoretical basis. Projecting itself onto that meta-epistemological plane of dramaturgical discourse, the German variation on the classical political theatre coincides with the production of an exacting critique of the existing conditions of social objectivity and the role played by theatrical representation in its material reproduction. It is this critical and theoretical orientation, in Germany, that will lead the transformation of the political theatre in its classical stage into something else. Erwin Piscator provided this critically informed theatre with a name: 'the new theatrical style that we had developed to give form to our revolutionary view of the world [is] the *epic* or political style.'[35] The political theatre is the epic theatre and with its development came 'elements for a dramatic theory of our times'.[36]

This led to a more precise way of accounting for theatre's alignment with politics. The political theatre must not only express itself by means of a directly interpretable political content, it must be 'activist, combative, political' – it must 'fight the political fight with artistic means'.[37] The emphasis on praxis further signified: it must have an appropriate form, capable of bringing that content into an indispensable relation with its audience; but also, for that content to have credibility with its audience, it must be situational and realistic (the 'settings were to be constructed as realistically as possible'[38]) – only then would the political theatre 'become a place offering real experiences, rather than illusions'.[39] In practical terms, as with the Russian agit-theatre, this meant the complete subordination of theatre to political goals. Hence Piscator placed on stage the politics he witnessed on the street; the stage became an inventory of the chants, imprecations, and slogans of protestors, their placards, their speeches, and their grievances. The political theatre, at least in its classical phase, could therefore scarcely afford to be

inconvenienced by the usual aesthetic misgivings over the wholesale incorporation of art by politics and the effect it would have on its autonomous
status. Quite the contrary, it unreservedly embraced its subordination: 'we
banned the word *art* radically from our program, our "plays" were appeals
and were intended to have an effect on current events, to be a form of
"political activity".'[40] Moreover, Piscator asserts, 'It was not a question of a
theatre that would provide the proletariat with art, but of conscious propaganda, nor of a theatre for the proletariat, but of a Proletarian Theatre.'[41]

The noteworthy distinction drawn, at this juncture, is between the 'theatre for the proletariat' and the 'Proletarian Theatre'. If for the former the
proletariat is simply a given, it is because the term 'proletariat' holds no
political significance for such a theatre. Its aim is simply to provide idle
distractions and mummeries for the masses that merely entertain them. In
the case of the latter, the Proletarian Theatre presupposes no such thing, and
it is precisely for this reason that it becomes an effective synonym for the
political theatre. The Proletarian Theatre did not assume the existence of the
proletariat as a political entity, it aimed to produce that identity. Its political
function can be described – no more, no less – than the political subjectification of the worker *as* proletarian.[42] The task of the political theatre was to
'make an educative, propagandistic impact on those members of the masses
who are as yet politically undecided or indifferent'.[43] For this reason, it presupposed three concurrent possibilities, without which it would have been
incapacitated at the outset. First, it supposed that a political subjectification
is possible through art; second, that the political subject does not yet exist, is
in some sense trapped in a 'pre-political' state of ideological dormancy; and,
third, that the theatre possesses the rhetorical means to awaken the political
consciousness of this phlegmatic pre-political subject, to bring their political
being into a state of full self-presence through which their historical destiny
is able to be realised. It is precisely for this reason, also, that the classical
political theatre discarded art for propaganda. For Piscator, propaganda
was understood in entirely positive terms: rather than statist, it specified the
pedagogical and didactic aim of political theatre and so did not possess the
pejorative sense that attaches to the word today. Correspondingly, the pedagogical stance of propaganda theatre was entirely oriented by the question
it posed: Through what form of praxis does emancipation become possible?

To array this cluster of ideas programmatically, three imperatives are
clearly determinative for the political theatre according to Piscator: (1) it
must have 'appropriate propagandistic aims'; (2) it must reject the 'bourgeois concept of art'; and (3) it must 'lay the foundation of the new (proletarian) art'.[44] The meaning of the first imperative is clear: it indicated
the 'Subordination of all artistic aims to the revolutionary goal: conscious
emphasis on and cultivation of the idea of the class struggle'.[45] The second,

however, is rather less straightforward, since to dismantle the bourgeois concept of art is to expose it not for what it consciously does but for what it unconsciously conceals (even from itself). Thus, to say that all theatre is political, but not all theatre is political in the same way, is also to indicate the peculiar signification the theatre has within the bourgeois state: that it is political in the sense that it eschews politics; that it does not present itself as being political as such; and indeed insofar as it accords with the bourgeois concept of art, that it is political by being 'anti-political'. It is anti-political precisely because it seeks the elevation of the 'spirit of man' as 'universal aesthetic experience', but at the cost of a loss of all self-consciousness of his material circumstances. For this reason, bourgeois art is ideologically inter-pellative without understanding itself to be so and, in this sense, it is exactly the opposite of propagandistic art: it inculcates beliefs, values, attitudes, and dispositions with unquestioning faith in the idea of reality as given in its own image. If the bourgeois theatre is political, not by professing a politics, but by concealing its ideological character, it is because it is the very embodi-ment of *the ideological theatre*; while, conversely, it is because the classical political theatre is expressly designed to reject the illusions of the ideological theatre, to castoff its ideological structures, so as to embrace the real move-ment of history, and to motivate its spectators to realise their true interests through it, that it is a *theatre of propaganda* – meaning, for Piscator, it is an avowedly self-conscious political art.

All the same, it remains unclear what a self-consciously political art *is*. Is it simply an art that serves a political agenda, or is it capable of being something else? That the political theatre expressed a need to address this question is surely implicated in Piscator's third imperative: the theatre of propaganda must serve the purposes of laying the foundation for a new art, attuned to the needs of the proletariat. It is evident that the political thea-tre will be compelled to surpass the limited focus of the theatre of propa-ganda if it is to realise itself as a new form of art. Let us extrapolate, as an example, the problem with propagandistic art from the critique offered by the German expressionist playwright, Ernst Toller. If the political theatre seeks to place art at the service of political goals, it must contend with the paradox that to function effectively as propaganda it must diminish art's *critical* power: where propaganda is associative, critical art is dissociative. It seeks to create a gap or interval between reality and its perception through reflective means. Propagandistic art, insofar as it serves the 'immediate goals of the day', has an opposing aim. Its function is to suture the space that separates the individual subject from the particular political investment or 'interest' of the party. It does so by playing directly on people's dislikes and disaffections: it urges people to act, not reflect. Seeking to escape this con-tradiction, Toller distinguished between 'artistic propaganda', whose aim is simply to 'impel the viewer to immediate action',[46] and political art – which, he said, although it may identify the same problems as the propagandist, and even advocate the same solutions, is also able to expose the 'tragic' dimension of reality, the finite and subjective limits that define both the ability to act in the world and the true nature of political experience. Toller's solution thereby interjected a 'critical' function into political art – and it is this shift towards a critical art that sees the end of the political theatre in its 'classical' phase.

This embrace of the critical power of political art, beyond an avowedly propagandistic function, is found in Brecht's description of realism, which makes it the very model for critical interpretation: 'true realism has to do more than just make reality recognisable in theatre. One has to be able to see through it too. One has to be able to see the laws that decide how the processes of life develop.'[47] It is not simply enough to seek to persuade the audience, one must also teach them to see reality for what it is, to peer through the surface veneer of the commodified world, for instance, or to penetrate the mystifications and illusions of theatrical representation, to see for oneself – in any case – the laws that govern reality's appearance. Only through such an act of critical or 'complex' seeing[48] (that 'method' with which Brecht's work was constantly grappling) is it possible to re-found the entire basis of aesthetic experience, thereby establishing a new relationship between politics and art. The considerable ambition of Brecht's vision is encapsulated in the *Messingkauf Dialogues* where he writes that through art 'man produces himself'.[49] What is implicated in this elliptical statement touches on the entire problematic of political theatre, even if it does not resolve it. On the one hand, a critical art must possess the power of dispelling all illusions. It must act in such a way that it counters that 'surrogate satisfaction', described by Adorno, that otherwise makes art an 'ally of repression'.[50] To do so it must, according to Brecht, possess the perspicuity and objectivity of a science: a truly realist art will be apt for a scientific age. On the other hand, it must lay the foundations of an art yet-to-come, and – with reality's imagined sublation through art – project a vision of society's future such that it conjures into being the revolutionary subject, who is capable of leading humanity to its eventual emancipation. It must therefore fuse the critical method with propagandistic aims so as to understand itself in the same way that the bourgeois theatre misunderstands itself – as a theatre of ideological inscription that is nonetheless founded on a true knowledge of the 'real'. To the extent that Brecht's epic theatre succeeds in manufacturing this alignment of 'science' and 'ideology', his must be viewed as the apotheosis of the political theatre in its classical stage. Still, the question that it seems to pose suffuses it with an abiding tension: to which reality does this theatre belong? – to present reality, which is the object of its critique, or to emancipated reality, which does not yet exist? The tension results from the logic of critique, which traps the very subject it seeks to emancipate under the dense mass of the reality it constructs – as a totality dominated by illusions that must first be dispelled, as an irresistible process of subjection, and as a self-concealing falsification of the real. It is because reality under bourgeois conditions of life is encountered as practised cynicism that Brecht's theatre works ceaselessly on two simultaneous fronts in the hope of reversing its effects. First, it targets the representational logics of the theatre, opening up theatre to its immanent critique so as to constitute a 'politics of the theatre'; second, it works on the spectator in order to forge a new positionality for the subject via a new mode of spectating – it produces a 'politics of the spectator'.

It is why, first and foremost, Brecht's political theatre, in its synthesis as epic theatre, must systematically dismantle the basic form on which the old dramatic stage relied: the complete subordination of events to the hero's worldview, its emphasis on the 'clash of forces' – on 'conflict' – that sweeps the spectator along in its wake, and the subtending of the scenic parts of the play in service to the appearance of a unified 'whole'.[51] The development of the techniques of the epic theatre, summarised by Walter Benjamin as a refusal to appeal to the 'spectator's capacity for empathy' so as to teach them to be 'astonished at the circumstances within which he has his being',[52] had the objective of showing reality, not as a seamless flowing dramatic development, but as spliced together, like a film, out of fractured and fragmented elements of disjointed time. The objective was to break with the composition of myth, with the structure of recognition that the dramatic theatre cultivates in its auditor, by breaking the link between ideology and the fixation of belief in the subject.

Brecht expresses the difference between the political (epic) theatre and the ideological (dramatic) theatre as follows:

> The dramatic theatre's spectator says: Yes, I have felt like that too – Just like me –
>
> It's only natural – it'll never change – The sufferings of man appal me, because they are inescapable – That's great art: it all seems the most obvious thing in the world.[53]

Where, for the ideological stage, suffering is naturalised, and fate becomes a substitute for history, the message is unequivocal: nothing can change the order of things – one must be resigned to whatever one's social fate prescribes, the encumbrances of life are inescapable. The epic theatre, by contrast, shows another way, one in which the deceit of fate is unmasked. It says: 'That's not the way – ... It's got to stop – The sufferings of this man

appal me, because they are unnecessary.'[54] Consequently, where the ideological theatre is predicated on an absolute identification ('I weep when they
weep, I laugh when they laugh'), the political theatre, in Brecht's nimble
hands, seeks the dis-identification of the audience with the classical heroic
paradigm of the dramatic stage and its fraudulent balance sheet that natu-
ralises modes of social and economic domination, separating humanity into
its winners and losers ('I laugh when they weep, I weep when they laugh').[55]
What Brecht's method insists upon therefore is two things. The first is that
the critical power of the theatre depends entirely on the technique of dis-
identification, which opens the way to a political consciousness at the level
of spectatorial practices; the second is that the capacity of theatre to produce a counter-interpellation requires an intervention within the order of
theatrical representation, accomplished by an intervention in the apparatus of the theatre itself. What Brecht anticipates thereby is the fundamental *displacement* of the political theatre and its transformation away from
the deadening effects of propaganda into a critical theatre whose eventual
mutation will produce a post-Brechtian 'politics of the theatre'. The latter
represents an important moment in the genealogy of the political theatre: it
produces a theatre capable of sustaining critique but without expressing any
overt political commitment; but for that very reason, the 'politics' that the
post-Brechtian theatre extols opens up the critical theatre to the paradox of
its reabsorption by the bourgeois stage.

2

Displacement effects: Althusser's 'Brecht' and the theatre of the conjuncture

A theatre of pure displacement – of diagnostic transpositions, tactical dislocations, and strategic dislodgements – this was essentially the way in which Louis Althusser conceived Brecht's contribution to the development of political theatre in an unfinished text, written in preparation for a public discussion held at the Piccolo Theatre in Milan in 1968.[1] Of particular interest is the way Althusser consolidated the image of Brechtian theatre as a theatre of dis-identification, as a theatre of critical ruptures, opting to translate Brecht's concept of *Verfremdungseffekt* by the term 'effet de déplacement' or 'effet de décalage' (displacement or 'shift' effect). In doing so, however, he foreshadowed, without ever intending to, what would later appear as the closure and even impossibility of the political theatre. Scepticism concerning representation will lead to the decentring of politics in theatre, and the evacuation of tangible content – something Althusser already discerned within the critical spaces that had been opened by the theatrical revolution Brecht inaugurated. If the *critical theatre* – the name assigned here to describe the post-Brechtian 'tradition' – emerges on the surface of Brechtian discourse, appearing there in complex and paradoxical ways, it is because it must itself be grasped as an effect of displacement through which the political theatre in its classical appearance would eventually be dissolved into a new articulation of the theatre as a 'critical politics of the theatre'. It is because it is the conventional form of theatrical production that is, above all, at fault that Althusser asserts that for Brecht it was 'necessary to effectuate a displacement within the *interior* of theatre'.[2] What is meant by 'interior displacement', and what consequences ensue from that meaning, is the principal focus of the discussion that follows. The emphasis on theatre's interiority, on an immanent critique of the theatre by means of the theatre, should not, however, be confused with the technical innovations with which Brecht is habitually associated. Althusser insists: 'it is safe to say that reducing the revolution of Brecht's theatrical practice to mere ... technical recipes is a betrayal of Brecht's revolution.'[3] Rather, at stake in Brecht, at least for Althusser, is the transformation of the entire way of making theatre.

Brechtianism is less a revolt against the theatre (as in early Piscator), than a revolution in theatre *practice*. Although this revolution in theatre practice aims to transform the ideological theatre, it also has immense implications for the political theatre. As it turns out, the displacement of the political theatre becomes the precondition for the emergence of a critical theatre. The closure of the former provides the opening for the latter. It is a revolution in the exact sense of the word: it turns the political theatre 180 degrees about on its axis. No longer is it a question of making political theatre, whose impossibility lies in the fact that theatre shares no identity with politics (theatre is not politics, any more than it is life, it always remains 'theatre').[4] Instead, Brecht makes theatre 'in a political way'.[5] What is implied in this distinction, however, is by no means obvious, although it will prove significant later. To make theatre in a 'political way' is to make theatre as social and ideological critique – a critique that is also, *a fortiori*, a social and ideological critique of the theatre and its apparatus.

That Althusser understands the critical theatre essentially as a form of ideology critique is clear from his identification of the respective approaches of Brecht and Marx to theatre and philosophy: 'Marx's philosophical revolution is in every way similar to Brecht's theatrical revolution.'[6] Just as Marx did not seek to subtract philosophy from his own thought, permitting it to play a determinate role, so Brecht's fidelity to the theatre is unwavering. Brecht does not seek to make theatre anew or produce an anti-theatre; nor even does he discard the repertoire, just as Marx by no means jettisoned Hegel or wrote an anti-philosophy. 'Brecht', Althusser writes, 'takes the theatre as it exists, and works on the interior of the theatre as it exists.'[7] Marx attempted, as is well known, the same thing with the German idealist tradition in philosophy, subjecting it to a materialist critique. Furthermore, each accomplishes this feat, in their respective fields, by prioritising practice over theory; and it is precisely because of their practical or rather materialist orientation that each can forge a path back to politics. Each critique reveals that what both philosophy and theatre have in common is their denial of being determined by politics ('Philosophy and theatre are fundamentally determined by politics, and yet they do their utmost to erase this determination, to deny this determination, to escape politics').[8] Philosophy claims that it is above history to the extent that it is utterly impassive in the face of class-based and other conflicts, and so sees itself as rising above mere political squabbles. Similarly, the ideological theatre, which in Brecht is designated the 'culinary theatre', understands itself as aesthetic play: its autonomy exempts it from politics. It is this aesthetic exceptionalism that elevates bourgeois theatre to the sphere of universal experience (whereas politics concerns only particularity). It is because of the mystifications that lead a particular subject position (specifically the bourgeois subject) to view itself as occupying a space of universality that it becomes imperative to disrupt the apparatus that produces the culinary theatre as an ideological theatre, in order to 'show the real function of the theatre'[9] – in short, to 'displace', fundamentally, its point of view ('il existe un déplacement fondamental … le *déplacement du point de vue*').[10] A displacement must occur that disrupts the aesthetic play of the culinary theatre, which conceals the voice of politics, so as to 'fix' the point of view of the theatre elsewhere, on the 'place of politics'.[11]

This does not mean that theatre succumbs to politics, that politics appropriates the stage for its own ends, as in the theatre of propaganda.[12] It denotes something entirely different. First, that the representations of the ideological theatre are placed in brackets: that the techniques that produce ideological effects, and spectatorship in the mode of the 'natural (spectatorial) attitude', are suspended. Second, that these ideological structures and representations are thereby turned over for critical scrutiny. A theatre of disrupted effects and representational critique – this is what Althusser had in mind when he wrote that the theatre is not identical to politics, that in Brecht theatre remains 'theatre', yet is nonetheless produced in a manner that discloses the political. Through disruption and critique, Brecht's theatre comes to occupy the place that represents politics. Or, otherwise expressed: to *dis*place the representational form of the ideological stage, the critical theatre must discover within itself the place, or *locus*, in which politics is founded. As with theatre, politics is a space of identifiable representations and a representational space in which the identification of the subject becomes possible (a 'distribution' of identities and social spaces – in effect, a spatial partitioning of the social, as Jacques Rancière would have it). To achieve its disruptive effect, displacement operates across the three spatial dimensions of the theatre simultaneously: its presentational space (the space of 'play'), its representational space (where theatre produces ideological and symbolic effects), and its social spaces of reception (shifting the point of view on itself it shifts the point of view of the spectator). This is why Brecht's well-known techniques do not define what Brechtianism is. It is only the entire ensemble of displacement effects that contribute to the transformation of the point of view of the theatre that truly defines Brecht's theatre. These are also the ensemble of effects through which a critical theatre practice begins to articulate itself according to three mobilisations that transform the theatre on immanent grounds.

(1) The critical theatre must break the link of complicity that is established between the ideological theatre and the spectator. For Althusser, its strategic aim is to transform the consciousness of what the theatre is, to 'displace the theatre in relation to the ideology of the theatre that exists

in the mind of the spectator'.[13] To produce a transformed consciousness of the theatre it is necessary to demonstrate the reality of the theatre situation beneath its representations. The 'real' of the theatre must puncture the fantasy and deception that the ideological stage perpetrates (that the auditorium exists in a continuum with actual life, when in fact it is constituted as a space of aesthetic exception). This means that the critical theatre emerges not through dramatisations that are critical of life, or of certain aspects of life – of its partialities, its exclusivities and inequalities, its biases, which are the social sources of conflict – but through more fundamental means: through stagings that demonstrate theatre's difference from life. In insisting on the gap between audience and stage, the theatre opens a space of critical distance, of analytical detachment, and it is precisely through making visible the differential between theatre and life that a viewpoint on the exceptional character of the theatre situation is obtained. Since this can only occur within the theatrical scene, all aspects of theatre production are necessarily implicated in the processes of displacement – scenography, the use of props, costume, lighting design, and so on. Only through a 'physical displacement', placing the emphasis on theatre's material level, is the 'mystified complicity' between the spectator and theatre's world of illusion dispelled. And so, writes Althusser, the critical theatre must constitute itself as a demonstration of 'what the theatre and the spectators do not want to see: that the theatre is not life'.[14]

(2) The critical theatre must decentre the play, it must rescind the authority of the text, and it must deconstruct the traditional supremacy of the drama as promoted by the ideological theatre. The reason Althusser gives for this has to do with the symbolic effect of the ideological theatre and what makes it ideological: namely, its capacity to produce ideology in the form of a 'spontaneous representation', with its ability to transform a contingent dramatic artifice into apparent nature ('reality'). Althusser writes that this 'displacement-effect consists essentially in … preventing the play from having the form of the spontaneous representation that the audience has of life, of its conflicts, in which the drama presents the solution'.[15] To speak of the production of ideology as spontaneity is to indicate the inherently self-concealing function of ideological processes; ideology seldom presents itself as ideology. It is not, therefore, a question, as some have claimed, of pointing to the faultiness of the 'message-receiver' model of theatrical communication, but the exact opposite. The problem with the ideological theatre is that its communicative (or 'interpellative') mechanisms work too well. The key to their success lies in their inexplicitness, however. If the contrivances of the ideological theatre work 'too well', it is not because it has a persuasive message that it advertises to its audience, and which the audience reads off its surface as though it were a text printed in indelible

ink on a sheet of paper, but because it functions at a deeper communicative level of recognition.

What, though, does it mean to distinguish between the levels of identification and recognition? And where exactly is recognition to be located in Althusser's concept of the spectator and their capture by ideology?

This is where things get considerably more complicated. Discussing the function of recognition in his earlier and better-known essay on Brecht and the 'Piccolo Teatro', Althusser offers an answer to this question through the critique of what he termed the 'identification model' of spectatorship: the 'dubious' idea that ideological attachment manifests itself in the form of a correlation, between the spectator's consciousness and the play's hero (what is, in effect, an 'imaginary' consciousness). Althusser notes that not only does this entail a naïve lapse into psychologism, which also disregards the fact that the ideological theatre by no means requires such a correlation in order to function (there is a world of difference between identifying *with* the hero, for example, and identifying what is at stake for them in the drama); it furthermore overlooks the fact that identification presupposes a prior moment of recognition (one can only identify that which has first been recognised, i.e., implicitly understood).[16] Specifically, the spectator, he writes, must first have recognised themselves 'in the ideological content of the play, and in the forms characteristic of this content'.[17] In order to speak of identification, 'cultural and ideological recognition' must be assumed.[18] This also means that recognition, which precedes identification, operates subliminally, on the subject's imaginary, thus at a pre-conscious level of ideological inscription or enculturation.[19] It is why the ideological aspect of the theatre is by no means reducible to the explicit content of the play; it resides also, and even more fundamentally, in its form. One is enculturated at the level of form, in other words, not simply through content. Form – and by this is meant also the whole raft of formal and informal conventions that constitute the experience of theatre – provides the mechanism for ideological recognition, which prepares for the possibility of any conscious act of identification. What is also clear from this is that recognition is not only carried in the form of the conventional dramatic text, although it most certainly is, but that it incorporates the enculturation of the subject as a theatregoer. Everyone who enters a theatre carries with them certain expectations whenever they do so and above all a certain 'desire for self-recognition' that must be satisfied.[20] As spectators 'we are', Althusser writes, 'first united by an institution'.[21]

Hence the fundamental power of the ideological stage has less to do with specific representations than with the way its modes of enculturation engender a mistaken faith, on the part of the subject, in representation as such, and in doing so mystifies the very space of representation by transforming an artifice into a spontaneous appearance of life. Since the play sits at the centre of the ideological theatre's institutional apparatus, constituting the moment of textual authority within the ideological space of the theatre, the critical theatre can no longer find its centre in the text. To resist its interpellative form, theatre must be turned inside out. If the ideological theatre identifies the play as the source of truth-effects, and through its modes of recognition the subjectification of the 'subject', the critical theatre finds its truth, according to Althusser, 'outside' of itself. The truth of the theatre situation can only be located outside of the theatre's representations ('hors d'elle-meme'), and outside of the interpellated subject of the ideological stage.[22] Its ultimate authority is the real. It is why, in relation to the Piccolo Teatro's production of Carlo Bertolazzi's play (*El nost Milan*, 1893) on Milanese social life in the 1890s, Althusser writes that the 'great confrontation at the end of the third act is more than a confrontation between Nina and her father, it is the confrontation of a world without illusions with the wretched illusions of the "heart", it is the confrontation of the real world with the melodramatic world'.[23] The 'real' must intrude on the space of recognition, to break the spell it casts on the spectator; it must dispel the sense of easy familiarity that absolves the enculturated subject from taking responsibility for what is seen in the theatre.

(3) The critical theatre must not only displace the play as the locus of the truth of the theatre, but it must also displace the locus of 'play' in the theatre so as to produce different truths 'playfully'. This third displacement effect has to do with Brecht's well-known approach to performance. The critical actor can no longer present themselves as the vector through which the *doxa* or *hegemon* expresses itself. To displace the 'play' of the actor is to systematically dismantle the expectations that both spectators and performers have regarding the proper function of playing in the theatre. Because the play of the ideological theatre is aimed at producing the spontaneous appearance of 'truth', the actor's technique must conceal the fact that what the actor does in performance is only play. For the ideological theatre, play must transcend its appearance as play – meaning both that the actor's play cannot be seen as play and that the actor who plays – their being, their corporeality, their consciousness, and all the contingent figurations that comprise their identity – will be subordinated, through techniques of mimetic substitution, to a represented reality, the prime character of which is that it is seen by its recipient, the theatregoer, as 'life-like'. The dialectic of 'reality' and 'play', their opposition, their contradictory appearance within one another, and the appearance of this contradiction in a mediated form that breaks the hold ideology has over the spectator's imaginary, is exactly what the critical theatre stages when the actor locates 'distance' in themselves. By establishing a distance from the character they play, the critical actor creates an *epistemic displacement effect* in which reality and play encroach on one another to

produce the contradictory space of the theatre, while confounding its representational claim on the real. The ultimate site for the displacement effect, made explicit through the aperture of theatrical play, and expressed through the doublet being-at-play/playing-at-being, is revealed as the ambiguous 'truth' of the theatrical situation.

Taken as an ensemble of effects, the whole problematic of the theatre of displacement comes down to one definitive aim: to bring about the end of the regime of identification that characterises the ideological theatre as a theatre that produces the illusion of spontaneous appearances. The Brechtian revolution in theatre practice seeks to establish a 'new relationship between the show and the audience';[24] and because of this the final displacement effect must be measured by the transformation of the audience, who are positioned as critical spectators of the theatrical event: 'The public must cease identifying with the scene they are being shown, in order to discover a critical position, to take upon themselves, the responsibility for judging, voting and deciding.'[25] What the critical theatre seeks to displace, at bottom, is the attitude of the audience toward what they are being shown – and so if, as Althusser remarks, the 'function of ideology is recognition (and not knowledge)'[26] then the function of the critical theatre is surely to reverse the effects of the ideological stage, to revoke its unitary appearance, and to shatter, once and for all, the old metaphor that the stage is a 'mirror' within which the spectator recognises themselves. One must dismantle the structure that produces recognition in order that the theatre situation becomes a site of knowledge production – a scenography of genuine discovery, rather than of ideological recognition (Benjamin also wrote: 'Epic theatre … does not reproduce situations, it discovers them'[27]).

But what exactly is it that the theatre situation discovers once these displacement effects have been mobilised? And what does it discover that expressly indicates the determination of theatre by 'politics'? On these questions, Althusser's unfinished text provides no clear answer. It must be sought elsewhere by placing it in relation to concepts found in his other writings. But also, and to maintain a degree of consistency with the idea of 'displacement' (itself a translation that displaces the meaning of 'alienation' in Brechtian theatre), the question should really be posed as follows: How does the critical theatre, in displacing the political theatre's immediate relation to militant politics, construct a relation between the theatre situation and the political situation? One productive way of answering this question requires mobilising two key Althusserian concepts by which the political situation is defined – those of the 'conjuncture' (a term he borrowed from Antonio Gramsci) and 'overdetermination' (from Sigmund Freud). It is to say that the critical theatre offers an insight into the present conjuncture of which the theatre is an overdetermined part.

What should be understood by the concept of the conjuncture? A conjuncture refers to the specific historical configuration or 'balance' of social forces at play in the material moment of the given present. Gramsci distinguished its character as 'occasional, immediate, almost accidental',[28] indicating that to be in the conjuncture is to be 'in the political moment'. The conjuncture is always ephemeral. It is transitive and aleatory – yet continually pressing; always contiguous with life-world imperatives and demands. However, while the conjuncture may be fugacious and impermanent, it also indicates, even if often in deceptive ways, the underlying complexity of the social formation that it expresses: its long-term tendencies, and the nexus of contradictions and contingencies by which it is constituted. It is why, for Althusser, the conjuncture must always be interpreted as 'overdetermined'. It is always the scene of a contradictory intersection, the 'fusion' and 'accumulation' of a 'number of realities'[29] that define the given historical moment in frequently perplexing and incoherent ways, yet always as the site in which social forces engage, moment to moment, in a relentless war for hegemonic control.[30] Put otherwise: the conjuncture names the moment when history and social forces coincide in the crisis of the present situation.

Enlisted in this context, the term 'displacement' takes on a new cadence, and a further conceptual articulation: it resides in the idea that where there is an overdetermined contradiction one typically finds either the pacification of contradiction, its dispersal within the social formation, enacted through forms of displacement that deprive contradictions of their antagonistic potential, or – in moments of crisis – its 'condensation', when those contradictions 'fuse' as happened during the Russian Revolution, creating an historic 'rupture'.[31] Further insight into the conjuncture, and its relevance for the theory of ideology, can be found in the work of the cultural theorist, Stuart Hall, who wrote: 'A social formation is a "structure in dominance". It has certain distinct tendencies; it has a certain configuration; it has a definite structuration.'[32] And yet, because they are overdetermined, there is no simple explanation for those tendencies. One cannot reduce them to one level of the social formation (typically understood as the economic level) without risk of oversimplifying them in an unconvincing and deterministic fashion. What the theory of the conjuncture envisages, instead, is a complex of determinations that not only belong to the social formation but are formative of it. Conjunctural analysis reveals, in other words, the social formation as the product of tendential movements, rooted deeply in long-term 'organic' social alignments and economic tessellations, whose realisation bears the weight and influence of their immanent contradictions and which can, under certain 'haphazard' conditions, erupt in political effractions ('fusions'). Hall writes, however: 'Structures exhibit tendencies – lines of force, openings and closures which constrain, channel and in that sense, "determine". But they cannot determine in the harder sense of fix absolutely, guarantee', and he adds – in a remark that holds great significance for those wishing to understand the fate of the political theatre – that what one cannot 'guarantee' is that 'classes will appear in their appointed political places'.[33] What Althusser's concept of overdetermination explains, for Hall, is how social, cultural, and political forces can no longer be explained in simple terms of economic contradictions, nor social struggle by 'class' destiny, grasped as the 'monistic' edifice of history as it once was by the orthodox left. Class struggle does not set history on a predictable and propitious course as if it expressed a positive law that made the outcome of that struggle all but inevitable; and so while complex social formations are never 'free or independent of determinations' (one should not deny the effects of economic reality) nor are they, for that matter, 'reducible to simple determinacy of any of the other social levels'[34] (it would be reductive to account for cultural phenomena as merely 'reflecting' the economic structure). It should also be said, that while, for Hall, there is 'no necessary correspondence', that is, no teleological law that guarantees the emergence of a 'ruptural force' based on class, equally there is 'no necessary *non*-correspondence' that entails that this could never happen under any circumstances. Such political articulations are always a possibility, even if they are not an inevitability.[35] Conjunctural conditions might be said to correspond to the peculiar morphological characteristics of plasticity as defined by the philosopher Catherine Malabou. They possess the 'capacity for deformation, re-formation, [and] explosion'.[36]

But how does this now well-known critique of what is essentially 'Kautskian' Marxism,[37] with its faith in the ineluctability of historical progress, powered by the engine of dialectical predetermination, and with all its smatterings of economism, help account for the emergence of the critical theatre? In fact, there are two immediate ways in which the critical theatre can be better and more precisely understood as a *critical theatre of the conjuncture* so as to draw out its association with the political. The first of these reveals its topological character. It is to understand the critical theatre as a theatre that necessarily exposes its own location within the conjuncture to which it belongs. In *dis*locating itself, the critical theatre disarticulates theatre as a representational space, as a pleonastic institution that simply reduplicates the given order of things. It thereby locates, in the precise sense that it identifies (and to the extent that it does so must risk), its structural emplacement within the given social formation, as well as its cultural authority, which it must jeopardise. Thus, the critical theatre employs displacement effects not just to critique the ideological theatre for being ideological, to resist its inveiglements, but also to disturb theatre's modes of habituation, its participation in and its complicity with the existing conjuncture – suspending, or perturbing, its capacity to produce representations that conceal or naturalise conjunctural contradictions. Rather than a space of recognition, it becomes a space for critical cognition. Even though it would be stretching things to say that the critical theatre is thereby able to expose the complex totality of social contradictions that comprise the conjuncture, which are typically concealed by the ideological theatre's system of representations and its mode of production, that totality nonetheless appears in the overdetermined form of the exposed theatrical *topos*. For the critical theatre, this occurs precisely when the ability of the ideological stage to dissipate or displace 'real' social antagonisms by means of its production of so-called 'cathartic' effects is deterred and the actual material basis of the theatre situation is revealed as a site of contradiction. Secondly: the theatre of the conjuncture engages, necessarily, in a form of cultural critique. In applying displacement effects to existing theatrical representations, the critical theatre not only disrupts the topological organisation of the theatre, and thus its forms of enculturation, it can only do so on the basis of its own conjunctural analysis of the wider social-political and historical context – and in ways that reveal further determinations of the existing social formation.[38] The critical theatre is no longer a mirror that reflects the world but a discursive surface refracting the intersecting levels of the social formation (legal, political, cultural, civil, and so on); it thereby operates in a mode akin to what Gramsci termed 'socio-historical criticism'.[39]

German director, Thomas Ostermeier and dramaturg, Florian Borchmeyer's production of Ibsen's play *An Enemy of the People* provides an exemplar of how the critical theatre of the conjuncture can appear to move that which is apparently unmovable: settled public opinion. It is not just that the production 'defamiliarises' Ibsen's play, but that in the process, Ostermeier sets apart the symbolic space of the theatre from the conformism that is prevalent within the public *doxa*. He does not reproduce the *doxa*, he produces it in its most volatile form – as incited by the powers of demagoguery. In this sense, the fictive political context of the play (which – to recall – concerns the struggle of Dr Stockmann to make known the truth about the political corruption he has discovered to the residents of the town, of which his brother is the mayor, concerning the industrial pollution of the spa waters upon which its economy relies) is produced in literal form when the fictional Stockmann calls an assembly that enlists the actual theatre audience as its members. Ostermeier does this not just in order to provoke the audience, to shake it free of its lethargy and its own inherent tendency toward conformity (enculturation), but to activate it *as a public*. How he is able to do so as a critical public, to what political end, and according to what theatrical means, will determine the extent to which Ostermeier's production can be understood as a critical theatre of the conjuncture. To begin the analysis, however, two preliminaries must be observed.

First, it is obvious that Ostermeier had no interest in the credulous idea that Ibsen's original text possesses an intrinsic political content that is reproduced simply in virtue of the play being staged. Still less does he view the political dimension of the play as a mere representation with no actual relevance to its audience beyond motivating the dramatic rivalry between the Stockmann brothers. On the contrary, Ostermeier's production proceeds on a different basis: that the political content of a play is 'unfixed', and so irreducible to the literal 'meaning' of the original text, whatever that may be, whatever its context, whatever effect the author intended it to have, or whatever dramaturgical function it serves in exposing the conflict between Thomas and Peter Stockmann. What this does not license, however, is the further claim that – in the name of defending the audience against illusions – the play thereby contains *no* political content, or at least no content that is relevant to the production. This is the second point. In fact, one can scarcely grasp how Ostermeier's production can be considered 'political' if one maintains that the political aspect of the theatre has nothing to do with it having a political theme. Peter Boenisch asks, for example, in an otherwise astute appraisal of Ostermeier – whether political theatre should be identifiable with 'any political content represented in a play or a performance'.[40] He is adamant it cannot: 'I insist', he writes, 'on theatre's vital force and capacity within the critical public sphere – yet, not by virtue of representing political action and socio-economic conditions and contradictions on stage.'[41] To be sure, much depends here on how one understands the idea of 'representation', and Boenisch is right to draw attention to the naïveté of assuming that a political content, present simply in virtue of the play's textural or semantic meaning, is sufficient for producing political theatre. It is no doubt also true that an anti-representational strategy, representing a break with pre-existing regimes of representation, can be understood to involve a critical politics of theatrical semiosis and its relation to 'signifier-signified' mediations. All the same, the critique of the sign system that revolves around the problem of the 'interpretant' (the semantic effect the 'sign' has on its experiencer) becomes all but meaningless politically unless it can be shown to engage somehow recognisably with the world of politics. It is difficult to see how, in short, a critical public sphere can emerge within the theatre without placing political and thus 'representational' content, through which political meanings are generated, 'on stage'.

There are two ways of understanding political content dramaturgically. First it can be understood as merely 'performed', where the salience of the political within the spoken content of the actor's speech is limited to a strictly semantic sense and is present only for the purpose of activating the dramatic conflict. Speech is understood both denotatively and connotatively as possessing a political meaning – yet it is political only in figurative terms;

the audience is not meant to experience it politically, and thus no political affects are produced. It is entirely possible to understand the speech that Thomas Stockmann gives to the fictional town assembly on the same basis as any speech given by, say, Pericles, or any other actual statesman – it is a political speech, with a political meaning. But that is as far as it goes: it is political in terms of its rhetorical use of certain 'figures of speech'. The second way of understanding that content is in relation to a specifiable referent where those figures of speech may take on a literal meaning for the person hearing it beyond a strictly dramaturgical function. The political content is here not determined by any essential meaning. The question is not whether the speech *possesses* a political content. Nor is it whether it is rhetorically 'political'. It is whether that content or meaning can possess any political significance for the audience – whether it is grasped beyond the merely semantic as possessing a 'real' import for them. To activate a theatre audience as a 'critical public sphere' depends entirely on the extent to which the latter is achievable. Boenisch is thus partially right when he asserts that the political theatre is not to be found in 'its political and ideological structures, conflicts and contradictions [... but] in the very core of theatre's unique aesthetic fabric: in the interstices between performing, spectating and living'.[42] But it would be better to have written: 'political theatre' is not to be found in those represented conflicts and contradictions *alone*. Only on this basis is the critical point able to be clarified: what Ostermeier's production reveals is how the political meaning of Ibsen's text, written as it was in the late nineteenth century, is nonetheless able to be reawakened through a particular conjunctural articulation of its content, i.e., such that it produces a critical public sphere, such that it becomes salient for a contemporary audience, such that it can produce actual political affects.[43]

There are a number of ways in which Ostermeier's production attempted to do this. The first noteworthy intervention involved the repositioning of the historical context of the original play. It is not just that Ostermeier updated the social and cultural milieu of the play's original scenario – a fairly standard device when producing contemporary versions of canonical texts. Nor is it that he reduced the age of its protagonists by casting actors in their thirties rather than fifties, so as to make it resonate better with the younger and hipper audiences who attend the *Schaubühne*. Rather it is that in doing so he transformed the play into a study of the contradictions that circulate within the affluent, liberal, and cosmopolitan professional middle classes of contemporary Berlin who comprise the audience. He sought to confront them with the politics of their own social formation. The production becomes a study of a class whose politics, in fact, reflect what can, when structurally viewed, be taken as the primary effect of the 'closure' of the political that occurred in the wake of the fall of the Berlin Wall in

1989, and which became the necessary precursor for the emergence of the subsequent hegemony of the consensus-based technocratic politics of the 'third way'. Borchmeyer, reflecting on the production, writes that he and Ostermeier reworked the play with the express aim of addressing

> the very specific situation of the generation that was politically socialized after 1989 ... a generation [that] considers itself to stand politically somewhere on the left, [who] feel the urge to be politically conscious and somehow engaged – but who [all] too quickly ... [disappear] within the mainstream: their 'political consciousness' instantly evaporates, and all of a sudden they adopt almost reactionary bourgeois attitudes.[44]

The production made visible the porosity of political frontlines that constantly renders the boundary between social liberalism and the pursuit of pure self-interest ambiguous. This is nowhere more poignantly revealed than in the closing moments of the production. Ibsen's original play ends when, in a quasi-Nietzschean avowal, Stockmann proclaims his defiance of all societal norms – 'the strongest man in the world is he who stands most alone.' In Ostermeier's version this line is jettisoned, with the result that the play is given a far more ambivalent ending. It leaves its audience with an image of Stockmann and his wife, Katharina holding the company shares to the very Spa Baths they have been trying to close. Not only have the share prices been depreciated by their accusations and warnings, it turns out that it is they who stand to benefit from the ensuing collapse in the market value of the spa – in fact, as it turns out, Stockmann's father-in-law, the industrialist responsible for the polluting of the water in the first place, has used Katharina's inheritance to purchase the Baths at a knock-down price on their behalf. It is not just that Stockmann has been wheedled by the cunning of his father-in-law into becoming complicit in an act of corruption, or into becoming an asset holder, whose interests are now those of a rentier and not the people, but that in contemplating the possession of the shares he is entirely prepared to discredit his own convictions, and in a sense has been all along – one might even say, he is structurally predisposed to do so in keeping with his class affiliation – and is entirely unconscious of his own latent tendency toward hypocrisy.

What this moment crystalises is the 'hipster' contradiction: that the capacity of the hipster to engage – or not (it is always elective) – on behalf of socially liberal issues – and therefore against vested interests is founded, materially, upon the same material interests of the position they seek to oppose. Hence, it presents its audience with a contradiction it has internalised, and the dilemma of the extent to which one can or is willing to relinquish one's own position within the social formation, to displace oneself materially within it. If the production thus ends on a cynical note, it also serves a critical function: it implicates Stockmann in a politics whose foundations are built, not on collective forms of solidarity, but on the quicksand of his own egoicity, leaving him entirely prone to the lures and baits of big business – in short, to being bought off. The adage, 'every man has his price' is disclosed both as the exasperating but real condition of Stockmann's 'subjective' mode of existence – and as a permanent accusation levelled against those who would believe in the solidity of political convictions in a 'post-ideological' age.

The third intervention has been the most widely discussed in critical responses to the production. It occurs when a section of text taken from the manifesto of the French anarchist collective, the Invisible Committee – *The Coming Insurrection* – is interjected into the performance in place of the original 'assembly' speech Ibsen had written for Stockmann in act four of the play. The original speech – notorious for its eugenicist assertions, its anti-democratic valorisation of the individual, and its invocation of the image of vermin in need of extermination to describe political enemies ('all who live by lies ought to be exterminated like vermin!') – while cut from Ostermeier's production finds something of a ghostly echo in certain aspects of the Invisible Committee's text, which 'advocates', as Borchmeyer notes, ' "eradicating the rotten roots" of society'.[45] All the same, the context is entirely distinct from the text that is said to have inspired *Mein Kampf*, and the force of the speech derives both from the acuity of its criticism of the contemporary conjuncture ('We've come to understand: The economy is not "in" crisis. The economy is the crisis'), as much as from the 'parrhesiastic' quality of Stockmann's performance – both of which win him considerable sympathy with the audience. That sympathy is itself an actual political affect: as noted earlier, Stockmann's assembly audience is by no means fictional since the production at this point deliberately breaks with the scenic integrity of the play so that the spectators come to occupy the position, quite literally, of the congregated members of the town meeting to which Stockmann gives his address. Boenisch writes, at this point the 'theatre situation and the play's fictional frame collapse into each other'.[46] This happens once Stockmann's speech reaches its conclusion with the proclamation, 'the worst enemy of the truth, this damned liberal majority!', whence a call is made for a show of hands to see who in the audience agrees with Stockmann's point of view. What occurs at this point is not, however, a formal collapsing of fictional and real 'frames'; it should be understood as an articulation of the theatre situation in light of the political situation – in light of the conjunctural present. The theatre 'fiction' provides the discursive surface for a condensation of the 'real'. Through the superimposition of past and present conditions, it sought a 'fusion' of actual and existing conjunctural elements, and an awakened consciousness of them, by exposing the audience to the organic tendencies it discovered buried in the text. Thus, it invited the audience to draw out the connections for themselves between the current state of politics – and their own disaffections – and the concern for economic mismanagement, political corruption, and media bias that can be found indexed at the centre of Ibsen's play.[47]

Ostermeier mobilised the stage so as to rupture the symbolic order itself, transforming the theatre into what Boenisch has described as a scene of Rancièrean dissensus. What this means is not simply that the theatre became disputatious, but that the critical theatre of the conjuncture stages an intervention within the hegemonic order itself. Boenisch writes, in relation to this performance, 'More than thematic extensions of motifs already articulated in [the play], these interventions … foster a "symptomatic actualization" of the (virtual) "whole" of the play – they come into the play, as it were, from its future of our present' – they historicise the spectatorial engagement with the play in ways that 'tap into the negative truth of the playtext, where it breaks through the established norms of our hegemonic order of the sensible'.[48] The canonical text is interrupted in order to open it up to its present discursive context, transforming the theatre – through a series of reframings – into a scenic demonstration of the contradictions and antagonisms that develop within the long-term 'organic' structure within which the social order of liberal capitalism resides. What such conjunctural strategies seek to expose, in a word, are the contradictions within the existing common sense by producing the space within the theatre for a critical consciousness of them. In an interview, Ostermeier indicated the necessity for being 'honest with the play, to get to the core of the text'.[49] To get to the core of the text, however, required the transformation of the play into a kind of Brechtian fabula in which the story of the poisoned spa water, upon which the town's economic health relies, as well as Stockmann's attempt to expose that scandal, and his derangement in the face of the attempt to cover it up, opens onto the real and persisting contradictions at the heart of liberal capitalism. Ibsen's play is thus recomposed as a system of historical and present-day trajectories, of flights of irrational desire (for instance, the pursuit of profit over environmental health) and as a revelation of those vested interests through which contemporary capitalism never ceases to give birth to its discontents.

There is one further way of understanding the location of the critical theatre inaugurated by Brecht, which problematises it further, and that is in light of the kind of institutional positioning it acquires within the conjuncture that provides it with its conditions of existence. It is to see that the emergence and development of the critical theatre (and its transformation into a critical politics of the theatre) is by no means simply a given but was produced as part of the wider conjunctural (and situational) tendency through which the political theatre was itself subject, over time, to the uneven processes of cultural-historical development. Since everything is subject to the vagaries of history, the political theatre can hardly be exempted. It is in this latter sense that one can begin to understand why the critical theatre prepares the way for the 'closure' of the political theatre, at least in its classical sense. In fact, as shall be seen later, the closure of the political theatre owes much to the wider conjunctural crisis of the period in which it becomes evident – certainly in the West, if not elsewhere. This crisis of the critical theatre is an inexorable product of a deeper political crisis that can be traced to the collapse of the post-war consensus toward the end of the 1970s, which leads to the closure of the political as such. It is why the critical theatre and its transformation, when viewed as an effect of the conjuncture, is as much a result of its aleatoric passage through events as it is their reflection; and it is why in an age in which politics has 'ended' it comes to believe that the impossibility of the political stage provides the only means for affirming theatre's political possibility.[50]

In fact, there are several conjunctural tendencies that come into play when accounting for the transformation of the political theatre into a post-Brechtian critical politics of the theatre. In the first place, it is obvious that for the political theatre to work, to produce its effects, the ideological theatre must be hegemonic. Even the theatre of displacement requires a hegemonic stage, without which it loses its critical force. But what if the ideological theatre is no longer the hegemonic cultural form? This is the question the poet and filmmaker Pier Paolo Pasolini posed in his *Manifesto for a New Theatre*, written in 1966. Pasolini argued that Brecht 'was the last man of theatre to be able to unleash a theatrical revolution within theatre itself'.[51] With the advent of mass media, with television, cinema – intensified today by the internet – 'something irreversible had taken place in the history of theatre'[52] that dismantled forever its cultural power. Even if it retains a degree of cultural prestige as an 'elite' art form, its purchase over the social imaginary has all but been extinguished. What results is a 'withering' away of the stage under the dominant forms of the mediatic state. The consequences of this for the political theatre is that it became increasingly irrelevant in direct proportion to the ever-waning power of the ideological theatre. Another way of putting this would be to say: once the theatre of the past is consigned to the past, then what of the 'theatre of the future', the theatre whose logic is that of the 'ruptural break'? Pasolini's verdict was stark: 'The days of Brecht', he wrote, 'are gone forever.'[53] With this, the power of the critical theatre to rent a hole in the fabric of culture becomes, at best, as with Ostermeier's *An Enemy of the People*, rupture at the 'local level' of a particular production; no longer can one speak of a global or revolutionary rupture in theatre practice as such. It is why Brecht, even if his is by no means the last word on the critical theatre, is certainly the last word on the political theatre in its classical appearance.

Pasolini's own solution to this dilemma, however, flounders on the second conjunctural tendency, which appears to invalidate it: the move from a critical theatre to a post-Brechtian politics of the theatre. Pasolini argued that a new type of critical theatre might be developed that would be able to connect the 'advanced element' of the bourgeoisie to the working classes.[54] What he envisaged, essentially, was a form of non-dramatic, non-spectacular, but highly conceptual theatre in which ideas or 'words' would become the 'real characters' on the stage.[55] In some respects, Pasolini's vision of a theatre in which there is an 'almost total absence of scenic action'[56] appears to be comprehensively vindicated with the development of postdramatic theatre in the late 1990s – the exemplar of a post-Brechtian 'critical' theatre. Unfortunately, the 'new' theatre did not forge a connection between the 'advanced' elements of the intellectual classes that produced it and the workers with whom they expressed their solidarity, as he had hoped when he wrote it in the 1960s. What it produced was an intellectually austere theatre that increasingly limited access to itself by requiring an exceptional level of interpretative ability on the part of the audience – a highly specialist 'advanced' theatre for an advanced audience equipped with enough cultural and educational capital to understand it. One can trace this development to an effect of the conjuncture that leads the critical theatre inexorably to produce a transformation of the aesthetic possibilities of the theatre more generally. Consequently, what began as a critical politics of the theatre, paved the way for an eventual incorporation of advanced theatre concepts that by no means undermined the dominant hegemony of the cultural formation to which it belonged; even as they rejected the bourgeois concept of representation, advanced works ascended to the exceptional status bestowed upon all works of art – they connected theatre production to the reflexive experiments that played endlessly with theatrical semiosis but what they did not do was connect it with life.[57] If anything they forged connections with 'elite' audiences across a number of rarefied spaces, which opened before them – the international theatre festival, the transnational touring circuit, made possible by the flows of globalised capital; they came to occupy prestigious arts venues, and found validation through the affirmation of academics. Through the 'advanced theatre', critical theatre finds its place in the world of the 'advanced' market, catering to advanced tastes. But all this confirms is that the validation of the advanced theatre was achieved on the grounds of the valediction of the political theatre, whose foundations had crumbled.

The third and perhaps most perplexing of the conjunctural tendencies for the prospects of the political theatre has to do with the waning of traditional political allegiances reflected in the collapse of the post-war social democratic consensus (significantly accelerated post-1989), and the 'closure of the political' as such. Where once it was assumed that the processes of proletarianisation would lead to the development of an historical class consciousness – the proletariat would become conscious of itself as labour power, as the producer of wealth, and as the only class capable of surpassing the existing system of exploitation – what transpired by no means led to the development of such an identity. There are several reasons for this that include the economic transformation to post-Fordist techniques of production and the growth of what Yan Moulier Boutang has described as the 'cognitive labour market'[58] – tendencies whose intricate developments are too complex to adequately deal with here. However, Andre Gorz provides a simple enough explanation that suffices for starters. The fact is, he wrote,

> [the] link between the development of productive forces and the growth of class antagonism has been broken. This does not mean that the internal contradictions of capitalism are not considerable. They have never been more spectacular. Capitalism has never been less able to solve the problems it has generated. Yet this inability has not proved fatal.[59]

I might add, however, that the problem is perhaps even worse than Gorz supposed, and that the real and decisive break lies with the assumption that proletarianisation would necessarily produce a proletarian consciousness, where in fact no necessary link exists. In other words, if the formation of political identities can be understood as an effect of the conjuncture it is not simply because the conjuncture determines which subject positions are available to individuals according to whatever contingent factors are presently in play, but also – and more fundamentally – it can only do so because every identity, including that of the worker, is overdetermined. The groundbreaking work of Ernesto Laclau and Chantal Mouffe has demonstrated that there is no complete and irreversible passage from the state of pre-political consciousness to that of 'proletarian man'[60] – an identity wholly defined by the political destiny of their social class 'as such'. Every identity remains contingent, and prone to any number of contending and contradictory social forces, and it is precisely this fact that makes the conjuncture what it is – the articulation of elements (social actors) whose identities are provisionally fixed by (and within) the given hegemonic formation. As such, and to refer again to Hall momentarily, if there is no guarantee that the proletariat will appear at its historically destined hour, in plain and simple terms, it is because there is no such thing as '*The* Proletariat' – there are only mutable and unstable identity positions, opened by the objective process of proletarianisation, but never wholly consolidated at the level of the subject. The fundamental point here is that class is not an ontological category but always an historical and political articulation, i.e., formed at and by particular sites of struggle. The proper name 'The Proletariat' is not the designation of a substantive identity, it describes the successful hegemonisation of one such struggle that occurred at a particular historical juncture within the development of industrial capitalism.[61] Since the political theatre developed precisely on the basis of a deterministic assumption that subsequently proved erroneous, it was eventually confronted with an irrevocable choice: either it would become otiose, or – admitting its intellectual insolvency – transform itself. The latter occurred once the conjunctural tendency to which the political theatre belonged reached a point of crisis, rendering it conscious of the equivocation that had constituted its founding presupposition.[62] It is why it would be more accurate to state that the closure of the political theatre is itself the product or consequence of a wider tendency that has led to the closure of the political as such. The development of the critical theatre and its transformation into a post-Brechtian critical politics of the theatre represents the process by which that consciousness – in truth, a consciousness of the crisis of the political – gained historical ascendancy over the political theatre, producing a final *effet de déplacement*.

3

Activist theatre of the conjuncture: Janam and the politics of the street theatre in India[1]

The closure of the political theatre, described in the previous chapter, by no means entails that the idea of a militant and activist theatre is therefore entirely swept from the board by the historical tendencies that overwhelmed the classical political theatre, or that its genealogy amounts only to the story of the erasure of actual politics from the taxonomic table of the theatre. It is to observe instead something quite remarkable: that despite the effects of the closure of the political theatre in Europe, an activist theatre persisted. That it did so in the Global South is hardly a coincidence. There, it did not pick up the message that it should put down its tools, pack up its bag of tricks, and go home. It took root in the favelas of Rio, in the townships of Cape Town, in the West Bank and refugee camps in Jenin, as well as in the working-class districts of New Delhi and Kolkata.[2] What accounts for its persistence is simple: wherever it appeared it is because the political and social situation necessitated its existence. Accounting for the activist theatre in its specificity, as a form distinct from the classical political theatre, is – however – by no means a simple matter. In fact, it is impossible to understand the appearance of the activist theatre (which is in any case as pluralistic as its contexts are singular and manifold) without also understanding the complex nexus of historical, political, institutional, and situational factors that led to its formation. This is to say, it must be grasped through the specification of its conjunctural determinations – something which considerably complicates the standard taxonomies of the political theatre as imagined from a northern perspective. The nature of that complexity can only be indicated here in outline form but its import for grasping what is to be understood by the political theatre more generally becomes clear once one asks whether it is possible to truly understand the political theatre without also understanding its relation to political strategy and tactics; without relating it to the terrain of actual political struggle.

Take in the first instance the problem of specification, which attends – not just to the fact that a politics is ascribed to a theatre or a play or its performance – but rather and more significantly to the precise manner of its entrance into the socio-political and cultural field. Understanding the way in which the present forces that occupy the political terrain are appropriated or modified by it – for example, the degree of political consciousness belonging to the audience – will have considerable implications for how one differentiates on strategic grounds between one form of political theatre practice and another. This is because the question of strategy concerns the given conjunctural mediations and elements that are activated within the given local context of an existing social formation, where 'making an entrance' into the field must be viewed as a tactical intervention, but whose deeper strategic problematic the theatre must necessarily be seen to embody for it to constitute its political articulation. It is this level of internal strategic and tactical complexity that tends to be overlooked in the well-worn criticisms of the activist theatre – i.e., that it exemplifies the reduction of politics to a narrowly defined 'issue', or that it frames art as an all-too-literal expression of politics. To understand the activist theatre as a form of political theatre, however, one must set the literalist and reductionist critiques to one side.

Consider for a moment what is in fact meant by the word 'issue', which is often grasped as the reduction of the complex social totality to a single delimiting factor or interest. An alternative way to look at this would be to understand issue-based politics as a form of populist reason, where an issue represents the rhetorical and popular idiom for what Ernesto Laclau termed a 'democratic interpellation'.[3] The implications of this immediately complicate standard understandings of the activist theatre and its tactical interventions. By articulating itself in relation to issues, the activist theatre constitutes itself as the site for the mobilisation of the popular democratic force otherwise known as 'the people'; and it does so in relation to a specifically defined articulation (an issue). It is the specificity of the articulation that enables the activist theatre to interpellate its audience around a grievance or wrong that possesses an emotional appeal for it, but also in such a way as to constitute them as representatives of the people, conceived as an imagined or projected totality. Seen thus, rather than epitomising the reduction of political speech to 'issue-based politics', in which the latter must be thought – as Michel de Certeau once expressed it – as 'merely an epidermal phenomenon',[4] the activist theatre constructs the symbolic site for the deeper popular movement it expresses. It can do this only because an issue represents a limited instance of the wider antagonism by which a popular force is itself constituted. An issue is thus misrepresented when viewed as merely subjective belligerence, incapable of grasping the bigger picture. Where genuine, it expresses the objective state of the political situation as mediated by a particular signified – the issue in question – which unites, in the form of an immediate popular demand, several otherwise distinct subject positions, whose differing interests nonetheless coalesce around a common grievance and a common identity – that of the *demos*. Now, this democratic procedure of convoking the people, in a coalitional and popular sense, consists in seizing or hegemonising what Laclau refers to as the 'empty signifier' (of the name) of the people. The denomination 'the people' is empty because strictly put it represents a 'universal signification' that is incommensurable with any particularity that seeks to occupy or claims to occupy its symbolic space. Laclau writes: 'this embodied totality or universality is ... an impossible object, the hegemonic identity becomes something of the order of an *empty* signifier, its own particularity embodying an unfulfillable fullness.'[5] In other words, the people can never be literalised, and all claims on the name of the people must be taken as being, in the final analysis, provisional. The provisional nature of the claim, however, does not imply a deficit in democratic politics. On the contrary, its constitutive emptiness indicates the condition of possibility for politics insofar as it constructs a universal space in which contending demands can encounter one another. Without this contingency, democratic politics would not be possible. Thus, if the name of the people assumes a determinate content, then – as Laclau notes – it can only do so in a figural not literal sense. This does not mean that political demands are fabrications without real substance; nor does it mean that they cannot possess a literal content. On the contrary, the specificity of the content is necessary: it provides the concrete means with which to construct that 'figure' that in reality can never assume a phenomenal immediacy, and for which every issue must be taken as its partial appearance. Without this moment of symbolic excess, no issue could be articulated on a strategic basis or serve a political function; it would amount only to a short-term preoccupation without any relation to a longer-term strategic enterprise. It is precisely this complex process of figuration, or – better-put – prefiguration, that is essentially at play in the activist theatre. It stages the figural appearance of the people *by means of* the conjunctural particularity contained in the issue around which it mobilises tactically. And it is for this reason that the activist theatre must be grasped as the figural presentation of the political and not its literal and reductive representation.

A different problem with conjunctural specification arises in relation to the problem of organic context, and it is here that we are required to attend closely to theatre's cultural and historical determinations. How does one account for the distinctive mediations that distinguish – and to an extent separate – the activist theatre in the 'Global South' from the earlier theatre of propaganda that emerged in Europe, particularly in Russia – no matter how influential it was – to avoid simply projecting the former as merely an epiphenomenon of the latter? One notable distinction, that will be argued for in what follows, is that in contrast to the latter, the tendency of the activist theatre in the Global South – particularly in response to the acceleration and global extension of transnational corporate power and the relative decline of traditional left alternatives – is not to pre-empt the political, democratic, or popular demand. It tends instead toward the recognition of a democratic demand that has already been embodied in a *demos*, and in relation to which its appearance constitutes a theatrical mode of approval.[6] For this reason, the activist theatre, as it developed beyond Europe, occupies its own distinct place within the taxonomy of the political theatre, which, although close to, should by no means be conflated with, the classical theatre of propaganda. Its difference from propagandistic theatre lies not just in its eschewal of the programmatic subordination of the theatre to the militant aims pursued by the political project that it was designed to explicitly promote; but, more specifically, it lies in its distinction from the earlier theatre's vanguardism, whose strategic aim – to which it must exhibit steadfast fidelity or else it is nothing – was not to approve but to *construct* a political demand. This democratic leaning of the activist theatre, its tilt to the knowledge already possessed by the people, and its orientation to the lifeworld, was indicated by the great Indian political theatre maker, Utpal Dutt, when he wrote: 'The audience is the link between life and theatre.'[7] To be in the vanguard is, by contrast, to place oneself in advance of any popular expression of a political demand: to direct the living – the proper meaning of didacticism for the classical political theatre. Even though it may be closely aligned with a set of strategic political aims, the activist theatre cannot be wholly determined by its adherence to them. I argue, rather, that it is defined by the democratic demand to which it gives its approval, and which embeds it within its conjunctural context. For this reason, it would be better to say that the activist theatre, rather than being *of* the party or political organisation, is better characterised as a democratic theatre of protest. Whether or not it is affiliated with a political party is less important to its definition than its specific form of militancy, which although agitational is by no means propagandistic, at least in the strict and somewhat limited sense that attaches to the didactic theatre.[8] What this compels is a further distinction that must be drawn between a critical theatre of the conjuncture (formed around the critique of a given ideological configuration) and what now might be termed an *activist theatre of the conjuncture.*

To admit the activist conception of political theatre is also to show that the development and transformation of the political theatre by no means proceeded as if it followed a syllogistic pattern which could be neatly arrayed and made specifiable as a logical sequence. Far better to specify the conditions that necessitate its distinct modalities: where the critical theatre emerges in relation to the chronic condition, the activist theatre can be seen as a response to the acute condition. It surfaces in relation to the specific dilemma, in each milieu that it seeks to address; it arises in direct reaction to the rapid elaboration of political developments that are scarcely foresee-able; it addresses itself to 'the things themselves' – to the political situation, to the strenuous demands of a sudden contestation. Thus, by dint of its very existence, it cannot feign ignorance of the world in which it becomes operative: on the contrary it must have an intimate knowledge of the world and its depredations. What takes form continually within it are convictions that are permanently attuned to the exigencies of its own lifeworld. Because it is compelled to act in the face of this or that impending 'crisis', its per-formers must be forever alert to the political moment. Not just performers, they are activists and strategists who have mastered the art of tactics. This is what makes it the most vigilant of all political theatres. If it is constantly shape-shifting, or variegated in terms of form, it is because it is continually adapted to respond to the novelty of the moment of its engagement; while the moment (because overdetermined) it recognises as always kaleidoscopic in character, as always alive – thus never entirely set or predictable in its manner of unfolding. To express this in the most emphatic terms: it seeks to harness the contingency that suffuses the conjunctural moment with politi-cal possibility, just as a turbine sail seeks to harness the power of the wind to generate the kinetic field that flows from it.

Hence, in seeking to trace a genealogical trajectory for the political thea-tre, one finds the road is pitted with potholes that do not make for smooth analysis; one sees that it is intersected by bifurcating paths whose mosaic-like pattern and complexity make it almost impossible to track or follow. No sooner is the political theatre named than the name must be renounced, and its denominations recast in new terms. Patrice Pavis writes – correctly – of the political theatre: 'This genre is constantly inventing new formulas and new disguises, as if the proliferation and diversification of forms were necessary for its survival. In reality, this is less a proliferation of forms than the permanent invention of new ways of doing politics.' How unfortunate then that in keeping with so many commentators he excludes activist theatre from any serious consideration: 'in theatre, politics is never given or acces-sible as a transparent and unambiguous message .... It cannot be reduced, except in agitprop or crude propaganda theatre, to a direct message.' What makes this all the more perplexing is that having summarily dismissed the most activist of all theatre practices he then notes: 'It is by seeking new and paradoxical political forms, not by fleeing conflict and problems that need to be solved, that political theatre can keep its strength and convic-tion, its interest and its contradiction.'[9] Of course no-one will deny that there are forms of activist theatre that are crude! But crudity of form, or the frankness of its message, offers no definitional precision by which to under-stand what the activist theatre of the conjuncture is or what it does. Nor does it do it justice as an aesthetic form attuned to the demands and to the contextual nuances of those to whom it addresses itself at ground level. Nor, finally, does such a dismissive approach comprehend what it is that makes the political theatre, in all its new and 'paradoxical' forms, both 'crude' and 'sophisticated' alike, 'political'.

So, what of this new entry that appears on the ledger sheet of the political theatre, and more to the point, what might one discover of the conjunctural problematic from a form of theatre that seeks to insert itself into the very heart of political and social realities?

I would like to offer, as an example of the activist theatre of the conjuncture, and if only in the limited form of an incomplete sketch, a conjunctural analysis of the world's most enduring activist theatres – the street theatre in India. To indicate something of the conjunctural problematic of the activist theatre as it emerged in India,[10] I begin with a little scene setting: the initial performance of the short twelve-minute play *Machine*, by Jana Natya Manch (the People's Theatre Front) or 'Janam' – which established it as India's foremost political street theatre troupe – before contextualising it (and Janam) in relation to wider issues of the conjuncture from which it derives its political significance.[11] The first performance took place on 19 November 1978, at the close of the All-India trade union conference, held at Delhi's Indoor Stadium, before 7000 delegates; it was then repeated the following day at a mass rally in support of workers at the old colonial Boat Club, a well-known site for protests and for expressions of political dissent.

To be sure, no sooner had the event begun than it was over. Even so, it would be a mistake to underestimate its significance or undervalue the force of its impact simply based on the show's brevity.[12] To place *Machine* within its immediate context: what this extraordinary piece of theatre announced was, in effect, the return of street theatre activism in India following the lifting of the state of emergency imposed by Indira Gandhi's government three years earlier. The Emergency (as it is now commonly called) was motivated in large part by a series of inflationary crises occurring between 1965 and 1974; it saw the suspension of civil liberties and the detention of political opponents, including several trades union leaders. It was also to have far-reaching consequences for India. The Marxist political theorist, Vijay Prashad, has argued, for instance, that it 'hastened the transition' to the 'era of liberalisation', and thus reoriented the Indian economy away from Nehru's policy of self-reliance to embrace instead export, foreign trade, and inward investment by international capital.[13] It hardly needs saying that the path to liberalisation was to be paved by policies and labour 'reforms' that deliberately weakened the worker's movement in India – or, indeed, that Gandhi's suspension of the constitution can be viewed as the first brazen step in that direction – a response, at least partly attributable, to the success of trades union activism prior to the imposition of the Emergency (the year

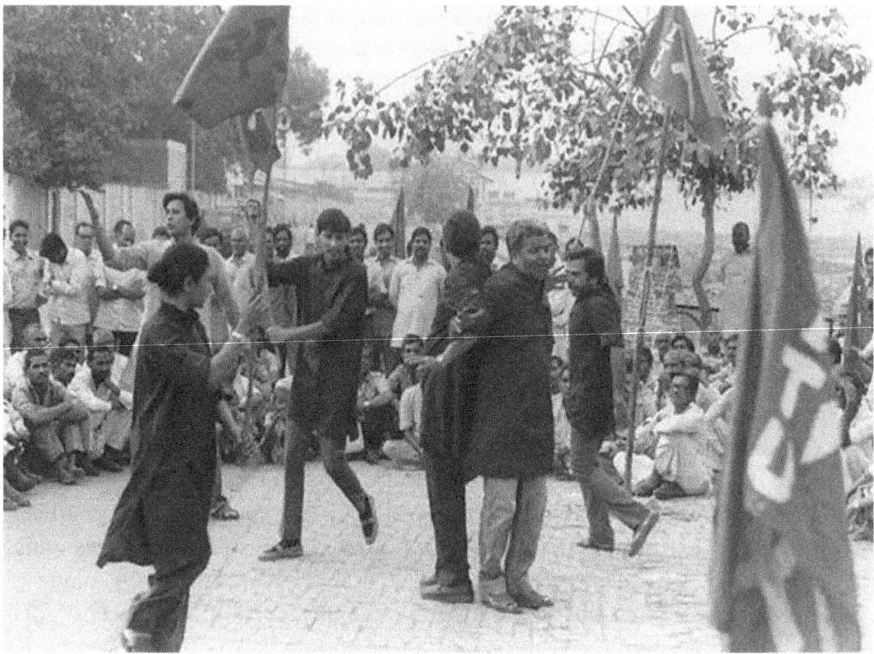

Figure 4 Safdar Hashmi in a performance of *Machine* with Moloyashree Hashmi and Lalit Ratan Girdhar, 1 May 1988.

before, 1974, had seen 1.8 million railway workers go on strike).[14] Viewed in light of this, *Machine* possesses a double significance. First, because it signalled a renewed and revitalised interest in the use of politically assertive street theatre and must be seen as a propitious moment for leftist theatre activism in India, although it is by no means the only example. Second, because of what was to follow economically, politically, and culturally, since *Machine*'s first performance was located at the dawn of what – at least if one follows Stuart Hall – must be viewed as the first flickering of a completely new conjunctural moment that would prove, eventually, to be far from propitious for the Left. It inaugurated a new period of political struggle that would be fought in the context of transformed cultural and economic realities and that would, with intensifying bitterness, test the resilience of the labour movement in India and the theatre associated with it.

It is scarcely accidental, therefore, that industrial and labour-related struggles have come to define the work of Janam – or that they have done so from the very outset. Safdar Hashmi, who stands at the centre of the story of Janam, later recalled in an interview how the production of *Machine* sought to respond to legislation for a new Industrial Relations Bill – an 'anti-people bill'[15] is how he described it – brought forward by the Janata government in response to a strike at the chemical factory in Ghaziabad in which six workers had been shot dead by private security contractors.[16] The legislation gave power to local authorities to suppress trade union activism, depriving workers of democratic rights by dismantling labour tribunals to resolve industrial disputes as well as inhibiting other consultative structures. *Machine* – politically terse and poetic (with its condensation of the contradictions of capital in the image of machinic production) – was Janam's response.[17] Hashmi portrayed the performance as follows: 'with our bodies we made a machine. Five people (three workers, the guard, and the owner) came on and started constructing a machine in motion, making all kinds of sounds.'[18] He then described how the machine malfunctions – how it eventually breaks down – with one of the workers peeling away from the group, declaring: 'I have stopped it, I could not tolerate it any longer.'[19] The worker, refusing further exploitation by the machine and its owner, and the oppression he has endured at the hands of the guard, solicits others to join him. Before long, the workers, having formed a united front, begin to issue their demands. Their protest, 'we won't work', however, is soon met with deadly force from the guards (as had really happened in Ghaziabad). But, although *Machine* reaches its climax with the murder of the workers, it is they who have the final word, when the narrator or 'Sutradhar' proclaims: 'No matter how many bullets you pump into us, the workers are not going to be defeated. They will rise again.'[20] And indeed the play ends with each of the workers rising from the ground, proclaiming their defiance in the face of the machine's barbarity with the emphatic declarative: 'Inquilab, Zindabad!' ('Long Live the Revolution!'). This familiar protest, of course by no means unique to India, nevertheless possessed a special significance for its audience. Not only did it express Janam's solidarity with those involved in an ongoing political struggle, but it was also made famous by Bhagat Singh, a martyr of the Indian Freedom Movement, executed in 1931 by the British colonial occupying authorities. Historical reference thus coincided with contemporary political sense. In articulating the conjunctural moment, it also asserted the historical nature of the struggle: that although individuals may perish, their sacrifices are not made in vain, since they continue to influence present possibilities, constituting a moment of mnemonic condensation for reparative demands, essential to the galvanising of progressive and popular forces.

It might be objected that what is described here can scarcely be differentiated from the earlier theatre of propaganda found in the theatrical work of Piscator or in the agitprop of revolutionary Russia. Hashmi appeared to endorse this view when he stated that the street theatre in India belongs to a lineage that can be traced directly back to the theatre of 1917, to work such as *Mystery-Bouffe* by Mayakovsky, and to the new mobile theatre that performed at factory gates, in dockyards, and in school playgrounds. Moreover, Janam's work was (and remains) closely tied to the trade union movement, and to the Communist Party of India-Marxist (CPI-M).[21] Hashmi would go so far as to assert the street theatre in India 'has more in common with the tradition of theatre developed by Piscator and Brecht [… than] with the traditional forms of theatre in India'.[22] But it also arises in a context of organic differences, conjunctural tendencies, institutional settings, and lifeworld imperatives that indicate a different genealogy of the political theatre, one that sometimes coincides with but also at times runs orthogonally to that of its European counterpart. This is to say that every political theatre must be understood, at least to the degree that it must be seen as a singular presentation of its situation, as a *sui generis* event. It derives it political meaning from the conjunctural circumstances particular to it.

There are several analytic implications that follow from this. First, to understand the political theatre in India, one must attend to what makes it distinctive: the organic terrain and political situation from which it grew – in a word, the radical context that saw the rise of political activism in India, which anchor its present-day possibilities, including those of the political theatre, within its historical conditions of emergence. Of these conditions, two should be immediately acknowledged as constituting the organic or historical basis that continues to be formative for ongoing struggles over India's political identity. The first arises in the nineteenth century, with the national struggle against British colonial rule that saw the birth of the Independence Movement in 1857, initiated by the 'Indian Mutiny' – although preceded by earlier mutinies such as the 'Poligar revolts' in what is now known as Tamil Nadu in 1799, and the Mutiny at Vellore in 1806.[23] The second comprises, less the stock of expressly articulable political experiences that are constitutive for India's sense of historical identity, than the wider reverberations of colonialism's endemic political and cultural aftereffects. These continue to represent what Hall would describe as long-term situational tendencies, which are rather more inchoate and dispersed in both form and structure. They bind the development of the organs of modern Indian civil society, as well as its economic, religious, and political institutions, according to particular historical constraints and contradictions. They embody the organic distribution of inequalities, some located, for example, in the caste system, and others deriving from the complex ways in which the latter intersected with colonial rule. Ashis Nandy – one of India's foremost analysts of the effects of colonialism on the construction of the modern Indian psyche – describes, among the primary narratives that continue to inform contemporary Indian political life, the way in which the colonial political economy favoured the Brahminic castes in government appointments and in the modern professions which it opened up around the middle of the nineteenth century. The traditional skills of these castes helped them to reconcile work, worldview and selfhood by reinterpreting traditions – which was their prerogative as well as specialization – and by ascribing meanings to exogenous bureaucratic, political, and juridical forms.[24]

But he also describes how, in the second half of the nineteenth century, a twofold transformation of colonialism – 'growing British chauvinism and [its] commitment to Europe's civilizing mission' – led to an adaptive 'split' within Indian elites. One half 'sought salvation in aggressive modernization, the other in an odd form of reactive Westernisation which wore the garb of cultural nationalism'.[25] What it has left India with today are two opposing forms, one of which Nandy identifies with both liberal and even radical variants of modernisation programmes, the other 'Hindu nationalism and revivalism' – in fact, a Hinduism that is co-opted into European notions of nation and national exceptionalism.[26] Under colonialism, in other words, existing inequalities of the caste system ossified, producing new and hybrid cultural forms, while emergent class divisions, imposed through the imperial form of government, and the introduction of capitalist modes of expropriation and subordination, hardened into a subaltern system. Since this system was by no means dismantled following Independence, it persisted as part of the socio-political inheritance and ongoing legacy of colonialism in contemporary India. Given the complex circumstances of modern Indian history, its forms of political activism, including the street theatre, must be understood in distinct ways to equivalent forms of struggle that took hold in Europe. Without wishing to overstate the obvious: the street theatre, as a theatrical, aesthetic, and political form, necessarily gives expression to the unique antagonisms that derive from the contradictions that characterise Indian modernity – that is to say, it can only really be understood in light of the organic basis of the given Indian conjuncture.

Thus, when Hashmi states that the street theatre 'identifies itself consciously with the needs of the modern world', but that it also, consequently, 'establishes a more critical relationship with the past',[27] he locates it, not simply within the 'tradition' of political theatre, but political theatre as it develops within its specifically Indian context, and insofar as that historical context pertains to present conditions. It is avowedly agitational ('a militant political theatre of protest'[28]) but it also has organic connections to a long Indian folk tradition of social satire, comic interludes, and 'humour at the expense of the religious or the secular establishments'[29] as found, for example, in the Sanskrit play, *Mrichchakatika* that mocked the sacred priest caste of the Brahmin. That said, the Indian context must also be articulated as historically responsive to inescapable social, economic, cultural, and political developments found on the wider world stage. Unquestionably, the street theatre owed its origin to the international workers' struggle, and to the emergence of the leftist movement in India; but even as it drew inspiration from the theatre of the Russian Revolution, it did so as a means of articulating the specific struggles within the national independence movement itself, by agitating for a socialist alternative to those bourgeois class interests that were becoming increasingly dominant within it. It must, therefore, be viewed according to the locality of the given circumstance in which it appeared. The street theatre did not simply appear from nowhere, it was a response to ground-level political pressures (the need to form a popular front to combat fascism was one pressing concern) as well as meeting burgeoning democratic demands (another). In the 1940s those cultural influences, historical compressions, and operative circumstances converged – Althusser would say 'fused' – to produce the Indian People's Theatre Association (IPTA)[30] – an organisation of writers and artists 'formed to co-ordinate and strengthen all the progressive tendencies that have so far manifested themselves in the nature of drama, songs and dances'.[31] And it was the IPTA that gave serious impetus to the street theatre as a political form. Its clear-cut aim was 'to draw the masses into the anti-imperialist struggle'.[32] But it was also avowedly democratic, as the title of the first bulletin of the IPTA, published in 1943, was to make clear: 'People's theatre stars the people.'[33]

However, although the IPTA emerged as a democratic rather than top-down movement, with 'its roots deep down in the cultural awakening of the masses of India',[34] it nonetheless embodied a contradiction that it was not able to adequately resolve. What the cultural movement anticipated and to an extent sought to establish was a new democratic social order, but it was precisely in seeking to realise this aim that it ran into difficulties. Malini Bhattacharya explains why as follows: to effectuate change, the IPTA had to work on the basis of the existing theatre – not least because the demands of the present were urgent. This required mobilising a theatre that was predominantly rooted in the cultural activity that thrived among the urban middle class in West Bengal. A new form of drama had to emerge that could both 'wean the urban middle class away … from the commercial theatre' and appeal to an audience that 'at least in some rural areas … had known nothing but traditional forms of folk entertainment before'.[35] What emerged was an 'intermediate product, reflecting the contradiction between the existing reality of Bengali theatre and the historical need for change'[36] – it had to reconcile both the contemporary reality of the masses, and its presentation in a dramatic form that was still bound, in large part, by imported European conventions, particularly those of melodrama and naturalism. Its most successful intervention came in response to the Bengal famine, with Bijon Bhattacharya's melodrama *Nabanna* in 1944. Although initially staged as a full-scale proscenium play, however, a shorter version called *Jabanbandi* ('Testimony') – better adapted to street performance – quickly followed, and was performed often to vast audiences in and outside Calcutta, in temporary and makeshift theatres, and deploying agitprop methods.[37] Nevertheless, it was not until 1948, when the political context had deteriorated drastically for the Left, with government suppression of the Communist Party and its allies, that the IPTA – at least according to Samik Bandyopadhyay – fully realised the street theatre form as a political response to a situation of extreme state coercion. In an 'emergency' that was no 'less severe and repressive and murderous than Indira Gandhi's', the proscenium plays [of the IPTA] were driven underground – and to the streets, where they were performed at great risk of violent reprisal from state actors to both performer and audience alike.[38] It is here that a theatre of the street comes to fully embrace the idea of a form of cultural production adapted entirely by the needs of the conjunctural moment, in defiance of 'legitimate' theatre, understood as either state subsidised, or commercial – and thus in opposition to existing political and cultural authority. Perhaps the influence of the IPTA on the street theatre that would later develop can be felt most acutely here, with a theatre, grasped as a form of cultural work, entirely acclimated by political necessity in its effort to meet a situation founded upon the direst adversity imaginable.

This is not to deny that the legacy of the IPTA is, as Bhattacharya argues, a difficult one. By the late 1940s and early 1950s, the organisation had already begun to fragment – not just in West Bengal but across a number of Indian states.[39] That said, the context of the 1950s, in West Bengal, is instructive for understanding the realignment of the political theatre in post-Independence India, and its development beyond the IPTA. In an important document, commissioned by the West Bengal branch of the IPTA, published in 1955, the film director Ritwik Ghatak wrote: 'Under the shadow of idealism, the culture and aesthetics of this land have grown up. So, we must understand the character and idiosyncrasies of this culture. It can be properly studied when the idealism of India, in its philosophy and religion, is sifted and weighed.' And he added: 'We must combat the manifestations [of idealism] in everyday life with the weapon of Marxism wedded to Indian Reality.'[40] What this signalled was a recognition that a new phase in the national struggle was needed – one that would address itself directly to the post-Independence situation in which the struggle for culture required the opening of a new hegemonic front and thus the creation of a 'democratic platform, based on democratic lines'.[41] Ghatak argued for the development of a theatre repertoire that would also '*break* the theatre by *doing* theatre' – and for this what was required was the formation of new methods of training, attuned to the necessity of collective action – the actor as a cultural worker operating within the context of a group. Ghatak writes:

> to act in the midst of mass action – on street corners, in labour halls, picket lines, processions – we need actors of such caliber which only group action and Repertoire can give birth to. Actually, to act under these conditions in villages, and at the same time, to be artistically in one piece an actor needs a special kind of training, which only a well-rounded approach can shape.[42]

Thus, despite the disintegration or dispersal of the IPTA in the early 1950s, what it led to was the formation precisely of the Group Theatre movement in Kolkata, which can be seen within the lineage, and as a direct heir, of the IPTA.[43] Hashmi himself was part of a group of young students who in the 1970s sought to revive the Delhi branch of the IPTA, inactive since the 1950s, by creating open air proscenium plays for mass audiences. And although his relation to the IPTA was short-lived, from it sprang Janam (formed in 1973). However, as always, it is important to observe the specificity of the conjunctural moment. Strictly speaking, Janam's politics owed much more to the novel circumstances of the period, than to the desire to reanimate the IPTA as an organisation. The experience of the student movement of the late 1960s and early 1970s, the spirit of protest that alighted with global opposition to the war in Vietnam, and the new social movements such as the women's movement from which it drew inspiration, all compelled a radical response to the immediate demands of the political moment, for which the old architecture of the IPTA proved inadequate.

In sum, then – and taken together as an ensemble of historical factors – it is from these innumerable streams and confluences of organic tendencies, from the immediate demands of various struggles, of the tactical ebb and flow of victories and defeats, and advances and retreats, that the Indian street theatre came to establish itself as the world's largest democratic street theatre movement. By the late 1970s, and if only achieved by circuitous means, it had realised the IPTA dream – to employ Hashmi's words – of establishing a 'people's theatre at the people's doorstep'.[44]

All the same, for the very reason the street theatre emerged as a democratic theatre for a 'non-theatre going audience',[45] to use Arjun Ghosh's succinct expression, it must be seen as being entirely circumscribed by the dilemmas of the very lifeworld that animates it. Indeed, how could it be otherwise? A theatre possessed of a progressive sense of India's political destiny, created as much with an activist as with a theatrical mentality – to reach out to 'an audience that [had] never been exposed to theatre and other art forms'[46] – establishes itself within a tradition steeped in Indian revolutionary praxis, where it articulates itself in relation to the tactical and strategic demands of an ongoing and concurrent emancipatory political struggle.[47]

These facts are inseparable for the democratic theatre; and nowhere is this more true than of Janam. It is also precisely because it derives its affective intensity from its engagement with the present moment, that it must bear within it the most salutatory lessons regarding the practical limits that inevitably restrict the possibilities of any activist theatre of the conjuncture. I would like, at this point, then, to examine how those limits necessarily express the conjuncture that imposes them. Ghosh notes, for example, that the 'strength or weakness' of troupes such as Janam cannot 'be viewed in isolation from the strength of the CPI(M) in particular and organisations of the left in general'.[48] What this statement alludes to are the specific infrastructural problems that are encountered by the political street theatre in India today; while these must, in turn, be seen as deriving from an ongoing conjunctural crisis for the Left, rendering the conditions under which Janam, and groups like it, operate increasingly adversative. Adversity, of course, has many faces – but one prominent face is that of capitalism under neoliberalism, whose insistent market-oriented policies, over the past forty years, have led to the evisceration of the trades union movement. The result, Prashad notes, could not be bleaker: 'Having lost one of its potential pillars of support, the workers and the Left are now thrown to the wolves.'[49]

If such desperate conditions are easy enough to assert (the effects of immiseration are hard to conceal), tracing their implications and origins is rather more difficult. From the perspective of a conjunctural reading, they situate the street theatre within the wider context of the global transformation of capital since the 1970s, the dismantling of the Bretton Woods system, in which India had been an active member, and the resulting hegemonic capture of the State by neoliberal political formations that actively subordinated its national interests to those of multi- and transnational corporations. What Hall described in 1979, in relation to the UK, finds its parallel in events that occurred in India more or less at the same time, producing trends that have continued to gain ground ever since. Not only did these forces 'destroy' that 'form of consensus in which social democracy was the principal tendency', they also 'polarised' the emerging political space, pushing it firmly 'to the right'.[50] The situation Arundhati Roy observed, twenty years ago, in the wake of the murderous anti-Muslim pogroms in Gujarat in the early 2000s, and on the eve of Bush's war in Iraq, has only worsened: 'the two arms of the Indian government have evolved the perfect pincer action. While one arm is busy selling India off in chunks, the other, to divert attention, is orchestrating a howling, braying chorus of Hindu nationalism and religious fascism.'[51] In fact, two 'twinned' tendencies might be observed here. On the one hand, there has been a pluralisation but also a fracturing of forces on the left, while, on the other hand, a homogenisation and consolidation of those on the populist right – the 'nationalism of tandoori pizza' and the rise of a 'virulent communalism'[52] – with dire consequences for the traditional left, as represented by a series of electoral defeats for India's communist parties. Prashad writes of the 'precipitous decline in West Bengal and the disarray in Kerala ... alongside a failure of an electoral breakthrough elsewhere in the country' – and this is 'despite strong and vibrant Left unity in Andhra Pradesh and Tamil Nadu, despite creative and essential Left mass struggles in Haryana and Maharashtra, and despite strong and brave Left units in Kerala and West Bengal'.[53]

For this reason, the street theatre movement in India has endured, in its own way, the consequences of the significant setbacks suffered by the Left over recent years. These can be related to such long-term trends that have seen, not only the collapse of the 'centrist' Congress Party giving significant electoral advantage to the Indian People's Party (BJP), who pursue an aggressive Hindutva (Hindu nationalist) ideology, but also, a corresponding failure on the part of the organised left to combat its popular appeal. For Aijaz Ahmad, the crisis of the Left has systemic and tactical origins: it can be traced back to the establishment of liberal, parliamentary democracy in India that posed an 'inescapable dilemma' for the Left – whether to pursue the path of revolution, thus eschewing parliamentary processes but thereby becoming electorally insignificant (as happened with the Maoist groups in India) or whether to follow a 'reformist' and non-revolutionary path, participating in parliamentary elections, but accepting the constitutional settlement from which they derive their legitimacy (the path pursued by India's communist parties). The latter brings with it inevitable compromises, and a legitimation crisis once power is attained – as happened in West Bengal where the Left Front government appeared to have accepted the 'parameters' of neoliberal policy in its effort to reindustrialise the state.[54] Ahmad calculates the consequences for the Indian Left as having produced a 'blockage at both ends'.[55] Arup Baisya has further described how the Left found itself out-manoeuvred by the Right, and that its emphatic embrace of secularism identified it with a liberal era that was superseded by a new epoch of religious sectarianism.[56]

However, although a failure of tactics no doubt accounts for the comparative weakness of the organised Left today in India, its primary cause – as already noted – must be traced back to the neoliberal reforms introduced by the Congress Party in the 1980s that saw a raft of anti-union legislation being introduced, designed to suppress effective political opposition. This period marks, according to Ghosh, 'a phase in which the Left and other democratic forces were on the retreat and on the defensive'. These labour reforms also instituted a vicious circle: they 'crippled the ability of trade unions and other mass organizations to carry out effective resistance to such policies'.[57] The result of this on the cultural work of groups such as Janam is as obvious as it is politically uncomfortable. When the social movement is weak, then the infrastructure on which cultural workers rely, provided by the organised Left, is invariably diminished. Even where mobilisation does occur at 'ground level', it becomes ever more difficult to convert that cultural work into political or electoral gain.[58] Writing on the Group Theatre(s), Parimal Ghosh notes that a 'theatre that draws its sustenance from politics'[59] will inevitably reflect its divisions and splits, its disillusionments and disappointments: 'The cultural sphere, at the end of the day, [is] only an adjunct of the political sphere. The former cannot prosper as long as the latter does not provide a clear-headed direction to it.'[60] The Left theatre movement could scarcely be expected to survive unscathed the disarray on the Left as such. It is why the crisis confronting the network of theatre troupes who comprise the Group Theatre cannot be viewed apart from the 'fallout of the much bigger crisis in the constitutional left movement of the country'.[61] And, finally, just as with the collapse of social democratic parties in the West, the predicament of the Indian Left can no doubt, likewise, be explained to a large extent by policy missteps when in government – this is particularly true in the case of West Bengal, where a Left Front government held power for over three decades.[62] Writing on the balance-of-payments crisis that afflicted India in the 1990s, Baisya observes:

> The left, in power in a few Indian states, especially in West Bengal, also succumbed to this pressure with policy paralysis .... The total abdication of its role by a supposedly pro-labor government in West Bengal further worsened the situation .... The unions and the state both remained a mute witness to the onslaught on workers during the decade.[63]

Ghosh perceives, however, a more subjective tendency at play that has driven the Left, in India, as elsewhere, not so much into a structural as an 'existential' crisis. As the 'fantasy of a revolution gradually faded away', he writes, so the Left was deprived of its traditional raison d'être.[64] It is owing to the sheer scale and complexity of the situation, leading the Left to a crisis of strategic purpose, that commentators such as Girish Shrivastava have lamented that the ' "Left's lack of political vibrancy" in the recent past has affected street theatre and groups like JANAM. One senses a loss of direction, a certain confusion.'[65]

One might think that a loss of direction, organisational collapse, and all around it a sense of political beleaguerment, would have proven fatal to the street theatre's continued prospects in India. The fact that it continues to operate effectively indicates a quite different and rather multifaceted reality; indeed, while the conjunctural moment continues to constitute a predicament for the Indian Left, as indeed is the case elsewhere, the demand for political alternatives has only gained traction as the drastic fluctuations in global financial markets over recent years have produced their inevitable bitter side-effects within the social sphere. Even Shrivastava sees reasons for cautious optimism, noting the emergence of new street theatre groups that, although less explicit, perhaps, than Janam in their political affiliations, nonetheless 'continue to perform in streets and spread the message of equality and freedom'.[66] However, a more specific reason for the street theatre's survival may well lie in the distinct relation it establishes as a form of cultural work to conjunctural problems, and which fundamentally differentiates it from the classical vanguardist theatre of propaganda (as well as propagandistic variants of the street theatre developed by the Right). The distinction – as delicate as it may be – is carefully teased apart by Pushpa Sundar when she distinguishes between the 'political theatre' and the 'theatre of protest':

> The term 'protest theatre' is often used as a synonym for political theatre, but it has a wider scope. Socially concerned theatre may raise consciousness about social ills for which individuals, and not the State, may be collectively responsible; thus, it may not be aimed at political authority at all.[67]

The concept of the 'political theatre' here assumes a rather more precise meaning than is generally allowed. It is limited to theatre that either challenges or reinforces state authority and power. By contrast, the theatre of protest addresses itself to a wider set of concerns, less focused on ideological criticism than on 'social criticism'.[68] Sundar adds a further clarification:

> [where political theatre deals with] political ideas and concepts usually in an attempt to attack or support a particular political position, [the] protest theatre merely raises certain issues, explores certain problems and asks certain questions; at other times, it may attempt to change the beliefs and opinions of the spectators, ultimately seeking political and social action based on those changes. But the essence of protest theatre is that it is directed towards the power of an authority – political, religious, or social.[69]

Protest theatre – whose prevalent form in India, for Sundar, is the street theatre – is 'politically oriented' theatre, then, but it is not 'Political Theatre' in its classical sense. It is the tactical and strategic use of theatre as a 'weapon of protest'[70] that is deployed and adapted in response to specific, situationally located injustices – hikes in bus fares, violence against women, or the plight of peasant farmers struggling against the interests of corporate agribusinesses. It is in this sense that an agile and mobile theatre, designed for the purposes of political and social mobilisation, a pluralistic theatre oriented by the demands of social movements, comes to define the *activist theatre of the conjuncture* and its political meaning.

In a recent paper, Bishnupriya Dutt has delineated the essential aim of the street theatre, with enviable precision. Drawing on Elaine Aston, she notes that it seeks to 're-animate political sources of desire' by 'indexing' itself to 'the material conditions of life' of its audience.[71] By indexing the material conditions of life the street theatre places itself in direct proximity to immediate lifeworld imperatives – indicating a second reason for its capacity to survive under conditions of extreme duress. It is not just that it is an authentically popular form of street entertainment but that it is popular in the genuine sense of being democratically founded – as such, it appears as an articulation of popular demands. In a context where working-class cultures are politically marginalised, where they are pushed to the periphery of mainstream political discourses, where they are ignored or discounted, or even abused and violently attacked by those in authority – and where their demands are left unmet no matter how valid – the street theatre constitutes an essential means for giving those demands a public expression. (There is, in fact, no demand without expression, and no expression without a means of articulation.) To say that they are expressions of the popular demand is to say the street theatre creates, even if only momentarily, a *res publica* – a public space within which communities of solidarity are able to appear, bound together not just by a shared sense of grievance, but by the affective state of co-belonging that is formative of a 'demos' – the street theatre engenders, in those who engage with it, precisely this 'phatic' political affect. One might argue, all the same, that the production of political affect in a transient audience is no guarantee that a political *effect* will follow, or that a 'people' will be convoked. Of course, that is true. But to insist on a guaranteed effect is to reduce the integral political quality of the activist theatre of the conjuncture – i.e., that it is an articulation of a popular demand – to its supposed instrumental aims. What this does is load the dice against it by reducing its political meaning to a single requirement: that it demonstrates its political consequences 'literally'. If it cannot do so then it must be useless; if it can, then it has condemned itself as 'mere propaganda' – either way, it will be damned.

It is a standard trope of theatre criticism that a self-consciously political theatre must be viewed as a 'lesser form' of theatre. In the words of Rustom Bharucha, to the theatre establishment, the 'street theatre is not theatre'.[72] Whereas, in fact, he argued, it should be seen as the most undiluted form of theatre – and precisely because it is a theatre that is unencumbered by a desire for 'ontological' purity. The theatre, Bharucha observed,

> is always already a representation of something that exists. Therein lies the terrible bind of artists who seek absolute purity in the theatrical idiom. They are destined to be impure. Fortunately, street theatre workers rarely suffer from delusions of their autonomy. Instead of concealing their affiliations and loyalties, they assert those links in their work.[73]

It is worth reflecting on the context that led Bharucha to write his short but penetrating paean to the street theatre. He was moved to do so on hearing the news of the murder of Safdar Hashmi, during a Janam performance on the streets of Sahibabad on Delhi's outskirts in 1989.[74] From this, one immediately grasps the extraordinary courage of India's cultural workers who perform in 'that most anonymous of battlegrounds and theatrical sites: the street'.[75] One immediately understands that the risks involved offer proof of its political salience – that 'there is no political theatre worth its name that is not innately dangerous'.[76] But nor should one neglect the aesthetic basis of the street theatre, which provides the means by which that 'battle' is fought – that at its best the street theatre possesses as much artistry, skill, and technical innovation as any other form of theatre, despite its poverty of means.

One should attend, in this regard, to the most scrupulous meaning of the 'aesthetic', understood as the production of a material *sensorium* – the mediated world, in other words. If the 'impure' street theatre is a 'pure' distillation of the theatre, rather than its negation, it is because it constitutes itself on the terrain of the world it finds itself in – the world of everyday dispossession, which it produces as theatre for the purpose of intervening in it. Thus, it enacts a spatial partitioning of 'the street', configuring it as a space of theatrical exception. With this aesthetic procedure, which is fundamental to it, these theatre opuscules, like brilliant constellations of light – capable of illuminating what otherwise would remain occluded by corruption and indifference – possess the power of *reconfiguring* the oppressive distributions of everyday life with its grinding sense of drudgery, poverty, and squalor; if they possess any power to disconcert or to captivate, it is because they cut through quotidian appearances as keenly as a sharpened blade cuts through wood. If troupes such as Janam take to the street to perform at great personal risk, it is not because they confuse art with life, but because – as seen earlier in Althusser's entanglement with Brecht – they understand full well that theatre is not life, and it is not politics. The street theatre is *theatre*: the construction of an aesthetic space in which the circumstances of life and politics are *staged*, and where the language game of politics can be examined and exposed to the extent that its real effects are able to be temporarily 'suspended'. The Janam performance, in 1988, *Halla Bol!* ('Attack!'), made in support of a strike called by CITU (Centre of Indian Trade Unions), provides a case in point. It features a comical depiction of a policeman who intervenes in the performance to try to persuade the actors to drop the politics and just do 'Some love story, a play of lovers, with some song and dance, and a bit of comedy'.[77] Reflecting on this show, Hashmi wrote, in actuality an 'ordinary person would never dare laugh at the police' – were they to do so, they would be rewarded with a beating.

But when the policeman enters the space of the street theatre as a satirised figure not only is the 'participation of the people … guaranteed', but the laughter becomes a 'weapon'. And he added: 'I think that laughter is a weapon in the hands of the people with which they destroy, an image which is hated.'[78]

Far more could be said on the aesthetics of the street theatre, on its method of staging agonistic confrontations, on its production of images that can capture the immediacy of the lifeworld problematic with an extraordinary intensity of expression, and on the commitment of its activists who 'resonate with total belief in what is being said'.[79] But let this suffice for now as an example of an activist theatre of the conjuncture.

From what has been said, the following is surely apparent: it is, above all, a theatre of extreme aesthetic mobility; its versatility is attuned to the overdetermined character of the conjuncture, which is to say, to a possible intervention in a conjuncture that, as Panagiotis Sotiris has written, is 'constantly open to transformation'.[80] If the activist theatre of the conjuncture is compelled to act at great speed, it is because capturing the material moment is like leaping aboard a moving train.[81] The fact that it is able to do so demonstrates the street theatre activist's essential skilfulness in 'catching' the conjunctural moment. It is this, finally, that makes the activist theatre of the conjuncture – essentially an agitational rather than propagandistic or didactic theatre – the most visible theatrical expression of the political distinction that exists between strategy and tactics. To fully elaborate this point, once again Gramsci offers a key insight: the conjuncture, he wrote, is 'closely linked to immediate politics, to "tactics" and agitation', in contrast to the 'situation', which 'relates to "strategy" and propaganda'.[82] From this one can venture a final, decisive distinction: where the theatre of propaganda is the servant of strategy, the activist theatre of the conjuncture is the master of tactics. If the conjuncture constitutes the exemplary site for hegemonic struggle – what Hall, echoing Gramsci, termed the 'immediate terrains of struggle'[83] – it is because it constitutes the terrain on which political action inescapably happens. It is the political terrain par excellence precisely because it embodies the effects of 'incurable structural contradictions'. It is, therefore – Gramsci concludes – 'upon this terrain that the forces of opposition organise'[84] in order to create a 'new reality [by shifting] the previously existing disposition of social forces'.[85]

When reflecting on his work with Janam, in one of his final interviews, Hashmi explained the essentially political pre-*disposition* of the street theatre, which exists within the nexus of living social forces with the aim of 'shifting' them: 'we responded with theatre', he said, 'to a real need.'[86] What is this 'real need' and what is this 'response' if it is not the simultaneous expression of a democratic demand stemming from the lifeworld and the recognition of its legitimacy with the approval given to it by the street theatre. What this democratic demand contains is both an instruction and an imperative to act by amplifying it according to the means made available by the street theatre. It is precisely because its entire existence is beholden to the democratic demand that the activist theatre of the conjuncture is, of all political theatres, 'political' in this directly democratic sense. Yet because it is conjunctural, it is also fundamentally 'occasional'. It is a theatre whose militant orientation is designed entirely to serve the occasion that expresses the singular and pressing needs of the present.

4

The 'closure' of the political theatre (and the critique of postdramatic reason)

Let us return to the vexed discourse on the 'closure' of the political theatre in Europe, which has dogged debates over recent decades. Having traced out a genealogy of the political theatre, albeit indicatively (there are innumerable gaps, elisions, and missing links ...), and having examined the conceptual and practical implications of its various shifts and turns, its displacements and transpositions, it is now time to locate the point at which the taxonomy of the political theatre is, as it were, fully decomposed or better still deconstructed. Of course, I am not suggesting such a point is reducible to a 'punctum' in time. As I have previously noted, the sense of the political theatre's closure derives from an extended historical process and is woven into a tapestry of multiple factors that take on the condition of determining constraints. Geographically it can be demarcated in terms of what have principally been European or Western theatre practices – although not exclusively so.[1] Nonetheless, the idea of a 'postdramatic crisis' of the political theatre emerges in relation to a largely Western discourse on the 'closure of the political' as such. At the same time, the concept of a theatre of political closure nonetheless asserts a degree of universal applicability (or so it sometimes seems when reading its principal proponents). It is a claim that finds its most explicit theoretical articulation in Hans-Thies Lehmann's highly influential treatise, published in 1999, on 'postdramatic theatre'. To understand what is at stake in the idea of theatre's political closure, and the extent to which that idea produces something of a theoretical impasse, means that a 'critique of postdramatic reason' is imperative. One of the difficulties in formulating such a critique, however, lies in the slippery nature of the very concept of the *post*dramatic, as indicated by the prefix 'post'. Postdramatic theatre defines itself ambiguously against what it is *not*, rather than in relation to what it *is*. Lehmann himself is at pains to show that a theatre that is 'post' drama is by no means to be confused with the sweeping negation of the dramatic stage. ' "After" drama', he writes, 'means that it lives on as a structure – however weakened and exhausted – of the "normal" theatre: as an expectation of large parts of its audience, as a foundation for many of its means of representation, as a quasi automatically working norm of its drama-turgy'.[2] The postdramatic maintains the memory of the dramatic theatre within its formulation, without which it could not furnish the meaning of a new mode of theatre that is still in the process of being adumbrated. Equally, when striving to assert or discover that identity, whose forms – unlike that of the dramatic theatre – are multiple and dispersed, appearing across a dizzying number of practices and genres (theatre, performance, and live arts), care must be taken not to reduce the postdramatic to mere polemicism. To make sense of the postdramatic is to make sense of it as a 'logic'. Since the post-dramatic logics that operate within the 'new theatre' are not polemical, they cannot be thought in the avant-gardist sense of constituting a 'break' with tradition.[3] It is why the theoretical analysis of postdramatic theatre moves away from avant-gardism to embrace post-structuralism: it represents, not a break with tradition, but a closure of the effects of representation.

But how, if it is not conceived as a rupture or a clean break with the past, is the idea of 'closure' to be understood?

An obvious point of reference, and a place to begin to answer this question, is found in Derrida's critique of Artaud's theatre of cruelty. The theatre of cruelty was envisaged by Artaud as a mode of theatre according to a discourse that constituted itself – or so claims Derrida – as the 'closure of representation'. It is the closure of representation that constitutes the precondition for the birth of this new theatre, which is 'outside' of representation and so, Derrida notes, is 'life itself, in the extent to which life [is] unrepresentable'.[4] What it presupposed was two things. First, it presupposed the possibility of escaping or evading representation by seizing on forms of immediacy (or what Helmut Plessner once termed the 'unfathom-ability of life'[5]) that could not be repeated in an 'iterative' structure, that is, captured within 'language'; and second, it presupposed that the domain of life could therefore only be conceived authentically as existence outside of discourse. However, what the closure of representation also indicated, Derrida argued, was a double limit located within the very form of representation, and which consists of the invariant feature of the sign insofar as it is constantly caught up in the temporal play or slippage of its two terms, those of the signifier and the signified. The possibility of representation is thus also bound by the impossibility of finding an 'outside' to representation. It is within the structure of the sign that a certain impasse of representation is discovered in the form of the impossibility of evading the iterability of the present. Derrida located this impasse of representation at the heart of the very theatre that announces its closure.

The theatre of cruelty is a theatre that seeks to affirm life by binding itself to the living moment – to reject the mimetic basis of theatre that reduces the-atre to a kind of 'sensory illustration' of a text already written and of a life already lived.[6] What it seeks, explicitly, is a theatre emancipated from the tyranny of the text. This meant, further: the emancipation of speech from character; of *opsis* from its classical subservience to dramatic action; of gesture and the body from choreographic order; of mise-en-scene from the law of scenic inscription; of the co-presence of the spectator and actor from the artificial separation of worlds – 'real' and 'fictive' – by the proscenium stage. By substituting theatre for a space of 'festival', the closure of representation discovers a theatre of life. It produces – in Derrida's terms – a 'stage whose clamor has not yet been pacified into words'.[7] The impasse that Derrida identifies within the theatre of cruelty, however, reveals that Artaud's dream of a theatre beyond representation cannot but be completely overwhelmed by failure at the exact moment it appears to succeed. The closure of representation turns out to be an enclosure of (life by) representation. It rests on the phantasm of an elusive presence that can nonetheless be seized upon, on the idea of the good infinity of the absolute present in contrast to the bad infinity of representation and its dispersal in time, in short, it rests on a desire for pure being. It also rests, for Derrida, on a 'dialectic' that the theatre of cruelty could not ultimately evade: 'the movement through which expenditure is reappropriated into presence'.[8] The claim that the moment of performance can be valorised as the moment of life teetering on the brink of its extirpation, and thus of an unrepeatable present, is itself beholden to an 'economy of repetition' – that is to say, to representation.[9] For something to be, it must be subject to an iterative structure – it must be temporally 'dispersed' – which dispels the possibility for the accomplishment of full self-presence, or of the inscription of being in the fullness of the present. The claim that performance is bound to death, i.e., to a unique present, to the expenditure of the moment in which its existence is somehow 'unmarked' by representation, and through which it slips the knots and binds of meaning, leaving behind no trace of itself – at least none that can be adequately grasped within language – is itself based on a misunderstanding of performance, which is inescapably menaced by repetition. What the impasse of the theatre of cruelty discovers thereby holds a twofold significance: first, that theatre is the exemplary site of the 'irrepressible movement of repetition';[10] and second, that within the very space of its closure, 'representation continues'.[11]

In what sense, though, should the closure of representation be understood as being operative within the logics of the postdramatic theatre?

A clue to answering this question lies in Lehmann's claim that the postdramatic theatre, like Artaud's 'energetic' theatre, 'would be a theatre beyond representation – meaning, of course, not simply without representation, but not governed by its logic'.[12] There are two counterparts to this anti-representational logic. It refers both to a metaphysical thesis concerning a time that is not bound or contained by representation *and* to a kind of 'immanent critique' of actual existing representational or 'mimetic' forms (gesturing towards Adorno). However, it is by placing the emphasis on the latter rather than the former that the idea of the closure of representation produces an understanding of the 'politics' that constitutes postdramatic theory's founding gesture. It is, as per this 'logic', a politics that leads nevertheless to a paradoxical outcome. It is not sufficient that the revolution in theatre practices must bring about the long-called-for closure of representation; it must, as a consequence, confront the political theatre for its complicity, knowing or otherwise, in systems of representation, and its collusion with the deceptions of *mimesis*. It must show that the political theatre is not so very different, after all, from the ideological theatre it claims to oppose – and that even the 'critical theatre' of Brecht, since it relied on the alienated 'distance' of the spectator, is compromised by the form of representation it installed at the heart of the critical gesture. It is why to fully embrace the closure of representation, which is the essential feature of what might be termed the 'postdramatic epochē' (the 'bracketing out' of the effects of mimetic substitution in the conventional dramatic theatre), the corresponding entailment follows as surely as a receding tide must in due course return to the shore: the closure of representation brings about the closure of the political theatre. This is not to say that postdramatic theorists are ignorant of the paradox of this 'politics of representation'; nor are they ignorant of its perils – accusations of a formalist turn and of a tendency toward pure self-referentiality fall wide of the mark.[13] What this logic leads them to is not the abandonment of politics but its attempted reinscription within the space of a theatre that has relinquished 'discursive, conceptual meaning *in toto*' – a political theatre without the presence of political themes or content.[14] Lehmann writes, as an example:

> [it] remains essential to acknowledge that the truly political dimension of theatre has its place not so much in the thematising of politically burning subject matters … as in the situation, the relation, the social moment which theatre is able to constitute.[15]

The gesture is essentially the same as Artaud's, while discarding the theatre of cruelty's political agnosticism. Postdramatic theatre rejects politics within theatre for being representational at the same time as it incorporates the 'political' by dispensing with representation's discursive logics. It is able to do this because, in liberating theatre from the representational stage, it discovers a theatre of 'situation'. As with the theatre of cruelty, the theatre of situation is the theatre emancipated from the law of mimesis; it is theatre as archi-theatre, or what Derrida termed, in relation to Artaud, the theatre in its 'multidimensional milieu' in which the 'closure of classical representation [becomes] the reconstitution of a closed space of original representation, the archi-manifestation of force or of life'.[16] This archi-theatre is only realised, however, at the point where the conventions of the dramatic theatre are suspended, including not only the thematic of the play – its narratological or allegorical meaning, but also the 'referential' meaning that makes it a 'mirror' or reflection of the 'world': 'what is enacted and said on stage refers to – and *defers* to – social and political realities outside the theatre.'[17] Contained within the idea of reference – the dirty secret of every representational theatre – is then an unspoken 'deferential' logic. It is this logic that the postdramatic epochē is designed to disrupt or 'suspend', and by doing so, establish a new relation between theatre and the political.

To 'defer' to something is to indicate a relation of subordination, of a lesser to a higher authority, and it is in this sense that the 'moral' of the ideological theatre or the 'message' of the political theatre are revealed as two sides of the same representational coin. In both cases, theatre acquiesces to the logic of representation; while representation, according to its logic, is deployed – just as Adorno had once observed – to make reality, not questionable, but 'comprehensible'. Representation establishes theatre's spectator in a cognitive relation to the world, while constituting the world as an interpretable 'object' that can be mastered through theatrical representations. Representation deprives reality of its ambiguity so that what once appeared opaque, even mysterious, is dissolved into something seemingly transparent: the representation itself. This presents the political and critical theatre with a peculiar problem: one cannot critique what one must simultaneously ratify; its modes of reproving reality contain tacit concessions to it. Even as it changes the representational 'content', it leaves intact the structure of discursive domination: the transformation of the world into representational knowledge. To refer/defer contains an accusation of egregiousness that is levelled against the political theatre precisely because it is compelled to realise itself in the milieu that Max Weber once described as world 'disenchantment'.[18] Since representational forms must invariably yield to the reality they represent, they can scarcely be expected to transgress its boundaries or norms; in fact, they cannot do so because those boundaries and norms are established, maintained, and communicated by representational means. To break with them would require breaking with the logic of representation as such – a performative contradiction. Even the critical theatre must consequently hold the world – the rational representational/ communicative system – in too much esteem. But it is also, and precisely because it is representational, an ineffectual means for transforming the world. Even on its own terms the political theatre offers too little, too late; the theatre of representation is in essence a 'dilatory theatre' that misses out on the opportune moment. The deferential, in this sense, also signifies representation's lateness.

There is a further reason why the political theatre, in all its forms, has reached a point of historical closure for Lehmann. To understand contemporary reality is to understand that today power can no longer be personified. Politics becomes problematic for the dramatic stage because 'social power', and its modes of distribution, has been reconfigured to the point of making its representation impossible.[19] Power, grasped by Lehmann in quasi-Foucauldian terms, no longer takes a juridical form; it appears as a 'microphysics, as a web'[20] in which economic and political processes have become detached from those who claim to command them. Structures of power are increasingly impersonal – one might say bound by machinic processes – with the consequence that the system of relations through which power is administered or distributed is made autonomous. Even 'political elites', Lehmann writes, have 'no real power'.[21] On this basis, he concludes: 'political conflicts increasingly elude intuitive perception and cognition and consequently scenic representation.'[22] Politics is displaced to a kind of noumenal rather than phenomenal realm. It can be intuited only indirectly, as a symptomology of fanaticisms and other pathological effects: '*non*-political terror, anarchy, madness, despair, laughter, revolt, antisocial behaviour' – each symptom is the expression of the '*momentary* suspension of normative, legal and political modes of behaviour'.[23] Because political behaviours no longer respond to norms, and since its juridical and rational basis has been exceeded, it becomes impossible to present politics on stage in the form of a dramatic conflict or as the struggle between individual wills. Since the political theatre, in both its classical and critical conceptions, rests on a mimetic logic of representation that is founded on the idea that politics plays out in an arena of staged conflicts, disputes, and – eventually – their public resolution, its capacity to comprehend contemporary political reality is not just limited but leads to its mystification.

One factor that Lehmann cites to account for this transformation in the way politics is experienced is the development of the mediatic state, where there can no longer be any possibility for establishing an organic connection between the forms of mimetic representation and the modes of power that circulate within the global networks that link contemporary informatics-based societies. It is why postdramatic theatre, in Brandon Woolf's words, can only ' "obliquely" [engage] the political *real*ities of our "mediatised and globalised" world' and must do so 'by refusing to "represent" a *real*ity which is no longer *real*ly representable as drama'.[24] It is this mediatic usurpation of politics – its Debordian spectacularisation, on the one hand, and on the other – the growth of a kind of techno-totalitarianism, with all the nihilistic excesses induced by contemporary modes of communication, that confirms the closure of the political theatre for Lehmann. And it is in light of this political catastrophe that postdramatic theatre is tasked with rethinking theatre's relation to the political:

> If we do not want to write off the political dimension of theatre altogether, we have to start with the diagnosis that the question of a political theatre changes radically under the conditions of contemporary information society. That politically oppressed people are shown on stage does not make theatre political. And if the political in its sensational aspects merely procures entertainment value, then theatre may well be political – but only in the bad sense of an (at least unconscious) affirmation of existing political conditions.[25]

To forestall the possibility of a 'bad' politics of representation, the postdramatic theatre proposes another: 'there is only one thing theatre can do: artistically deconstruct the space of political discourse as such.'[26] What does it mean to deconstruct the discursive space of the political? It means repealing its 'authoritarian construction'[27] – but not on the basis of the approach of the old 'critical theatre' of Brecht, since politics in theatre only works, as Lehmann asserts, *'modo obliquo'*.[28] It is precisely for this reason that postdramatic logic in all its obliqueness comes to exemplify the idea of a critical theatre of the politics of the theatre: 'It is not through the direct thematisation of the political that theatre becomes political but through the implicit substance and critical value of its *mode of representation*.'[29]

That logic also imposes a series of proscriptions to ensure there can be no return to a theatre that is, as it were, 'modo recta': do not thematise; do not produce messages; do not seek to influence anyone through direct appeals to the audience; do not proselytise or seek to teach them; disrupt every attempted communication; beware the power of spectacle; think twice about its affirmations; do not desire the subject or seek their interpellation, since in converting them one must bring them under the law of representation – how, one might ask, given these commandments, is postdramatic theatre's critical engagement with theatre's 'mode of representation' to lay claim, even if obliquely, to the political? The answer Lehmann gives reveals just how close the postdramatic theatre remains to the position of the avant-garde, even if that proximity is expressed surreptitiously. The solution is to be discovered in theatre's irregular matriculation into the space of the aesthetic exception. Lehmann writes: 'there is an insurmountable rift between the political, which sets the rules, and art, which constitutes, we might say, always an *exception*: the exception to every rule, the affirmation of the irregular even within the rule itself.'[30] Now the aesthetic exception installs art in a realm of autonomy, which preserves it from the instrumentality of the world of work and of politics. It suspends the world of practical engagements and pragmatic effects. Occupying the space of the aesthetic exception, a work of art derives its status as 'art', but it does so at the cost of losing its power to affect the social.[31] The avant-gardist gesture, which Lehmann embraces, so as to claim the political dimension of the postdramatic theatre, rests on the idea that the limit of art, established by the aesthetic exception, separating it from social reality, can be 'transgressed'. In other words, the space established by the aesthetic exception must be traversed, its effects disrupted by the act of 'crossing' the line that demarcates the frontier of art. Without a formal relation between rule and exception, of course, no transgression would be possible, and it is why Lehmann insists that the 'transgressive moment is … essential for all art, not just political art'.[32] Elsewhere he writes: '[Theatre] takes place where the limit of what we imagine as being theatre is reached and crossed. Art cannot be art if it is just art.'[33] This does not license, however, a return to a socially activist praxis in which theatre abandons art to become 'engagée'. On the contrary, in an age where political reality evades representation, the only means left to theatrical practices by which theatre might disturb that reality, are to be found in the one remaining power that belongs to it as art: the power to transgress the law that is immanent to it – and in the case of theatre, this can only be the law of *mimesis*.

To transgress in this instance means to breach the boundary established by the aesthetic exception, but to do so indirectly – 'modo obliquo'. For postdramatic theatre, to make that breach requires that it adopt a critical stance toward reality while refraining from offering a 'critique' of reality, which would collapse it back into a representational mode. The alternative transgressive path to critique lies in exposing theatre to the 'real' that is secreted within the theatre situation itself. To understand what this complex manoeuvre entails is by no means straightforward. The first step requires a logical substitution: the 'performative' is substituted for what Lehmann calls the 'afformative', which is a logic that is diametrically opposed to that of politics and its representation. The reason for making this substitution is buried here, as are its consequences:

> As long as we view the political about theatre as a counterforce that is political – as a counter-position and – action and not as a non-action and interruption of the law – we are putting the wrong kind of game on the agenda.[34]

What this says is that theatre cannot be political in the sense that the political is positional. To occupy a 'position' on the terrain of politics, is not just to enter it as an actor but to enter the political as a field of representation, in which different and opposing subject positions become available to individual actors. Not only is theatre unable to do this, but it has never been able to do so, according to Lehmann; to think otherwise is simply to perpetuate the same old misconception that confounded the political theatre in the first place. Theatre's mode of performance is not in truth performance, it is only 'pretending to perform'.[35] The common misconception to the contrary testifies to the peculiarity of theatre as a form of art. Although it inhabits the space of the aesthetic exception, it also claims to 'mirror' reality in highly misleading and disingenuous ways. After all, the very term 'actor' contains an equivocation that makes it all too easy to confuse the levels of reality and representation. There are indeed 'real political actors', Lehmann writes, who though they may not fully know what they are doing, are nonetheless able to know that 'what they are doing at least *is* a doing' – but he adds: 'Not so the theatre.'[36] Theatre is all pretence, all illusion, all charade in which non-action passes itself off as real speech and actual deed; and that is why the postdramatic theatre, which rejects the equivocation at the heart of dramatic modes of representation, does not claim to be performative but 'afformative': the afformative indicates the 'non-performative in the proximity of performance'.[37] It is in embracing the attitude of non-action and by inserting non-performance into the sphere of actuality – rather than simply 'representing' and 'repeating' it as conventional theatre does – that postdramatic logics enact, not just the closure of representation, but the gestures through which the 'performative' is conspicuously interrupted. However, this does not explain why the afformative (rather than affirmative) gesture should be taken as a specifically political interruption.

To understand how it becomes political, at least in Lehmann's terms, requires understanding how postdramatic theatre reconceptualises politics. Theatre's 'political engagement', he writes, 'does not consist in the topics but in the forms of perception.'[38] What he means by this can be summarised thus: if the postdramatic theatre's politics cannot be located at the level of a referent, nor in a system of signification, it is because theatre's politics are not 'discursive' – they are to be found in the disruption of the very logics of discursivity (the field of representation). Thus, Lehmann writes that the 'politics of theatre … is to be sought in the manner of its *sign usage*. The politics of the theatre is a *politics of perception.*' This somewhat elliptical move is qualified by a further remark: 'we have to remember that the mode of perception in theatre cannot be separated from the existence of theatre in a world of media which massively shapes all perception.'[39] Here, it seems, two 'mimetic' systems are made to coincide – the *mimetic* understood as a theatrical system of representation, and the *mimetic* understood as a system of mass communications. From this, two problems ensue. The first refers back to the problem of representation under the 'mediatic regime' of the image; the second, to the kind of intervention that theatre can make through its own politics of perception insofar as it is able to disrupt that regime – indicating the nature of the 'political' encounter that is realised in postdramatic theatre's 'theatre of situation'.

Because of the intricate web Lehmann spins here, I will take each point in turn.

(1) Following Samuel Weber, Lehmann develops the notion that the effects of mediatic forms of communication have resulted in a fatal separation of the 'real' event from its perception. This becomes increasingly noticeable in terms of mediatic modes of reception, particularly in relation to the twenty-four-hour news cycle. What this produces is 'an erosion of the act of communication'.[40] The argument is a familiar one, recalling Walter Benjamin's thesis that the development of modern communications saw experience depreciate in value[41] (resulting in the impoverishment of 'communicable experience').[42] Lehmann's emphasis is placed on the negative effects that this impoverishment has on the community of media experiencers: 'The consciousness of being connected to others and thus being answerable and bound to them ... in the medium of communication itself recedes in favour of communication.'[43] No longer can one speak of an ethical communion through communicative acts, since communications – reduced to the circulation of information – has become the very medium of our alienation from one another and from the world. What it alienates, specifically, is the relation between the subject of perception and the subject of the event: although catastrophe upon catastrophe piles up before the bewitched eyes of the consumer of mediated news, they can no longer bear witness to what has been experienced or lived; its reception is conditioned instead by the way mediated images place the viewer at a 'radical distance' from the represented event, reducing them to a mere 'onlooker'.[44] Worse still: reception induces indifference in the consumer since the consumer of news images is no longer 'answerable' for what is conveyed to them: 'Produced far from its reception and received far from its origin, [[mediatic communication] imprints indifference onto everything shown.'[45] It is at this point that one can begin to understand why Lehmann insists that the political 'function' of the postdramatic theatre lies in its practice of 'suspending' or 'interrupting' the law of the signifier – its 'designating function'.[46] To disrupt the order of signification becomes political in the sense that postdramatic theatre disorders the signifier as an ordering principle of communicative reason as such. It 'does not create orders of power', Lehmann writes, 'but introduces chaos and novelty into the ordered, ordering perception'.[47] To transgress the signifier is to interrupt its ability to designate a signified; it is to detach language from the twin production of sense and reference through which the world and its events are syntactically and grammatically ordered. Because the political effect of this transgression cannot itself be presentable in the form of another 'truer' representation, it can only be revealed in making visible those 'ideological structures in our everyday way of seeing the world'.[48] This is where the postdramatic theatre demonstrates an

affinity with Brecht's critical theatre, and – as Lehmann notes – Althusser's reading of it, which is its claim to disturb or challenge a certain 'mindset', or what Althusser termed, a certain 'melodramatic consciousness'.[49] In this sense, the postdramatic theatre shares with the critical theatre the exact same object of analysis: the ideological mechanism through which reality is constructed *as* representation ('Ideology is essentially misunderstanding. In this respect theatre must necessarily find ways to confront this habit of perception').[50] Where it departs from Brecht's critical theatre, is that it does not claim to counter the melodramatic (or mediatic) consciousness with another consciousness that has been led to a critical understanding of what it has been shown, or to another order of reality that can also be somehow represented. Postdramatic logics are post-Brechtian to the precise extent that they reject Brecht's 'answer of presenting the political problem in epic distance to an audience'.[51]

(2) What the politics of perception develops in place of the *mimetic* is an 'aesthetics of response-ability'. The postdramatic solution to the problem is, in this sense, literally 'self' referential. Its politics are not to be found at the level of what is communicated but insofar as it makes manifest the 'real' moment contained in the communicative act as such, as that which is fundamentally emancipated from all subordination to representational logics and which appears only with the disruption of the ideological mechanism of reception – namely, the pure auto-affectivity of the spectator as 'response-ability'. It seeks to break with the ideological dimension of atrophied experience, so as to produce another experience – one that reverses the reification contained in mediated communications – or what Lehmann describes as the 'mutual' implicatedness of both actors and audience in the 'theatrical production of images'.[52] What it generates, or stages, is an 'ethico-political' experience for the audience and the actors. This experience is no simulacrum, Lehmann asserts, and so by definition is an experience of the 'real'. It is this experience that defines and distinguishes the 'theatre of situation' from the theatre of representation. What assures Lehmann that this is an authentic encounter rather than another piece of theatrical phantasmagoria, and how it can be interpreted as an experience of the postdramatic, can be illustrated through the firsthand account he gives of his own response to a performance by Egyptian artist, Laila Soliman, *No Time for Art*. The performance documents, and attests to, those killed in Cairo during the protests against Mubarak's government in January of 2011, as well as condemning those responsible for the brutal level of violence used by the police against anti-government protestors. The work comprised two moments: first, each member of the audience received an envelope addressed to the International Court of Human Rights in The Hague, which demanded that those responsible for the violence be brought to justice. The second moment required

each audience member to read aloud 'the name, age, circumstances, and place of death of a martyr' before passing the microphone on to the next person – a routine that continued until every person present at the performance had spoken.[53] This simple act of testifying to the traumatic killing of the protestors, according to Lehmann, produced an 'awareness and engagement' (with a contemporary tragedy), but it was also, he adds, an experience of a 'moment, very strictly, of *theatre*'.[54] It was theatre without the acting out of a dramatic story: a theatre without 'theatre'. But it was also 'without propaganda, or even political statement'.[55] What it was, however, was a theatre that placed a direct *demand* on each member of its audience, as Lehmann concedes: 'I feel the demand which this envelope is addressing to me. And I feel uneasily confronted with my not doing anything about this reality.'[56] It is by means of this demand that the theatre situation is punctured by the 'real'.

What is important therefore is to understand how Lehmann interprets the nature of this demand given the postdramatic logic of the closure of the political in theatre. To begin with, Lehmann situates it in relation to the problem of tragedy, understanding this, not as a genre, but as indicative of a mode of transgression that 'leads us to a recognition of the radical possibilities of the human being to transcend itself and its world and at the same time to choose the path where self-destruction awaits'. This transgression 'constitutes the tragic dimension' of politics.[57] The 'tragic' dimension of postdramatic theatre must, Lehmann insists, be distinguished from tragic drama. The idea that tragedy is essentially a dramatic form installs a false origin in every appearance of tragedy that founds it on representation, reducing it to a mimetic dramaturgical construct. In doing so, the original 'experience' of the tragic is betrayed. It is only in recuperating the tragic in the context of the archi-theatre, only in defying the law of representation, that it becomes possible to rediscover tragic experience anew: 'the articulation of tragic experience … is not bound to dramatic procedure – but to theatre.'[58] How, though, does this recuperation of tragic experience return theatre to an authentic encounter with the political? It is because the gesture of the postdramatic, the very suspension of the representative function of the dramatic theatre, produces the theatre of situation as the transgression of the 'autonomy' of the 'aesthetic sphere'. And only insofar as theatre has been discovered as a situation is it possible to 're-invest the sphere of the real into the aesthetic domain which systematically is defined precisely by the exclusion of the real: Ethico-political responsibility re-enters into the aesthetic experience.'[59] The idea here of ethico-political responsibility suggests that the rupturing of aesthetic experience by that which transgresses art's autonomy belongs properly speaking to the subject who has been exposed to the 'shock' of encountering something inassimilable within the frame of aesthetic experience (as that which is distinguishable from life). It is only with this element of shock, with the intrusion of the real, that 'tragic experience' becomes possible for the subject. It is an experience that is transgressive for a further reason: it is an experience that pushes the subject to encounter the very 'edge of what is culturally acceptable'.[60] In other words, it is transgressive in the conventional sense that transgression must entail the breaking of a social taboo (rather than simply the terms of the aesthetic exception). Although there is no political theatre as such, then, in postdramatic theatre what is discovered is an ethico-political dimension of the subject, which occurs with the confrontation of the spectator and the real: a confrontation that constitutes the theatrical situation as a situation in which the conventional 'aesthetic contemplative mode' of spectating is fundamentally unsettled in the form of an authentic encounter with that which is radically exterior to representation. The postdramatic does not define itself as political precisely because it is not a theatre of agency. But it is a theatre that is 'ethico-political' in the sense that it induces in its viewer a 'concrete questioning of the self'.[61] It is at this point, however, that a troublesome question begins to appear: Why should this experience of the tragic, this responsibility for bearing the weight of the production of images, and the revelation of the 'response-ability' of the spectator, be seen in a specifically *political* sense?

One can understand full well how the theatre experience as described by Lehmann, which places the subject at the 'centre' of the theatre situation, but also as being existentially 'in question', can be described in relation to the ethical. But is that enough to pronounce the experience ethico-*political*? Does it provide a sufficient understanding of how the theatre of situation opens the spectator up to a sense of their own political being? The question that niggles here is this: How is theatre able to present a 'political experience' without any recourse to political representation? Remember, the issue is not only the exclusion of a particular form of representation from postdramatic theatre, specifically 'dramatic' form, but also of representational logics, whose nucleus is that it is the bearer of a 'content' or 'referent'. The answer, according to Lehmann, is that postdramatic theatre draws the spectator out of the transcendence of representation (the desire for fictive dramatic worlds and for 'meaning') and into the immanence of the theatre situation itself in which something 'real' happens and for which the spectator, along with the performer, shares equal 'responsibility'.[62] The theatrical experience, viewed outside of representation, in short, is the experience of the archi-theatre: it is that of an 'encounter' – the auto-affection of the co-presence established between performer and spectator, where a consciousness of one's mutuality entwines with a sense of the evanescence and friability of the performance event, constituting the essential truth of theatre's communal entelechy. It is precisely why, for that encounter to be described as ethico-political, it must be experienceable not simply as an abstract co-presence but through the 'reality' of an actual *demand*. For Lehmann, it is the demand that invokes my 'response-ability' – but ability to respond to what specifically and how? There is only one way to answer this question and that is to establish the limits of the demand that is placed on the spectator; only on this basis can postdramatic experience be adequately understood in ethico-political terms. The extent to which an experience can be designated ethico-political already indicates the extent to which representational content must already tacitly permeate the field of postdramatic experience (even though Lehmann wants to maintain it is not its determining logic). If it is an 'experience' then it must be an experience *of* something. Experience must be accounted for via the specificity of that which, as phenomenology tirelessly demonstrated, must be seen in terms of the 'aboutness' of the experience. After all, every audience encounter is an encounter between people in a determinate space, according to which it can be characterised *as* an encounter somewhere and with someone; every experience is an experience *of* something that can be stated or described *as* a singular situation, defined by its own unique set of structuring conditions. Each level of description provides not only the set of determinations that makes the situation what it is; it situates the experience of a demand within a determinate context penetrated by other mediations (i.e., representations). Lehmann's case for the ethico-political status of the postdramatic theatre rests, in other words, upon its capacity to function 'representationally'; despite his own definition of a post-representational theatre, representation re-enters surreptitiously by the back door.

Also, consider what the structure of the demand itself mediates. Insofar as it is 'ethico-political', the demand that the postdramatic theatre stages must be grasped as having a twofold structure. It is 'ethico-political'. What this denotes are two types of demands falling under the sign of a double designation. There are ethical demands and there are political demands; or, if preferred – there are demands that can be read as both ethical *and* political. Although these are made to converge in the compound form 'ethico-political', they must also be distinguishable, at least in principle, insofar as they each answer to distinct criteria. The issue for the postdramatic theatre, and the central consideration here, is specifically that of the political aspect of the demand, given the post-dramatic theatre's exclusion of the criteria of politics – that is to say, of its refusal to be determined by political categories insofar as to do so would return theatre to a representational form.

Several observations might be made at this juncture.

First, it is hard to see how a theatre that is deprived not just of a political content or 'message', but also of its ability to construct itself 'positionally', a theatre that refuses to countenance theatre's 'determination by politics', can articulate itself nonetheless *as* political. It is why a post-Brechtian theatre, reconfigured as theatre 'made in a political way', but eschewing political content, will always struggle to reinscribe the 'political' back into the very form that operates under the sign of representation's 'closure'. Just as there is no theatre situation that is not an actual situation, and just as there is no demand without a particular mediation, so there is no experience of the political (an ontological category) without an 'ontic' context in which it is realised as actual politics. This means: every experience of the political is tied to specific political contexts and conflicts in which its particularised demands are seen to be representative. In short, to deprive the theatre of an ability to position itself, is to suspend its relation to the dimension of the conjunctural where politics is articulated and within which the theatre situation acquires its political character because it is 'situated' on a particular terrain of struggle.

This is not to deny that a 'tragic' or 'transgressive' demand, within postdramatic theatre, cannot be understood as ethical. It reveals, however, that in embracing the closure of representation postdramatic theatre, as it is conceptualised by Lehmann, must foreclose its claim on the political or risk misrepresenting it. In its exclusion of the criterion of politics – the articulation of adversative positions within a social terrain – there is simply no means of determining the demand that the postdramatic encounter stages as political. What it risks, however, in attempting to reinscribe the political within the space of theatre's originary 'co-presence', its face-to-faceness, is the collapse of politics into the ethical. The understanding of the ethical as a transgressive form within art must itself be seen vis-à-vis the subject's exposure to that which is radically exterior to the aesthetic sphere, which nonetheless intrudes onto the space of art, where it is experienced as the transgressive moment of the 'tragic', while assuming the form of a demand without political content. The demand that unsettles one's sense of self, which produces response-ability, without hope of locating within oneself an action that is adequate to it (as Lehmann reports in his response to Soliman's performance), which could meet or fulfil it, has more than a passing resemblance to the infinite demand, associated with the philosopher Emmanuel Levinas.[63] Ethical experience arrives as the transgression of the subjective borders of experience. It is the experience of a disturbance that cannot be contained within its boundaries, in which the subject loses sight of itself, precisely before the face of an alterity, whose demand cannot be met, but which is nonetheless felt to be compelling. A political demand, by contrast, addresses itself – not to the other qua 'other' – but to specific sites of representational exclusion and grievance.

The question that arises, however, is on what basis might the postdramatic theatre re-admit a political content without conceding everything to the 'bad' old theatre of the past, or collapsing the political into the ethical? There are several reasons that suggest it can do so provided it is willing to accept a degree of determination (call it determination in the last instance) by representation. To begin with, one might recall Lehmann's own problematisation of the theatre: If it is not to be defined by the 'dramatic', then how is theatre to be distinguished in and for itself? What is it that makes postdramatic theatre 'theatre'? To reprise what was previously established: in dismantling the mimetic stage, postdramatic theatre discovers theatre in the 'archi-form' of the theatre of situation. This 'Ur-theatre' is defined as a site of encounter, of the face-to-face. But why should the encounter per se constitute theatre in its Ur form? Without wishing to stray too far into problems of etymology, theatre is also, of course, a *theatron*. It is always bound up with the problem of that which is shown and of the seeing of the 'show'. It is because of this obvious fact that Lehmann can say, after all, that theatre's politics rest on the problem of perception. This pronouncement does not deliver a decisive verdict on the political theatre however: every perception is an embodied perception constituted within a relational field, which reveals itself in the act of disclosing its other. Even at its most minimal, there is always a perceiver and a perceived, both polarities are enveloped and co-constituted in the concrete space of visibility that the perceptual act must circumscribe. Just as the perceptual act must disclose the relative position of the perceiver to themselves, so theatre is also made visible to itself ... – stands in a reflexive relation to what is made visible through it. In this sense, it is indeed a structure of 'response-ability'. A space of seeing and of being seen; a space also in which something is shown to someone, whether an object, an image, a piece of political oratory, a discourse, an action, a demonstration. The *theatron* is thus not strictly speaking a space of representation; but it is a space in which things – sometimes including 'representations' – are brought forth to be shown. What can be surmised from this is only that the archi-theatre discovers in the idea of the encounter in a situation (performance's 'face-to-faceness'), and in the opening of a space of speaking and hearing and seeing and showing (*theatron*), the *necessary* conditions of any theatre whatever. All the same, there is no reason to assume that such a definition of theatre implies a relation to the political as such. For such a possibility, something further is required – the very thing, in fact, that Lehmann appears to prohibit when he proclaims:

> For a politics of perception in the theatre, it is not the thesis (or antithesis) that counts, not the political statement or engagement (both of which belong in the

domain of real politics not represented politics), but rather a basic disrespect for tenability of positive affirmation.[64]

What this assertion appears to deny is that a 'politics of perception' requires a specifiable political 'content'. This prohibition bars explicit political statements but also politically motivated modes of engaging issues that trouble the 'real' world. The theatre of perception is political, not because it says anything that can be construed in political terms, then, but solely in virtue of the attitude it internalises. It is political because of the way it *sees* its object according to an *intentional stance* that is motivated by a 'basic disrespect' for (uncritical) 'affirmations', i.e., representations of the world. Still, it is hard to see how such a basic stance can escape the suspicion that it covertly reintroduces a political content through the very form of its negations. For there to be a negation, after all, there must also be a 'negated' object. And it is only in relation to such a negated content, i.e., the 'object' of the negating act, that any 'situation' – theatrical or otherwise – can be defined *as* political. What is discovered in this unremarkable 'as' is not a generalisable impulse but rather the *sufficient conditions* that enable the attitudinal act to be characterised as a political attitude. It is an attitude through which one experiences the concretion of social antagonism, which insofar as it enters the theatre transforms it into a 'real' situation. It can only claim to do so, however, when the spectator experiences that antagonism as an immediate 'affect' in relation to *what* they are shown, and that implicates them as part of the situation. Consider, in this regard, how the negating attitude of 'disrespect', which for Lehmann attaches to an abstract generality (the 'tenability of positive affirmation'), can be seen to converge with postdramatic theatre's tragic sense of transgression, as discussed earlier. To disrespect something that has been socially affirmed is to understand transgression in a specifically political sense – so while there can be all manner of possible transgressions, what interests the postdramatic theatre must be politically salient transgressions – the transgression of 'socially' inscribed norms in which the social totality is somehow incriminated through the act of its being transgressed.

A theatre that breaks society's taboos (rather than affirms its norms – the norms of 'affirmative culture'[65]) is a theatre that inevitably confronts its audience with a situation that compels it to renegotiate the relationship of spectator to spectacle. This is because the spectator–spectacle relation is made 'unstable' as soon as the 'theatrical content' can no longer be fixed by the discursive hierarchies established by the norms of representation. Those norms cannot be thought independently of their regulatory function within the wider social formation – their function in terms of articulating the social topography through which the order of the symbolic is instituted – i.e., the 'law' that regulates the general economy of representation, as well as their constitutive role in the identity-formation of the subject, particularly through forms of imaginary acts of identification – i.e., the ideological inscription of the subject into the symbolic order ('the imaginary relationship of individuals to their real conditions of existence').[66] It should be clear that transgression is always a relational form that breaches, or at least disturbs, the binary space established by both norms and taboos (whether understood as a socially codified set of expectations that limit individual behaviours or as arising from customary practices). In this sense, when theatre breaks a taboo or disrespects a norm it has already 'abolished' the 'aesthetic distance between stage and auditorium'[67] – or to put it otherwise, it has transgressed the border that separates art from social practices as established by the terms of the aesthetic exception. It breaches the exception by means of a 'transgressive relationality'. It is this transgressive movement that transforms the theatre from a site of contemplative (autonomous) spectating into that of a 'situation' where one does not simply interpret reality, and where one's sense of reality is set upon – is directly assailed and provoked.

What the postdramatic theatre produces, then, is not a critical theatre in the old 'hermeneutic' sense. It is not a theatre of 'readings' in which one can 'interpret' reality but a theatre that elicits affective responses to the theatre situation that have specifiable political analogues. But it remains an open question how it can generate such affective responses in an audience by breaking with the norms that it embodies and that constitutes it as an 'abstract community' (cohering around a set of imagined attitudes, beliefs, and values), without also believing it is possible to transgress the limit that preserves theatre from politics.[68] Lehmann's distinction between 'real' and 'represented' politics appears to be a strained one at best. Where theatre genuinely transgresses, it has already incited a political response, and it does so because it has trespassed onto the domain of the real of the political that lies beneath hegemonic representations: the real of social antagonism, in other words, that culture constantly seeks to dispel through its 'affirmations'. If it could not claim to do this, it could hardly be considered transgressive, let alone 'situational'. By the same token, one cannot break a taboo without invoking the particular context to which that taboo applies, which has its basis in existing social and lifeworld practices. The alignment of norm and taboo and the acts that transgress them is always determined by their cultural location. Both norms and taboos are tied to the political because they are used to place limits on what is tolerable in respect of what can be seen, said, or done (whether in the domain of 'real life' or within the space of representation). This is not to deny that there are forms of representation in which the breaking of a taboo is socially acceptable – the representation of incest, for instance, is accepted if the aesthetic exception effectively preserves the difference between the domains of life and art thereby protecting both from each other (as in stagings of *Oedipus Rex*). But where a representation strains at the limits of what is socially accepted, one always finds, invariably, that an illicit traversal of the space of the aesthetic exception has occurred, and this is what is meant by the term 'transgressive' in the context of art. There is no transgression that does not, consequently, in one way or another, imply a volatile and antagonistic relation to a political content (or content that can be politicised). The very form of a transgressive act mediates a socially inscribed content. It incorporates the norm it breaches or tests to destruction within itself. This by no means entails a return of the theatre to the most conventional form of *mimesis* – 'drama' (although nor does it necessarily preclude such a possibility). It is to say that there can be no 'inscribing' of the political into the situation of the theatre without recourse to a representational content. It is the 'content' of representation – to the extent that it condenses the law of the discursive and semantic field within it – that makes it the bearer of a political 'charge'. Finally, insofar as such a content must be concretely specifiable, it should be thought – in the last instance – in relation to the specificity of the conjunctural moment in which its political charge is able to be discharged. Equally, it shows that for any theatre to be designated 'political', it is always a determinate political content that provides it with its *sufficient conditions* – and thus the possibility of a political articulation. It might, of course, be objected that this idea of content is far removed from what Lehmann envisages in his refusal of politics understood as an explicit statement of positionality – contained in the 'message' of the play, for example. Clearly that is true. There are two ways of responding to this. The first is to observe that if that is all Lehmann has in mind, then his argument is trivial to the extent that it trivialises the idea of the political (in theatre) by reducing it to the narrowest meaning of the word 'politics'. The second concerns the problem of a positionality that need not take the form of an explicit message for it to be considered nonetheless political. Indeed, positionality is implicit within postdramatic theatre's attitude of negating affirmative culture. Owing to the inescapable positioning that any attitude necessarily compels its bearer to adopt, with respect to the facticity of their 'situation', it can be transcoded into the terms of a political intention. It is why, finally, Soliman's performance is able to be understood in ethico-political terms. It is not just that it invoked the 'response-ability' of the spectator; in doing so it articulated the spectator into a particular moment of conjunctural crisis through the political demand it placed on them – a demand that urged them to *take* responsibility. The 'message' was received, in other words, 'loud and clear' precisely because what had been closed (in the theatre) was once again opened by the appearance there of a political demand.

5

The political theatre 'redefined'

From the foregoing discussion, the decomposition of the taxonomy of the political theatre appears to stem, not only from the incoherence and flaws of the taxonomic idea itself, but from the internally fragmented dream of the possibility of a political theatre as such. As with any 'dream-work', the term 'political theatre' provides a screen upon which a number of unconscious fantasies continue to be projected. Hence all and sundry are free to assert that everything is political when it comes to the theatre. For such a relative perspective, the end of the classical conception of the political theatre, far from being lamented, revealed a cornucopia of possibilities. Those who have adopted this expansive view, however, have forgotten that what seems capacious today would have been dismissed, for good reason, as capricious yesterday. The thought that everything is political is itself an effect of the 'post' political crisis of politics. There are two ways of explaining the idea of a 'post political' conjuncture. The first is that the theatre is now liberated from politics to be political in whatever way corresponds to its fluctuating motivations. To a degree this is an understandable development. Once the political theatre became untenable, the theatre that saw itself in political terms tended to be defined according to a different formulation – that of a 'politics of …' etc. The second appears as the problematic underside of the first claim. It states that politics has been unshackled from the political; the latter has become a 'floating signifier', whose content fluctuates ambiguously according to its usage. It is in relation to the presently parlous state of the political that the preceding pages attempted to prise current contrarian positions (in theatre) free from their footholds in 'post politics'. It has not sought to assert that the political theatre is therefore once again a possibility by blithely pointing out that it exists here and there as an empirical fact; but to show instead that the general taxonomy of the political theatre, from its classical formulation to its eventual dissolution into a 'critical theatre' and beyond, has something important to say concerning the nature of what is possible today and under what vexed conditions the theatre can be said to be political. It shows that this genealogy not only continues to circumscribe but also continues to constrain theatre's political possibilities through both historical (material) factors and conceptual limits that, however contingent they may be, are nonetheless determinative of its meaning.

A genealogy of the political theatre seeks to establish those limits. It maintains that in no way does the political theatre ever emerge *ex nihilo*. Nor is it always 'there', loitering in the wings, waiting for an opportune moment to show what it is capable of doing. In relation to the persistence of the eternal recurrence of the phantom of the political theatre, one must insist instead on its conjunctural character. Thus, first: not only should any political theatre be accounted for in terms of the specificity of its own conjunctural moment, but also, second: the problem of what gets *called* 'the political theatre' should always be seen as indebted historically to a particular conjunctural moment. That problem must be grasped originally in relation to the circumstances and needs that emerged with the Bolshevik present of 1917 (a present that haunts the century that follows). Regarding the first point: the political theatre, as with any mode of political expression, should be understood as 'conjuncturally' conditioned, as something beholden to a determinate situation, as an effect of the conjuncture. It arrives on the scene, materially bound by the contingent circumstances of its context (as seen in the Indian street theatre). The political theatre therefore appears *sui generis*, and it is in those terms that it should be understood. To borrow from its legal denotation, this means: every political theatre installs itself in the 'exception'. But viewed more broadly as a genealogical problematisation: the specificity of the conjuncture of 1917 introduced something novel, something fundamentally unseen before in theatre's long history, insofar as it carried within it the prospect of a radical rupture with that past. It is true that the revolutionary theatre had its antecedents; that it was preceded by the somewhat vague idea of a 'people's theatre'. It is true also that there are a number of instances of theatre in the past that served some political purpose (a notable example would be the theatre of the suffrage movement).[1] The precedent, however, in this case, provided no clear guide as to the reality of what was actualised in 1917 with the attempt to inaugurate a proletarian and revolutionary stage in post-Tsarist Russia. It is not just that the revolutionary theatre expressed itself in opposition to the development of the 'ideological' theatre that emerged in the nineteenth century but that the vanguardist disposition marked the political theatre's arrival as a ruptural force within the field of the aesthetic. This theatre belonged not to theatre's past but to a new phase of history: it proclaimed a fundamental 'break' with all theatre that had gone before. That the radical nature of the historical break turned out to be chimerical only revealed the contradictory meaning of the conjuncture to which the political theatre in its classical 'revolutionary' phase belonged. It showed that the political theatre, however radical it claimed to be, could not escape the fact that it remained tethered to the 'theatre'. Another way to express the same point is to say that the radical historicity of the revolutionary moment could not for long conceal, in its modes of subjectivation, the necessary subordination of the present to (rather than the emancipation from) the 'organic' claims of the past. The new theatre encountered this in the form of a setback that revealed the limited nature of the historical break it claimed to represent – it possessed no repertoire of its own. Platon Kerzhentsev was candid enough to concede this as early as 1918, writing: 'we must admit that the proletarian theatre's repertoire is not yet created.'[2]

The classical period of the political theatre thus turned out to be short-lived. If the term 'classical' can nonetheless be said to convey something of the true character of the 'political theatre', it is because the truth it announced belonged to an epochal struggle in which the fundamental contradiction of history, taking the form of the class struggle, would finally resolve itself according to preordained laws of the historical dialectic. So long as theatre was swept along with the forward march of the proletariat, the political theatre remained possible. Once the class whose interests made the worker the natural bearer of that truth began to fragment, and once, as happened over the subsequent decades, new struggles emerged, supplanting the old social formations with new ones that possessed differentiated identities, and which in turn transformed and multiplied the sites of political contestation, so also the political theatre found itself dispersed according to centrifugal forces it could not master. To exacerbate matters: by the 1950s, what had also become increasingly apparent were the inadequacies of the critical theatre that had by now separated itself from the propagandistic character of the political theatre's earlier vanguard phase. Unable to proceed with the exuberance that motivated the revolutionary spirit that produced theatre at 'year zero', it turned inward to take a critical look at the theatre as it already existed. The problems it incurred as a consequence had to do with the extent to which this self-reflexive theatre nonetheless remained tied proximately to the world from which it distanced itself. This is true as much of the 'unpolitical' Beckett, as it is of the 'committed' Brecht. The problem comes down – in the final analysis – to concerns surrounding the nature of theatricality; it derives from the fact that theatre's exceptionality appears quite unlike that of other artistic practices – it is shot through with an ambiguity that comes from being unable to quite escape the suspicion that it constitutes a mimetic supplement to the real, that it is always – no matter how self-critical – indebted to the old idea that it is the illusory 'mirror of the world'. The limits of the critical theatre were established precisely around this mimetic fault-line, which began to demarcate the uneven transition from a Brechtian to a post-Brechtian theatre, and in which the closure of representation provided the unstable ground for a new articulation of theatre's anti-illusionistic 'politics'. The controversy in which the idea of a political theatre remains mired today owes as much to the incomplete nature of this transition as it does to what the previous chapter described as the 'closure' of the political itself.

For sure, there was a time, characterised by the critical modernity of Brecht, when theatre stood beside itself; it offered itself as a corrective to theatre's long history of misdemeanours, and to that extent convinced itself it had found the solution to the dilemma of theatre's inherent falsity. It presented itself as knowledge of the world and at the same time as knowledge of the extent to which the spontaneous appearance of everyday reality had masked the penetration of life by ideology. If the critical theatre presided over the processes of reality, by dismantling the production of its own representations, it was because it was happy to lay bare its own powers of mediation, which it boldly revealed to the public. It rejected the naïveté and lies of mimetic fabulation in order to expose the truth of representational form, in which the spectator is prepared by ideology for their (unconscious) assimilation into a world of unfreedom. This self-reflexive stance assured it of its critical task. In Brecht theatre became both a space of representation in which 'enjoyment' of the spectacle was encouraged, and a machine that interrupted the very mechanism that produced that enjoyment to the extent that it suspended the profitable expenditure of desire in the ideological theatre's illusory satisfactions. It constituted, thereby, a contradictory representation whose effect served to distance the spectator from the source of their pleasure. Since it could not resolve the contradiction it staged, however, it remained indebted to the problem of representation. Thus, while the political theatre was the first theatre to become fully conscious of the terrible power the stage wielded (that the desire theatre inculcated in the audience, through its representations, also produced monsters), the critical tendency drove it ever further toward the logic of the closure of representation itself. The rigorous nature of that logic would eventually lead theatre to the abandonment of all 'content'. Only on this basis could the 'reality' of the theatre situation be authentically realised. The theatre situation – no longer reliant on the old artifice of the stage – was to be distilled from theatre's own immanent ethical substance instead. Through the ethical it expurgated the mimetic supplement to theatricality, and escaped representation altogether. It is in respect of this ethical rather than critical perspective that the postdramatic stage left Brecht in its wake, and all those held captive by theatre's representative function. Even for Brecht the spectator remained an accomplice of the great crimes that make up theatre's regular stock in trade – the trade in spectacular suffering before which the audience derives the supercilious pleasure of condemning the guilty without any thought of having also implicated themselves. And so (as the previous chapter attempted to show) the critical politics of the theatre was compelled by the logic of immanent critique into attempting the final step that even Brecht's critical theatre had failed to make, to frustrate not just the pleasure of the audience, but their sense of moral impunity. What resulted, however, led to the impasse of the closure of the political theatre itself, in which a critical politics of the theatre denied the possibility of a theatre that could speak directly about 'politics'.

I have proposed in responding to this genealogical narrative, this 'taxonomic' experiment, a different way of approaching the problem of the political theatre. By conceiving its transformations in light of the permutation of the historical contradictions it passively embodied, and in relation to the emergent sources of social antagonism it could hardly evade, or according to the unpredictable effects of the logic of aesthetic displacement internal to its mediations, the political theatre was consequently redefined as a response to the problem of the conjuncture. According to this methodological presupposition, the idea of a theatre of the conjuncture provides a means of defining both the minimal conditions that a political theatre must meet to be described as 'political' and the series of concrete specifications or 'determinations' in relation to which its instances should be analysed. The very formulation of the 'theatre of the conjuncture' can be interpreted in several ways, of course. On the one hand, it is necessary to grasp the theatre as part of a given conjuncture – taking it as a privileged moment constituted against the background of a larger object of analysis: the theatre as a scene of condensation for a chaotic and complex nexus of social, historical, economic, and political forces. This is to account for the necessary contextual aspect of the 'political theatre' insofar as it belongs to a distinct discursive formation (its distinctiveness deriving from what Raymond Williams once termed, 'structures of feeling' – the affective structuration of the present – and Gramsci the 'common sense' which is hegemonic at a given time, although never achieving absolute dominance[3]). The analysis of the theatre of the conjuncture thus imposes its own 'discipline', to adapt a phrase from Stuart Hall, on anyone who seeks to understand it. On the other hand, to account for the political aspect of a piece of politically aware theatre is to ask how it understands itself as *articulating* the conjuncture of which it is a part. In this respect, no political theatre is possible that has not arrived at its own understanding of the conjunctural predicament of its own time. Whatever techniques it makes use of to do so, and regardless of whether its aim is to 'intervene', to 'interrupt', or to 'represent', the key to its analysis, if it is to activate the dimension of the political, necessarily bears on the question posed by Hall of 'how different forces come together, conjuncturally, to create the new terrain on which a different politics must form up'.[4]

The lesson to be drawn here is clear: the possibility of the political theatre comes down to the question of whether or not one believes in the possibility of politics. When all is said and done, there is no possible political theatre that does not attach itself to the idea that a change in the balance of social forces, with a view to the fundamental transformation of the structure of feeling of the age, is a possibility for it.

Immediately in response to this, however, one senses the old incredulity reappearing just as surely as aerophagia produces the need to eruct. What hope does this conjunctural theatre have of effectuating a change in the overall hegemonic disposition of its time through which the balance of social forces is held in check by a preponderant power? Why not let the world sort itself out, and let theatre be theatre? To this one might add a further objection, not one with such quietist leanings, perhaps, although also voiced *sotto voce* – in the cool and calculating intonations of the seasoned sceptic: What resources, in truth, does the theatre have at its disposal to conduct a sufficient enough analysis of its own conjuncture to be politically salient, to make it of any *use* to politics? And finally, there is a question that is suffused with the anxiety of our present age, which will focus the discussion on the most troubling contemporary aspect of the problem. This question, whose weight bears heavily on the dilemma of the 'present conjunctural hour', is where I would like to conclude this book: How, given the global expansion of economic forces, over recent decades, which exceed even the capacity of the most powerful of nation-states to control them – let alone the protests of individuals (who might just as well be whistling in the wind) or those social movements that rise like great transversal waves only to be swallowed up by deeper ocean currents – can one speak of the political theatre (or art for that matter) as a meaningful possibility today?

To the first question, the answer is straightforward enough. It is not a matter of anything so credulous as hope, which is only the flipside of the incredulity and despair that arises from false expectations. It is a matter of articulating the theatre as part of a broader strategic undertaking. If it *is* political, it is because it contributes to a dissident culture whose immediate and individual effects are seldom easily calculated (which is not the same thing as saying it does not possess any). The idea that the world of politics and that of the theatre can be sanguinely oblivious to one another is an inherently fatuous one, as history amply shows.[5] To the second question, I would say, without wishing to seem overly dismissive, it is not important whether the theatre can demonstrate a comprehensive or even theoretical estimation of the conjuncture. The reason for this – not least – is because by its overdetermined nature no comprehensive purview of the conjuncture is available to anyone. Of necessity, one starts from where one is within it – understanding one's grasp to be inevitably partial. Heidegger once observed when discussing the problem of the hermeneutic circle that what matters most is how one enters it (not that it is circular). The same principle applies. On the one hand, the theatre of the conjuncture must let itself be attuned by the antagonistic character of the conjuncture, of which it is already a part – to become aware of the social consequences of its contradictions, and the crisis tendencies that it manifests as the play of antagonisms; on the other hand, it must be prepared to respond to the conjuncture, and in doing so, to risk failure, scorn, censure, and even political repercussions, without which it cannot claim to possess a political character of its own.

The third question, however, which strikes at the heart of the present crisis, poses a more substantive dilemma that cannot be easily evaded. It touches on what Peter Osborne has described as the 'disjunctive conjuncture' of globalisation's remorseless 'present' – a conjuncture, if you will, comprising a 'new kind of totalizing but immanently fractured constellation of temporal relations'.[6] It can be represented but only as a 'conceptual space for which there is no available *social* occupant, insofar as the subject position that unifies the process of globalization (that of a globally mobile capital) is not that of a possible social agent, or subject of action'.[7] If globalisation constitutes an historical process that lacks a subject, then beyond mere 'damage control' – Gayatri Spivak's bleak assessment[8] – what is to be done? I don't believe for one moment anyone today thinks there is an easy answer to this question. All the same, if one is not to abandon the belief that politics is possible, then firm steps along the path that leads out of the morass must be taken. One opening can be found, albeit implicatively, in Osborne's own analysis of the 'conjunctively disjunctive' *structure* of globalisation. Globalisation is a contradictory structure-in-difference whose logic captures alterity by temporalising it in a form Osborne describes as 'contemporaneity', i.e., 'temporally totalized but disjunctive unities'.[9] If it is permissible to extrapolate from this description, I hope without doing it too much of an injustice, this might well be thought as follows: the geopolitically differentiated regions of the globe, though constituted by globalisation as 'co-eval', bear within themselves distinct historical realities. These realities are composed, not only out of unique geographical contexts and cultural trajectories that precede the emergence of 'world history' (the history of capital), but also out of the historical antagonisms, the struggles and resistances, already found striating the development of global capital itself: through past and ongoing suppression of indigeneity, for example, as well as through the experience and legacy of the transatlantic slave trade and later European colonial expansion and settler occupation. How such differences (antagonisms) come to be 'unified' – absorbed into and neutralised by capital – belongs to the work of the ideological, political, and economic processes that underpin globalisation. It is these processes that reproduce the mutable form of globalisation's structural nexus, a form composed of ever tightening but also constantly expanding and multiplying interdependencies, an interlocking of all the regions of the globe into the world system of transnational markets and capital flows. Globalisation's modus operandi – to return to Osborne – consists in 'combining' these historical specificities with 'social structures that produce geopolitically totalised presents that are constitutively problematic: unified only in *images* of ideal, speculative or fictional "subjects" purporting to occupy the same kind of historical space as the alienated ideality of the value form of capital, in its seeming self-determining movement'.[10] It is precisely, however, the constitutively problematic character of globalisation that opens up possible ways of contesting its ideological unity – the 'unity' of its images – to disclose within the apparently 'seamless' movement of capital, the crisis tendencies that animate it and that constitute its elemental and primitive driving force (the tendency to 'overaccumulation' – more on this below).

To be effective, however, such contestations must also propose ways of destabilising globalisation's perpetual present. It is in relation to this that Spivak offers the suggestive thought-figure of 'planetarity'. Beyond globalisation's unity-of-differences, its systemic production of sameness everywhere through value exchange, the concept of planetarity discovers 'another system' that we 'inhabit' but 'on loan'.[11] After all, we do not 'possess' the planet, it possesses us to the extent that it sustains the very possibility of life. The planet – rather than globe – names the precondition for humanity's continued existence, and the key to its future prospects. With this thought-figure, Spivak writes: 'I propose the planet to overwrite the globe.'[12] Now it is this tactic of overwriting the ideological production of the 'fiction' of globalisation as a totalising and 'englobing' form of ceaseless consumption and overproduction that interests me insofar as it provides a means of displacing the very idea of globality through a 'fictive' or '(im)possible' (as Spivak writes) sublation: the idea of a planetary way of living replacing the real of globalisation's death drive. And so, in response to the third question, posed above, I would like to add to the taxonomy of the political theatre the name of a 'futural' political theatre – the 'theatre of the planetary conjuncture' – in order to examine how a political engagement with globalisation (that process without a subject) might nonetheless be imagined as a possibility through theatre. Spivak concludes her essay on planetarity by writing: 'The "planet" is, here, as perhaps always, a catachresis for inscribing collective responsibility as right.'[13] Likewise, then, I will broach this theatre of the planetary conjuncture as a 'catachresis' – admitting it only as the strained and inadequate name for a political theatre of the future, a theatre of collective responsibility whose time is nonetheless overdue.

6

The theatre of the planetary conjuncture: Milo Rau's *Congo Tribunal*

To assert (rather than to invent) a theatre of the planetary conjuncture is not to indulge in the marginal pleasures of a recondite theoretical endeavour. It is not a question of idly imagining a speculative theatre that does not yet exist. The task is not *conjectural* – it is urgent, in Lenin's sense: 'conjunctural'. It demands the uncovering of a theatre of the not-yet-existent that addresses itself explicitly to globalisation's conjunctural present. The task, which is here one of an attempted culmination – of sorts … is to distinguish this theatre whose practice is already 'of the future' insofar as it pushes hard against globalisation's perpetual 'now'. This theatre of the planetary conjuncture is a theatre that takes its orientation from the utopia of globalisation's imagined end. (How else could it orient itself as a politics?) For it to be political, it must *have* a politics, however. This means it must have a horizon upon which it projects an alternative image of reality as a futurity – the utopianism of an imagined futural present (the phalanstery of Fourier, for instance, stands as one historical example of utopic 'horizontalisation' upon which a politics might be projected). But it must also show that reality as it is presently conceived constitutes a dead-end that must be confronted and resolutely defeated so as to make way for such a future – the non-utopian and 'real' moment of its future temporalisation. It is this above all else that entitles it to proclaim itself a pre-eminently 'political theatre'. That it is 'theatre', and that it trades in a *poiesis*, matters little. If it is of the planetary conjuncture its character is political through and through. As *poiesis* it already suggests a flowering with real term consequences, an overwriting of the now. What it overwrites is the presentism (and pessimism) of globalisation. It overwrites the ideology that there is 'no alternative' (but the ceaseless movement of the productive-consumptive present) by a temporality that is exposed to a historicity that comes to it from a future whose possibility is – were it not for the theatre – otherwise barred. It is a time that is always overdue. This theatre is thus a theatre in which the accounts of the present are not simply left unsettled, but are endowed with a negative particularity, where justice is not speciously recuperated, or piously proclaimed, but shown to be permanently in arrears. A utopian theatre whose temporality is that of the overdue, and which overwrites the present with the overdue, is exactly how the theatre of the planetary conjuncture will be imagined in what follows.

To add a little flesh to the bones of this idea, an example.

There is one theatre maker whose work today encapsulates, although he is by no means the only one, the kind of theatrical projection of an alternative futural horizon of the kind I have in mind – who directly addresses the global conjuncture, and who consequently comes closest to articulating the idea of a theatre of the planetary conjuncture – the Swiss director Milo Rau.[1] One finds a certain explicitness in Rau's own discourse, for a start, not least his avowed utopianism, that makes him particularly conducive to the task of enumerating such a theatre.[2] Indeed, Rau understands his work explicitly – and not just in a practical sense but also with a clear awareness of its utopian undertaking – as 'an education for a global we'.[3] In opposing what he calls the 'aesthetic approach' to theatre making (theatre made simply for the sake of the art of theatre), Rau's theatre is never just 'theatre'; nor was it ever 'just' theatre. Quite the opposite. What it reveals is that theatre's integral space of exception stands in a problematic relation to the autonomy of the 'aesthetic' since it is always oriented by a sociality that it can never quite evade and that essentially marks its distinction from other art forms. With that sociality, theatre's production of exceptional space cannot entirely escape the social responsibility placed upon it, which thereby inclines it towards the gravitational field of the political. It is not that theatre must always be aligned to the pursuit of political ends, but that the tragic magnitude it is capable of bearing cannot be divorced from the harrowing nature of the reality it summons. This is what Rau's theatre reasserts – a reminder that with the 'word', not only is the world created, along with speech, oratory, and poetry, but so too therefore are both politics and theatre. Mere play thus once again assumes the dimension of tragic risk in Rau, and a means of intervening in that world. It is why, for him, the theatre idea is a 'social phantasy' which, he says, 'is active, it has an urge to realise itself. It wants to take the entire world in its arms and, above all else, it wants to change the world.'[4] For Rau this does not mean a theatre that restricts itself to a critical analysis of existent reality – one that offers itself as evidence for (or is reproduced in the form of a document of) a political situation that has occurred elsewhere, beyond the stage, as an event in 'real life' (reinstalled in its distinction to the 'nonreality' of theatre). It means, instead: the 'transitioning' away from the literal facts of the story in order to stage 'something like a real situation that speaks for itself'.[5]

This emphatically experiential approach, the desire to 'encounter the existential reality of life at eye level',[6] explains Rau's well-known preference for the technique of staging 'reenactments'. His 2011/12 production, *Hate Radio*, for example, sought to discover, through reenactment, the effects of degraded and abject political discourse that would lead eventually to the Rwandan genocide of 1994. It did so by recreating the Hutu extremist radio station Radio-Télévision Libre des Mille Collines (RTLM) in the form of an exact facsimile or 'simulacrum'. It then populated the surrogate RTLM with actors playing Hutu extremists – DJ Joseph, Valérie Bemeriki, Kantano Habimana, whose speech – and casual disregard for human dignity and decency – they reproduced, along with the Italian-Belgian radio host, Georges Raggiu, whose presence made the station palatable to middle-class Hutus (Raggiu and his fellow *animateurs* were later convicted of crimes against humanity).[7] *Hate Radio* confronted its audience, not with a documentary, but with a faithful copy of a two-hour radio broadcast from 1994 in which pop songs and sports news were interspersed with solicitations to the audience to kill anyone from the Tutsi minority as well as any moderate Hutu who stood in their way (it also incorporated video projections of victim and perpetrator testimonies).

Since *Hate Radio* eschewed the mere act of documenting reality, the question it posed was not 'what happened?' but rather: 'How does mass murder happen?'[8] The question displaced the focus of the theatre away from the analysis of facts and onto the problem of audience complicity

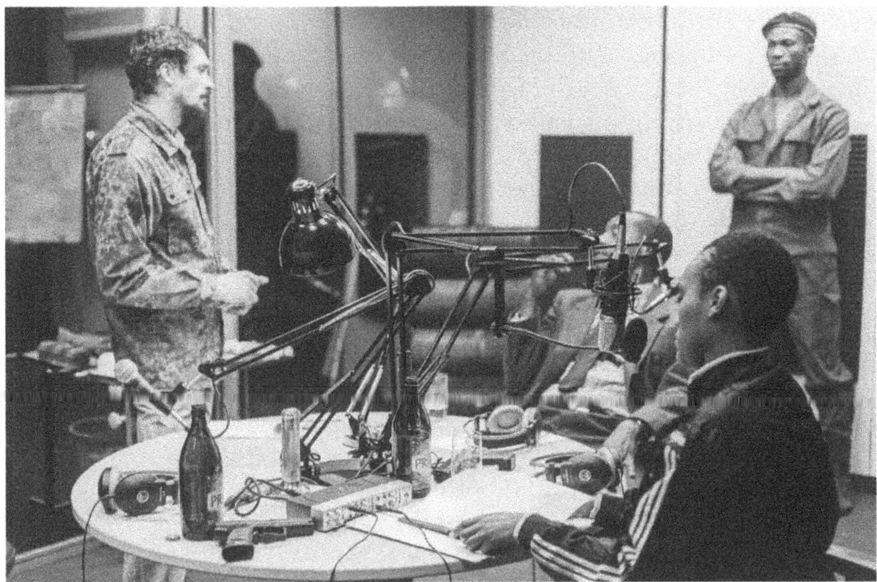

Figure 5 Milo Rau, *Hate Radio*, 2012.

(RTLM was instrumental in mobilising the civilian Hutu population who listened to it in the genocidal war against their Tutsi neighbours). In providing an exceptional space in which the 'call for mass murder' appears once again 'legitimated' by means of a simulation that is 'oversaturated' by the real,[9] the 'barrier', as Rau expresses it, 'between passive watching and active comprehension is crossed, in which the spectator also becomes complicit in something that they, from a purely factual point of view, are not directly involved in'.[10]

I have noted, previously, that for the theatre spectator, complicity is the unacknowledged presupposition in the enjoyment of the acts they watch. Aware of it or not, audiences possess a share of responsibility for the staged malfeasance of theatre's bad intentions, even as it solicits their sympathy with the suffering endured by its incumbent victims. In the case of *Hate Radio*, the audience complicity possessed a double character that disabled theatre's usual means of exoneration. It resisted any facile attempt at empathic identification with the victim as well as theatre's fabled amplitude for moral condemnation ('poetic justice'). The literal invocation to kill was not a mere theatrical representation but the repetition of debased reality in simulated form. *Hate Radio*'s reenactment did not entrust its audience with the documented facts of the matter for them to be calmly assayed as though presented as neutral capsules of evidence; it staged a discomforting experience of RTLM's charismatic radio hosts, drinking beer while casually enjoining their audience to commit acts of unimaginable horror and cruelty. It is as if Arendt's banality of evil were incarnated by this theatre *in propria persona*. Rau's aim was thus not to bring the 'facts' to light (they are already widely known) but to bring the nature of audience complicity to light: to turn back or repel the identification enjoyed by the audience, the theatre's structured pleasure in taking delight in the suffering of others, and to transform that pleasure into a motive for dis-identification. The experience embraced both theatre's 'heliotropism' through which the theatrical event draws its spectator into ever closer proximity with the source of its own 'terrible enjoyment' – the lure of the image – and the exorcism of that pleasure by means of the awareness it produced in its audience of the 'distance that is always present between the self and the image, the play, or another – and in which something like "guilt", "attitude" or "catharsis", where all these forms of an emotional or moral analysis can develop'.[11] The experience of theatre's pleasure and the failure to achieve the 'jouissance' that is promised to the spectator, makes possible a space for the development of both critical and affective intelligence. It is why, for Rau, 'analysis is not enough' – if a political theatre is to be credible, it must be autoptic: its observations must also be experienced as personal by its audience.[12]

But of course, there is more to be said with respect to this approach especially if what is to be elucidated is to exceed the distanciated space established by the old critical theatre. In this sense, the aspiration behind Rau's political theatre is both 'critical' and 'classical'. The political theatre must be understood as making an actual intervention in reality. It must 'really intervene in the transmission of the world, in the transmission of history'.[13] And so for Rau its mode of performance cannot be reduced to the act of simply documenting reality (as is found in the tradition arising with the theatre of Peter Weiss) but to demonstrate that reality can be altered. Theatre's representations are not to be thought as ordered in accordance with pre-existing facts whose fixed essence they would merely reproduce as historical statements, as discourse, or as commentary. On the contrary, conceived as a *poiesis*, theatre is ill-conceived when thought in straightforwardly representational terms. It is a staging of the becoming true of truth; the becoming real of reality. The emphasis placed on becoming rather than being indicates that reality and truth are not 'states' or 'conditions' of the way things are. They are contestable productions and processes within which an intervention (and invention) is always conceivable. The contingency of events is the constitutive precondition for reality's appearance; just as the knowledge carried by that contingency that things might be otherwise provides an epistemic motive for political action. When it comes to the world and to politics, and especially when it comes to how historical events are understood, nothing is wholly set in perpetuity; nothing entirely fixed in its place. This is to say that to understand the now in conjunctural and overdetermined terms is to understand present reality in its provisional character as much as through its determinations and entanglements. 'The present is simply a transitional space', Rau writes, 'in which the future has to be realised.'[14] It cannot be a simple space, however. If the idea of transitional space is understood as conjuncturally determined, the metaphysical language of an empty or formal space through which an indifferent time flows, devoid of content, must be rejected. It is the space of real historical contestations, of political actions with actual social forces in play, as well as – and this is where a space of representation remains essential – possible judgements on those actions and their consequences. If political theatre, in Rau's sense – part classical, part critical, part activist[15] – provides a means for 'bringing to light all [reality's] consequences and thus showing [that reality] in action'[16] – he means to reveal its processes, its forms of appearance, its modes of determination, its historical attributions, but also its unpredictable and unstable character – thus the possibility for its transformation.

The idea that theatre brings truth 'to light', however, might be seen as something of a tired metaphor; the idea that it does so in the form of a simulacrum might also be seen as pushing it into the sphere of an ill-fated paradox. It is important therefore to understand what these two terms 'truth' and 'simulacrum' mean and how they are related to one another in Rau's theatre. When Rau differentiates the specificity of 'artistic truth'[17] – who's medium of conveyance is, as it were, a theatrical 'simulation' – I propose to understand this in the following way: it is simulacral truth that overwrites reality as it is normally recognised (and accepted) by another attitude, and for the sake of producing another truth. Here it is important to grasp two things. First, that the assertion of the nonreality of the theatre rests on an amphibology since the theatre constitutes its own reality, through which it glimpses the *other* of reality, the other 'present' to *this* present .... Theatre is a fantasy of the real, through which the real is conjured in simulated form – through a kind of séance or possession. The theatrical simulation is thereby not deployed to demonstrate that which merely *is* (a copy), it appears as a premonstration – a showing forth in advance. And what it places 'in advance' of reality is that which is 'overdue', where the overdue must be understood as possessing the force of an apodictic truth (a truth that is beyond dispute). In fact, second, the overdue indicates an ontological presupposition: both a deficit and an excess in the order of being. The overdue is not simply a lack, a condemnation, an absence – but also the deferred promise of a plenitude-to-come, in which that which is sworn to being is finally honoured. A planetary politics operates within this differential of the overdue. It operates within the space of the exceptional demand that it produces and that it constructs; and as the friction that the incomplete present generates as social antagonism.

Related to this: one can understand the artistic tactic of overwriting reality with the overdue (not rewriting but reparative writing) in light of two ways in which the problem of the simulacrum can be thought in relation to either a politics or an anti-politics.

The first, which is how Rau understands the term, is associated with the thinking of Roland Barthes for whom the 'simulacrum describes the paradox or impossible work of a representative double',[18] essential nonetheless to any scientific demonstration. Applied to the reenactment, Rau states: this means 'an artistic practice that is completely exposed to the impossibility of depicting reality [as discovered through] the depiction of something that has happened'.[19] In this sense, Rau's theatre simulation might be understood according to the kind of 'expository protocol'[20] employed by Barthes, that transcribes the past (an injustice) into the space of the present (the overdue) in order to adumbrate the possible future it foreshadows (justice due). What it does not refer to is a simulacrum in the sense established by Jean Baudrillard – essentially an anti-politics – of an 'unattached, artistic world of signs without referents'.[21] The power of the reenactment derives from the paradoxical relation reenactment establishes to a real content that is irrefutable, yet which cannot be made to coincide with the moment of its appearance *as* reenacted reality, or as representation. Nor can the real therefore be entirely comprehended or made to account for itself through its documented image: its documented form is merely the ellipsis of that which is overdue. In making sense of this claim, one must further distinguish between two 'levels' that establish the play and the staging of a simulacrum. On the one hand, there is the level of a real content that is posited but that cannot be immediately grasped – a real that is unilaterally determinative of the simulacrum's appearance insofar as it possesses the force of a truth that becomes tangible through it (*apodixis*). On the other hand, there is mediated 'reality' (the ideologically 'closed' present) whose modes of givenness, and apparent objectivity, are to be deconstructed by means of a simulated demonstration (exposure of the present to an ideologically 'open', infinite discourse – let us call this the 'science' of the simulation). The nonoriginality of the clone/double, the irreducible character of the simulacrum, constitutes a negation of the authority of sanctioned reality by making its epistemic claim on the 'real' – its knowledge of the real – problematic. The real is not an illusion, then. It is not a *mere* simulacrum, a phantom presence, a hyperreal, a gravitationless nebula; it can be approached but only in the same way that Orpheus was advised to approach Eurydice – obliquely and not frontally. What this means is that the real constitutes the ungraspable limit condition for the possibility of a theatre that finds its inspiration in the social truth content concealed in the image of reality. It is here that the political potential of the theatre simulation reveals itself in its most poignant artistic form. The point of this 'documentary' theatre is not to render reality transparent, but to show – through the exposure of reality to the real – that the prevalent ways in which reality is understood, comprehended, or depicted involve failures of comprehension, and that the terms in which reality is couched offer at best only partial understandings. If art's simulacral 'image' thereby works *on* the social imaginary, it does so 'politically' in ways that aim to reinstate reality's forsaken indebtedness to the real. This becomes a possibility only when preconceptions of reality and its modes of reception are able to be suspended through theatre's simulated epochē. Only by operating within and upon the ideological space within which the social imaginary is produced, through the deconstruction of its symbolic registers, and by dismantling the authority it possesses over the real, can a utopian theatre hope to realise its political aims.

To be clear, this theatre is utopian but not in a romantic sense: not because it presents an image of a reconciled and harmonious social order, or because it stakes a claim on a lost origin that might be regained through art – the harmony of the faculties – but because it contains within it the promise of the overdue. Thus, if its images are not produced to make reality more comprehensible, it is because they aim to show its truth as reprehensible. To make the comprehensible incomprehensible is to deplete the power that 'reality' is invested with and weaken the symbolic grip through which it maintains its hold over the social imaginary. Only at the extreme point of torsion, in which the order of knowledge twists to the point of unravelling, in which its symbolic resources are revealed as threadbare, can theatre make possible those (re)imaginings that comprehension has already foreclosed. Theatre's utopian horizon of the overdue is 'utopian' in the sense that it projects a simulated world that does 'not yet' exist – is an imaginary projection of what might be possible as can only be inferred from its presentation in a simulation-image. But it is a *real* utopia – or rather constitutes that 'moment' of a real demand ('ellipsis', 'lack') that appears within the theatre image and that makes the defiance of its utopian thought a compelling one. To state this thesis as baldly as is possible: what the not yet, the overdue, designates, within the simulacrum of an image, is the real of an injustice through which present and historical reality become indictable. It is for the sake of animating a genuine demand for justice that the political theatre must undertake its 'Orphic' descent into Hades so as to retrieve disavowed and subjugated truth. Contrary to what one might assume, when Orpheus ascends from the world of shadows, having failed to bring Eurydice back with him, he doesn't return empty handed: the real is not entirely lost.[22] Quite the reverse, in fact, since loss bears within it the trace of the real that determines it as 'loss'. What Orpheus possesses is his dispossession. Thus, his lament comes with the overbearing affective power of *what* he has lost; but what that loss itself testifies to is not just that which is lacking within reality, it points to its profound unfairness, and to the fact that reality is constituted not by the imaginary appearance of plenitude but by a real privation. Once again, the overdue character of the conjuncture comes to the fore through the image of a lack. Unlike Orpheus, however, the political theatre does not console itself with a lamentation: it cannot afford to be melancholic. It must find its motivation within the light of the artistic truth of a planetary future contained in the expression 'not yet' (quite distinct from the 'as if') ... – Consequently, if present reality is overwhelmed by an affect it cannot contain, it is made questionable by a 'fiction of the real' that overwrites it with the indomitable image of a utopian 'justice-to-come'.

I shall take just one example to illustrate this idea of a theatre of the planetary conjuncture – a piece made in 2014 by Rau and his collaborators entitled *The Congo Tribunal*. Taking the form of a people's tribunal, created in the spirit of the post-war prosecution of leading Nazis at Nuremburg by an internationally convened criminal court, *The Congo Tribunal* staged a series of quasi-legal hearings that charged the Congolese state, multinationals, and the Bretton Woods economic monetary system – comprising the World

Bank, World Trade Organization (WTO) and International Monetary Fund (IMF) – of complicity in the 'systematic aggression' perpetrated by militias, rebel warlords, and neighbouring state actors (Rwanda, Burundi, Uganda) against Congolese civil society. The aim of the tribunal was to examine the 'causes and consequences' of a twenty-year conflict known as the 'second' Congo war in the mineral rich region of the Great Lakes in Eastern Congo.[23] The tribunal adopted two approaches to this crisis: first in relation to the prosecution of a number of specific human rights violations (such as the forced deportation of artisan miners[24]); and secondly – as shall be seen – through the incrimination of the global conjuncture, identified as the general cause of the conflict. Georges Nzongola-Ntalaja has written poignantly of the war: 'No region of the African continent has known as much political strife, loss of life and social dislocation during the last 42 years as the Great Lakes region.'[25] Triggered by the Rwandan genocide of 1994, as well as the 'disintegration of the Mobutu regime' in 1997, 'and the state decay associated with it',[26] the 'Congo war' remains the greatest conflict of the era of globalisation. Indeed, while no exact figures are available, estimates suggest it may have claimed between six and seven million lives to date. Among the many contingent factors that caused the conflict, a single word accounts for its protracted nature: 'profiteering'. In fact, the global trade in conflict minerals such as coltan, the raw material from which tantalum and niobium minerals are extracted – essential for digital miniaturisation and found in consumer products such as mobile phones[27] – is the immediate or 'efficient' cause of the crisis in the Democratic Republic of Congo (DRC). Again, as Nzongola-Ntalaja writes, the most significant factor in the war is 'the logic of plunder in the new era of globalization, which has to do with the growing tendency of states, mafia groups, offshore banks and transnational mining companies to enrich themselves from crises'.[28]

The first of Rau's hearings, which examined these issues, took place over a period of three days in the DRC, at the old Jesuit Collège Alfajiri, founded in the town of Bukavu in 1938, while a second set of hearings occurred a month later in Berlin.

The tribunal form itself belongs to the long history of the trial employed as a dramaturgical strategy wherein theatre and law coincide in agonistic processes of litigation, commencing with ancient Greek tragedy – for instance, Hecuba – and extending up to more recent tribunal plays – the first of which was Weiss's *The Investigation*, based on transcripts made of the Frankfurt Auschwitz trials (1963–1965). Rau writes: 'The law, or more concretely, the format of the trial or tribunal is a kind of tournament, a framework of rules in which *truth* becomes possible in a completely basic, specifically antagonistic sense.'[29] A significant qualification should be observed, however, in respect of *The Congo Tribunal*'s use of the trial form: those who

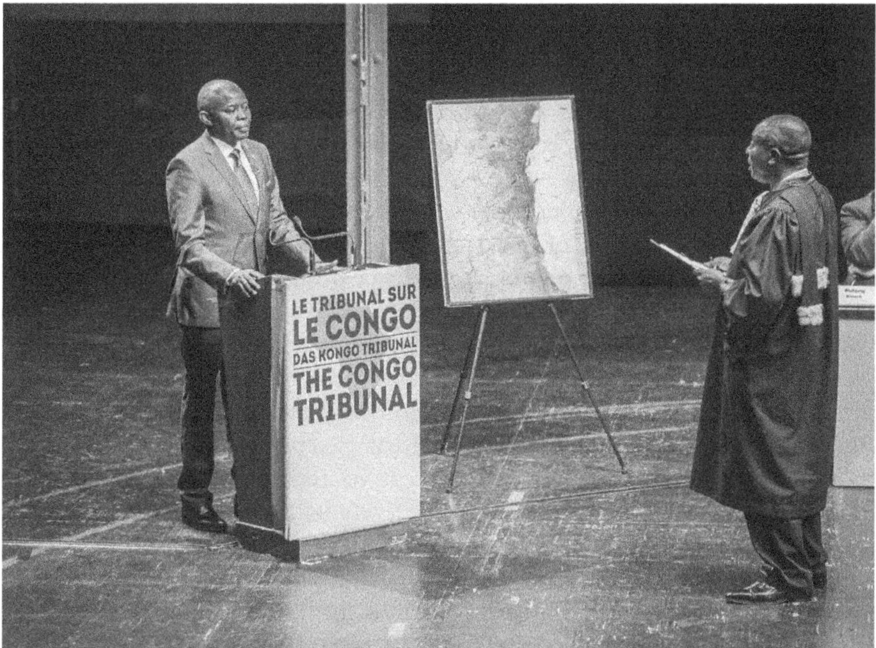

Figure 6 Milo Rau, *The Congo Tribunal*, 2014.

gave testimony during it were neither actors nor performers speaking words already uttered by others but actual victims and perpetrators of the conflict, as well as government officials, police chiefs and generals, politicians, economists, and philosophers. The hearings were presided over by Jean-Louis Gilissen, an advocate in international criminal law, involved in the preparation of the UN-report about Eastern Congo that declared the situation genocide, and the case prosecuted, not by means of a 'scripted' narrative, but by means of a process of litigation led by a chief investigator, Sylvestre Bisimwa, also a specialist in international criminal law and human rights abuses. The jury comprised a number of experts – among others: Séverin Mugangu, a legal professor; Gilbert Kalinda, Deputy of the Province of North Kivu, representing national and international mining companies; Colette Braekman, Africa correspondent for the Belgian newspaper, *Le Soir*; and Vénantie Bisimusa Nabintu, a Congolese human rights advocate. One might well ask, given Rau's situational 'realism', in what sense the *Congo Tribunal* constituted a 'theatre' at all, when to all intents and purposes the tribunal acted as a de facto court of law.

In fact, the answer to this question speaks directly to the concept of theatre's overwriting of reality by means of a simulation. It is because it is a simulation that *The Congo Tribunal* (a 'preenactment' rather than reenactment insofar as it preceded any actual prosecution) remains on the side of 'theatre' – and it is a simulation insofar as it deploys theatre's peculiar ability to 'clone' space, to superimpose one space upon another – in this case the space of law, the court, which was theatrically 'cloned' for a performance that was real in every respect except for the fact that it did not possess the 'force' of law (nothing was enforceable, no-one confronted any immediate consequences or sanction, as a consequence of its judgement). One might recall at this point the paradox noted by Derrida in his essay *The Force of Law*, with its invocation of Pascal's dictum: 'There is no law without enforceability'[30] – but also that while a certain 'founding' violence, which precedes all questions of justification, establishes the law and makes it enforceable, the question of the relation between justice and law is nonetheless rendered ambiguous by an instituting act of violence for which the law cannot give an account.[31] To this it can be added that for Rau's 'people's tribunal', the law is not present at all, merely its appearance in the form of a simulation (the court had no statutory authority), but that through the simulation what became present was the claim of justice – in other words, a demand that possesses the singular force of truth, if not of law.

Again, it is important to note, in this regard, that Rau's tribunal was never intended to be viewed as an exact representation of legal processes, reproduced only for the sake of theatrical verisimilitude. The structural ambiguity of the clone lies in the fact that it is not reducible to a representational counterpart of reality to which it stands in a 'corresponding' relation. What is replicated in the simulation is not a correspondence but the integral identity of the original – the clone possesses everything in common with the original except its authority upon which its efficacy depends (i.e., its capacity to produce 'felicitous' speech in Austin's sense). This is not to say, however, that it is without consequences or truth. The clone dispossesses the 'original' of its location, so as to take possession of what is normally prohibited from appearing there. This is what distinguishes the nonidentical duplication of the space of law in Rau's use of simulation, from the Baudrillardian simulacrum (which discloses only the semblance of a rotten referent lying at the heart of every referential meaning), and it is precisely for this reason that it insists on the incontrovertible presence of the real as presented by means of the cloning of the space of law. The clone is a presentation of the real, not a representation of reality. It is this insistence on the real that enabled an overwriting of present reality with the claim of a truth that has yet to be acknowledged. 'It is a theatrical tribunal,' Rau would proclaim, 'but everything is real.'[32] The theatrical overwriting of the present in the form of a simulation can be understood as 'real' in the supplementary sense that, while the court possessed no legally binding authority, no jurisdiction, nonetheless it acted as a surrogate for the space of law that was 'not yet' available to the victims of the conflict. In this sense the cloning of the space of the court was constituted through an appropriative use of international criminal law, as well as the ritual aspects of court procedures, and so cannot be viewed as the theatrical representation of a trial – it was a 'real trial', insisted Rau. At the same time, it was also theatre – 'not real' in this first sense – yet as a simulacrum nonetheless able to get at the truth in ways that an actual trial would not be able to. Rau asserts 'The Congo Tribunal made something real, which was not imaginable in anyone's wildest dreams.'[33]

There are several related aspects to this claim – to Rau's wildest of dreams – that require elucidation, and that will help to unravel the complex operations involved in the politics of overwriting reality. The first concerns the relation of the particular to the universal. What exactly is the nature of that relation? Wherever one deals with matters of law, the problem of the subsumption of the individual as a particular case falling under the universal applicability of the rule of law constitutes the basic operation of legislative power in general, of the authority of the court, and of the legitimate use of force in upholding decisions founded on law. At the same time, the law – an abstract generality – can only be realised through the individual and particular instance. I will resist delving too deeply into the philosophical implications of the conflict that arises between the particular and the universal, as they function in law, or that arises with the inscription of the particular into the apparatus of legal institutions, except to note that what tends to be observed with respect to the almost mystical communion of universal (abstract) and its realisation in the particular (concrete) is the emergence of a caesurae or gap or better still incommensurability between the generality of law, grasped as a legal representative system, and the singular presence of the victim – what has been referred to, in relation to Derrida, as the law's 'other'.[34] The representational violence of law resides in its reduction of the singular to a mere 'case' that reveals the dissymmetry or inadequation that exists between the law and the point of its application, that overwrites the 'idiomatic' language of the victim through their inscription into the universal language of the general rule. Although the application of a rule that complies with the law is confirmed in the legal decision, justice is by no means assured (and not only because there are more bad laws than good ones). For the law to function, for it to actually deliver justice, Derrida observes, it must undo itself – it must simultaneously be 'conserved' and 'destroyed': 'Each case is other, each decision is different and requires an absolutely unique interpretation which no existing, coded rule can or ought to guarantee absolutely.'[35] The claim of truth – that is, the demand of justice (understood beyond its limited meaning within the restricted economy of law) – necessarily undoes the universal pretension of law to transcend the reality it adjudicates. What the force of truth exposes, in relation to the universalising character of law, is this inherent *aporia* of law: the fundamental contradiction it embodies when the general is applied as a facticity. It is precisely this deconstructive dynamic that is mobilised in *The Congo Tribunal* in its indictment of the system of globalisation.

For example, when Rau states that the 'universality of *The Congo Tribunal* is contained in the complete subjectivity of the testimonies, taken from the often cruel and inhuman everyday life',[36] he does not mean that it is enough to attend to the speech of the 'other', to pay the debt of a responsibility owed to the other through the solemn acknowledgement of their singularity, still less, to swathe their speech in those ethical hues that paint the liberal sensibility of the West in a half-flattering light. He is drawing attention to a contradiction that exists between the idiomatic speech of the victim, which conveys a definite demand for justice, and a legal system whose universal and indefinite character is so constituted that it is incapable of confirming that demand – thus is unable to recognise the prerogative of an injustice, or the redress it can offer it. There is, among several shocking incidents related in *The Congo Tribunal*, one atrocity that bears particular mention in this regard: a massacre of breathtaking depravity committed against the civilian population of the village of Matarule in the South Kivu province of the DRC, close to the city of Bukavu, in June 2014, that left over thirty women and children dead. Rau described what he saw as 'Old Testament reality' – a catastrophe of immeasurable suffering that was met largely by official indifference from the government in Kinshasa (accusations of indifference were further exacerbated when it was later revealed that both Congolese military personnel and United Nations peacekeepers were stationed in the area but had failed to intervene). What makes the magnitude of the crime so grave is not just the terrible and frankly unspeakable facts of the event – the slaughter of pregnant women in a hospital, for example. It is that such atrocities are a commonplace in Eastern Congo; just as it is a commonplace that the demands for justice go unheard, as if the speech and anguished cries of its victims were somehow inaudible, despite their deafening volume; thus, these crimes, with a few notable exceptions, are left untouched by law and unpunished. And so, to transcode the particularity of this incident in the terms of the general problem of the conjuncture, which is what Rau, I think, is trying to suggest in the piece: insofar as the demand for justice seeks a hearing it must undo the law by revealing its central contradiction; it stages a demand whose particular force of truth can only be heard on the basis of a general ('universal') indictment of the global pretence of which the law constitutes a fundamental part within the system of globalisation. It is for this reason that the singular and specific nature of the demand for justice, as presented through *The Congo Tribunal*, must ultimately be grasped in political terms and as a political act – that is, in relation to the terrain of conjunctural struggle – for it to acquire its full meaning. Every particular indictment is in the final instance inseparable from, indeed becomes an emblem of the general political indictment of the system of globalisation. Each atrocity reveals the wretched face of what is in fact the physiognomy of permanent horror. And this is not simply because it can be identified as the cause of one injustice after another, but because each, in its own way, reveals injustice to be a primary element of the conjunctural conditions that sustain globalisation's existence. Insofar as it is appended to economic power, the international apparatus of law becomes an accomplice to the crime, as Rau indicates when he observes:

> Constitutional law and every single legal act ensures that different concurrent legal systems remain in balance. A simple example: According to the Congolese mining laws, the deportations explored in *The Congo Tribunal* are legal; however, according to the Congolese constitution, land laws and many other legal systems, they are not. This is true for everything: To kill a person can be either a heroic act or self-defence or a murder. However, there is no court in the Congo to protect its people from the law and specifically from the mining law – which were forced on the Congolese state by the World Bank – by protecting the diversity of the law itself, or, in other words, by adding the corrective of justice to the law.[37]

Thus, *The Congo Tribunal* constitutes an indictment of the global conjuncture, where the appearance of multiple injustices must itself be seen as a constitutive rather than accidental feature of globalisation. What it demonstrates is not so much the absence of law as the abject failure of an entire system of laws, or effectiveness in sustaining their disavowed purpose. In transcoding the language of law and that of the 'universal' into the specificity of the conjuncture two things become apparent: first, that the universal always has a concrete geopolitical character in which its abstract appearance serves entirely ideological purposes; and, second, that when one speaks of 'global modernity' – the universalising aspect here indicates nothing as lofty as the 'universal rights' of the Enlightenment, but rather the absolutising of the interests of capital, as protected in international courts. The conflict – on the other hand – in which the contradictions of globalisation are materialised in the form of brutal crimes perpetrated against the population of the Eastern Congo must be accounted for according to its modes of particularisation and the insidious tendencies they express. Rau identifies these tendencies, entirely appropriately, with the processes of 'development' – in reality, underdevelopment. It is also why the hearings of

The Congo Tribunal, for Rau, dialectically 'anchor' conflicts of development, whose global causes it shows to be profoundly implicated in the local consequences of globalisation, in what Stuart Hall terms the '"law" of capitalist modernization: uneven development, organized disorganization'.[38]

I would like to touch – finally – on some of these 'organised-disorganised' tendencies of the global conjuncture, which *The Congo Tribunal* tries to make visible for its audience, and through which the conjunctural dynamics that sustain the crisis of globalisation, and its ongoing and destabilising effects, are inscribed in what might be termed the 'politics of the overdue'. The first thing to note is the organic basis of the crisis, which is rooted in a long history of imperial expropriation of Africa. That history is summarised by Walter Rodney in his classic study of 1972, *How Europe Underdeveloped Africa*, in which he argued the necessity of viewing 'development-underdevelopment' as a *dialectical* relation when accounting for the process that continues to underscore the present conjunctural crisis:

> Because of the superficiality of many of the approaches to 'underdevelopment' and because of resulting misconceptions, it is necessary to reemphasize that development and underdevelopment are not only comparative terms, but that they also have a dialectical relationship one to the other: that is to say, the two help produce each other by interaction. Western Europe and Africa had a relationship which insured the transfer of wealth from Africa to Europe. The transfer was possible only after trade became truly international; and that takes one back to the late fifteenth century when Africa and Europe were drawn into common relations for the first time – along with Asia and the Americas. The developed and the underdeveloped parts of the capitalist section of the world have been in continuous contact for four and a half centuries. The contention here is that over that period, Africa helped to develop Western Europe in the same proportion as Western Europe helped to underdevelop Africa.[39]

The dialectical relation between development and underdevelopment henceforth requires two apparently separate processes to be regarded, not as external to one another, but as co-constitutive: each is established on the basis of the other; each is mutually implicated in a single and totalising organic structure. To understand the present structuration of globalisation as a historical form, however, it is necessary to highlight the two interwoven totalising phenomena out of which it is hewn.

I shall describe the first of these 'sculptings' in relation to the *longue durée* of 'world history' – as indicated by Rodney above – but in which one sees a transformation in the organic character of global capital and its forms of brokerage over the past seventy years. This occurs in the wake of the processes of decolonisation, which gathered pace in the middle of the last century, when the old imperia of Europe – in particular, Britain, Belgium, and France – were displaced by (and absorbed within) powerful new economic blocs, possessing new concentrations of cultural, social, and political (and military) capital. During this period of transformation, no real emancipation took place. Such dreams were bitterly and swiftly dispelled: just as soon as the reins of the old imperialism were let loose, they were seized up by new administrative hands. On this basis a new global formation emerged, eventually developing the radical institutions of neoliberalism, supra-state multinationals, as well as the transnational financial networks that today comprise the brokers of the so-called 'advanced' world, i.e., the primary beneficiaries of globalisation. Although this transformation has given rise to new actors on the stage of global capital (initially the US from the 1950s and more recently China), the practice of wealth extraction from the South to the North is both lynchpin and constant variable, regardless of such immense geopolitical shifts and the replacement of one elite by another – hence its 'organic' character, which must be taken as being rooted in deep-seated historical processes and tendencies.

The problem of the organic or entrenched nature of these processes and their tendencies has recently been described in terms directly indebted to Trotsky's analysis of the 'backward' character of Russia at the turn of the twentieth century. Trotsky nominated it the problem of 'uneven and combined development'. Alexander Anievas and Kerem Nişancioğlu, for example, have argued that 'uneven and combined development offers a cogent means of theoretically explaining the differentiated social forms and historically distinct agencies emerging from a single, unified process of socio-historical development, as well as the geosocial effects of their interactive differences'.[40] What their revision of Trotsky's theory demonstrates is that development does not follow a 'unilinear path'[41] but rather a complex and variegated path, producing asymmetries of power in the global system. Asymmetry is hard baked into globalisation not least because development is subject to the brute circumstances of the world's diverse natural environments and their associated habitats. Thus, different societies emerged according to distinct and wide-ranging ecological and geographical variances that ensured unevenness was embedded within the historical processes of their development (long before the arrival of capitalism). In short, the relative factors of abundance or scarcity dialectically conditioned the ways in which distinctive social formations and their various cultures emerged on an adaptive basis. Viewed in organic terms – and thus of its political consequences – uneven development, comprising differences both within and between societies, established the conditions for what Anievas and Nişancioğlu describe as 'structural competitive [relations] between societies';[42] capitalism did not invent these organic asymmetries, but it would exploit them through the construction of a global competitive market based on 'free trade' and the projection of economic and military power.

The 'combined' element describes the active processes of interaction that exist between cultures (essential to their co-formation) while 'unevenness' describes the potential for the expropriation of one by the other – each aspect having a decisive influence over the way differential relations between the regions of the globe structured 'world history', producing the 'globe' as the stage upon which the game of economic and political domination was and continues to be played out. The immanent and dynamic process of uneven and combined development therefore underpins both the historical formation and the continual structural enlargement of globalised capitalism – as Anievas and Nişancioğlu write:

> From its inception, capitalism's expansion … took a 'combined' character, fusing with the plurality of existing sociological forms through its internationally mediated emergence. In so doing, distinctly capitalist processes would come to progressively gain control over this extant unevenness, reconstituting its fundamental quality as it unified the various instances and forms of uneven development into a single, causally integrated world-historical totality.[43]

Let us turn our attention to the second phenomenon that must be invoked, in addition to that of organic transformation, to fully understand why injustice is a constitutive rather than constituent element of globalisation. Rodney termed this phenomenon 'the factor of dependency'. Dependency, he argued, is 'primarily responsible, for the perpetuation of the colonial relationship into the epoch that is called neocolonialism'.[44] Rather than the organic structure and dual processes of uneven and combined development, what dependency brings into view are the historical tendencies that derive from them, that underpin them, and that are articulated (and experienced) in the form of the conjunctural crises produced by them. Two related tendencies are particularly salient insofar as they show how capitalism, as an economic system, inhabits and exploits the process of 'development' through a form of crisis management. The first describes the tendency of capital to 'overaccumulate' surplus value to the extent that it leads to a crisis of devaluation (resulting from the 'falling rate of profit'); the second tendency appears in the consequent form that seeks to resolve the crisis of overaccumulation: 'neocolonial' investment (in 'new' markets) or capital transfers (in the form of debt relief through structural adjustment programmes). David Harvey explains the process as follows: if the 'pervasive tendency of capitalism [is] to produce crises of overaccumulation' then capitalism needs 'spatio-temporal fixes' to manage them.[45] I will focus on the spatial fixes here for reasons that should become obvious. Now, crises of overaccumulation occur in a number of ways: when surplus capital, taking the form of commodities within a given territorial market, exceed demand – pushing down prices and resulting in a loss of profits – producing a crisis of 'devaluation'; or, alternatively, when surplus value exceeds the capacity of the market to absorb it, generating a crisis of excessive financial liquidity. A fundamental contradiction of capital appears with the latter: if there are insufficient opportunities to reinvest surplus capital then the very thing that enables capital to function as capital is undermined (i.e., its capacity to produce growth through profitable investment). Among the possible ways of resolving such crises, Harvey writes, are spatial 'fixes' – the 'opening up [of] new markets, new production capacities and new resources, social and labour possibilities elsewhere'.[46] In short, crises of overaccumulation are resolved through the conduit opened up by the territorial expansion of capital through which value can once again freely flow in the form of new investment opportunities: 'the opening up of new and cheaper resource complexes, of new dynamic spaces of capital accumulation, and the penetration of pre-existing social formations by capitalist social relations and institutionalized arrangements'.[47] Hence, according to Harvey, it is precisely the logics of overaccumulation crises that leads to the 'fix' that drives the 'narrative of uneven geographical development and imperialist politics'.[48] More to the point: uneven development provides a ready means for resolving a specific crisis of capital in one region through commercial predation in another, in which resources such as natural minerals, diamonds, or gold – all found in the Great Lakes region of the DRC – are expropriated with, at best, a minimum level of investment in the host's civil society.

Harvey's apposite term for this parasitical activity of resource extraction is 'accumulation by dispossession'.[49] Dispossession occurs precisely because the system of capital investment exacerbates and exploits the 'dependencies' that result from the asymmetries of uneven development. Patrick Bond describes this process in even blunter terms: it is 'looting'.[50] If it is looting, however – and one should always call a spade a spade – its proceeds are nonetheless legitimated and sanctioned by global institutions, its processes administered through legally binding structural adjustment programmes, its regimes imposed under the benign sounding name of debt relief. Debt relief and Africa's historical indebtedness (the legacy of colonialism), as many commentators have observed, constitute two sides of the same neoliberal coin. In 2005, for instance, the G5 finance ministers agreed to write off $40 billion in debt belonging to the eighteen poorest countries in exchange for neoliberal 'reforms'. One should recall, all the same, whose interests 'neoliberal conditionality' is designed to safeguard, and that what results from those safeguards is a lightly regulated field in which '[tax] fraud, transfer pricing and other multinational corporate techniques [ensure the systematic extortion of] Africa's income'.[51] These are the wages of (the sin of) 'extraction-resource dependency' in which the 'power of a dominant economic bloc to extract surpluses from weaker blocs' guarantees the weaker blocs are themselves 'locked into non-capitalist social relations'.[52] On the one hand, the weaker bloc is denied the opportunity to develop, while African elites – co-opted as the comprador enablers of the multilateral system – collude in the draining of resources;[53] on the other hand, the imposition of market conditions ensures a clash of interests occurs between local populations who derive little benefit from entering into the system of commodity exchange with the profitmaking interests of international corporate power. The cost incurred by this ruinous process, as is seen in the case of the DRC, is state failure. The reason is simple, brutally so: the 'comprador' state in which transnational capital and its agents parasitically operate have little need of normal state functions beyond the minimal provision of security. On the contrary, they benefit from the hollowing out of its civic, legal, and demo-cratic institutions, leaving it prostrate before all comers.[54] The failed state, whose existence is condensed into the 'deployment of pure power', as Bond puts it,[55] in the service of 'extractive commerce', manifests the inner logic of the conjunctural crisis of globalisation, while at the same time confronts it with its direst consequences.[56]

It is hardly a surprise, given the scale of the calamity, that recent years have seen various attempts by global institutions to rein in the excesses through the imposition of new laws and a system of regulative checks and balances. The OECD Due Diligence Guidance for Responsible Supply Chains of Minerals from Conflict-Affected and High-Risk Areas in 2011 sought to impose a regulatory system on importers of certain minerals, as did the US 'conflict minerals' law, passed in 2010 (Section 1502 of the Dodd-Frank Wall Street Reform and Consumer Protection Act), that intended to improve transparency throughout the supply chain. These acts were followed by the European Union memorandum in 2014 that aimed to 'reduce the financing of armed groups and security forces through mineral proceeds in conflict-affected and high risk areas' and support 'responsible sourcing practices' within EU-based companies.[57] Needless to say, the results have been vari-able. According to a report by the Responsible Sourcing Network (Mining the Disclosures, 2019, RSN), an analysis of the mineral supply chain of 215 US companies 'found many have fallen short of the obligations and the conflict minerals Rule'.[58] '[M]ediocre levels' of adherence, the report's authors found, have '[weakened] efforts to tackle the financing of armed groups'; one reason for this: the 'incentive for companies to implement the law [was] eliminated'[59] by the actions of the Trump administration that threatened to abandon the Dodd-Frank act and which led subsequently to the US Securities and Exchange Commission's decision to suspend enforce-ment of the law.[60]

These, then, are some of the principal factors – the organic processes, glo-balising forms and structures, and long-term historical tendencies, as well as more recent political, economic, and commercial decisions – that provide the backdrop for the conflict in the DRC. And it is in relation to these conjunctural crisis conditions that *The Congo Tribunal* must be interpreted. I have argued that *The Congo Tribunal* provides a means for elaborating a 'politics of the overdue' that articulates a 'futural' theatre of the planetary conjuncture. The political task of such a theatre is to overwrite the present with another possibility for the present, with a different sense of futurity, with a different temporality to that of production/consumption, and thus with a different historicity to the current historical trajectory that defines the 'necropolitical' character of the global now, to employ Achille Mbembe's incisive term.[61] That the latter need not be inexorable is the first axiom of the theatre of the planetary conjuncture; the second axiom is that the transformation of the present requires the overwriting of the present by the overdue. It is why *The Congo Tribunal* should not be viewed as merely staging a theatrical prosecution in lieu of the 'real' prosecution it hopes for. More precisely understood, it is a demonstration that the possibility of justice concerns present conditions that must be fundamentally transformed (and transformed by 'futural' means). Hence Rau proclaims the tribunal's theatrical form as a 'presentational space for the present' but whose function is to 'illuminate the future practice of an international administration of justice for the Congo ... not as an artistic allegory, not through fictional characters, but as a real situation erected in the presence of the real political and social actors and based on real, valid legislation'.[62] One understands the emphasis on the real as that which contains truth in itself, but which is also and can only be a negating force *for* justice. Justice overdue means: the jurisdiction of international law and courts constitutes part of the problem, reflecting ideological biases and a 'strategic political bias'.[63] 'Justice first' is the imperative reality forces upon it. How to define that reality? In Rau's condensed formulation, it is that of a 'second imperialism' – thus: 'eternal peace in the imperial centres, eternal war or rather the state of exception in the external spaces'.[64]

On this basis, one also understands that *The Congo Tribunal* comprises not just a specific instance, or a glitch in the system, but a general model within which the crisis of the global conjuncture operates, and that it is consequently to be understood as a 'symbolic, ultimately interchangeable location for the economic policy of globalisation'.[65] It is worth considering in detail what the implications of this are since it touches on the context of our general insecurity, and also our general complicity with regard to the global situation: weak states, inadequately developed civil society, corruptible elites, unchecked economic power of multinationals – establishing a hegemony of corporate power unfettered from all accountability, responsibility, and liability. This is the global reality that *The Congo Tribunal* seeks to highlight. In Rau's analysis, two deadly logics are revealed through it. The first is the 'downward dialectic'[66] placed on failed states by globalised forces such as the World Bank or the neocolonialism of new actors, etc.; the second concerns the logic of *stasis* that results – of inner turmoil, civil strife, and political pathologies such as genocide resulting from interethnic violence – that enables the new imperialism and is exacerbated by it. This is also the meaning of the new cosmopolitanism: not perpetual peace but perpetual conflict. It is this logic and these consequences that *The Congo Tribunal* discovers 'behind the beautiful scenery' of global capital, as Rau puts it, 'of the UN, NGOs, the World Bank and their statistics'.[67]

In this sense, and to conclude – the theatre of the planetary conjuncture also contains within its utopian explorations of a possible co-inherited world – of what Mbembe has termed 'the project of the *in-common*' – a sober warning.[68] It comes in the form of an open question: What does the future look like? The answer to this question shows why the Congo appears before us as testament to the horror that stems directly from averting one's eyes in the face of reality. It reveals historical forces that not only manifest themselves in the immediate past, but which are actively determining the future. Thus, Rau is right to assert – and here is where I will end: 'The gaze on what happens in the Congo, is not a gaze into the past, it's a gaze on our collective future.'[69]

This is what the future looks like, in other words: as with the Eastern Congo, we will see the 'dismantling of state structures on behalf of free trade, the subjection of vast regions to the authority of the World Bank, the trituration of all the approaches taken by the civil society for the implementation of the profit rhythms of financial capitalism controlled in New York, Beijing, Boston, and Brussels, the creation of protectorates under the watch of UN troops [... all] will soon be a reality in other global regions as well'.[70]

7

On taxonomic strategies

And what finally are we left with? Not, it seems, with a definitive classificatory system of the political theatre, as one might anticipate from a taxonomic exercise. A disappointment then? (Wasn't it already understood that this was an exercise undertaken in bad faith?) Was it merely a labour in vain? Then, to what end?! Do we possess anything other than a limited and rudimentary sense of the object of study? And in any case hasn't it been established that any such substantive form or practice probably does not exist, and that it is even questionable whether it ever did? If the conclusion is: there is no such thing as the 'genre' of political theatre – and that does seem to be *a* conclusion one might draw – then it is a deflationary one. When confronted with the question of its 'substance', so many fluctuating doubts linger as to *what* it *is* as to make the existence of the political theatre appear little more than protean. We seek to identify its unique features in vain, we skirt around its circumference without ever constituting its centre: it is little wonder that what at first seems tangible quickly becomes intangible once its assumptions are probed, and the ground it grows in dug over. The political theatre is too mutable to be a genre, too inconstant to be a form, too irregular to be a style (although in some respects 'style' is what it has been reduced to more often than not – for instance, the 'Brechtian' style of political theatre; the 'Boalian' style; the 'postdramatic' style, etc.). Naturally, then, we become suspicious of the validity of any type of theatre that *styles* itself as 'political'. There is a certain critical attitude that may even feel itself to be vindicated by such a thought. It argues political theatre has no political substance because it has no political consequences; there is therefore no such thing as the political theatre. This is what the chorus proclaims too: theatre and politics are two different things! But it is the same chorus that also decrees: *all* theatre is political because *everything* is. Everything is different; nothing is different!

It may perhaps be remarked, despite such demurrals, that the question of the political theatre will not be so easily bottled-up: it constantly renews itself whenever politics becomes a pressing concern beyond the theatre. And regardless of this have we not explored enough of the topic to know that a positive result does not reside in simply dismissing the idea of the political theatre out of hand – one cannot derive a positive from a mere negation. Despite well-founded doubts, it is hubristic to suppose that the political theatre is simply a meaningless designation and that all that remains is simply 'theatre', minus the pejorative connotations of the adjective 'political' that was once ostentatiously attached to it (during a period apparently more naïve than our own). What is the alternative approach? Might one forge a middle path by making a certain concession here, a minor compromise there? Might one not be tempted to seize therefore upon a recuperative solution, by admitting: 'there is no such thing as "The Political Theatre" – okay! *BUT* there *are* nonetheless political theatres.' The benefits of such a standpoint are palpable: not only has the dirty bathwater been drained, but the baby has been saved ... – but as a solution this is only superficially tempting. It is not as if 'The Political Theatre', grasped in grand and singular form (precisely the rhetorical contrivance I avoided earlier when I used the designation the 'classical political theatre') finds its counterpart in the idea of a multiplicity of theatres, each adopting distinct political approaches, methods, styles, or what have you. Political theatre in the plural may be less egregious a formulation, it may even possess greater descriptive precision, it may accord better with the reality of existing and historical practices, but it doesn't absolve us of the work of confronting the fundamental problem. This is because by locating 'The Political Theatre' and the idea of 'political theatres' as obverse sides of a strict semantic coin that neatly divides them, not only have we failed to resolve the problem, but we have missed it entirely. The *problem* of the political character of the political theatre pertains to both sides equally: hence they are precisely two sides of the *same* coin, regardless of whether the political theatre is conceived as singular or plural. At the same time, I think this brings us somewhat closer to the heart of the matter, and to the heart of the problem with which I have been contending in this essay.

It is perhaps better to enquire, then, as to their inner connection, as to their relation, in other words, to view the matter 'historically'. Over the course of little more than a century, the political theatre appeared on the scene, it overturned the old assumptions of what theatre was thought capable of being and what it should do, it shattered the consensus around whose interests it should serve, it established itself in dismal circumstances – not as belief incarnate but with its back up against the wall. It articulated theatre as part of a wider struggle, and thereby became part of the struggle. It installed itself within the space of the exception that was all too real – it fled the safety of the aesthetic exception to intervene in the state of exception – and in a way that no other art form had the power to do. It thus seized upon the power of the stage to wage a war on the society of the stage. It heralded within theatre's spaces of theatrical exception, the exceptional situation of the conjunctural moment it saw beyond itself, but also found within itself. At the same time, it operated ceaselessly on the operations of the theatre: it transformed the theatre, and thereby it transformed itself. That the classical political theatre proved ultimately a chimera does not disprove the reality it attested to – and that as with any other political thing, the political reality of the theatre is nothing other than its conjunctural reality.

It is this political reality of the theatre that comprises the central discovery of this taxonomic exercise, this thought experiment – and where this book concludes: the political theatre is always a theatre of the conjuncture (the same can be said of every 'political' work of art). Equally, the over-determined nature of the political theatre – its inability to be decided 'in the last instance' – has meant that the 'reality' of a conjunctural theatre could only be articulated according to the field of problematisations that arose with it. The theatre of the conjuncture possesses no reality in itself; its reality is founded on the form of its social mediations – not on the basis of its 'autonomy'. In this sense I concede 'taxonomy' is no doubt a poor word – too arid, too technical, too methodological – to describe what I have tried to do here. The purpose it served was to indicate the problematic to the extent that it compelled us to ask what is *meant* by the term 'political theatre'. That term did not serve as a pretext for a structuralism of the theatre; it necessitated instead the opposite: a genealogy of the political theatre.

A genealogy of the political theatre!? What is meant by this?

I have taken the idea of a genealogy as indicating the historical dimension of the problem rather than constituting a history as such. A genealogy of the political theatre is not a history *of* the political theatre. If it was, it would rightly be seen to have failed. What has been elaborated here would be a poor cousin of the history of the political theatre. But nor should genealogy be viewed as the history of the *idea* of the political theatre – since the latter is always tacitly contained in the former. I have not been tempted into writing the story of the 'rise and fall' of the political theatre. On the contrary, the genealogical approach I have taken could scarcely commence with something that covertly installs at the outset a name that serves the purposes of identifying an origin. In other words, if the name of the political theatre appears outside the problematic by which it is constituted – that is, outside its own historical field of emergence – then its conceptual purpose is to act as the sovereign term governing the continuous line of development over which it reigns. What it does not do is designate a 'problem'. Better to view the name of the political theatre, instead, as the basis for the genealogy of a conjunctural problem.

But are we not then led back to the absurdity of supposing a discontinuous line of development – either the object of a genealogy is constant, or the genealogy is constantly changing its object, and so provides no basis from which to describe anything? My answer to this objection is that the problem of the political theatre, which appeared at the commencement of the previous century, took the form of an event – not an object; and that the consequent ramifications of that event, insofar as they played out over time, constituted the historical trajectory of a problem – questions of form or genre were some of the ways in which the problem was articulated through practices. It is more likely, in fact, that the various struggles with aesthetic form, over the past century and into the next, arose precisely because the political theatre remained caught inside an event whose meaning could not be decided, and that through its various permutations the name of the political theatre came to traverse the entire century. In short, the event of the political theatre constitutes the advent of the problem of the political theatre. It is why the problem of the conjuncture with which theatre has engaged in a perpetual struggle itself resides within the context of the lengthier organic question of an underlying 'tendency'. It predisposed the theatre toward an engagement with, and at times, a direct intervention in, the sphere of the social; that tendency was born of the political orientation set by the event (whose varied points of emergence, running deep into the nineteenth century, like the veins and arteries of a body, finally fused during the Russian Revolution), and located it within a milieu of progressive struggle – that is to say, the struggle for democracy.

For this reason, also, when one speaks of the political theatre, one is speaking of a problematic that consists of two intersecting axes. The first axis, as I have said, is conjunctural: the theatre is political, irrespective of whatever form it takes, *whenever it exceeds being a mere 'effect' of a particular conjunctural moment and seeks to transform its present in some way*. The second axis is tendential: the theatre is political if it bears within itself *the organic problematic of the political*, which predisposes it, in virtue of the 'event' of the political theatre toward the new – in other words, toward the future it anticipates.

There is one final observation I would like to make. If it is worth raising these questions today, it is because the genealogy of the political theatre cannot but ultimately trace the epistemic problem of the political, whose impasse has been reached in the form of the crisis of the 'post political'. Hence the series of questions I have asked are neither new, but nor are they irrelevant: What is politics? What is the conjuncture? What is ideology? What is reality? And how has theatre tried to articulate these questions – in short, what can it do? While I do not think there is a definitive way of answering these questions, to pose them for ourselves is important if we are to direct ourselves to the conjunctural present. For that same reason, there can be no definitive way of stating what the political theatre is, can, or should be. What can be said, however, is that the 'constant' of the conjuncture, as that which continually presses in on the present moment, compels the question of the political theatre. To address that question today, is also – I would suggest – to address the specific nature of the conjunctural crisis of the post-political: the disappearance or loss of a utopic horizon upon which a politics might be projected. To the extent that such a horizon is still occluded – smothered by what appears to be a dense layer of atmospheric fog – the question of the political will remain frozen in a state of enduring 'crisis'. The theatre may seem a meagre resource in the face of such a calamitous moment, and an inadequate response to so much of the ensuing suffering. But it also provides, as I hope the theatre of the planetary conjuncture indicated, a social means of experimenting with *what might be*. In this sense, the political theatre continues, as it has always done, to address the dilemma of the present in a form that anticipates the possibility of the future – a future that it brings into the present in simulated form.

Notes

Introduction: The horizon of the aesthetic

1 See, for instance, Ed Pilkington and David Smith 'Bernie Sanders Warns of "International Oligarchy" after Paradise Papers Leak', *The Guardian* (6 November 2017). Available at: www.theguardian.com/news/2017/nov/06/bernie-sanders-paradise-papers-leak-international-oligarchy (Accessed: 14 February 2023).

2 See Jacques Rancière, 'Artistic Regimes and the Shortcomings of the Notion of Modernity' in *The Politics of the Aesthetic*, trans. Gabriel Rockhill, 15–25 (London: Bloomsbury, 2021).

3 Nicolas Bourriaud, *The Exform*, trans. Eric Butler (London: Verso, 2016), 43.

4 Rancière writes: ' "art" is not the common concept that unifies the different arts. It is the *dispositif* that renders them visible.' Jacques Rancière, *Aesthetics and its Discontents*, trans. Steven Corcoran (Cambridge: Polity Press, 2009), 23.

5 Peter Osborne, *The Postconceptual Condition* (London: Verso, 2018).

6 Rancière, *Aesthetics and its Discontents*, 8.

7 Alexander Gottlieb Baumgarten, *Aestheticorum* (Hildesheim: George Olms Verlag, 1986 [Ionnis Christian Kleys, 1758]), section 1, 1 ['scientia cognitionis sensitiuae']. Although Baumgarten first designates the aesthetic as a distinct sphere, he was influenced by the publication of Christian Wolff's *Empirical Psychology* in 1732. Wolff outlined a metaphysical concept of the beautiful, in which beauty finds its foundation In the beauty of an object: 'Beauty consists in the perfection of a thing, by virtue of that power it possesses to produce pleasure in us' ('Pulchrituda consistit in perfectione rei, quatenus ea vi illius ad voluptatem in nobis producendam apta' Christian Wolff, *Psychologia Empirica, Methodo Scientifica*, section 544 (Frankfurt and Leipzig: Libraria Rengeriana, 1732), 420.

8 Baumgarten, *Aestheticorum*, section 423 ('Tertia cura fit rebus eleganter cognitandis ... sed aesthetica, i.e. veritas quatenus sensitiue cognoscenda est'), 269.

9 Immanuel Kant, *Critique of Judgement*, trans. James Creed Meredith (Oxford: Clarendon Press, 1952), 236 and 80.

10 Ibid., 80, fn. 1.

11 Ibid., 42.

12 See Jürgen Habermas's Adorno Prize address delivered in 1980 published as: 'Modernity versus Postmodernity' in *New German Critique*, vol. 22, Winter, 1981, 3–14.

13 Jay Bernstein, *The Fate of Art: Aesthetic Alienation from Kant to Derrida and Adorno* (Oxford: Polity Press, 1992), 225.

14 Ibid., 5.

15 Ibid., 4.

16 Ibid., 4, 9.

17 Ibid., 5.

18 Theodor W. Adorno, *Aesthetic Theory*, trans. Robert Hullot-Kentor (London: Continuum, 2002), 136.

19 Raymond Geuss, *Philosophy and Real Politics* (Princeton, NJ: Princeton University Press, 2008), 25.

20 Rancière, *Politics of the Aesthetic*, 12.

21 Ibid., 9.

22 Rancière, *Aesthetics and its Discontents*, 36.

23 Ibid.

24 Ibid.

25 Jacques Rancière, *Dissensus: On Politics and Aesthetics*, trans. Steven Corcoran (London: Continuum, 2010), 140.

26 Theodor W. Adorno and Max Horkheimer, *Dialectic of Enlightenment*, trans. John Cumming (London: Verso, 1997), 83–84.

27 Peter Bürger, *Theory of the Avant-Garde*, trans. Michael Shaw (Minneapolis, MN: Minneapolis University Press, 2009).

28 Rancière, *Dissensus*, 142.

29 Jacques Rancière, *The Emancipated Spectator*, trans. Gregory Elliott (London: Verso, 2009), 82.

30 Ibid., 82.

31 Ibid., 60.

32 Adorno, *Aesthetic Theory*, 232.

33 Alan Read, *Theatre, Intimacy & Engagement: The Last Human Venue* (Basingstoke: Palgrave Macmillan, 2009), 26.

34 Ibid., 25.

35 Ibid., 186.

36 Ibid., 186 (emphasis added).

37 Liz Tomlin, *Political Dramaturgies and Theatre Spectatorship: Provocations for Change* (London: Methuen Drama, 2019), 2.

38 Ibid., 11.

39 Ibid., and Rancière quoted in Tomlin, ibid., 11. Elsewhere she writes: 'Rancière understands the politics of aesthetic efficacy to [mean …] the individual's autonomy from the artist's intention to construct their own meaning', 44.

40 Ibid., 101.

41 Ibid., 49.

42 Ibid., 112.

43 Rancière, *Emancipated Spectator*, 74.

44 Fredric Jameson, *The Political Unconscious: Narrative as a Socially Symbolic Act* (London: Routledge, 1983), 25.

45 Jacques Rancière, *The Method of Equality*, trans. Julie Rose (Cambridge: Polity Press, 2016), 175.

46 Rancière, *Politics of the Aesthetic*, 58.

47 Ibid., 57.

48 Ibid.

49 Ibid., 58.

50 Bonnie Honig, *Political Theory and the Displacement of Politics* (Ithaca, NY: Cornell University Press, 1993), 2.

51 Ibid., 4.

52 Rancière writes: 'Politics exists when the figure of a specific subject is constituted, a supernumerary subject in relation to the calculated number of groups, places, and functions in a society.' Rancière, *Politics of the Aesthetic*, 47–48. Or, elsewhere: 'Political subjectification produces a multiple that was not given in the police constitution of the community, a multiple whose count poses itself as contradictory in terms of police logic.' Jacques Rancière, *Disagreement: Politics and Philosophy*, trans. Julie Rose (Minneapolis, MN: University of Minnesota Press, 1999), 36.

53 Stuart Hall, 'Marx's Notes on Method: A "Reading" of the "1857 Introduction"' in *Selected Writings on Marxism*, ed. Gregory McLennan, 19–61 (Durham, NC: Durham University Press, 2021), 30.

54 Jameson, *Political Unconscious*, 25.

55 Ibid., 26.

56 Ibid.

57 The theory of articulation derives from Althusser and Balibar's reading of Marx – see Louis Althusser and Étienne Balibar, *Reading Capital*, trans. Ben Brewster (London: NLB, 1970) – for instance, Balibar writes of the 'articulation of the instances of the social formation', 207, fn. 5; Althusser employs the metaphor of a body: 'the structure of the whole is articulated as the structure of an organic hierarchized whole. The co-existence of limbs and their relations to the whole is governed by the order of a dominant structure which introduces a specific order into the articulation (*Gliederung*) of the limbs and their relations', 98.

58 Ernesto Laclau, *Politics and Ideology in Marxist Theory: Capitalism, Fascism, Populism* (London: Verso, 2011), 7.

59 'The unity which they form is thus not that of an identity, where one structure perfectly recapitulates or reproduces or event "expresses" another; or where each is reducible to the other; or where each is defined by the same determinations or have exactly the same conditions of existence; or even where each develops according to the effectivity of the same conditions of existence; or even where each develops according to the effectivity of the same contradiction ....' Stuart Hall, 'Race, Articulation, and Societies Structured in Dominance' in

Essential Essays, vol. 1, ed. David Morley, 172–221 (Durham, NC: Duke University Press, 2019), 196.

60 Ibid., 197.

61 Stuart Hall, Chas Critcher, Tony Jefferson, John Clarke, and Brian Roberts, *Policing the Crisis: Mugging, the State and Law & Order* (London: Red Globe Press, 2013 [1978]), 3.

62 Ibid., xv.

63 Produced as part of a series of prints entitled *Genocide and Democracy III*, 2015.

64 See Slavoj Žižek, *The Metastases of Enjoyment: Six Essays on Women and Causality* (London: Verso, 2005), 54.

65 Reinhart Koselleck, ' "Space of Experience" and "Horizon of Experience": Two Historical Categories' in *Future's Past: On the Semantics of Historical Time*, trans. Keith Tribe, 255–275 (New York: Columbia University Press, 2004), 258.

66 Peter Osborne, *Expecting the Unexpected: Once More on the 'Horizon of Expectations'*, lecture, 16 May 2019. Available at: www.youtube.com/watch?v=amStWD9jJm0 (Accessed: 6 January 2022).

67 Koselleck, 'Space of Experience', 268.

68 Ibid., 267.

69 See for example: Dipesh Chakrabarty, *The Climate of History in a Planetary Age* (Chicago, IL: University of Chicago Press, 2021).

70 Gayatri Chakravorty Spivak, *Death of a Discipline* (New York: Columbia University Press, 2003), 73. In the face of the dystopic future 'around the corner', Spivak argues for a 'utopic' form of planetary living, whose imperative is 'Think, therefore, the planet ....' Gayatri Chakravorty Spivak, 'Imperative to Re-imagine the Planet' in *An Aesthetic Education in the Era of Globalization*, 335–350 (Cambridge, MA: Harvard University Press, 2012), 343.

71 See also Achille Mbembe, *Out of the Dark Night: Essays of Decolonization* (New York: Columbia University Press, 2021) – Mbembe writes: 'To reopen the future of our planet to all who inhabit it, we will have to learn how to share it again among humans, but also between humans and nonhumans, between the multiple species that populate our planet', 41.

72 Hannah Arendt, *The Human Condition, Second Edition* (Chicago, IL: University of Chicago Press, 1998 [1958]), 12.

73 Aristotle, 'Politics' in *The Complete Works of Aristotle*, The Revised Oxford Translation, ed. Jonathan Barnes, vol. 2, trans. B. Jowett, 1986–2129 (Princeton, NJ: Princeton University Press, 1986), 1283b, 42–1284a, 1, 2037.

74 Ibid., 1280a, 31–32, 2031–2032.

75 Ibid., 1280a, 33, 2032.

76 Arendt, *Human Condition*, 13.

77 Ibid.

78 Peter Weiss, *The Aesthetics of Resistance*, vol. 1, trans. Joachim Neugroschel (Durham, NC: Duke University Press, 2005), 64.

Part I: The aesthetic exception

1 Matthew Arnold, *Culture and Anarchy and Other Writings* (Cambridge: Cambridge University Press, 2010), 62. See also Alain de Botton, 'Should Art Really Be for its Own Sake?', *The Guardian* (20 January 2012). Available at: www.theguardian.com/commentisfree/2012/jan/20/art-museums-churches (Accessed: 14 February 2023).
2 Pierre Bourdieu, *The Rules of Art*, trans. Susan Emanuel (Cambridge: Polity Press, 2019), xiv.
3 Ibid., xv.
4 Alain Badiou, 'The Common Preoccupation of Art and Philosophy' in *Badiou and his Interlocutors: Lectures, Interviews and Responses*, ed. A.J. Bartlett and Justine Clemens, 31–38 (London: Bloomsbury, 2018), 35.
5 Ibid., 36.
6 Were it possible to do so, one would confront an entirely distinct 'regime' of the arts, as Jacques Rancière would say.

The paradox of the aesthetic exception

1 Giorgio Agamben, *What Is an Apparatus?*, trans. David Kishik and Stefan Pedatella (Stanford, CA: Stanford University Press, 2011), 11. See also Michel Foucault, 'The Confession of the Flesh' in *Power/Knowledge, Selected Interviews and Other Writings 1972–1977*, ed. and trans. Colin Gordon, 194–228 (Essex: Longman, 1980).
2 Tristan Tzara, 'Manifeste Dada' in *Dada 3* (Zurich: Mouvement DADA, 1918). Available at: www.ubu.com/historical/dada/dada.html (Accessed: 5 May 2022).
3 Bourdieu, *Rules of Art*, 288.
4 Giorgio Agamben, *Homo Sacer: Sovereign Power and Bare Life*, trans. Daniel Heller-Roazen (Stanford, CA: Stanford University Press, 1998), 181.
5 Edward Coke, *The First Part of the Institutes of the Laws of England*, Lib. II, 'Of Villenage', Sect. 199, vol. 1 (London: R. Brooke, 1738), 130.
6 William Blackstone, *Commentaries on the Laws of England in Four Books*, vol. 1 (Clark, NJ: The Lawbook Exchange, 2007), 121.
7 Giorgio Agamben, *The State of Exception*, trans. Kevin Attell (Chicago, IL: University of Chicago Press, 2005), 4.
8 Stuart Hall, 'The Work of Representation' in *Representation: Cultural Representations and Signifying Practices*, ed. Stuart Hall, 13–74 (London: Sage, 2002), 28.
9 Samuel Beckett, *Endgame* (London: Faber & Faber, 1972), 39.
10 Stéphane Mallarmé, 'Un coup de dés jamais n'aborlira les hazard' in *Un Coup de Des & Other Poems*, trans. A.S. Kline, 76–110 (Poetry in Translation, 2009), 77. Available at: www.poetryintranslation.com/klineasmallarme.php (Accessed: 22 April 2021).

11 One example of this radicalisation of the exception that attained an early theoretical articulation can be found in the Russian Formalist notion of 'liter-
   ariness' – indicating, according to Silvija Jestrovic in her detailed analysis of
   the Russian avant-garde, the 'eminent quality of a literary work' which paral-
   leled the 'term "theatricality" as theatre's intrinsic and self-referential quality', Silvija Jestrovic, *Theatre of Estrangement: Theory, Practice, Ideology*
   (Toronto: University of Toronto Press, 2006), 43. Jestrovic provides an excellent analysis of how the exception is radicalised with the Russian Futurists conception of 'Zaum' – a 'radical instance of poetic language that defamiliarizes
   the notion of aesthetic communication [… giving] rise to new meanings', 48.
12 Mallarmé, *Un Coup*, 77.
13 Kélina Gotman, 'Mallarmé's "Livre": Notes towards a Schizotheatre', in
   Textual Practice, vol. 33, no. 1, 2017, 1–20, 12, 3.
14 Ibid. (original emphasis).
15 See for instance Bürger's classic work *Theory of the Avant-Garde*.
16 Jean-Luc Nancy, 'Masked Imagination' in *The Ground of the Image*, trans. Jeff
   Fort, 80–99 (New York: Fordham University Press, 2005), 84.
17 Ibid.
18 Ibid.
19 Kant, *Critique of Judgement*, 168 (emphases are Kant's).
20 Ibid., 164.
21 Ibid., 168.
22 Ibid., 169, 171.
23 Ibid., 169.
24 Ibid., 167.
25 Ibid., 168.
26 Ibid., 172 (original emphasis).
27 Ibid., 171.
28 Ibid., 181.
29 Ibid., 164.
30 Ibid., 166.
31 Ibid., 173.
32 Ibid., 174.
33 Ibid.
34 Ibid., 165.
35 Ibid., 161.

Crossing the threshold

1 Tzara, 'Manifeste Dada', 4. Tzara writes: 'Liberté: DADA DADA DADA,
  hurlement des couleurs crispées, entrelacement des contraires et de toutes les
  contradictions, des grotesques, des inconséquences: LA VIE', 4.
2 Giorgio Agamben, 'Archaeology of the Work of Art' in *Creation and
  Anarchy: The Work of Art and the Religion of Capitalism*, trans. Adam Kotsko,
  1–13 (Stanford, CA: Stanford University Press, 2019), 3.

3 Bürger, *Theory of the Avant-Garde*, 51.
4 Ibid., 87.
5 Agamben, 'Archaeology', 12.
6 Ibid., 12.
7 Marcel Duchamp quoted in Thierry de Duve, 'Echoes of the Readymade: Critique of Pure Modernism' in *The Duchamp Effect: Essays, Interviews, Roundtable*, ed. Martha Buskirk and Mignon Nixon, 93–130 (Cambridge, MA: MIT Press, 1999), 104 (original emphasis).
8 Hence the Readymade occupies the peculiar position of being both autonomous in the sense it is extracted from the world of things, but non-autonomous in that it denies the 'autonomy' of artistic labour. This is one reason why the concept of autonomy presents difficulties in interpreting the work of art – a difficulty that is more fully explained in relation to the problematic of the aesthetic exception.
9 Marcel Duchamp, *The Blind Man*, no. 2, May 1917, New York, 4.
10 Thomas McEvilley, 'Doctor, Lawyer, Indian Chief: "Primitivism" in Twentieth Century Art at the Museum of Modern Art' in *Art & Otherness: Crisis in Cultural Identity*, 27–56 (New York: McPherson and Company, 1992), 27.
11 Robert Goldwater, *Primitivism in 20th Century Art* (Cambridge, MA: Harvard University Press, 1986 [1938]), 250.
12 Ibid., 252.
13 See Edward W. Said, *Orientalism* (New York: Random House, 1978), 1.
14 Ibid., 6.
15 Ibid., 3.
16 See for an extended discussion Souleymane Bachir Diagne, *African Art as Philosophy: Senghor, Bergson and the Idea of Negritude*, trans. Chike Jeffers (London: Seagull Books, 2011), 45–96.
17 Guillaume Apollinaire, 'Exoticism and Ethnography' in *Apollinaire on Art: Essays and Reviews 1902–1918*, trans. Susan Suleiman, 243–246 (London: Thames & Hudson, 1972 [1912]), 244, 246.
18 Andre Malraux, *Picasso's Mask*, trans. June Guicharnaud (New York: Da Capo Press, 1976), 114.
19 Goldwater, *Primitivism*, 9.
20 Hal Foster, 'The "Primitive" Unconscious of Modern Art' in *October*, vol. 34, Autumn 1985, 45–70.
21 Malraux, *Picasso's Mask*, 170.
22 Ibid., 168.
23 Goldwater, *Primitivism*, 159. According to Goldwater, Picasso misunderstood African art, appropriating it as violence when in fact it is highly rational and static.
24 Malraux, *Picasso's Mask*, 171, 96.
25 Ibid., 99.
26 Ibid., 98.
27 Ibid., 166.
28 Rasheed Araeen, 'Modernity, Modernism and Africa's Authentic Voice' in *Third Text*, vol. 24, no. 2, 2010, 277–286, 284.

29 The reality is that a pan-African consciousness permeates early twentieth-century modernism, constituting itself as a force of political incursion, aesthetic transformation, and epistemic rupture, from Harlem to Martinique, from Cuba to Senegal – this is nowhere more forcefully asserted than through the Negritude movement and the poetry of Aimé Césaire – see for example, his masterpiece *Notebook of a Return to My Native Land/ Cahier d'un retour au pays natal*. As Stuart Hall once observed, modernism cannot be thought as a set of 'triumphal artistic practices ... located in ... the West ... In reality, the world is absolutely littered by modernities and practicing artists, who never regarded modernism as the secure possession of the West, but perceived it as a language which was both open to them but which they would have to transform' Stuart Hall, 'Museums of Modern Art and the End of History' in *Modernity and Difference*, Annotations 6, ed. Stuart Hall and Sarat Maharaj, 8–23 (London: INIVA, 2001), 19.

30 Diagne, *African Art as Philosophy*, 52.

31 Ibid., 52.

32 Ibid., 53. It is, according to Diagne, the Negritude poets who would resolve the riddle: 'Art is the evidence of African philosophy and, conversely, we do not attain full comprehension of African art without understanding the metaphysics from which it proceeds. This metaphysics ... is a metaphysics of *rhythm* which, according to Senghor, is at the core of African thought and experience', 54–55.

33 Ibid., 198.

34 Ibid., 8.

35 Michel Thévoz, 'Preface' to Lucienne Peiry, *Art Brut: The Origins of Outsider Art*, trans. James Frank, 7–8 (Paris: Flammarion, 2001), 7.

36 Jean Dubuffet quoted in Peiry, *Art Brut*, 11.

37 Jean Dubuffet, 'Asphyxiating Culture' in *Asphyxiating Culture and Other Essays*, trans. Carol Volk, 7–12 (New York: Four Walls, 1988), 10.

38 Ibid., 12.

39 Ibid., 8.

40 Dubuffet writes: 'Just look at the care that artists take (with their vestimentary disguises and their individualistic behavior) to be known as such and clearly distinguish themselves from the common people', ibid., 9.

41 Michel Foucault, *The Archaeology of Knowledge and the Discourse on Language*, trans. A.M. Sheridan Smith (New York: Pantheon Books, 1971), 50.

42 Bourdieu, *Rules of Art*, 244.

43 The artist is not simply a producer of art but increasingly, a collector, a curator, and a critic.

44 Bourdieu, *Rules of Art*, 246.

45 Ibid., 245.

46 Dick Higgins, 'Against Movements' in *Something Else Newsletter*, vol. 1, no. 6, May 1967, 1–4, 3.

47 Joseph Kosuth, 'Art after Philosophy' in *Art after Philosophy and After: Collected Writings, 1966–1990*, ed. Gabriele Guercio, 13–32 (Cambridge, MA: MIT Press, 1993), 16.

48 Ibid., 15.
49 Donald Judd quoted in ibid., 17.
50 Ibid.
51 Ibid.
52 Ibid., 18.
53 Ibid.
54 Ibid.
55 Ibid.
56 Ibid., 19–20.
57 Ibid., 20. See Kosuth's critique of realism where realist art, because it is not analytic but 'synthetic', requires an 'empirical' mode of verification: 'one is flung out of art's "orbit" into the "infinite space" of the human condition', ibid., 21.
58 Ibid.
59 Ibid., 24.
60 Ibid.
61 I refer here to Andrea Fraser's reflections on the problem of institutional critique in art, which I do not have space to develop further. However, this is no doubt pertinent: 'Representations of the "art world" as wholly distinct from the "real world", like representations of the "institution" as discrete and separate from "us", serve specific functions in art discourse. They maintain an imaginary distance between the social and economic interests we invest in through our activities and the euphemized artistic, intellectual, and even political "interests" (or disinterests) that provide those activities with content and justify their existence. And with these representations, we also reproduce the mythologies of volunteerist freedom and creative omnipotence that have made art and artists such attractive emblems for neoliberalism's entrepreneurial, "ownership-society" optimism. That such optimism has found perfect artistic expression in neo-Fluxus practices like relational aesthetics, which are now in perpetual vogue, demonstrates the degree to which what Bürger called the avant-garde's aim to integrate "art into life praxis" has evolved into a highly ideological form of escapism. But this is not just about ideology. We are not only symbols of the rewards of the current regime: In this art market, we are its direct material beneficiaries', Andrea Fraser, 'From the Critique of Institutions to an Institution of Critique' in *ArtForum*, vol. 44, no. 1, Sep 2005, New York, 278–285. Available at: www.marginalutility.org/wp-content/uploads/2010/07/Andrea-Fraser_From-the-Critique-of-Institutions-to-an-Institution-of-Critique.pdf (Accessed: 3 March 2021).
62 Allan Kaprow, 'Nontheatrical Performance' in *Essays on the Blurring of Art and Life*, ed. Jeff Kelley, 163–180 (Berkeley, CA: University of California Press, 2003), 174.
63 Dick Higgins, 'Intermedia' in *Something Else Newsletter*, vol. 1, no. 1, February 1966, 3.
64 Allan Kaprow, 'Performing Life' [1979] in Kaprow, *Essays*, 195–198, 195.
65 Ibid., 195.

66 Michel Foucault, 'The Subject, Knowledge, and the "History of Truth"' in *Remarks on Marx*, trans. R. James Goldstein and James Cascaito, 43–82 (New York: Semiotext(e), 1991), 48.

67 Martin Jay, 'The Limits of Limit-Experience' in *Constellations*, vol. 2, no. 2, 1995, 155–174, 159.

68 Allan Kaprow, 'The Legacy of Jackson Pollock' [1958] in Kaprow, *Essays*, 1–9, 4.

69 Ibid., 7–9.

70 Kaprow, 'Performing Life' [1979], 195.

71 Ibid.

72 Ibid., 196.

73 Ibid., 198.

74 Allan Kaprow, 'Art Which Can't Be Art' [1986] in Kaprow, *Essays*, 219–222, 219.

75 Ibid., 220–221.

76 Ibid., 222.

The institution of art

1 Bürger, *Theory of the Avant-Garde*, 50.

2 Ibid., 12.

3 Jürgen Habermas, 'Habermas: Questions and Counterquestions' in *Habermas and Modernity*, 192–216 (Cambridge: Polity Press, 1985), 197.

4 Bürger, *Theory of the Avant-Garde*, 50.

5 Nicolas Bourriaud, *Relational Aesthetics*, trans. Simon Pleasance and Fronza Woods (Dijon-Quetingy: Les Presses du Réel, 2006), 44.

6 Herbert Marcuse, 'The Affirmative Character of Culture' in *Negations: Essays in Critical Theory*, trans. Jeremy J. Shapiro, 65–98 (London: Mayfly Books, 2009), 97.

7 Bürger, *Theory of the Avant-Garde*, 13.

8 Ibid., 42.

9 Ibid., 13.

10 Ibid., 24. Bürger, extending Marcuse's argument on affirmative culture, writes: 'works of art are not received as single entities, but within institutional frameworks and conditions that largely determine the function of the works', 12.

11 Alain Badiou, *Handbook of Inaesthetics*, trans. Alberto Toscano (Stanford, CA: Stanford University Press, 2011), 11.

12 See Alain Badiou, 'Thèses sur l'art contemporain/ Fifteen Theses on Contemporary Art' in *Performance Research*, vol. 9, no. 4 (On Civility), 2004, 86.

13 It is worth recalling Jacques Rancière's criticism of Badiou's 'well-guarded fortress', when he writes: 'We can then ask if Badiou's own classification of the arts is not designed to ensure the inviolate "specificity" of art and that which

is not art – whether it is philosophy or the misery of the world – to a residence, to the borders. We shall ask, by the same token, whether there are no tensions to be found at these borders that undermine the tying of Platonism and modernism under the rubric "inaesthetics"', Jacques Rancière, 'Alain Badiou's Inaesthetics' in *Aesthetics and its Discontents*, 63–87, 81.

14 Pierre Bourdieu, *Distinction: A Social Critique of the Judgement of Taste*, trans. Richard Nice (London: Routledge, 1986), 226. One could, no doubt, understand the impasses of institutional critique as discovered in art practices in relation to this sociological reduced entelechy, where art is nothing but its framing conditions, against which it must nevertheless rebel – leading critique into either the monotony of institutional discourse, or wild flights into the wilderness beyond the institution that nonetheless tacitly reproduce those framing conditions under the ruse that the work must be seen 'partes extra partes'.

15 Ibid., 227.

16 Ibid., 228.

17 Ibid., 240.

18 Ibid., 246.

19 See Bourdieu's *Language and Symbolic Power*, trans. Gino Raymond and Matthew Adamson (Cambridge: Polity Press), 2011.

20 Bourdieu, *Distinction*, 250.

21 Ibid., 239–240.

22 Bourdieu, *Rules of Art*, 242.

23 Ibid.

24 Ibid.

25 Ibid., 243.

26 Adorno, *Aesthetic Theory*, 182.

Part II: Political art after the communicative turn

1 Theodor W. Adorno, 'Commitment' in *Notes to Literature*, vol. 2, trans. Shierry Weber Nicholson, 76–94 (New York: Columbia University Press, 1992), 93–94.

2 Ibid., 76.

3 See Janelle Reinelt, 'Resisting Rancière' in *Rancière and Performance*, ed. Nic Fryer and Colette Conroy, 171–194 (London: Rowman & Littlefield, 2021), 172.

4 Ibid., 173.

5 See Tony Fisher, 'Introduction: Performance and the Tragic Politics of the Agōn' in *Performing Antagonism: Theatre, Performance and Radical Democracy*, ed. Tony Fisher and Eve Katsouraki, 1–23 (London: Palgrave Macmillan, 2017), 15–16.

6 I am grateful to Antoinette Burchill for introducing me to this artist. For Burchill's own analysis of Scott's work, see Antoinette Burchill, 'Conflictual Sociability? A Paradoxical Approach to Politicized Street Theatre' in *Art & the Public Sphere*, vol. 10, no. 2, 1 November 2021, 165–173.

The classical debate revisited

1 Georg Lukács, 'Realism in the Balance', trans. Rodney Livingstone in Theodor W. Adorno et al., *Aesthetics and Politics*, ed. F. Jameson, 28–59 (London: Verso, 2007), 38.
2 Bertolt Brecht, 'Against Georg Lukács', trans. Stuart Hood in Adorno et al., *Aesthetics and Politics*, ed. Jameson, 68–85, 82.
3 Jean-Paul Sartre, *What Is Literature?*, trans. Bernard Frechtman (London: Routledge, 1993), 210–211.
4 Ibid., 236.
5 Ibid., 212.
6 Ibid.
7 Ibid., 216.
8 Adorno, 'Commitment', 80.
9 Theodor W. Adorno, *Minima Moralia: Reflections from Damaged Life*, trans. E.F.N. Jephcott (London: Verso, 1984), 224–225.
10 Adorno, 'Commitment', 77.
11 Ibid., 78.
12 J.L. Austin, *How to Do Things with Words, Second Edition*, ed. J.O. Urmson and Marina Sbisà (Oxford: Oxford University Press, 1976), 22.
13 Adorno, 'Commitment', 79.
14 Ibid., 93.
15 Ibid., 81.
16 Ibid., 82.
17 Ibid.
18 Ibid., 84.
19 Ibid., 82.
20 Ibid., 83.
21 Ibid., 84.
22 Ibid., 85.
23 Grant H. Kester, *Art, Activism, and Oppositionality: Essays from Afterimage* (Durham, NC: Duke University Press, 1998), 17.
24 Bourriaud, *Relational Aesthetics*, 43.
25 Claire Bishop, *Artificial Hells* (London: Verso, 2012), 27.
26 Shannon Jackson, *Social Works: Performing Art, Supporting Publics* (Abingdon: Routledge, 2011), 60.
27 Ibid., 35.
28 Paolo Virno describes the difference as follows: 'In Fordism, according to Gramsci, the intellect remains outside of production; only when the work has been finished does the Fordist worker read the newspaper, go to the local party headquarters, think, have conversations. In post-Fordism, however, since the "life of the mind" is included fully within the time-space of production, an essential homogeneity prevails', Paolo Virno, *A Grammar of the Multitude: For an Analysis of Contemporary Forms of Life*, trans. Isabella Bertoletti, James Cascaito and Andrea Casson (South Pasadena, CA: Semiotext(e), 2004), 103.

29 Ibid., 56.
30 Chantal Mouffe, *Agonistics: Thinking the World Politically* (London: Verso, 2013), 86.
31 Ibid., 87.
32 Ibid., 85–86.
33 Hans-Thies Lehmann, 'A Future for Tragedy? Remarks on the Political and the Postdramatic' in *Postdramatic Theatre and the Political: International Perspectives on Contemporary Performance*, ed. Karen Jürs-Munby, Jerome Carroll and Steve Giles, 87–109 (London: Bloomsbury, 2013), 108.
34 Mouffe, *Agonistics*, 90.
35 Tania Bruguera, 'Art as a Verb' in *We Are Many: Art, the Political and Multiple Truths*, ed. Jochen Volz and Gabi Ngcobo, 152–163 (London: Koenig Books, 2021), 154.
36 Ibid., 154–155.
37 Rancière, *Politics of Aesthetics*, 59.
38 Rancière, *Method of Equality*, 175.
39 Reinelt, 'Resisting Rancière', 173.
40 Ibid.
41 Ibid., 181.
42 Ibid., 173, my italics.
43 Fisher, 'Introduction', 193.
44 Lehmann, 'A Future for Tragedy?', 107.
45 Ibid., 108.
46 Mouffe, *Agonistics*, 93.
47 Ibid., 93–94.
48 Ibid.
49 Bojana Kunst, *Artist at Work: Proximity of Art and Capitalism* (Winchester: Zero Books, 2015), 61.
50 Ibid., 52.
51 Jackson, *Social Works*, 30.
52 Ibid., 13.
53 Jen Harvie, *Fair Play: Art, Performance and Neoliberalism* (Basingstoke: Palgrave Macmillan, 2013) .
54 James Thompson, *Performance Affects: Applied Theatre and the End of Effect* (Basingstoke: Palgrave Macmillan, 2009), 118. Thompson writes: 'working with a group of refugees, for example, has a politics that needs to be questioned, but it is not, by some default process, one that is inherently critical, or one that can claim an automatic contribution to social change', 5.
55 Emile Durkheim, *The Division of Labour in Society*, trans. G. Simpson (London: Macmillan, 1964), 1.
56 Ibid., 64.
57 Bourriaud, *Relational Aesthetics*, 28.
58 Jackson, *Social Works*, 21.
59 Ibid., 72.

60 But perhaps it will be objected that the political and the social form an indissoluble package – we speak of the socio-political as a compound noun, after all, and as such it would seem to be senseless to distinguish between them. The political is founded on the *socius*, on the continuance of existing traditions, on life-praxes that determine the general conformity of individuals within society, and which taken in their literal sense indicate the agreement established between people living in community with one another, from whence society springs; thus politics must find its definition in relation to what Michael Oakeshott described as 'the activity of attending to the general arrangements of a collection of people who, in respect of their common recognition of their manner of attending to its arrangements, compose a single community' Michael Oakeshott, 'Political Education' in *Rationalism in Politics and Other Essays*, 43–69 (Indianapolis, IN: Liberty Fund, 1991), 56. The activity of politics is determined not by the whim of an individual will; nor does it stem from ideological motives that arise in pursuit of particular interests, but – as he puts it – from 'the existing traditions of behaviour themselves. And the form it takes, because it can take no other, is the amendment of existing arrangements by exploring and pursuing what is intimated in them', 56. What does this mean but that politics is just the process of negotiating how institutional arrangements are modifiable through shared processes underpinning how societies are governed, taken in both broad and narrow senses: how those arrangements may be amended, jettisoned, and replaced by something else – but, whatever the result, that process is founded axiomatically on the principle of a 'communitas'. For this reason, a community living together in a polity is thus inseparable from the social condition of being human. Each, on this view, has a share – in some degree – of the *bios politikos*. But Oakeshott's conservative formulation presupposes the very thing that politics places in question: in other words, if we define the political from the perspective of the *pluralism* of the social, then we can no longer assume *commonality* founds the political. On the contrary, we discover the principle by which talk of commonality is necessarily limited by multiplicity, and where 'tradition' reveals itself to be an articulated structure, composed of contingent practices whose apparent necessity is constitutively prone to conflicting social imperatives.

What this leads to is an analytic distinction: when we speak of a politics, what we have in mind is a discrepancy between a plurality of viewpoints; a discrepancy that at the same time signals a relation of power and a relation of excess in which the ground of the social as given is not sufficient to satisfy the (democratic) demands placed on it. That excess expresses itself as a demand for the negation of an existing arrangement, and as such brings it into conflict with opposing interests. So, while I agree that the social must always be viewed in socio-political terms, in virtue of the inherent pluralism of the social, that does not entail that the political can be defined on the basis of a presumed sociality that we 'share in common', but on the divisions that serrate that sociality.

Art of the communicative turn

1 Jürgen Habermas, *The Theory of Communicative Action: Reason and the Rationalization of Society*, vol. 1, trans. T. McCarthy (Cambridge: Polity Press, 2004), 386.
2 Jürgen Habermas, *The Philosophical Discourse of Modernity*, trans. F. Lawrence (Cambridge: Polity Press, 2002), 296.
3 Ibid., 29.
4 Habermas quoted in Bürger, *Theory of the Avant-Garde*, 25.
5 Habermas, *Communicative Action*, 274.
6 Ibid., 278.
7 Ibid., 294.
8 Ibid.
9 For example, see Chantal Mouffe's essay 'Radical Democracy: Modern or Postmodern' in *The Return of the Political*, 9–22 (London: Verso, 1993).
10 Habermas, *Communicative Action*, 287.
11 Ibid., 288.
12 Ibid., 287.
13 Ibid., 289
14 Austin, *How to Do Things*, 107.
15 Habermas, *Communicative Action*, 293.
16 Louise Owen, 'Identity Correction: The Yes Men and Acts of Discursive "Leverage"' in *Performance Research*, vol. 16, no. 2, June 2011, 28–36, 32.
17 Yes Men, BBC on YouTube, 2 January 2007. Available at: www.youtube.com/watch?v=LiWlvBro9eI (Accessed: 3 April 2019).

What is the proper way to display a US flag?

1 Bronisław Malinowski, 'The Problem of Meaning in Primitive Languages' in C.K. Ogden and I.A. Richards, *The Meaning of Meaning: A Study of the Influence of Language upon Thought and of the Science of Symbolism* (New York: Harvest, Brace & World, 1923), 296–336. Malinowski observed: 'phatic communion … serves to establish bonds of personal union between people', 316. To the extent that it seeks to collectivise the subject, one finds a phatic moment in every political address, but the reverse is not always true: phatic sociality is by no means necessarily political.
2 Available at: www.dreadscott.net/works/what-is-the-proper-way-to-display-a-us-flag/ (Accessed: 19 April 2019).
3 Ernesto Laclau and Chantal Mouffe, *Hegemony and Socialist Strategy: Towards a Radical Democratic Politics, Second Edition* (London: Verso, 2013), 97.
4 An Act to Prohibit Desecration of the Flag, [82 Stat.] Public Law 90-381-July 5, 1968. Available at: www.govinfo.gov/content/pkg/STATUTE-82/pdf/STATUTE-82-Pg291-2.pdf (Accessed: 15 March 2019).
5 Foucault, *Archaeology of Knowledge*, 50.

6 Michel Foucault, *The Government of Self and Others*, Lectures at the Collège de France 1982–1983, series editor: Arnold I. Davidson, trans. Graham Burchell (Basingstoke: Palgrave Macmillan, 2010), 61.

7 Michel Foucault, *The Courage of Truth: The Government of Self and Others II*, Lectures at the Collège de France 1983–1984, series editor: Arnold I. Davidson, trans. Graham Burchell (Basingstoke: Palgrave Macmillan, 2012), 35.

8 United States v. Eichman, 496 U.S. 310.

9 U.S. Supreme Court, United States v. Eichman, 496 U.S. 310 (1990). Nos. 89-1433, 89-1434. Argued 14 May 1990. Decided 11 June 1990. Justia US Supreme Court. Available at: https://supreme.justia.com/cases/federal/us/496/310/ (Accessed: 15 March 2019).

Part III: Taxonomy of the political theatre

1 Karen Jürs-Munby, Jerome Carroll and Steve Giles, 'Introduction' to *Postdramatic Theatre and the Political: International Perspectives on Contemporary Performance*, ed. Karen Jürs-Munby, Jerome Carroll and Steve Giles, 1–30 (London: Bloomsbury, 2013), 9.

Foundational problems and problems of foundation

1 This is not to say such histories have not been suggested in the past. Notable examples include Siegfried Melchinger's *Geschichte des Politschen Theatres* (Hannover: Velber, 1971), in which he identified the tragic drama of Sophocles and Aristophanes as originating political theatre; also Arnold Hauser's 1951 study, *The Social History of Art* argued: 'Greek drama was in the strictest sense "political drama"', Arnold Hauser, *The Social History of Art: From Prehistoric Times to the Middle Ages* (London: Routledge, 2003), 78.

2 Alain Badiou, *Rhapsody for the Theatre*, trans. Bruno Bosteels (London: Verso, 2013), 36.

3 Ibid., 51 (original emphasis).

4 Romain Rolland, *The People's Theatre*, trans. Burrett H. Clark (New York: Henry Holt and Company, 1918), 4.

5 Ibid., 4.

6 Ibid., 35.

7 Ibid., 58.

8 Ibid., 8.

9 Ibid., 80. Rolland looked back to Rousseau, the Festival of the Supreme Being, and Michelet.

10 Vsevolod Meyerhold, 'Theatrical Moscow 33' [1920], 14. *Stat's, pis'ma, rechi, besedy*, 2:37–43 in Laurence Senelick and Sergei Ostrovsky, *The Soviet Theatre: A Documentary History*, ed. Laurence Senelick and Sergei Ostrovsky, 118–119 (New Haven, CT: Yale University Press, 2014), 119.

11 Althusser's commentary on Lenin's reflections on the revolution is pertinent here: 'if the general contradiction [between the forces of production and the relations of production ...] is sufficient to define the situation when revolution is the "task of the day", it cannot of its own simple, direct power induce a "revolutionary situation", nor *a fortiori* a situation of revolutionary rupture and the triumph of the revolution. If this contradiction is to become "*active*" in the strongest sense, to become a ruptural principle, there must be an accumulation of "circumstances" and "currents" so that whatever their origin and sense (and many of them will *necessarily* be paradoxically foreign to the revolution in origin and sense, or even its "direct opponents"), they "*fuse*" into a *ruptural unity* ... [revolution] presupposes the "fusion" of an "accumulation" of contradictions', Louis Althusser, 'Contradiction and Overdetermination' in *For Marx*, trans. Ben Brewster, 89–128 (London: Verso, 1999), 99.

12 Edward Braun, *Meyerhold: A Revolution in Theatre* (London: Methuen, 1998), 165.

13 Vsevolod Mayakovsky, 'The Proletariat and Art', 22 and 29 December 1918, in Senelick and Ostrovsky, *Soviet Theatre*, 60. In 'An Open Letter to the Workers', published in *Gazeta Futuristor* (*Futurist Gazette*), 15 March 1918, in Senelick and Ostrovsky, *Soviet Theatre*, 56, Mayakovsky would proclaim: 'Only the eruption of the Spirit of Revolution will rid us of the rags of antiquated art.'

14 Anatole Lunacharsky, 'Address to the Actors and Workers of the State Theatre of Petrograd' 1917 in Senelick and Ostrovsky, *Soviet Theatre*, 44.

15 Anatole Lunacharsky, 'The Proletkult and Soviet Cultural Work' in *Proletarskaia Kul'tura*, no. 7–8, April–May 1919, 1–3 in *Amateur and Proletarian Theatre in Post-revolutionary Russia: Primary Sources*, ed. Stefan Aquilina, 37–40 (London: Methuen, 2021), 38.

16 Ibid.

17 Ibid.

18 Ibid., 39 (original emphasis).

19 Valentin Tikhonovich, 'The Proletarian Actor', *O Teatre*, 1922, 89–91 in Aquilina, *Amateur and Proletarian*, 165–166, 165.

20 Ibid. (original emphasis).

21 Ibid., 166 (original emphasis).

22 René Fülop-Müller, 'Spirit and History of Bolshevism', Zurich 1926 in Senelick and Ostrovsky, *Soviet Theatre*, 93.

23 Unknown author, 'On Staging Agit-Trials', *Moscow Proletkult*, Iskusstro v rabochem klube, 1924, 96–99, in Aquilina, *Amateur and Proletarian*, 174–177, 174.

24 Ibid.

25 Unknown author, 'The Dramatization of a Living Newspaper', *Moscow Proletkult*, source: Iskusstor v rabochem klube, 1924, 66–71, in Aquilina, *Amateur and Proletarian*, 167–173, 168.

26 Lars Kleberg, *Theatre as Action: Soviet Russian Avant-Garde Aesthetics*, trans. Charles Rougle (London: Macmillan, 1993), 58.

27 V.V. Ignatov, 'Report of Comrade Ignatov "On the Proletarian Theatre"',
delivered at the First Moscow Municipal Conference on Proletkult, 23–38
February 1918 – originally published in the Report of Comrade Bartinsky,
'On the People's Theatre', STDM 17–21, 239–230 in Senelick and Ostrovsky,
Soviet Theatre, 46–47, 47.

28 Vsevolod Meyerhold, 'On Work and Recreation', 7 August 1918, in *Stat'I,
pis'ma, rechi, besedy* [Articles, letters, speeches, talks] (Moscow: Iskusstvo,
1968), vol. 2, 4–5 in Senelick and Ostrovsky, *Soviet Theatre*, 49.

29 Ibid.

30 Nikolai Evreinov, 'The Storming of the Winter Palace' *Krasnyi militsioner*,
1920 (14/15), trans. David Riff in *The Storming of the Winter Palace*, ed. Inke
Arns, Igor Chubarov and Sylvia Sasse, 23–25 (Zurich: Diaphanes/ University
of Zurich, 2016), 24, 25

31 Arns et al., 'Preface' in Arns et al., *Storming of the Winter Palace*, trans.
Bernard Heise, 7.

32 Konstantin Derzhavin, 'The Mass as Such', *Zhizn' iskusstva*, 12 November
1920, trans. David Riff in Arns et al., *Storming of the Winter Palace*, 61–63, 62.

33 Vsevolod Meyerhold, 'Speech at an Open Debate on *The Dawn*' in Edward Braun,
Meyerhold on Theatre, trans. Edward Braun, 215–216 (London: Bloomsbury,
2016 [1920]), 216.

34 Meyerhold's influence on the German debate can hardly be under-estimated: the
new political context of the Russian theatre under revolutionary conditions
demanded a fundamental re-evaluation of the art of the theatre, including the
work of the actor: '*We need to change not only the forms of our art but our
methods too*. An actor working for the new class needs to re-examine all the
canons of the past. The very craft of the actor must be completely reorganized',
Meyerhold in Braun, *Meyerhold on Theatre*, 243.

35 Erwin Piscator, *The Political Theatre*, trans. Hugh Rorrison (Bath: Methuen,
1980), vi.

36 Ibid., ix.

37 Ibid., 17, 14.

38 Ibid., 22.

39 Ibid., vii.

40 Ibid., 45 (original emphasis). What this articulates touches on the fundamental
dilemma posed by the aesthetic exception, when mobilised in the form of political art: the 'non-art' character of political theatre must nonetheless constitute
itself within the space of the exception, thus placing itself under the *dispositif*
of art.

41 Ibid., 44–45.

42 Piscator writes: the 'fundamental idea of the proletarian theatre [was to form] a
community which shared not only human and artistic but also political values',
ibid., 49.

43 Ibid., 46.

44 Ibid., 51.

45 Ibid., 45.

46 Ernst Toller, 'Remarks Concerning German Post-War Drama' in *Essays on German Theatre*, ed. Margaret Herzfeld-Saunder, 177–181, trans. Joel Agee (New York: Continuum, 1985), 178.

47 Bertolt Brecht, *The Messingkauf Dialogues*, trans. John Willett (London: Methuen, 1978), 27.

48 Bertolt Brecht, *Brecht on Theatre*, trans. John Willett (London: Methuen, 1964), 44.

49 Brecht, *Messingkauf Dialogues*, 95.

50 Adorno, *Aesthetic Theory*, 238.

51 Bertolt Brecht, 'Theatre for Pleasure or Theatre for Instruction' in *Brecht on Theatre*, 69–77, 70.

52 Walter Benjamin, 'What Is Epic Theatre? (Second Version) in *Understanding Brecht*, trans. Anna Bostock, 15–25 (London: Verso, 1992), 18.

53 Brecht, 'Theatre for Pleasure', 71.

54 Ibid.

55 Ibid.

Displacement effects

1 The text is published under the title 'Sur Brecht et Marx' in *Écrits Philosophiques et Politiques*, vol. 2 (Paris: Editions STOCK/IMEC, 1997), 561–577 – all the quotes that follow are from my own translation.

2 Ibid., 569 (original emphasis).

3 Ibid., 572.

4 Ibid., 570.

5 David Barnett writes for instance: 'Often, "political theatre" is taken to mean "theatre with political content" …' – as in plays by David Hare, for example – 'Brecht proposed a different way of understanding the political on stage: he was not making political theatre but making theatre politically', David Barnett, *Brecht in Practice: Theatre, Theory and Performance* (London: Bloomsbury, 2015), 32.

6 Althusser, 'Sur Brecht', 565.

7 Ibid.

8 Ibid., 567.

9 Ibid., 569.

10 Ibid. (original emphasis).

11 Ibid., 570.

12 Walter Benjamin writes, similarly, that 'A political tendency is a necessary but never sufficient condition for the organizing function of a work' and that '[art's] organizational usefulness [must in no way] be confined to their value as propaganda', Walter Benjamin, 'The Author as Producer' in *The Work of Art in the Age of its Technological Reproducibility and Other Writings on Media*, trans. Edmund Jephcott, 79–85 (Cambridge, MA: Harvard University Press, 2008 [1934]), 89.

13 Althusser, 'Sur Brecht', 571.

14 Ibid.

15 Ibid.

16 Althusser's distinction here is more or less the same as the distinction made by Heidegger in *Being and Time* between 'understanding' (*Verstehen*) and 'interpretation' (*Auslegung*), which makes what is understood explicit. Thus, Heidegger suggests the latter is the derivative phenomenon that presupposes the former: 'In interpretation understanding does not become something different. It becomes itself. Such interpretation is grounded existentially in understanding; the latter does not arise from the former', Martin Heidegger, *Being and Time*, trans. John Maquarrie and Edward Robinson (New York: Harper & Row, 1962), 188.

17 Louis Althusser, 'The "Piccolo Teatro": Bertolazzi and Brecht, Notes on a Materialist Theatre' in *For Marx*, trans. Ben Brewster, 131–151 (London: Verso, 1999 [1962]), 149. In an interesting analysis of Althusser's essay, Étienne Balibar argues that Althusser used the analysis of Strehler's production as a way of reformulating the problem of ideology, away from a straightforward notion of ideology critique (which presupposed a position outside of ideology). Rather, the Bertolazzi production constituted a process of what might be termed 'dis-enculturation' – the 'interpellation *out of ideology*, by the "real", as it were, which is present or embodied on the stage by the character of Nina and her opposition to the crowd' Étienne Balibar, 'Althusser's Dramaturgy and the Critique of Ideology' in *Differences: A Journal of Feminist Cultural Studies*, vol. 26, no. 3, 2015, 1–22, 9. The point being that Nina frustrates the desire for reconciliation within the audience and instead instils within them a consciousness of contradiction. The play does not so much repel the audience as provide it with a demonstration of the misrecognition involved in acts of recognition: 'the machine that makes the ideological fabric visible is also the one that forces a subject called a spectator to break with its conformism', 8.

18 Althusser, 'Piccolo Teatro', 149.

19 It is a process that describes how the subject experiences their real conditions of existence in the form of an '(overdetermined) unity' such that the real relations underpinning social existence are 'invested in the imaginary relation … rather than describing a reality', Louis Althusser, 'Selected Texts' in *Ideology*, ed. Terry Eagleton, 87–111 (Essex: Longman, 1996), 89.

20 Althusser, 'Piccolo Teatro', 149, fn. 6.

21 Ibid., 150.

22 Althusser, 'Sur Brecht', 572.

23 Althusser, 'Piccolo Teatro', 134.

24 Althusser, 'Sur Brecht', 572.

25 Ibid., 573.

26 Ibid., 575.

27 Benjamin, 'Author as Producer', 90.

28	Antonio Gramsci, 'The Modern Prince' in *Selections from Prison Notebooks*, trans. Quintin Hoare and Geoffrey Nowell Smith, 122–205 (London: Lawrence & Wishart, 1986) , 177.

29	Althusser, 'Contradiction and Overdetermination', 99, 115.

30	Althusser elsewhere writes: 'To think in terms of the category of conjuncture is not to think on the conjuncture, as one would reflect on a set of concrete data. To think under the conjuncture is quite literally to submit to the problem induced and imposed by its case', Louis Althusser, *Machiavelli and Us* (London: Verso, 1999), 18 – the conjuncture renders a 'political objective, a practical task', ibid., 19.

31	Ibid., 104–106.

32	Stuart Hall, 'Signification, Representation, Ideology: Althusser and the Post-Structuralist Debates' in *Critical Studies in Mass Communication*, vol. 2 no. 2, June 1985, 91–114, 91.

33	Ibid., 96.

34	Ibid., 91.

35	Ibid., 94 (original emphasis).

36	Catherine Malabou, *What Should We Do with Our Brain?*, trans. Sebastian Rand (New York: Fordham University Press, 2008), 15.

37	Karl Kautsky (1854–1938) was a leading figure in the German Social Democratic Party and proponent of the economism understood as a defining tenet of 'orthodox' Marxism. For an in-depth analysis of Kautsky, see Laclau and Mouffe, *Hegemony and Socialist Strategy*, 14–29.

38	Jeremy Gilbert provides a useful definition of conjunctural analysis, writing in relation to Stuart Hall's work: 'The aim of conjunctural analysis is always to map a social territory, in order to identify possible sites of political intervention. Such interventions need not actually be made, or be made on behalf of any particular political project or tendency, for the analysis to have validity; but its potential utility to anyone wanting to intervene in a given situation is the key criteria according to which conjunctural analysis can be judged', Jeremy Gilbert, 'This Conjuncture', in *New Formations*, vol. 96/97, 2019, 5–37, 15.

39	Gramsci, 'The Prince', 178.

40	Peter M. Boenisch, ' "An Actor, But in Life": Spectatorial Consciousness and Materialist Theatre: Some Notes Apropos Althusser' in *Performing Antagonism: Theatre Performance and Radical Democracy*, ed. Tony Fisher and Eve Katsouraki, 81–99 (London: Palgrave Macmillan, 2017), 83.

41	Ibid.

42	Ibid., 83.

43	Likewise, it is perfectly plausible to distinguish between the production of political effects and the understanding of something as possessing a political meaning – a piece of theatre or art can possess a political meaning, yet not claim to be producing a determinate political outcome (if by this is understood the term 'effect').

44	Florian Borchmeyer in Peter Boenisch and Thomas Ostermeier, *The Theatre of Thomas Ostermeier* (Oxon: Routledge, 2016), 80–81.

45 Ibid., 81.

46 Boenisch, 'An Actor', 90.

47 Borchmeyer reflects: 'I am … convinced that the production would have equally functioned in exactly the same way before the 2008 financial crisis' (Boenisch and Ostermeier, *Theatre of Thomas Ostermeier*, 83) yet at the same time in each iteration the production 'immediately triggers a concrete and very specific interpretation wherever we perform' (ibid.). From this one understands that the production is not 'about' specific conjunctural moments but rather is structured in such a way that it can be articulated in relation to them: a conjunctural articulation is possible because the production opens up the text to the present crisis of the conjuncture.

48 Peter M. Boenisch, *Directing Scenes and Senses: The Thinking of Regie* (Manchester: Manchester University Press, 2015), 185.

49 Thomas Ostermeier, 'Ibsen meets Snowden: Thomas Ostermeier on An Enemy of the People', interview with Simon McBurney in *The Guardian*, published 24 September 2014. Available at: www.theguardian.com/stage/2014/sep/24/thomas-ostermeier-interview-theatre-ibsen-enemy-of-the-people (Accessed: 27 March 2021).

50 As Alan Read writes, 'Performance and the political are incommensurable if not downright contradictory' and he goes on to state: 'I would suggest that to politicize performance requires us to do away with the idea of political theatre, if not political theatre itself', *Theatre, Intimacy & Engagement*, 27.

51 Pier Paolo Pasolini, 'Manifesto for a New Theatre' in *PAJ: A Journal of Performance and Art*, trans. Thomas Simpson, vol. 29, no. 1, January 2007, 126–138, 127.

52 Ibid., 134.

53 Ibid.

54 Ibid., 127.

55 Ibid., 128.

56 Ibid., 129.

57 I have elsewhere in this volume examined this phenomenon in terms of the paradox of avant-gardism and the aesthetic exception.

58 Yann Moulier Boutang, *Cognitive Capitalism*, trans. Ed Emery (Cambridge: Polity Press, 2011), 124. Boutang also observes: 'The good old "people" of the revolutions of old becomes uncouth and multiplies. Like light, which we perceive as white but which diffracts into the thousand colours of the rainbow as soon as it encounters a prism. An end to the good old "national" flag of the nineteenth century, which was rarely capable of embracing more than three colours at a time. And also an end to the blood-red flag of the revolutions of the twentieth century', 126.

59 Andre Gorz, *Farewell to the Working Class: An Essay on Post-industrial Socialism*, trans. Michael Sonenscher (London: Pluto Press, 1997), 14.

60 Laclau and Mouffe summarised their findings thus: 'We have demonstrated that there is no logical and necessary relation between socialist objectives and the positions of social agents in the relations of production; and that the

articulation between them is external and does not proceed from any natural movement of each to unite with the former. In other words, their articulation must be regarded as a hegemonic relation ... the direction of the workers' struggle is not uniformly progressive: it depends, *just as with any other social struggle*, upon its forms of articulation within a given hegemonic context', Laclau and Mouffe, *Hegemony and Socialist Strategy*, 86–87.

61 I am grateful to Tom Six for his critical observations here.

62 Objectively, the term proletariat indicates a position of subordination within capitalist relations of production. Subjectively viewed, however, it does not constitute an identity independent of those relations: the identity of a class that exists 'in and for itself' – it designates a *position* that can be occupied (that of 'worker') but not an *identity* that is thereby free of other determinations or conditioning factors that would prevent individuals from occupying other, often contradictory, positionalities that are equally authoritative for them (for instance, religious identities, any number of cultural affiliations, or simply identities based on consumerist dispositions).

Activist theatre of the conjuncture

1 I am extremely grateful to Ms Komita Dhanda, a political theatre activist and PhD researcher, for her generosity in taking the time to discuss with me her work with Janam, its current activities, and its historical context. Much of what is written in what follows is steered by the insights she offered during our conversation and in subsequent communications. Whatever errors are present, they are entirely my own – I make no pretence of being an expert in Indian theatre, history, or politics. If I have ventured this far, it is because I believe it is important to acknowledge the street theatre within any understanding of political theatre and its possibilities (indeed obstacles) today.

2 I do not deny that activist theatres exist, or have existed, in the Global North, only that – for historical reasons that must be accounted for – they are far more advanced and indeed prevalent in parts of the Global South.

3 Ernesto Laclau, 'Towards a Theory of Populism' in *Politics and Ideology in Marxist Theory: Capitalism, Fascism, Populism*, 143–198 (London: Verso, 2011), 176.

4 Michel de Certeau, *Culture in the Plural*, trans. Tom Conley, (Minneapolis, MN: University of Minnesota Press, 2001 [1974]), 120. De Certeau adds: 'Just as in the political theatre, statements rarely correspond to what is happening ... however necessary it may be, the reintroduction of political problems in literary expression bring forth the sign of an urgency. But in itself, even if scandal or censure brings notoriety, that expression is sterile and without consequence. Every one of the movements that have attempted to make a statement through collective "consciousness-raising" in similar situations – such as Paulo Freire's in Brazil – has run up against the same barrier. From the moment when, through its own process, an action begins to change the balance

of forces, it is interrupted by repression organized by the established powers … the consciousness-raising retreats in view of inevitable political aggression', ibid., 120. It is important to note, however, that de Certeau does not simply dismiss out of hand the possibility for a cultural politics. His point is not that there can be no cultural politics but that there can be no cultural politics 'unless sociocultural situations can be fashioned in terms of present forces and commonly known oppositions' (ibid., 121) – in the language developed here – without a conjunctural understanding. The further question he poses is salutatory and unavoidable: 'It remains to be seen if the members of a society – today drowned in the anonymity of discourses of which they are dispossessed, and subject to conglomerates whose control exceeds their grasp – will find, along with the power of locating themselves in a game of acknowledged forces, the means of capturing speech', ibid.

5 Ernesto Laclau, 'The "People" and the Discursive Production of Emptiness' in *On Populist Reason*, 67–128 (London: Verso, 2007), 71.

6 Here, I distinguish between two kinds of demand that nonetheless possess cognate structures: the democratic or 'popular' demand and the ethical demand, as developed by Simon Critchley. Critchley describes the structure of the demand as follows: 'ethical experience begins with the experience of a demand to which I give my approval. There are two key components to ethical experience: *approval* and *demand*', Simon Critchley, *Infinitely Demanding: Ethics of Commitment, Politics of Resistance* (London: Verso, 2007), 14. I argue that democratic demands, likewise, require – or at least seek – approval, which constitutes the basis for forms of solidarity with those issuing demands based on specific injustices or grievances. When I express solidarity for a cause that is not necessarily my own, for instance, I am approving a democratic demand. The difference between ethical and democratic demands (which I can only indicate here) is that whereas the ethical demand (as Critchley expresses it) is 'articulated through the *hetero-affectivity* of an unfulfillable, one-sided and radical demand' (ibid., 56), the popular or democratic demand can in principle be *met* or 'fulfilled'. It is finite, concrete, and specifically located in the material circumstances of the lifeworld from which it is generated.

7 Utpal Dutt, *Towards a Revolutionary Theatre* (Calcutta: Seagull Books, 2009), 19.

8 To be sure, the distinction here is a difficult if important one to make – it mirrors the difference in Gramscian terms between a 'war of manoeuvre' (an aggressive war of direct combat) and a 'war of movement', which belongs to the struggle to mobilise mass social movements. The activist theatre belongs to the latter; the theatre of propaganda is part of the former. One might also add the critical theatre is closer to what Gramsci termed the 'war of position' – a struggle fought against an existing hegemony on the basis of intellectual and cultural resistance operating through forms of ideology critique and from within specifiable institutional sites.

9 Patrice Pavis, *The Routledge Dictionary of Performance and Contemporary Theatre*, trans. Andrew Brown (Oxon: Routledge, 2016), 183.

10 The obvious question here is: *which* theatre of the conjuncture do you mean? What kind of activism? What political context? Etc. I concede entirely the partial nature of my account. Not only is there no 'end' to the unfolding of conjunctural determinations, thus any conjunctural analysis is provisional and partial – the question is always whether or not it is sufficient for its purpose ..., but also the choice of the example is itself limiting. It is no doubt entirely legitimate to complain that alternative examples are occluded – why not this or that theatre instead? I am embarrassed that so much has been omitted here that should be included. My analysis, however, does not claim to be exhaustive. It is an invitation to think the political theatre according to a certain analytic strategy and in relation to categories appropriate to it – the examples I give are the examples that seemed to me appropriate for that purpose.

11 Although political street theatre can be found extensively throughout India, my primary example concerns Delhi-based Janam – the primary reason for doing so, aside from space, lies in the nature of Janam's work, which is focused on urban and industrial-based activism. However, to avoid distorting the character of the street theatre, it is important to indicate something of its history and scope – accepting the purpose here is not to give a full account but rather to alert the reader to the wider context beyond Janam's work. Street theatre in India has a long and complex history indeed. For brevity's sake, let us take just one federal state, as an example – West Bengal – where a touring/street theatre emerges in the 1940s and 1950s (for instance the theatre activist Tarapada Lahiri toured a small troupe around villages in the 1950s). However, theatre practitioners in West Bengal, inspired by the cultural front in Russia, used theatre to promote the anti-imperial struggle across the state as early as the 1930s. For example, the Student Federation sought to inspire the ideals of the revolutionary struggle in the rural peasantry in 1938, through street theatre, partly in response to the need to combat fascism (see Bulbuli Biswas and Paramita Banerjee's 'Street Theatre in Bengal: A Glimpse' in *Seagull Theatre Quarterly* [STQ], vol. 16, December 1997, 33–37. Influential early practitioners of the form include the theatre maker Panu Pal, who deployed street-corner plays for propagandistic ends, and indeed pioneered the use of street theatre in electioneering strategies – a practice that continues to this day. His theatre also developed an activist orientation, as seen in his play 'Chargesheet' that protested the detention of the leadership of the Communist Party in 1948–1949 – see Samik Bandyopadhyay 'Theatrescapes' in *STQ*, 1997, 25–30; also, Aparna Bhargara Dharwadker's *Theatre's of Independence: Drama, Theory, and Urban Performance in India* (Iowa City, IA: University of Iowa Press, 2005), 21–53. During the 1960s and 1970s, West Bengal saw the emergence of the Group Theatre movement, comprising – as Partha Chatterjee observes – 'several dozen groups, large and small, mostly linked to one or the other political parties of the left, [producing] plays that were both theatrically novel and politically and socially progressive', Partha Chatterjee, 'Theatre and the Publics of Democracy: Between Melodrama and Rational Realism' in *Theatre Research International*, vol. 41, no. 3, 2016, 202–217, 210. However, not all

theatre groups were aligned to political parties – for example, the non-aligned leftist theatre group *Silhouette*, which emerged at the commencement of the so-called 'Third Theatre' movement in Kolkata in the 1980s, as well as the influential street theatre of Badal Sircar, whose experimental style incorporated both folk form and martial arts, though tended toward the apolitical. Perhaps the most influential practitioner of politically oriented street theatre was Utpal Dutt, who began producing street theatre in the early 1950s. Dutt reflecting on his considerable practical experience described the complexity of the form: rather than a simple didacticism, in which the audience is the recipient of the author's message, as conveyed by the performers, Dutt argued that the role of the audience contributed to its meaning in a three-way dialectic: 'This is what the audience does to the contradictions of the theatre – it brings the actual life-experience to bear upon the stage', Dutt, *Towards a Revolutionary Theatre*, 19.

12 It is estimated that around 160,000 people saw *Machine* and its iterations at the Boat Club – see Safdar Hashmi, *The Right to Perform: Selected Writings of Safdar Hashmi* (Delhi: Sahmat, 1989), 167.

13 Vijay Prashad, *No Free Left: The Futures of Indian Communism* (New Delhi: LeftWord Books, 2020), 39.

14 Ibid.

15 Hashmi, *Right to Perform*, 160.

16 See Arjun Ghosh, *A History of the Jana Natya Manch: Plays for the People* (New Delhi: Sage, 2012), 35.

17 Janam still performs the play today. Here one should note two things: first, that the theatrical imagery of the capitalist expropriation of labour transcends the particularity of its first performances – but that, second, its contemporary political salience derives from its ongoing ability to be articulated according to new conjunctural conditions.

18 Hashmi, *Right to Perform*, 160.

19 Ibid.

20 Ibid., 161. In correspondence with Komita Dhanda, she explains: 'Sutradhar is a common figure in traditional Sanskrit theatre and folk theatre in India. Likewise, in street theatre also a Sutradhar is someone who narrates the story and takes it forward. Sutra literally means a string/thread and that's what a Sutradhar essentially does – stringing the story. In some of Janam's plays, Sutradhar take the story forward [through] songs. There is sometimes more than one Sutradhar in a play.'

21 There are a significant number of leftwing political parties in India. The CPI-M is the largest, formed out of a split in 1964 from the CPI. The reason for the split, according to Prashad, had to do with a conflict over whether to align with the Soviet bloc – the CPI-M favoured an independent trajectory; the CPI did not (see Prashad, *No Free Left*, 158). There are, also, a number of other leftwing groups including – among others – the All India Forward Bloc, the Revolutionary Socialist Party, the Revolutionary Communist Party of India, as well as various Maoist groups.

22 Hashmi, *Right to Perform*, 9.

23 For a fuller account of these struggles in the context of early colonial expansion in India, particularly during the period of the East India Company, see Amar Farooqui, *The Establishment of British Rule, 1757–1813* (New Delhi: Tulika Books, 2014).

24 Ashis Nandy, *Time Warps: Silent and Evasive Pasts in Indian Politics and Religion* (London: Hurst & Company, 2002), 16. Nandy writes elsewhere, for example, of attempts during the nineteenth century to Christianise Hinduism – see *The Intimate Enemy: Loss and Recovery of Self Under Colonialism* (Delhi: Oxford University Press, 1983), 25 – one of many 'invidious modes of Westernization', ibid., 24.

25 Nandy, *Time Warps*, 18.

26 Ibid., 18, 20.

27 Hashmi, *Right to Perform*, 9.

28 Ibid.

29 Ibid., 7.

30 The IPTA arose as a grouping out of the Indian Progressive Writers' Association (IPWA) that arose in 1936 as an anti-fascist organisation of leftwing writers and intellectuals. For more information, see: Binayak Bhattacharya, 'Looking Back: Some Historical Anecdotes of the Indian People's Theatre Association in Bengal' in *The Visva-Bharati Quarterly*, vol. 22, nos. 3–4, October 2013–March 2014, 88–100.

31 'People's Theatre Stars the People', Indian People's Theatre Association, Bulletin no. 1, July 1943 in Sundhi Pradhan, *Marxist Cultural Movement in India*, compiled and edited by Sudhi Pradhan (Calcutta: Santi Pradhan, 1960), 124–129.

32 Hashmi, *Right to Perform*, 6. A draft resolution prepared by Anil de Silva for the first All India People's Theatre Conference, 25 May 1943, proposed that the IPTA 'recognises the urgency of organizing a people's theatre movement throughout the whole of India … revitalizing the stage and the traditional arts and making them at once the expression and organiser of, our people's struggle for freedom, critical progress and economic justice', in Pradhan, *Marxist Cultural Movement in India*, 130–132, 130.

33 Quoted in Malini Bhattacharya, 'The IPTA in Bengal' in *Journal of Arts & Ideas*, no. 2, January–March 1983, 5–22, 5.

34 Ibid., 6.

35 Ibid., 7.

36 Ibid.

37 Ibid., 10. I thank Bishnupriya Dutt for drawing my attention to *Jabanbandi*.

38 Samik Bandyopadhyay, 'Theatrescapes' in *STQ*, 1997, 25–30, 26.

39 Binayak Bhattacharya adds two useful points in relation to the tensions within the IPTA, but also its ongoing significance for political theatre in India. The first is identified with the challenges that resulted from a new hardline leadership of the CPI in 1948 that alienated many progressive intellectuals and writers, with its 'orthodox' views on culture. As a consequence, Bhattacharya writes,

a 'good number of the front-rankers in the IPTA started leaving the organisation from this time to form several independent theatres or other cultural groups like *Bohurupee*, *The Little Theatre Group* and so on', Bhattacharya, 'Looking Back', 98. The second point pertains to a more general influence of the experience of the IPTA: the 1940s, and in particular, the IPTA's humanitarian response to the Bengal famine, brought India's progressive intelligentsia into a direct relation with popular politics for the first time. Bhattacharya writes: 'I consider it most significant because as an alternative to the Gandhian mode of accommodating the "subaltern" in the nationalist political practice, this mass-cultural efforts [sic] led by the progressive Bengali intelligentsia tried to reform and reconstitute the terrain of cultural construction of [Bengal]', i.e., it developed, within the progressive Left, a properly democratic disposition that would outlast the IPTA, ibid., 98.

40 Ritwik Kumar Ghatak, *On the Cultural 'Front'*, Kolkata: Ritwik Memorial Trust, 2006 [1954]), 51–52.

41 Ibid., 57.

42 Ibid., 79.

43 Bhattacharya, 'IPTA in Bengal', 5.

44 Hashmi, *Right to Perform*, 16. That said, a distinction should be observed with respect to different *uses* of the 'street theatre'. Hashmi had already distinguished 'between democratic street theatre and reformist and sarkari street theatre' (ibid., 14) – the latter indicating officially sanctioned governmental and NGO appropriations of the form for the purposes of policy dissemination – for instance around family planning, where street theatre indeed assumes a propagandistic function. For Hashmi, this kind of development constitutes not only a misunderstanding of the street theatre, but also, he argues, the 'form itself resists such efforts at takeover', ibid., 9. However, this last claim is somewhat troubled by a more recent development that has seen the 'appropriation' of the street theatre 'format' for the purposes of pursuing the agenda of Hindutva nationalism. Here we find a turn to a propagandistic rather than democratic use of the form – explored in an important article by Aparna Mahiyaria in which she describes how the street theatre is deployed as part of a cultural front within the political project of the contemporary Indian Hindu nationalist right. Mahiyaria describes how in 2016, a nationalist right-leaning street theatre competition was launched on the campus of the University of Delhi, a 'project aimed at creating a "counter-hegemonic" practice to the conventionally Left-progressive Street-theatre', Aparna Mahiyaria, 'Right Wing and Street-Theatre: From Censure to Co-option' in *Studies in Theatre and Performance*, vol. 41, no. 3, 2021, 305–320, 309. This was an attempt to 'reroute Street-theatre from its anti-imperialist and working class legacies towards a narrowly defined nationalism', ibid. Mahiyaria shows how the Right frequently conceals its true intent by moderating the content of these plays to downplay its more extreme ideological commitments. Thus, to understand its specific mode of appropriation by the Right, Mahiyaria argues, it is necessary to understand it as an appropriation of the street theatre form *to* an underlying organisational

constant that it is designed to promote. In short, to understand the emergence of the Right-wing street-theatre requires grasping the activist intent as part of the Right's war of position: its aim is to expand its organisational reach to 'effectively [attract] new associates to the *Hindutva* project', ibid., 312, 313.

45 Arjun Ghosh, 'Cultural Intervention and Cultural Resistance' in *Economic and Political Weekly*, vol. 46, no. 24, 11–17 June 2011, 69–75, 69. In an interview with Moloyashree Hashmi, co-founding member of Janam, she observes how she was struck by the fact that when the street theatre began '90% of the audiences [had] never seen any play in their lives', Janam is People Theatre Forum, Interview with Moloyashree Hashmi, Sahapedia, 2 May 2016. Available at: www.sahapedia.org/janam-peoples-theatre-forum (Accessed: 22 March 2021).

46 Ghosh, 'Cultural Intervention', 73–74.

47 Ibid., 74.

48 Ibid., 73.

49 Prashad, *No Free Left*, 22.

50 Stuart Hall, 'The Great Moving Right Show' in *Selected Political Writings*, ed. Sally Davison, David Featherstone, Michael Rustin, and Bill Schwarz, 172–186 (Durham, NC: Duke University Press, 2017 [1979]), 177.

51 Arundhati Roy, 'Confronting Empire' in *The Ordinary Person's Guide to Empire*, 69–77 (London: HarperCollins, 2004), 71.

52 Prashad, *No Free Left*, 52.

53 Ibid., 143.

54 Ibid., 239–240.

55 Aijaz Ahmad, 'India: Liberal Democracy and the Extreme Right' on *Indian Cultural Forum*, 7 September 2016. Available at: https://indianculturalforum.in/2016/09/07/india-liberal-democracy-and-the-extreme-right/?fbclid=IwAR3xDQcpP10jtEhrCXau60uoRcCRpikbJyoNroAsEVCTAwui4Fnb3hFUPKE (Accessed: 22 April 2021). For a 'Gramscian' analysis of the rise of the Indian far right, drawing parallels with Mussolini's Italy – both lay claim to the reinvention of the classical past (Brahminical classicism in the case of India) – see Aijaz Ahmad, 'Fascism and National Culture: Reading Gramsci in the Days of *Hindutva*' in *Lineages of the Present: Ideology and Politics in Contemporary South Asia*, 129–166 (London: Verso, 2000), 131.

56 Arup Baisya, 'Strategic Dilemma of the Indian Left' in *Economic and Political Weekly*, vol. 49, no. 47, 22 November 2014, 13–16, 14.

57 Ghosh, *A History of Jana Natya Manch*, 110. Prashad makes a similar if broader point: 'A weakened trade union movement meant of course a weakened left' (Prashad, *No Free Left*, 221); the correlate point here being that the strength of the street theatre movement is very much decided by the fate of the wider political movement to which it belongs.

58 Once again, I thank Dhanda for her incisive observations here.

59 Parimal Ghosh, 'Rise and Fall of Calcutta's Group Theatre: The End of a Political Dream' in *Economic and Political Weekly*, vol. 47, no. 10, 10 March 2012, 36–42, 40.

60 Ibid., 42.

61 Ibid., 42.

62 The fate of the CPI-M-led Left Front in West Bengal (1977–2011) has a particular importance here and is analysed in some depth by Prashad. Having held power for three decades made it easy for its opponents – Mamata Banerjee's anti-communist All India Trinamool Congress – to 'define it as elite', Prashad, *No Free Left*, 131. Banerjee mobilised a wide range of popular grievances – capturing the very classes who 'were supposed to be central to the Left base', ibid.. She achieved this by using powerful populist rhetoric – slogans such as 'Maa, Mati, Mannash' (Mother, Motherland, People) thereby 'usurping' the space of the Left (ibid., 252), even though, as Prashad notes, she promoted 'budgets that would do nothing' for the people, ibid., 131. Right populism achieved its victory over the Left, but not far beneath its surface, Prashad notes, lies the 'gangsterism inherent in this sort of populism', ibid., 133. And he adds: 'The grammar of street violence is essential to Banjeree's form of populism. It gives the appearance of plebeian democracy, while behind the scenes the work of business is conducted to the satisfaction of the business class. In another era, this would be called fascism', ibid.

63 Baisya, 'Strategic Dilemma', 14–15.

64 Ghosh, *Rise and Fall*, 42.

65 Girish Shrivastava, 'Can Street Theatre Survive without the "Left"?', in *National Herald*, India, 24 June 2018. Available at: www.nationalheraldindia. com/theatre/can-street-theatre-survive-without-the-left (Accessed: 1 February 2021). It is perhaps also worth noting one of the dilemmas that arose for the street theatre, at least in West Bengal, since 1977 when the Left Front government won the state through a coalition of leftist parties led by the Communist Party of India-Marxist (CPI-M) – as Biswas and Banerjee observed in the late 1990s: with the state now governed by a leftwing grouping, the 'tradition of protest movements inspired and led by leftists [was] totally coopted into uncritical support for the ruling left', *Street Theatre in Bengal*, 37. What had emerged, according to Chatterjee, was effectively a form of state-sponsored theatre that was 'repetitious, predictable and non-threatening'; what it revealed were the 'limits of activist political theatre', *Theatre and the Publics of Democracy*, 212.

66 Ibid.

67 Pushpa Sundar, 'Protest through Theatre: The Indian Experience' in *India International Centre Quarterly*, vol. 16, no. 2, Summer 1989, 123–138, 123.

68 Ibid., 123.

69 Ibid.

70 Ibid., 125.

71 Bishnupriya Dutt, from a paper given at 'Social Movements, Performance and Democratic Practices, Indo-Canadian Dialogue' at the Shastri Indo-Canadian Institute Golden Jubilee Online Conference, 25–27 March 2021.

72 Rustom Bharucha, 'Letter to the Dead' in *Economic and Political Weekly*, vol. 24, no. 15, 15 April 1989, 780–782, 781.

73 Ibid.
74 For a full account of the political murder of Safdar Hashmi, see Ghosh, *History of Jana Natya Manch*, 86–91.
75 Bharucha, 'Letter to the Dead', 780.
76 Ibid.
77 Quoted in Ghosh, *History of Jana Natya Manch*, 88.
78 Hashmi, *Right to Perform*, 169.
79 Bharucha, 'Letter to the Dead', 781.
80 Panagiotis Sotiris, *A Philosophy for Communism: Rethinking Althusser* (Leiden: Brill, 2020), 200.
81 See ibid., 308.
82 Gramsci, 'The Prince', 177, fn. 79.
83 Hall, 'Great Moving Right Show', 173.
84 Gramsci, 'The Prince', 178.
85 Ibid.
86 Hashmi, *Right to Perform*, 167.

The 'closure' of the political theatre (and the critique of postdramatic reason)

1 Ashis Sengupta has written extensively on the development of 'postdramatic theatre' in India for example, which began with the performative turn in the 1990s. He writes: 'Indian theatre-makers experimented with their new forms not being conscious of Lehmann, but what they did in their own contexts fall much in line with some aspects of the kind of theatre that he highlights while theorizing the "postdramatic"' – only more recently has there been a self-conscious effort to combine European postdramatic ideas with the 'eclectic performance traditions of India', producing the postdramatic, not as an imitation, but in an Indian idiom, Ashis Sengupta, *Postdramatic Theatre and India* (London: Methuen, 2022), 19.
2 Hans-Thies Lehmann, *Postdramatic Theatre*, trans. Karen Jürs-Munby (London: Routledge, 2006), 27.
3 Ibid., 28.
4 Jacques Derrida, 'The Theatre of Cruelty and the Closure of Representation' in *Writing and Difference*, trans. Alan Bass, 232–250 (London: Routledge, 1985), 234.
5 Helmut Plessner, *Political Anthropology*, trans. Nils F. Schott (Evanston, IL: Northwestern University Press, 2018 [1931]), 49.
6 Derrida, 'Theatre of Cruelty', 237.
7 Ibid.
8 Ibid., 246.
9 Ibid.
10 Ibid., 247.
11 Ibid., 250.

12 Lehmann, *Postdramatic Theatre*, 38.

13 See Florian Malzacher, 'No Organum to Follow: Possibilities of Political Theatre Today' in *Not Just a Mirror: Looking for the Political Theatre of Today*, ed. Florian Malzacher (Berlin: Alexander Verlag, 2015), 20.

14 Jürs-Munby et al., *Postdramatic Theatre and the Political*, 7, 6.

15 Lehmann quoted in ibid., 7.

16 Derrida, 'Theatre of Cruelty', 237, 238.

17 Jürs-Munby et al., *Postdramatic Theatre and the Political*, 16.

18 Max Weber, 'Science as a Vocation' in *From Max Weber: Essays in Sociology*, ed. and trans. H.H. Gerth and C. Wright Mills, 129–156 (London: Routledge, 1991), 148

19 Lehmann, *Postdramatic Theatre*, 175.

20 Ibid.

21 Ibid.

22 Ibid.

23 Ibid.

24 Brandon Woolf, 'Toward a Paradoxical Parallaxical Postdramatic Politics?' in Jürs-Munby et al., *Postdramatic Theatre and the Political*, 43–44 (original emphasis).

25 Lehmann, *Postdramatic Theatre*, 178.

26 Ibid., 177.

27 Ibid.

28 Lehmann, 'A Future for Tragedy?', 108 (original emphasis).

29 Lehmann, *Postdramatic Theatre*, 178.

30 Ibid., 178.

31 Discussed in detail in the first section of this book.

32 Ibid.

33 Hans-Thies Lehmann, 'Akira Takayama: To Hide, not to Disappear' in Malzacher, *Not Just a Mirror*, 166–170, 167.

34 Lehmann, *Postdramatic Theatre*, 179.

35 Ibid.

36 Ibid.

37 Ibid.

38 Ibid., 184.

39 Ibid., 185.

40 Ibid., 184.

41 Walter Benjamin, 'The Storyteller: Reflections on the Works of Nikolai Leskov' in *Illuminations*, trans. Harry Zorn, 83–107 (London: Random House, 1999).

42 Ibid., 84.

43 Lehmann, *Postdramatic Theatre*, 184.

44 Ibid.

45 Ibid., 185.

46 Ibid., 179.

47 Ibid.

48 Lehmann, 'A Future for Tragedy?', 108.

49 Ibid.
50 Ibid.
51 Ibid.
52 Lehmann, *Postdramatic Theatre*, 186.
53 Soliman quoted in Lehmann, 'A Future for Tragedy?', 88.
54 Ibid., 89.
55 Ibid.
56 Ibid.
57 Ibid., 93.
58 Ibid., 97.
59 Ibid., 100.
60 Ibid., 106.
61 Ibid., 109.
62 Lehmann, *Postdramatic Theatre*, 124.
63 See, for example, Emmanuel Levinas, *Totality and Infinity: An Essay on Interiority*, trans. Alphonso Lingis (Pittsburgh, PA: Duquesne University, 2002). Levinas writes: 'The Other remains infinitely transcendent, infinitely foreign', 194. See also Simon Critchley: 'the Levinansian ethical subject is a subject defined by an experience of an internalized demand that it can never meet, a demand that exceeds it, what he calls infinite responsibility', Critchley, *Infinitely Demanding*, 10.
64 Lehmann, *Postdramatic Theatre*, 186.
65 See Herbert Marcuse's essay 'The Affirmative Character of Culture' in which he writes: 'The truth of a higher world, of a higher good than material existence, conceals the truth that a better material existence can be created in which such happiness is realized. In affirmative culture even unhappiness becomes a means of subordination and acquiescence', Marcuse, 'Affirmative Character of Culture', 89.
66 Althusser, 'Selected Texts', 101.
67 Lehmann, *Postdramatic Theatre*, 187.
68 See Marcuse, 'Affirmative Character of Culture', 92.

The political theatre 'redefined'

1 See Naomi Paxton's comprehensive study: *Stage Rights!: The Actresses' Franchise League, Activism and Politics 1908–58* (Manchester: Manchester University Press, 2018).
2 Platon Kerzhentsev, 'The Repertoire of the Proletarian Theatre' (1918) in Aquilina, *Amateur and Proletarian Theatre*, trans. Anastasia Lesnikova, 88–93, 93.
3 Raymond Williams, *Marxism and Literature* (Oxford: Oxford University Press, 2009), 134; Gramsci, 'The Study of Philosophy' in *Selections from Prison Notebooks*, 321–377, 323

4 Stuart Hall, 'Gramsci and Us' in *The Hard Road to Renewal*, 123–149 (London: Verso, 1990), 163.

5 See Tony Fisher, *Theatre and Governance in Britain, 1500–1900. Democracy, Disorder and the State* (Cambridge: Cambridge University Press, 2017).

6 Osborne, *Postconceptual Condition*, 16.

7 Ibid., 12.

8 Quoted in Osborne, ibid., 11.

9 Ibid., 19.

10 Ibid., 19.

11 Gayatri Chakravorty Spivak, *Death of a Discipline* (New York: Columbia University Press, 2003), 72.

12 Ibid.

13 Ibid., 102.

The theatre of the planetary conjuncture

1 See, for example, Stephen Ogheneruro Okpadah's essay 'Politics, Oil, and Theatre in Africa' in *Environmental Postcolonialism: A Literary Response*, 47–59 (London: Rowman & Littlefield, 2021) for an analysis of Nigerian poets (such as Tunde Fatunde and Ibiwari Ikiriko) responding to what he terms the 'squandermania' (52) over oil reserves in the Niger Delta that have led to violent suppression of local peoples at the hands of the Nigerian government and multinational oil companies – for example, the Odi Massacre that occurred in November 1999.

2 I understand utopianism in the specific sense described in the book's introduction: the attempt to conceive a horizon of horizons able to displace the current 'horizon of expectations'.

3 Milo Rau, *Globaler Realismus/ Global Realism* (Gent and Berlin: Verbrecher Verlag, 2018), 195.

4 Ibid., 157.

5 Ibid., 163.

6 Ibid., 164.

7 Rwandan journalist, Kennedy Ndahiro reflecting on RTLM wrote: 'At the beginning of 1994, it was evident that the country's leadership was planning something sinister, on a much larger scale than had ever been imagined. Just a month before the genocide, RTLM's Noël Hitimana gave the first hint over the radio: "On the day when people rise up and don't want you Tutsi anymore, when they hate you as one and from the bottom of their hearts … I wonder how you will escape." The government's propaganda machinery had carried out its task meticulously. Four weeks later, all the demons descended on Rwanda. Blood was flowing on the streets. The Tutsi were hunted down without mercy; they were killed in schools, churches, hospitals, and even prisons', Kennedy Ndahiro, 'In Rwanda, We Know All about Dehumanizing Language', *The*

Atlantic, 13 April 2019. Available at: www.theatlantic.com/ideas/archive/2019/04/rwanda-shows-how-hateful-speech-leads-violence/587041/ (Accessed: 30 August 2021).

8 Rau, *Global Realism*, 163.

9 Ibid., 174.

10 Ibid., 170.

11 Ibid., 172.

12 Ibid., 157.

13 Ibid., 183.

14 Ibid., 185.

15 It seems to me that Rau's theatre as a 'poiesis' lacks the directness of the activist theatre of the conjuncture – it is not a 'praxis' – yet to the extent that it intervenes conjuncturally contains an activist dimension.

16 Rau, *Global Realism*, 158.

17 Ibid.

18 Ibid., 174.

19 Ibid.

20 Roland Barthes, *How to Live Together: Novelistic Simulations of Some Everyday Spaces. Notes for a Lecture Course and Seminar at the Còllege de France (1976–1977)*, trans. Kate Briggs, text annotated by Claude Coste (New York: Columbia University Press, 2013), 136.

21 Rau, *Global Realism*, 174. According to Baudrillard, 'the hyperreal of simulation is translated by the hallucinatory resemblance of the real to itself' – everything that is solid is dissolved into sign, resemblance, hallucination – Jean Baudrillard, *Simulacra and Simulation*, trans. Sheila Faria Glaser (Ann Arbor, MI: University of Michigan Press, 2004 [1981]), 23.

22 See Baudrillard, *Simulacra and Simulation*, 7.

23 The periods of the two Congo wars are 1986–1997 and 1998–2003.

24 During the period of the second Congolese war artisanal mining in the Great Lakes region was massively expanded, as global demand – driven by the digital revolution for minerals such as tantalum, used to manufacture electronic capacitors – increased drawing more and more people into the mining industry. Most miners were artisanal, mining minerals by hand, using panning techniques. Often working under harsh conditions, often involving child labour, and without labour protections, the artisan miners found themselves easy prey for militia groups – and the State – who would levy 'taxes' on their yields to fund the purchase of weaponry (and to enrich themselves). When multinational mining corporations were granted exploitation rights, violence intensified with the forced removal of artisan miners from many mining sites.

25 Georges Nzongola-Ntalaja, *The Congo: From Leopold to Kabila. A People's History* (London: Zed Books, 2003), 215.

26 Ibid.

27 A memorandum of the European Parliament is unequivocal on the implications of this for consumers: 'such minerals, potentially present in consumer products, link consumers to conflicts outside the Union. As such, consumers are

indirectly linked to conflicts that have severe impacts on human rights, notably the rights of women, as armed groups often use mass rape as a deliberate strategy to intimidate and control local populations in order to protect their interests', *Amendment 6, Proposal for a Regulation, Recital 8, Union System for Self-certification*, P8-TA (2015) 0204. Available at: www.europarl.europa.eu/doceo/document/TA-8-2015-0204_EN.html (Accessed: 24 August 2021).

28 Nzongola-Ntalaja, *The Congo*, 227.

29 Rau, *Global Realism*, 214.

30 Jacques Derrida, 'The Force of Law: The "Mystical" Foundation of Authority' in *Deconstruction and the Possibility of Justice*, ed. Drucilla Cornell, Michel Rosenfeld, and David Gray Carlson, 3–67 (New York: Routledge, 1992), 6.

31 Derrida asks: 'How are we to distinguish between the force of law of a legitimate power and the supposedly originary violence that must have established this authority and that could not itself have been authorized by any anterior legitimacy, so that, in this initial moment, it is neither legal nor illegal', Derrida, 'Force of Law', 6.

32 Milo Rau, 2014, the-congo-tribunal.com (Accessed: 22 August 2021).

33 Rau, *Global Realism*, 223.

34 See for an interesting and in-depth discussion of Derrida's 'Force of Law', Jacques de Ville, *Jacques Derrida: Absolute Hospitality* (New York: Routledge, 2011): 'Justice, as expounded by Derrida, seeks to undermine the *rule* of law as well as the rule of *law*. Liberal legal theory, which dominates in the world today, sees only "cases", which must be dealt with in terms of existing rules and legal principles. There is no space, possibility, or allowance here for going beyond law, resisting law, in deciding a "case", even a "hard case". Derrida's analysis of the structure of law, on the other hand, allows for the "suspension" of the *rule of law*. In other words, in an actual case that comes to court, the judge (especially in an apex court), representing the community, has to, in revolutionary fashion, "abolish" law and the state (that is, sovereignty) as mechanisms which institute and maintain a restricted economy', 163.

35 Derrida, 'Force of Law', 23. Derrida also writes: 'To be just, the decision of a judge, for example, must not only follow a rule of law, or a general law but must also assure it, approve it, confirm its value, by a reinstituting act of interpretation, as if nothing previously existing of the law, as if the judge himself invented the law in every case', ibid.

36 Rau, *Global Realism*, 262.

37 Ibid., 216.

38 Hall, 'Gramsci and Us', 165.

39 Walter Rodney, *How Europe Underdeveloped Africa* (London: Verso, 2018 [1971]), 86.

40 Alexander Anievas and Kerem Nişancioğlu, *How the West Came to Rule: The Geopolitical Origins of Capitalism* (London: Pluto Press, 2015), 53.

41 Ibid., 45.

42 Ibid.

43 Ibid., 48.

44 Rodney, *How Europe Underdeveloped Africa*, 286.

45 David Harvey, 'The "New" Imperialism: Accumulation by Dispossession' in *Socialist Register 2004: The New Imperial Challenge*, vol. 40, 63–88, ed. Leo Panitch and Colin Leys (London: Merlin Press, 2004), 63.

46 Ibid., 65.

47 Ibid., 65–66.

48 Ibid., 70.

49 See ibid., 64; alternatively: 'accumulation based on predation', ibid., 74. Harvey describes the effects of dispossession as including: 'the commodification and privatization of land and the forceful expulsion of peasant populations; conversion of various forms of property rights – common, collective, state, etc. – into exclusive private property rights; suppression of rights to the commons; commodification of labor power and the suppression of alternative, indigenous forms of production and consumption; colonial, neo-colonial and imperial processes of appropriation of assets, including natural resources; monetization of exchange and taxation, particularly of land; slave trade; and usury, the national debt and ultimately the credit system', ibid.

50 See Patrick Bond, *Looting Africa: The Economics of Exploitation* (London: Zed Books, 2006).

51 Patrick Bond, 'Global Uneven Development, Primitive Accumulation and Political-Economic Conflict in Africa: The Return of the Theory of Imperialism', in *Journal of Peacebuilding & Development*, vol. 4, no. 1, March 2008, 1–14, 5.

52 Ibid., 6

53 Bond notes: 'Instead of an organic middle class and productive capitalist class, Africa has seen an excessively powerful comprador ruling elite whose income has been based upon financial-parasitical accumulation, which in turn is subject to vast capital flight', Bond, *Looting Africa*, 6–7.

54 Nzongola-Ntalaja notes: 'with state decay and the breakdown in law and order, the Congo has once again become a wild frontier to which everyone is free to fetch whatever they can' (*The Congo*, 235) – and he adds: mining transnationals embarked on a 'new scramble for mining concessions and exploration rights all over Africa', ibid., 236.

55 Bond, *Looting Africa*, 113.

56 Bond summarises the situation as follows: 'with an estimated three million dead in Central African wars, partly because of their proximity to zones of access to coltan and other mineral riches, conflicts worsened between and within the Uganda/Rwanda bloc, *vis-à-vis* the revised alliance of Kabila's Democratic Republic of Congo (DRC), Zimbabwe, Angola, and Namibia. Only with Kabila's assassination in 2001 and Pretoria's management of elite peace deals in the DRC and Burundi are matters settling, however briefly, into a fragile peace combining neoliberalism and opportunities for mineral extraction', Bond, *Looting Africa*, 115. Elsewhere he writes: 'The bottom line is enhanced profit for international capital and despotism for the citizenry', Bond, 'Global Uneven Development', 3.

57 Explanatory Memorandum, 2014, *Proposal for a Regulation of the European Parliament and the Council Setting up a Union System for Supply Chain Due Diligence Self-certification of Responsible Importers of Tin, Tantalum and Tungsten, their Ores, and Gold Originating in Conflict-affected and High Risk Areas, European Parliament.* Available at: https://eur-lex.europa.eu/legal-content/EN/TXT/?uri=CELEX%3A52014PCO111 (Accessed: 20 June 2021).

58 Source: Responsible Sourcing Network (RSN) Report quoted in 'Companies "Disregard Responsibility" over Conflict Minerals: Report', posted 23 October 2019, *Mongabay, News & Inspiration from Nature's Frontline.* Available at: https://news.mongabay.com/2019/10/companies-disregard-corporate-responsibility-over-conflict-minerals-report/ (Accessed: 20 June 2021). The RSN Report, *Mining the Disclosures*, 2019, An Investor's Guide to Conflict Minerals and Cobalt Reporting in Year Six, examined the extend of compliance among US companies with the Dodd-Frank Act and noted a 'trend [that] is disconcerting and demonstrates the relegation of 3TG [conflict minerals] due diligence to a lesser corporate concern and a blatant disregard to implement U.S. federal legislation'. Available at: www.sourcingnetwork.org/mining-the-disclosures (Accessed: 5 August 2021).

59 RSN, *Mining the Disclosures*, 2019.

60 Human Rights Watch recently reported a 'downturn in 2020' where, in eastern Congo, 'numerous armed groups, and in some cases government security forces, attacked civilians, killing and wounding many'. The humanitarian situation in the country remained alarming, with 5.5 million people internally displaced. Nearly 930,000 people from Congo were registered as refugees and asylum seekers in at least twenty countries as of November, Human Rights Watch, Democratic Republic of Congo, Events of 2020. Available at: www.org/world-report/2021/counter-chapters/democratic-republic-congo (Accessed: 7 June 2021).

61 See Achille Mbembe's description of the necropolitical as the 'subjugation of life to the power of death', Achille Mbembe, 'Necropolitics', trans. Libby Meintjes in *Public Culture*, vol. 15, no. 1, Winter 2003, 11–40, 40. Of relevance in the context of this essay, he gives the example: 'Increasingly, war is no longer waged between armies of two sovereign states. It is waged by armed groups acting behind the mask of the state against armed groups that have no state but control very distinct territories; both sides having as their main targets civilian populations that are unarmed or organized into militias. In cases where armed dissidents have not completely taken over state power, they have provoked territorial partitions and succeeded in controlling entire regions that they administer on the model of fiefdoms, especially where there are mineral deposits', 34–35.

62 Rau, *Global Realism*, 187.

63 Ibid., 260. Rau adds: the truth the Tribunal testifies to is the 'truth of a political economic war that is fought every day against Congolese communities … a war waged through forced relocation, massacres and … even new laws', ibid., 261.

64 Ibid., 186.

65 Ibid., 193.
66 Ibid., 193.
67 Ibid., 217.
68 Achille Mbembe, *Critique of Black Reason*, trans. Laurent Dubois (Durham, NC: Duke University Press, 2017), 183.
69 Rau, *Global Realism*, 184.
70 Ibid.

Index

EU authorised representative for GPSR:
Easy Access System Europe, Mustamäe tee 50,
10621 Tallinn, Estonia
gpsr.requests@easproject.com

www.ingramcontent.com/pod-product-compliance
Ingram Content Group UK Ltd.
Pitfield, Milton Keynes, MK11 3LW, UK
UKHW021826150726
7214IPUK00017B/341